Ecotourism in Sub-Saharan Africa

Since its first mention in the academic literature, ecotourism has been endorsed by nongovernmental organizations and governments as the most environmentally sound and locally beneficial method of tourist development. Over the last 30 years, sub-Saharan Africa has adopted ecotourism as the primary focus for tourism development; research into this has demonstrated mixed results. In this publication, we seek to explore the actual outcomes for African countries that have developed their tourism policy around the principals and values of ecotourism. The sheer scope and magnitude of the task means that a complete evaluation of ecotourism in Africa is impossible. Instead, included here are spot assessments of various aspects of ecotourism related to conservation, policy development, environment, governance, community, and indigenous peoples in southern Africa. The studies cover a wide array of countries, including Botswana, Kenya, Tanzania, Uganda, Ghana, Zimbabwe, and South Africa. Though this is only the beginning of a needed long-term evaluation of the positives and negatives of ecotourism, it provides a starting point from which to move forward. This book was originally published as a special issue of the *Journal of Ecotourism*.

Kenneth F. Backman is a Professor at the Department of Parks, Recreation and Tourism Management and Fellow of the Institute for Parks, Clemson University, SC, USA, and Associate Editor of the *Journal of Ecotourism*. His research areas are sustainable tourism development and ecotourism.

Ian E. Munanura is an Assistant Professor at the Department of Forest Ecosystems and Society, Oregon State University, Corvallis, OR, USA. He teaches ecotourism, and sustainable tourism planning. He also conducts a program of research on family well-being constraints influencing destructive forest use behavior in rural communities, and the mitigation potential of ecotourism.

Ecotourism in Sub-Saharan Africa

Thirty Years of Practice

Edited by
Kenneth F. Backman and Ian E. Munanura

LONDON AND NEW YORK

First published 2017 by Routledge

2 Park Square, Milton Park, Abingdon, Oxfordshire OX14 4RN
52 Vanderbilt Avenue, New York, NY 10017

Routledge is an imprint of the Taylor & Francis Group, an informa business

First issued in paperback 2018

British Library Cataloguing in Publication Data
A catalogue record for this book is available from the British Library

ISBN 13: 978-1-138-63796-2 (hbk)
ISBN 13: 978-0-367-22021-1 (pbk)

Typeset in TimesNewRomanPS
by diacriTech, Chennai

Publisher's Note
The publisher accepts responsibility for any inconsistencies that may have arisen
during the conversion of this book from journal articles to book chapters, namely
the possible inclusion of journal terminology.

Disclaimer
Every effort has been made to contact copyright holders for their permission to
reprint material in this book. The publishers would be grateful to hear from any
copyright holder who is not here acknowledged and will undertake to rectify any
errors or omissions in future editions of this book.

Contents

CONTENTS

Citation Information

The following chapters were originally published in the *Journal of Ecotourism*, volume 14, issues 2–3 (June–November 2015). When citing this material, please use the original page numbering for each article, as follows:

Chapter 1

Introduction to the special issues on ecotourism in Africa over the past 30 years
Kenneth F. Backman and Ian E. Munanura
Journal of Ecotourism, volume 14, issues 2–3 (June–November 2015) pp. 95–98

Chapter 2

Neoliberalism in ecotourism? The new development paradigm of multinational projects in Africa
Carol S. Kline and Susan L. Slocum
Journal of Ecotourism, volume 14, issues 2–3 (June–November 2015) pp. 99–112

Chapter 3

Analysing governance in tourism value chains to reshape the tourist bubble in developing countries: the case of cultural tourism in Uganda
Bright Adiyia, Arie Stoffelen, Britt Jennes, Dominique Vanneste and Wilber Manyisa Ahebwa
Journal of Ecotourism, volume 14, issues 2–3 (June–November 2015) pp. 113–129

Chapter 4

Conservation tourism and landscape governance in Kenya: the interdependency of three conservation NGOs
Arjaan Pellis, Machiel Lamers and René Van der Duim
Journal of Ecotourism, volume 14, issues 2–3 (June–November 2015) pp. 130–144

Chapter 5

Good governance strategies for sustainable ecotourism in Tanzania
Liliane Pasape, Wineaster Anderson and George Lindi
Journal of Ecotourism, volume 14, issues 2–3 (June–November 2015) pp. 145–165

Chapter 6

Community-based ecotourism: a collaborative partnerships perspective
Moren Tibabo Stone
Journal of Ecotourism, volume 14, issues 2–3 (June–November 2015) pp. 166–184

Chapter 7
*Community agency and entrepreneurship in ecotourism planning and development in the
Great Limpopo Transfrontier Conservation Area*
Chaka Chirozva
Journal of Ecotourism, volume 14, issues 2–3 (June–November 2015) pp. 185–203

Chapter 8
Ecotourism in Botswana: 30 years later
Joseph E. Mbaiwa
Journal of Ecotourism, volume 14, issues 2–3 (June–November 2015) pp. 204–222

Chapter 9
*Ecotourism implementation in the Kakum Conservation Area, Ghana: administrative
framework and local community experiences*
Patrick Brandful Cobbinah, Rosemary Black and Rik Thwaites
Journal of Ecotourism, volume 14, issues 2–3 (June–November 2015) pp. 223–242

Chapter 10
*Factors that influence support for community-based ecotourism in the rural communities
adjacent to the Kgalagadi Transfrontier Park, Botswana*
Naomi Moswete and Brijesh Thapa
Journal of Ecotourism, volume 14, issues 2–3 (June–November 2015) pp. 243–263

Chapter 11
A review of ecotourism in Tanzania: magnitude, challenges, and prospects for sustainability
John T. Mgonja, Agnes Sirima and Peter J. Mkumbo
Journal of Ecotourism, volume 14, issues 2–3 (June–November 2015) pp. 264–277

Chapter 13
*The influence of homestay facilities on tourist satisfaction in the Lake Victoria Kenya
Tourism Circuit*
Eliza Buyeke Ogucha, Geoffrey K. Riungu, Frimar K. Kiama and Eunice Mukolwe
Journal of Ecotourism, volume 14, issues 2–3 (June–November 2015) pp. 278–287

The following chapter was originally published in the *Journal of Ecotourism*, volume 15,
issue 2 (2016). When citing this material, please use the original page numbering for the
article, as follows:

Chapter 12
*Climate change risks on protected areas ecotourism: shocks and stressors perspectives in
Ngorongoro Conservation Area, Tanzania*
N. P. Mkiramweni, T. DeLacy, M. Jiang and F. E. Chiwanga
Journal of Ecotourism, volume 15, issue 2 (2016) pp. 139–157

For any permission-related enquiries please visit:
http://www.tandfonline.com/page/help/permissions

Notes on Contributors

Bright Adiyia is a scholar at University of Leuven, Belgium. His research interests are tourism in developing countries, poverty, regional development, and spatial analysis.

Wilber Manyisa Ahebwa is a Senior Lecturer on the Tourism Programme, Makerere University, Uganda. His research interests are in sustainable tourism, tourism, conservation and development, entrepreneurship in tourism, tourism planning, and policy analysis.

Wineaster Anderson is based at Department of Marketing of University of Dar es Salaam, Tanzania. She has researched and published widely in the areas of innovation and sustainability in natural resources and tourism, internationalization for poverty alleviation, international business and trade as well as gender and marketing. She was formerly the Dean of University of Dar es Salaam Business School and Director of Quality Assurance for the University of Dar es Salaam, Tanzania.

Kenneth F. Backman is a Professor at the Department of Parks, Recreation and Tourism Management and Fellow of the Institute for Parks, Clemson University, SC, USA, and Associate Editor of the *Journal of Ecotourism*. His research areas are sustainable tourism development and ecotourism.

Rosemary Black is an Associate Professor at Charles Sturt University, Australia, and undertakes research in sustainable tourism, tour guiding, heritage interpretation, sustainable behaviors, and adventure tourism. Prior to joining Charles Sturt University, Australia, she worked in protected area management, adventure travel, and community conservation. She has worked in academic for the past 20 years, and published four books and several referred publications.

Chaka Chirozva is a Lecturer at the Department of Environmental Science, Bindura University of Science Education, Bindura, Zimbabwe, and a graduate student at the School of Environmental Sciences, Charles Sturt University, Albury, Australia. Researcher/ practitioner in community-based natural resources management and trans-boundary resource governance, with a focus on active community participation in governance. Most recent work focused on innovative and deliberative research methodologies in empowerment of marginalized communities living within trans-frontier areas.

F. E. Chiwanga is a Lecturer in Foreign Languages at Sokoine University of Agriculture, Tanzania. His research interests include foreign languages, tourism, and conservation.

Patrick Brandful Cobbinah is a Lecturer in Planning at the Department of Planning, Kwame Nkrumah University of Science and Technology, Ghana. He holds a PhD degree in human geography. He is a member of the Ghana Institute of Planners and an Adjunct

Research Fellow of the Institute for Land, Water and Society, Australia. His research is focused on sustainable development and urban and regional planning, and environmental management.

T. DeLacy is a Professor in Sustainable Tourism and Environmental Policy at Victoria University, Melbourne, Australia. He was previously Director of the Australian Government-established, national, Sustainable Tourism Co-operative Research Centre. Terry presently leads a group researching the green growth transformation of tourism destinations.

Britt Jennes was a master student in the Master in Tourism, University of Leuven, Belgium, during 2012–2013.

M. Jiang is a Senior Research Fellow at Tourism and Events Research Group, College of Business, Victoria University, Australia. Her research interests include sustainable tourism, tourism adaptation to climate change, tourism and the green economy, and water governance. Her previous work has focused on Australia, China, and the South Pacific.

Frimar K. Kiama is a faculty member at the Department of Tourism and Hospitality Management, KISII University, Kisii, Kenya.

Carol S. Kline is an Associate Professor of Hospitality and Tourism Management in the Department of Management at Appalachian State University, Boone, NC, USA. Her research interests focus broadly on tourism planning and development and tourism sustainability, but cover a range of topics such as foodie segmentation, craft beverages, agritourism, wildlife-based tourism, animal ethics in tourism, tourism entrepreneurship, niche tourism markets, and tourism impacts to communities.

Machiel Lamers is Associate Professor at the Environmental Policy Group at Wageningen University, the Netherlands. His main research interests are in new modes of governance for sustainable tourism and conservation tourism, particularly in marine and polar environments.

George Lindi is Senior Lecture at Department of Marketing of University of Dar es Salaam. He was former Associate Dean of Faculty of Commerce and Management of University of Dar es Salaam, Tanzania.

Joseph E. Mbaiwa is a Professor of Tourism Studies at the Okavango Research Institute, University of Botswana, Botswana. His research interests are on tourism development, conservation, and rural livelihood development. He holds a PhD in Park, Recreation and Tourism Sciences from Texas A&M University, College Station, TX, USA. He is also a Research Affiliate of University of Johannesburg, School of Tourism and Hospitality, Faculty of management, South Africa.

John T. Mgonja is a tourism Lecturer in the Department of Tourism and Recreation at Sokoine University of Agriculture, Tanzania. He obtained his PhD in 2015 from the Department of Parks, Recreation and Tourism Management (PRTM) at Clemson University, SC, USA.

N. P. Mkiramweni is a Lecturer in sustainable tourism at Sokoine University of Agriculture, Tanzania. His research interests include: conservation of natural resources, promoting local community's livelihoods, climate change, tourism, and the green economy. His previous work has focused on agricultural economics.

Peter J. Mkumbo has over eight years of experience in the fields of sustainable natural resources and environmental management and tourism industry. He is currently a graduate student pursuing PhD in Parks, Recreation and Tourism Management at Clemson University, SC, USA. He is interested in Performance Metrics of Tourism Marketing, Destination Management and Marketing, and Visitor Dimensions (satisfaction, motivation, education, impacts, and management) in Destination Facilities and Attractions.

Naomi Moswete is Senior Lecturer in the Department of Environmental Science at the University of Botswana, Botswana. Her interests include tourism as a strategy for rural development, community-based natural resources management, and trans-frontier park-based tourism.

Eunice Mukolwe is an Assistant Lecturer at the Department of Tourism and Hospitality Management, KISII University, Kisii, Kenya.

Ian E. Munanura is an Assistant Professor at the Department of Forest Ecosystems and Society, Oregon State University, Corvallis, OR, USA. He teaches ecotourism, and sustainable tourism planning. He also conducts a program of research on family well-being constraints influencing destructive forest use behavior in rural communities, and the mitigation potential of ecotourism.

Eliza Buyeke Ogucha is a Lecturer at the Department of Tourism and Hospitality Management, KISII University, Kisii, Kenya.

Liliane Pasape is Lecturer at Nelson Mandela African Institution of Science and Technology (NM-AIST), Tanzania. She is currently the Dean of School of Business Studies and Humanities at NM-AIST.

Arjaan Pellis is a PhD student at the Cultural Geography Group of Wageningen University. In his PhD research, he is exploring the important and productive role of conflicts emerging in practices of conservation tourism.

Geoffrey K. Riungu is a lecturer in the School of Tourism, Hospitality and Events Management, Moi University, and is currently a PhD candidate in the Department of Parks, Recreation and Tourism Management at Clemson University, SC, USA. His research interests are in human dimensions of outdoor recreation, conservation and area management, sustainable tourism development, and microfinance and banking.

Agnes Sirima is a Lecturer and Head, Department of Tourism and Recreation in the College of Forestry, Wildlife and Tourism, Sokoine University of Agriculture, Tanzania. She is also the coordinator of research and consultancy activities within the College. She teaches and conducts research in areas of tourism and recreation planning, community capacity building, and leisure studies.

Susan L. Slocum specializes in sustainable economic development, working with communities to enhance backward linkages between tourism and traditional industries. In particular, she is interested in balancing policy development and integration to provide a more bottom-up form of planning within tourism destinations and has approached sustainable tourism from a contemporary view, which includes the addition of institutional reform and social justice.

Arie Stoffelen is a Research Foundation-Flanders (FWO) scholar at University of Leuven, Belgium. He researches tourism landscapes, governance, and regional development in cross-border contexts.

Moren Tibabo Stone is a Lecturer of Environmental Science and Tourism Studies at the Department of Environmental Science, University of Botswana, Botswana. His research interests include sustainable tourism development and management, ecotourism, community-based tourism, protected areas conservation, and community livelihoods improvement through tourism engagements.

Brijesh Thapa is a Professor in the Department of Tourism, Recreation and Sport Management at the University of Florida. He is also an Affiliate Faculty in multiple academic units: School of Natural Resources and Environment, Warrington College of Business, Center for International Business Education and Research, Center for African Studies, Center for Latin American Studies, Water Institute, Transportation Research Center, and the Graduate Program in Sustainable Development Practice.

Overall, his research theme is within the nexus of tourism, conservation, and sustainability. In this context, he has explored specific issues and associated linkages from a developed and developing country's standpoint largely among key stakeholder groups (e.g., visitors, residents, tourism industry, and policy makers). Among developed countries, his research has been based from a U.S. perspective examining specific themes such as, environmentalism, recreation behavior, planning and management issues at various nature-based tourism settings managed by the state and federal government.

Rik Thwaites is a Human Geographer in the School of Environmental Sciences at Charles Sturt University, Australia. He has taught across the fields of ecotourism, sustainable development and environmental management, community development, recreation and land use planning, and social research methods. His research interests focus largely around the nexus of community development and environmental management and conservation, as well as the implications of global environmental policies for local communities in less developed countries.

René Van der Duim is Professor at the Cultural Geography Group of Wageningen University, the Netherlands. In the last 10 years his research focused on the relation between tourism, conservation and development, especially in sub-Saharan Africa.

Dominique Vanneste is a Professor of Geography and Tourism at University of Leuven, Belgium. Her research interests are regional/destination development, governance, and cultural heritage.

INTRODUCTION

Introduction to the special issues on ecotourism in Africa over the past 30 years

Kenneth F. Backman[a] and Ian Munanura[b]

[a]Department of Parks, Recreation and Tourism Management, Clemson University, Clemson, SC, USA; [b]Department of Forest Ecosystems and Society, College of Forestry, Oregon State University, Corvallis, OR, USA

Tourism is one of the fastest growing sectors of the global economy. At 4.1% growth rate, tourism is expected to generate 1.6 billion tourists by the year 2020 (Christie, Fernandes, Messerli, & Twining-Ward, 2014). As Weaver and Lawton (2007) state, the term Ecotourism began to appear in the tourism journals in the late 1980s. Ecotourism was in the beginning seen to have the goals of ecological and economic impact for all stakeholders in this type of tourism, but it was questioned whether these goals are being achieved (Lawrence, Wickins, & Phillips, 1997; Lindberg & McKercher, 1997). In conjunction with this was the United Nations agreement on the establishment of the Millennium Development Goals that focused on rural development that reduced poverty, improved health and empowered women and children (Butcher, 2011). One of the main catalysts for achievement of the Millennium Development Goals and rural development was seen to be ecotourism (Butcher, 2011; Das & Chatterjee, 2015). Thus the purpose of this special issue of the Journal of Ecotourism is to report on how ecotourism is doing with the achievement of its goals in sub-Saharan Africa.

Africa's share of tourism growth is modest at 2%, based on year 2014 statistics (UNWTO, 2015). Since its introduction over 30 years ago, ecotourism has been central to tourism growth in Africa. As Gössling (2000) suggests, ecotourism is the fastest growing component of tourism industry. Ecotourism growth in Africa is particularly exceptional because of wildlife diversity and abundance of charismatic wildlife species (Lindsey, Alexander, Mills, Woodroffe, & Romanach, 2007). Over the last 30 years, Africa has experienced significant success in ecotourism application. Such success is manifested through significant revenue generation, foreign investment and other socio-economic benefits, which have led to significant appeal of ecotourism in Africa (Boyd & Butler, 1996). In fact, such economic opportunities of ecotourism have also generated support for wildlife conservation from non-traditional actors in public and private sector institutions. In addition, ecotourism has tremendously enhanced community wellbeing, development and support for wildlife conservation in communities coexisting with wildlife in Africa (Scheyvens, 1999). Multiple community conservation and community-based initiatives have emerged from ecotourism with both ecological and socio-economic benefits to many rural communities and nations in Africa.

In spite of tremendous success, ecotourism in Africa has experienced a number of constraints and limitations over the past 30 years. For example, most countries in the east and central part of Africa have been ravaged with civil wars, which have undermined ecotourism growth trajectory and potential. Poor infrastructure has rendered many countries with diverse wildlife and abundant charismatic species inaccessible, affecting their ecotourism potential. Institutional and human capacity has been a significant impediment to effective management of ecotourism in Africa. Capacity limitations have hindered the ability of practitioners in Africa to effectively monitor and mitigate potential negative impacts of ecotourism. Shortages of financial capital and entrepreneurship skills among local communities coexisting with wildlife have also constrained the potential of ecotourism practitioners in Africa to take full advantage of a growing ecotourism market. Corruption and top down governance approach to wildlife and protected area management has also been a limitation to the success of ecotourism in some African countries with tremendous ecotourism potential.

This issue is intended to put the success and constraints of ecotourism in Africa over the past 30 years into perspective. Through experiences of practitioners and scholars, this issue presents lessons learned over the years. Such rich experience will allow us to learn, adapt and continue to shape ecotourism as a tool for sustainable development in Africa.

The articles that are contained in this special issue are all reflections of what ecotourism is or has accomplished in various countries in sub-Saharan Africa only, and then just a sample of the countries it comprises. The first articles are an assessment of some of the many stakeholders involved in ecotourism in Africa. Kline and Slocum's (2015) 'Neoliberalism in ecotourism? The New Development Paradigm of Multinational Projects in Africa,' identifies four overarching organisational values required for successful ecotourism development these being: sensitivity to local needs/culture; organisational partnerships; capacity building and monitoring. In the second article Adiyia, Stoffelen, Jannes, Vanneste, and Ahebwa (2015) 'Analyzing governance in tourism values claims to reshape the tourist bubble in developing countries: The Case of Cultural Tourism in Uganda,' this article assesses the effect governance has on the tourism value chain with establishing local linkages to reshape the social and spatial boundaries of the tourist bubble in Uganda. Their results show that cultural activities can reshape the social boundaries of the tourist bubble and can act as a catalyst for development, but this tends to be less successful.

The third article focusing on governance and organisation is Pellis, Lamers, and Van Der Duim (2015) Conservation Tourism and Landscape Governance in Kenya: The interdependency of three conservation NGOs. In this article they assess organisational strategies and practices between 2007 and 2013 to demonstrate how conservation NGOs worked as intermediators of various forms of conservation tourism are subjected to multi-actor interdependencies. They found that mismatched scale-making hampers organisational objectives and contributes the reshaping of conservation tourism landscapes. The authors do show how their approach to governance has been successful using multiple conservation NGOs.

The fourth article focusing on governance strategies by Pasape, Anderson, and Lindi (2015) 'Good Governance Strategies for Sustainable Ecotourism in Tanzania,' identify that the factors most likely to jeopardise ecotourism are inadequate transparency, poor accountability practices and weak integration mechanisms between ecotourism operations and the country's development plans. This results in ecotourism development that has had unproductive planning and mismanaged ecotourism resources.

The next group of articles focus on community-based ecotourism within the African context. The fifth article by Stone (2015) 'Community-based Ecotourism: A Collaborative Partnership Perspective,' reveals in this study that in Botswana ecotourism has brought mixed results regarding biodiversity conservation and community livelihoods due to the involvement of too many stakeholders in designing, planning, and implementing ecotourism projects. But, even with mixed findings the article offers a progressive example of how stakeholders approach to natural resource management is evolving to be more successful.

The sixth article by Chirozva (2015) 'Community Agency and Entrepreneurship in Ecotourism Planning and Development in the Great Limpopo Transfrontier Conservation Area,' this article demonstrates that even in the transfrontier conservation areas, innovative community leaders have demonstrated imagination, have embraced and to some extent exploited ecotourism opportunities and are successful when they engage in social networking to promote local cultural tourism development.

The next group of articles in this special issue focuses on ecotourism development in a sample of African countries and provides an assessment of the success and problems in those countries. The seventh article is by Mbaiwa (2015) 'Ecotourism in Botswana: 30 years later.' This article describes that where ecotourism has succeeded, it generated economic benefits which had produced positive attitudes of residents toward ecotourism and conservation. Where ecotourism failed, the reason for failure was due to lack of entrepreneurship and managerial and marketing skills of local communities. With the results suggesting ecotourism can be a 'tool' to improve livelihoods and conservation if communities have the right socio-economic and political dynamics.

The eighth article by Cobbinah, Black, and Thwaites (2015) 'Ecotourism Implementation in the Kakum Conservation Area, Ghana: Administrative Framework and Local Community Experiences,' this article describes that due to the implementation of ecotourism without acknowledging community involvement and participation as relevant to successful ecotourism development, the Kakum Conservation Area has generated mixed experiences for local residents.

The ninth article by Moswete and Thapa (2015) 'Factors that Influence Support for Community-based Ecotourism in the Rural Communities Adjacent to the Kgalagardi Transfrontier Park, Botswana,' highlights the diverse array of factors that likely influence resident perceptions and their support for community-based ecotourism. The findings reveal that the factors that most influence residents are environment, economic, socio-cultural, and their knowledge of ecotourism.

The tenth article by Mgonja, Sirima, and Mkumbo (2015) 'A Review of Ecotourism in Tanzania: Magnitude, Challenges and Prospects for Sustainability,' identifies that ecotourism is highly localised and relatively minimal because of accessibility problems in some protected areas, inadequate infrastructure, and insufficient marketing and promotion. The fix for these problems is for more regulatory authorities to articulate clear policies, regulations, and guidelines that delineate strategies on the positive implementation of ecotourism.

The eleventh article which focuses on one type of ecotourism activity becoming more popular in Africa by Ogucha et al. (2015) 'The Influence of Homestay Facilities on Tourist Satisfaction in the Lake Victoria, Kenya Tourist Circuit,' assessed homestay facilities and found visitors tended to not be satisfied with their homestay experience. This was mostly due to inadequate facilities to meet the expectations of this type of visitor to this area of Kenya. This suggests that before implementation of a new tourism product into the marketplace, first ensure that the infrastructure to meet these wants and needs is in place.

My co-editor, Ian Munanura and I want to complement and thank all the authors of the articles in this special issue for their contribution to our better understanding of what the state of ecotourism development is in each of the countries in Africa studied. It can be seen that ecotourism and the principals behind ecotourism are in various stages of refinement with some successes, but many failures; how ecotourism can be brought to the point where its use as a tool for conservation and livelihood improvement has not yet been achieved in Africa, but the path to success for all stakeholders in ecotourism development to succeed is a little clearer due to the information in the articles found in this special issue.

References

Adiyia, B., Stoffelen, A., Jennes, B., Vanneste, D., & Ahebwa, W. M. (2015). Analysing governance in tourism value chains to reshape the tourist bubble in developing countries: The case of cultural tourism in Uganda. *Journal of Ecotourism, 14*, 2–3 (in press).

Boyd, S. W., & Butler, R. W. (1996). Managing ecotourism: An opportunity spectrum approach. *Tourism Management, 17*(8), 557–566.

Butcher, J. (2011). Can ecotourism contribute to tackling poverty? The importance of 'symbiosis'. *Current Issues in Tourism, 14*(3), 295–307.

Chirozva, C. (2015). Community agency and entrepreneurship in ecotourism planning and development in the Great Limpopo Transfrontier Conservation Area. *Journal of Ecotourism, 14*, 2–3 (in press).

Christie, I., Fernandes, E., Messerli, H., & Twining-Ward, L. (2014). *Tourism in Africa: Harnessing tourism for growth and improved livelihoods.* Washington, DC: World Bank.

Cobbinah, P. B., Black, R., & Thwaites, R. (2015). Ecotourism implementation in the Kakum Conservation Area, Ghana: Administrative framework and local community experiences. *Journal of Ecotourism, 14*, 2–3 (in press).

Das, M., & Chatterjee, B. (2015). Ecotourism: A panacea or a predicament? *Tourism Management Perspectives, 14*, 3–16.

Gössling, S. (2000). Sustainable tourism development in developing countries: Some aspects of energy use. *Journal of Sustainable Tourism, 8*(5), 410–425.

Kline, C. S., & Slocum, S. L. (2015). Neoliberalism in ecotourism? The new development paradigm of multinational projects in Africa. *Journal of Ecotourism 14*, 2–3 (in press).

Lawrence, T., Wickins, D., & Phillips, N. (1997). Managing legitimacy in ecotourism. *Tourism Management, 18*, 307–316.

Lindberg, K., & McKercher, B. (1997). Ecotourism: A critical overview. *Pacific Tourism Review, 1*, 65–79.

Lindsey, P., Alexander, R., Mills, M., Woodroffe, R., & Romanach, S. (2007). Wildlife viewing preferences of visitors to protected areas in South Africa: Implications for the role of ecotourism in conservation. *Journal of Ecotourism, 6*, 19–33.

Mbaiwa, J. E. (2015). Ecotourism in Botswana: 30 years later. *Journal of Ecotourism, 14*, 2–3 (in press).

Mgonja, J. T., Sirima, A., & Mkumbo, P. J. (2015). A review of ecotourism in Tanzania: Magnitude, challenges and prospects for sustainability. *Journal of Ecotourism, 14*, 2–3 (in press).

Moswete, N., & Thapa, B. (2015). Factors that influence support for community-based ecotourism in the rural communities adjacent to the Kgalagadi Transfrontier Park, Botswana. *Journal of Ecotourism, 14*, 2–3 (in press).

Ogucha, E., Ruingu, G., (trying to get this author's name) (2015). The influence of homestay facilities on tourism satisfaction in the Lake Victoria Kenya Tourism Circuit. *Journal of Ecotourism, 14*, 2–3 (in press).

Pasape, L., Anderson, W., & Lindi, G. (2015). Good governance strategies for sustainable ecotourism in Tanzania. *Journal of Ecotourism, 14*, 2–3 (in press).

Pellis, A., Lamera, M., & van der Duim, R. (2015). Conservation tourism and landscape governance in Kenya: The interdependency of three conservation NGOs. *Journal of Ecotourism, 14*, 2–3 (in press).

Scheyvens, R. (1999). Ecotourism and the empowerment of local communities. *Tourism Management, 20*(2), 245–249.

Stone, M. T. (2015). Community-based ecotourism: A collaborative partnerships perspective. *Journal of Ecotourism, 14*, 2–3 (in press).

UNWTO. (2015). *UNWTO tourism highlights 2015 edition.* Real Madrid: United Nations World Tourism Organization.

Weaver, D. B., & Lawton, L. J. (2007). Twenty years on: The state of contemporary ecotourism research. *Tourism Management, 28*, 1168–1179.

Neoliberalism in ecotourism? The new development paradigm of multinational projects in Africa

Carol S. Kline[a] and Susan L. Slocum[b]

[a]Hospitality and Tourism Management, Walker College of Business, Appalachian State University, Boone, NC, USA; [b]Tourism and Event Management, College of Education and Human Development, George Mason University, University Blvd, Manassas, VA, USA

As a global phenomenon, ecotourism is influenced by numerous stakeholders ranging from local charities to international governments and non-governmental organisations (NGO). Within the continent of Africa, multinational NGO and government involvement is at the forefront of ecotourism development as a strategy for natural resource management, economic gains, and increased quality of life. While many African countries are attempting to create a 'self-reliant' society, they still encourage extensive direct foreign investment. This paper asserts that, as the international voice that attempts to link conservation with domestic and foreign audiences, multinational agencies control the power structures that invariantly reinforce the concept of neoliberal conservation. It is argued that there is a need to better understand a multinational agency's role in ecotourism development; therefore, through an analysis of six multinational conservation agencies headquartered in Washington, DC, this paper presents an analysis of prevailing approaches to ecotourism development in Africa. The qualitative findings relay four overarching organisational values: sensitivity to local needs/culture, organisational partnerships, capacity building, and monitoring. Additionally, policies and protocols that encourage the sustainability of these values are presented, along with lessons learnt.

Introduction

Ecotourism is increasingly being used as a funding mechanism for conservation and community development initiatives. The main drivers for ecotourism projects are the economic benefits that support the management of natural areas, revenue expansion for governance, educational opportunities for tourists, and jobs and small businesses that provide residents new opportunities and decrease pressures on traditional uses of natural resources (Duffy, 2013; Honey, 2008). However, many of the decisions to incorporate ecotourism have been based in the philosophy of neoliberal conservation, which Büscher (2010) identifies as 'where nature and poor communities can be represented the way they "ought to be" in order to convince investors, tourists and policy makers of their value' (p. 261).

As a global phenomenon, ecotourism is influenced by numerous stakeholders ranging from local and regional charities to international governments and non-governmental organisations (NGO). Development of ecotourism destinations is complex, but generally involves the acquisition of donor funds from the Global North through multinational agencies, which in turn are passed to local or regional groups (often in the Global South) in the form of grants for local development projects. A transnational or multinational organisation refers to agencies with relationships across country boundaries and that have outposts around the world to deal with specific issues in a variety of countries (Willetts, 1996). Examples include the Overseas Development Institute, the World Conservation Union, the World Wildlife Fund, and the US Agency for International Development. These multinational agencies, which exist in all three economic sectors (public, non-profit, and private), may provide services in the form of conservation specialists, governance best practice, regional lobbying, marketing, and education to ensure that donor funding is appropriately allocated and investment produces the desired outcomes (Honey, 2008). These multinational agencies are referred to as the 'global governance' system, which has shaped the way in which ecotourism is represented and valued (Büscher, 2010, p. 262). Slocum and Backman (2011) write that increased reliance on these agencies in the tourism field, 'is changing the political climate in which governance occurs' (p. 284).

The continent of Africa provides an interesting case study as multinational agency involvement is at the forefront of its recent economic gains (Slocum & Backman, 2011). Many African countries have implemented community-based natural resource management as a strategy to reduce centralised management systems and ease open-access use of the country's natural resource base (Jones & Murphree, 2004) in an attempt to boost economic gains and increase quality of life. While many African nations have included policy agendas addressing a more 'self-reliant' society, they still encourage extensive direct foreign investment (Slocum & Backman, 2011). Ecotourism is no exception. Africa is dependent on the unique flora, fauna, and traditional communities in its tourism message. The historical centralised approach to development has provided limited in-country resources and increased the dependence on outside agencies to conserve and promote Africa's destinations (Kimbu & Ngoasong, 2013). However, the success of such governmental and non-governmental partnerships is still highly contested. Bawa (2013) writes:

> Despite criticisms of development NGOs in the Global South, these organisations provide crucial social services to people in many deprived communities. Given NGOs' peculiar positioning in development practice, it is important to neither dismiss nor blindly praise NGO involvement in the development process; rather, a critical appraisal of some issues central to NGO operations, . . . is crucial to understanding their activities and proposing new strategies of engagement with NGO activity in Africa. (p. 527)

While the integrity of multinational agencies in ecotourism development has generated extensive debates, the roles of these organisations are often overlooked. This paper asserts that, as the international voice that attempts to link conservation with domestic and foreign audiences (Slocum & Kline, 2015), multinational agencies control the power structures that invariantly add to the concept of neoliberal conservation. Through a qualitative analysis of six multinational conservation agencies headquartered in Washington, DC, this paper presents a summary of the priorities and lessons in ecotourism development in Africa. It is argued that, although it is difficult to tackle all of the issues facing Africa, there is a need to better understand the enablers within the current development paradigms, especially the multinational agency's role in ecotourism development.

Literature review

Neoliberal conservation has become a controversial issue in relation to natural resource management and the need for economic growth in developing regions (Büscher, 2010; Dressler & Roth, 2011; Jones, 2012). Büscher (2008) defines neoliberal politics as the ideology that aims to subject political, social, and ecological affairs to capitalist market dynamics. Neoliberal ideology models embrace the notions of market efficiency and specifically promote (1) an emphasis on material growth and capital accumulation as the antidote to poverty; (2) a rational, scientific approach to resource management; (3) emphasis on privatisation, competition, and individual entrepreneurship; and (4) commodification of landscapes as 'natural capital' (Fletcher, 2009, p. 270). Jones (2012) writes, 'neoliberal economic policies ... not only privilege particular strategies of industrial development but also shape the ways in which "sustainability" and "conservation" are promoted and contested' (p. 251).

The emergence of these models in the 1980s occurred as a result of a loss in confidence in the ability for newly emerging states to effectively manage their own economies (Lemos & Agrawal, 2006). Neocolonial ideologies and the perceived need for political control held by global governance organisations (the World Bank and International Monetary Fund) began steering public and private development funding from the Global North towards these newly emerging economies in the Global South. The core rationale was that scarce funds should be spent on activities where the greatest economic and social gains would result (McAffee, 2012). However, as corruption and mismanagement reduced the impact of development funding, neoliberal ideology supported the reduction of state involvement as a means to facilitate private interests, the expansion of market-based systems, and the privatisation of public services (Duffy, 2013). Neoliberal reforms in the Global South opened the door for foreign direct investment into natural areas, prompting multinational NGOs to commodify natural resources as a revenue stream (Benjaminsen, Goldman, Minwary, & Maganga, 2013). Benjaminsen et al. (2013) write:

> European ideas about vital wildlife resources being threatened by the African peasantry were not only important elements of colonial ideology but informed policies from early in the independence period, and continue to exert an influence on the wildlife and tourism sector today. (p. 1092)

The increasing power of foreign agencies in the protected areas and neighbouring communities of the Global South has driven the promotion of conservation and nature-based tourism to the Global North. The recent inclusion of 'community-friendly' programmes has drastically altered the social organisation and the politico-legal structures in areas around these protected areas (Garland, 2008). The response to these neoliberal ideologies has generated much debate in many academic disciplines.

Critics accuse neoliberal conservation as an avenue to commodify natural areas through tourism for the benefit of state agencies, conservation organisations, and private enterprises (Büscher, 2010; Igoe & Brockington, 2007). Igoe and Kelsall (2005) believe that the growth of the NGO 'industry' is a direct result of neoliberal policies and that the flow of donor investment through these NGOs has shifted the balance towards preservation rather than economic inclusion.

Evidence suggests that neoliberalism gives government agencies increased power to coerce residents, further alienating them from traditional resources (Dressler & Roth, 2011). Neoliberal changes in conservation have had a double-barrelled effect on local communities. Not only do they lose access to the natural resources that become isolated into reserves (Segi, 2014), but they also bear the brunt of negative tourism impacts, such as pollution, the loss of forests for tourism-related construction, and economic leakages through international tour operators. Furthermore, when tourism activities become more concentrated, new social hierarchies emerge, modifying traditional relationships between groups of people and resources (Garland, 2008).

Others warrant the growth in power inequalities to these new market-based valuation systems that privilege investors (the 'haves') over residents (the 'have-nots') (Duffy, 2013; Igoe & Brockington, 2007). Through the transformative process that brings former community resources under the umbrella of international protection, the relationship indigenous peoples have to the land is transformed, with lifestyles and cultures altered, creating insecurity, economic hardship and adversity to new conservation efforts (Dressler & Roth, 2011). Often nature becomes playgrounds for western visitors, investors or other foreign entities at the expense of local populations (Igoe & Brockington, 2007). Büscher (2010) reminds us that modern African history is 'littered with examples of expulsions and other human tragedies under conservation interventions that have sought to reconstruct local realities according to "Garden of Eden" images of "unspoilt" wilderness' as a result of modern conservation principles (p. 260). Fletcher (2009) writes:

> Observing that ecotourism is both practiced and promoted predominantly (although not exclusively) by white, professional-middle-class members of post-industrial Western societies, ... suggests that ecotourism can also be viewed as a discursive process, embodying a culturally specific set of beliefs and values largely peculiar to this demographic group that promoters, often unwittingly, seek to propagate through ecotourism development. (p. 269)

However, many scientists and advocates are seeing new possibilities for communities under the neoliberal paradigm. Lemos and Agrawal (2006) suggest that market systems can lead to increases in democracy and the empowerment of local communities. By uniting businesses, governments, NGOs and communities, conservation is now a shared responsibility that is giving rise to new models of conservation and development. Brown and Hall (2008) write, 'New forms of tourism have emerged, some of them at least with an ethical dimension, as a result of a shift from a product-driven to a consumer driven approach' (p. 842). Under new forms of neoliberal conservation, the greening of capitalism and the move towards social consciousness is growing, especially in relation to sustainable tourism, ecotourism and responsible tourism development (Ojeda, 2012). Therefore, market-based systems must be more responsive to consumer trends as the pressure towards ethical development grows.

While many attribute ecotourism's rise to demand-side factors and a social consciousness, there is also evidence that there is a simultaneous increase of service providers and trade associations along with the creation of national ecotourism plans (Honey, 2008). Schilcher (2007) believes that ecotourism, by the very nature of its dependence on tourism infrastructure, draw conservation sites and neighbouring communities into the neoliberal global economic system. She writes, 'organisations that need more tourism are bound to emphasise tourism's pro-poor potential to donors while promoting neoliberal approaches in which the industry can flourish' (p. 174). However, Duffy (2008) argues that ecotourism grew directly from the dissatisfaction with early neoliberal policies, especially in the Global South.

Neoliberalism in Africa

Neoliberalism and ecotourism are natural partners in academic discourse, especially relating to Africa; however, there is no consensus on the outcomes from neoliberal conservation policy. Duffy (2008) argues that ecotourism in Madagascar is highly political, even when situated as a neoliberal solution that brings together stakeholders. She emphasises that 'eco-tourism . . . is not politically, economically or socially neutral' (p. 140).

Tanzania has also struggled to unite neoliberal policies and ecotourism as a development tool. Nelson (2004) found that rural Tanzanian groups resisted restrictive regulations and seized the opportunity to sell land to safari companies, resulting in significant revenue and the ultimate restructuring of local governments. Later, conservation corridors, promoted by conservation scientists within the emerging neoliberal framework, 'became mired in the politics of conservation and land, and ultimately were rejected by community members' (Goldman, 2009, p. 343). State-protected areas in Tanzania continue to increase even though the national rhetoric is decentralisation and the strengthening of local rights to benefit from wildlife (Nelson, 2012). However, the government is not the only entity in question. Levine (2002) stated 'today there is little difference between the environmental strategies of international development agencies and those of the major conservation NGOs' (p. 1043).

Over a decade later, Bawa (2013) offered similarities in Ghana where 'local NGOs are themselves not as autonomous as they should be to promote ownership of poverty allevia-tion programmes' (p.535). She challenged that multinationals contribute to marginalisation by promoting 'victims' of poverty. In an assessment of the branding of Trans-boundary Natural Resource Management programmes throughout southern Africa, Büscher (2010) noted 'capitalist realism of trying to trumpet and advertise the value of nature and rural communities by focusing on idealized, harmonious human–nature constructions has in effect radically relocated this value and opens it up for speculation' (p. 273).

While grassroots organisations are prevalent in tourism studies, multinational agencies are often only mentioned in passing. NGOs and federal government agencies are involved in international conservation activities including scientific research, policy formation, edu-cation, and developing projects that add value to the protection of a natural resource (Slocum & Kline, 2015). The controversy lies in the appropriate levels of market-based structures in the conservation–preservation debate and the governance structures that inform, entice or coerce local communities to participate (Zerner, 2000). The new core of neoliberal conservation is in 'how' governance agencies approach the problems of human and nature interactions and if market-based solution should come passively or if new economic avenues should be built into conservation projects from the onset. Moreover, the market solutions implemented in restrictive conservation policies are often engineered by foreign proponents of conservation rather than the local groups most affected (Büscher, 2008). This paper looks at multinational organisations, their current philosophies in relation to neoliberalism and their role in conservation and community development. It is argued that they appear to be more in tune with the opportunities neoliberalism offers in the realm of conservation advancement and poverty elimination. The research questions for this study are:

(1) What is the state of affairs regarding ecotourism development in Africa?
(2) What policies, protocols, and practices are in place to ensure that the projects remain true to ecotourism principles?

Methods

The data were collected during the summer of 2011 through five semi-structured interviews and one focus group with representatives from Washington, DC-based organisations that operate in Africa (Table 1). Selection criteria for the six organisations included key goals of natural resource conservation, employing tourism development as strategy, and being currently and historically active on the African Continent. Selection criteria for the organisations' representatives included familiarity with tourism as a conservation strategy and direct involvement in a leadership role of relevant programmes. Interviews lasted between 60 and 90 minutes and informants received no incentive for their participation.

Five organisations identified capacity building (training, mentoring, and providing technical assistance) as core activities and goals. Another five directly participated in conservation science, while the sixth implemented programmes that supported conservation as a key community goal. All were involved with enterprise development within ecotourism and spent substantial effort on long-term partnerships to realise the principles of ecotourism. While five directly provided funding to conservation and tourism-related projects, all of them engaged with local communities on ecotourism project planning.

An interview guide was used to ensure that participants answered a similar set of questions, allowing for comparison between interviews during the analysis stage (Bernard & Ryan, 2010). The questions were developed collaboratively by the research team and were drawn from themes in ecotourism literature (Honey, 2008). Questions probed the organisation's involvement with ecotourism development, their policies and protocols on staff activities within the context of ecotourism development, and the nature of staff–community interaction. Interviewees were provided the questions prior to the meeting.

The interviews were recorded and transcribed. The data were analysed in three stages: research team members analysed the data independently; team members discussed the interpretation of findings and potential data codes; and a second round of coding was conducted with agreed-upon codes using Atlas TI 7.1.

Findings

While the missions of the organisations in the study differed, their stated approach to development included involving ecotourism and local communities through economic incentives (donor funds) as a means to enhance conservation principles and improve quality of life for residents. However, this neoliberal approach included not only elements of wildlife and habitat conservation, but education, empowerment, and poverty alleviation. More importantly, the values of all six bear similarities. These values, which can translate into programme outcomes or techniques, serve as the structure for the findings.

Table 1.   Interview descriptions.

Interview	Interview type	Points of contact	Gender	Type of organisation	Funding sources
A	Individual	1	Female	NGO	Grants; gifts; revenue generation
B	Individual	1	Male	Private	Contracts from US government & foreign governments
C	Individual	1	Female	NGO	Grants from US government & foreign governments
D	Individual	1	Male	Government	Taxes; grants
E	Individual	1	Male	Government	Taxes; grants
F	Focus Group	5	4 Female/ 1 Male	Government	Taxes; grants
Total		10			

The samples were all active on the African continent. Their tourism markets include safari tourists, scientific and academic tourists, voluntourirsts, luxury ecotourists, and sport hunters. Projects comprise ecolodge development, home stays, tour development, cultural events, 'people to people' experiences, indigenous food experiences, and value-added agricultural and heritage products, what might be described by Brown and Hall (2008) as a product-driven approach. An informant from the focus group (Interview F) outlined his involvement this way:

> It runs the gamut from consultations to helping to design ecotourism and scientific tourism on a national level. In terms of scientists, about 50% of our work is with the masses of scientists running around Africa. So, it runs the gamut from design, right down to infrastructure suggestions and I've recently worked with a couple of high end ecotourism companies that were looking at sites off the coast of Gabon. We're interfacing on what is their clientele, what is their market niche, how do they approach it, and what do they need.

This statement demonstrates the diversity in ecotourism project clientele (Honey, 2008) and helps to explain the growing customer base of multinational agencies. Their increasing involvement with 'markets' also suggests their neoliberal conservation approach. When discussing their current projects, all of the informants emphasised that the approach is critical, citing sensitivity to local needs and culture throughout the interviews.

Sensitivity to local needs/culture

The multinational development community, including ecotourism project managers, has been accused of considering local people secondary in their role in conservation (Bawa, 2013). This holds especially true on the African continent. Informant E puts it into light:

> Particularly back in time ... the element of biological research [acted] as if people are not part of the ecosystem. ... Over the last 10, 20 years, in the entire conservation community, there's a growing recognition that people are part of the ecosystem and that they are both the threat and the opportunity for management.

An expanding practice is to embed local, trained staff into the heart and management of a project. Informant A noted that her organisation primarily employed staff local to the country or region of focus (80% of the staff); Informants B, C, and F relied heavily on local partners for efforts to be successful. Each of the organisations agreed that their expatriate staff had a strong awareness of themselves as non-residents and consequently needed to respect the historic activities, local context and official structure of conservation work in the region. On the surface, these approaches seemed to contrast Bawa's (2013) concerns that ownership of projects is primarily out of the hands of locals and promotes victimisation of locals as 'poverty-stricken' residents of the Global South being helped by friendly neighbours of the North. Additionally, this attitude implies a convergence towards Lemos & Agrawal (2006)'s conclusion that neoliberal policies must promote democratic principles and community empowerment if locals are valued as stakeholders in ecotourism.

Informant A discussed 'cultivating trusted go-betweens', knowing the local language, and understanding the historic relationship between countries:

> For example, in Tanzania it is always more prudent to have a Tanzanian as the head of delegation, not a Kenyan. No matter what the qualifications of the Kenyan are, the Tanzanian

will be much more readily accepted. It's the same thing you could see anywhere here in the United States, it's one of those seemingly unfounded prejudices that exist there just as much as they do here.

Another way to foster and demonstrate sensitivity is by entering into projects for the long term in order to ensure that economic gains and conservation principles are sustainable. All of the informants emphasised the extended relationships they have with local governments, civic groups, and local NGOs. Informant D noted:

> We have a responsibility to do no harm, certainly. And to be sensitive to their community's ways of doing things in addition to seeding further development that comes down the road that we want to be compatible with. Especially if you're going to be there for a while, which hopefully you are, then you want to start it off right.

Informant E agreed, 'To be successful, you have to be cross-culturally sensitive.'

Neoliberal practices have given rise to a new view of suppliers and other stakeholders as a form of corporate 'customer'. Therefore, the challenges of conservation projects have brought a new focus on the needs of communities within ecotourism development (Brown & Hall, 2008). A stakeholder focus has put pressure towards an 'ethical' approach to development that incorporates effective inclusion channels of communication (Ojeda, 2012). While causality cannot be assumed, Africa has made great strides in economic development while simultaneously multinational agencies are changing the way they view local communities within ecotourism development (Slocum & Backman, 2011).

Organisational partnerships

During the course of the interviews, all of the informants named numerous partners at an organisational and project level. Collaboration was inherent in their fieldwork, funding structures, administration, and monitoring systems. Rather than regarding partnerships as an overt public relations strategy, the informants presented the narrative of partnerships as part of their organisation's value system. A member of the focus group (Interview F) stated:

> We give grants and provide technical advice, but we are a networking organization because in this age of specialization and high demands for technical skills, the key to complex answers, and conservation usually requires a network, grouped approach where people will learn to work in teams. You bring various things to the table and that requires knowing where particular expertise lies. So, one consummate skill is to bring together kindred spirits and that's a valuable function in today's reality.

Partnerships included African national governments, US and other foreign governments, local governments, foreign investors, local and foreign universities, local scientists/ researchers, international and local NGOs, cooperatives or civil society groups, foreign and local tourism operators, travel media, local naturalists, park managers or guides, and the Global Sustainable Tourism Counsel.

Informant B describes their partnerships with local professionals:

> [Scientists are] helping to identify and validate conservation threats; it is done in a participatory way where you bring community members, park staff, NGO staff, and tour operators into the room together. The other area where we often work with scientific NGO's is training. We

almost always work with local naturalist guides who might help us compile training materials, whether it's on the history of parks or local ecosystems or species, they'll help us do those trainings.

Without further grassroots investigations, it is difficult to know if these partnerships are 'mired in politics' as Goldman (2009) observed. Duffy (2008) recognised a need for new solutions to conservation issues; multinational agencies are in a position to solicit help from a variety of networked sources unavailable to individual conservation areas. While neoliberal politics are most certainly a part of the development process, the question remains how these politics manifest and who is involved in positions of power and voice. Multinational agencies are still foreign entities with agendas that focus on project success and increasing donor aid (Büscher, 2008). Therefore, while gaining recognition is an important element of success, it is still unclear how the power structure affects the reaction to adversity inherent in neoliberal landscapes (Igoe & Kelsall, 2005).

Capacity building

Capacity building came in the form of technical assistance, training, mentoring, and other activities to encourage, empower, and aid in the local control of projects. When informants were asked to describe the programmes of their organisation, four mentioned capacity building by name while the others described capacity-building activities. Informant C explains their role this way:

> Our grantees are often the leading conservation development organization of that area. So it's not like a group coming in not having any relationships, not knowing the local reality, and as soon as the grant ends, they leave. Our grantees are going to stay there with or without us. And we see our role as building their capacity ....we are here to support civil society and make sure that when we leave they are strong enough to be sustainable.

Informant A describes their approach:

> A hallmark over the years has been the priority of building African national capacity, so we have prioritized African national researchers, first and foremost. Generally, people are from these communities or close to them, better able to engage with local communities, and, generally, the data and the knowledge stays there in a more permanent form.

She elaborates that while they work with African wildlife managers as a primary stakeholder, 'when we say capacity builders, we're thinking about our community partners, thinking about our government partners, and again just trying to broadly help everyone make better decisions about natural resource management.'

The focus group members all agreed that capacity building is critical to their work:

> I would suggest that capacity building is our greatest tool to do conservation because it's education but it's more than just technical skills. It's about enlightening self-interest in regard to conservation and the environment and how to treat the Earth, which is very important to do if we're going to do conservation sustainably. Now, whose capacity are we building? The folks who live there and make the decisions at whatever level. It can be a villager with a crop or a minister deciding policy. We are trying to raise the capacity of individuals who make the decisions that affect the resources we're trying to protect. If a Nigerian woman is working for their national parks, and since what she can do is frequently limited by the institution she works for, we try to work with key institutions to build institutional capacity, since that's frequently a defining parameter.

Capacity building is seen as a path towards long-term management by locals. In this regard, it supports the notion of empowerment and ownership of local governments, civil society, and individuals (Bawa, 2013; Lemos & Agrawal, 2006; Ojeda, 2012). It seems the informants are working to prevent their projects becoming 'playgrounds' for tourists, investors or other foreign entities at the expense of local populations (Igoe & Brockington, 2007). However, they are extensively involved in most aspects of the project (Slocum & Kline, 2015; Zebich-Knos, 2008), which may not lend itself to local 'ownership'.

Monitoring

The informants suggest that monitoring their own activities and the activities of their grantees and partners is a fundamental value they try to embody (Interview A, C, D, and F). At least two mentioned their organisation's adoption of the World Bank's safeguards. Informant C expressed:

> Anyone who received World Bank funding must have them. [Some] thought it was too big of an imposition. But I've seen how the indigenous safeguards have really helped to strengthen a project.

Additionally, one NGO builds in funding to its grantees to support monitoring (Interview C).

Informant E was adamant that his organisation mandates strict environmental guidelines stating that 'no implementing mechanism grant contract can go forward unless there's been an environmental review.' In addition to the monitoring of natural resources, his agency examines social science issues, such as attitude and behavioural changes. Informant C concurred: 'We are trying to strengthen our monitoring in terms of measuring community benefits, benefits to individuals, and clearly ecotourism is an important tool to achieve that.' However, Informant D states: 'There used to be a social impact assessment requirement. There isn't any more, but one of the personnel that I work with actually is working on trying to revive that.'

A member of the focus group (Interview F) explained their monitoring:

> Were we reviewing a grant proposal that had potential impacts on a community, we would attempt, within the parameters available to us, to assure against a situation that would be negatively impactful on the environment, animals as individuals, or societies, and that is codified. Intrusive behaviors, things that would be deliberately culturally inflammatory, where there is a predictable sort of danger zone, would be a part of our review process. Now, this isn't necessarily codified, but due diligence implies that negative impacts on a wide variety of potential targets are duly considered as part of our action.

In addition to managing project impacts, informants discussed the mechanisms for the monitoring of visitor impacts. Informant B outlines his organisation's work with local guides:

> It is that person's job to observe, monitor, and instruct when that code is not followed and for that code to be communicated to that visitor. Especially if it's a sensitive activity, it happens through promotion materials, guided interpretation, and guided experience with someone telling you what to do and what not to do. It happens through signage. At the end of the day, that's a selling point for the markets that we are targeting.

However, a member of Interview F wonders if enough is being done to monitor the impacts of specific markets:

> We definitely fund a lot of researchers and are interested in focusing on research tourists and getting tourists to come in, collect a lot of data, but also finding facilities for them and hoping that they will benefit local national parks. But I am really curious if researchers are going to come and what will the impacts be for the communities.

As the global governance system for conservation (Duffy, 2013), monitoring and evaluating impacts is increasingly being incorporated into project funding and administrative mechanisms. With limited in-country funding (Kimbu & Ngoasong, 2013), international agencies have taken the lead to ensure that ethics are incorporated into this neoliberal governance system. While frequently uncodified, informants recognise the need to formalise these practices to ensure compliance on a wider and more consistent scale. How these values become operationalised will need future investigation.

Policies and protocols

Policies and protocols, to ensure sustainability, are increasingly being introduced within these multinational agencies. These include research protocols, data ownership, and codes of conduct for staff and tourists. On the macro level, organisational staff and partners were all expected to conduct their professional and personal activities with local sensitivity. Informant E considers this type of conduct aligned with basic human decency.

> We would hope that your aunt and uncle that are going to Kenya will be culturally sensitive and that [scientists] going to Gabon to work with the Smithsonian Research Center would have the same ethical responsibilities. When we are talking about scientific integrity and ethical behavior, all humans should practice good ethical behavior.

He notes that a subset of scientific integrity includes human and animal subject protocols and intellectual property, including genetic materials. All six of the informants stressed the importance, from an ethical perspective, that local communities have access to the data collected in their region. This and policies on human trafficking, respect of indigenous populations, and the use of environmental safeguards are codified in their policies, as well as their agreements with partners.

The discourse on policies included mitigation of impacts created by tourists. All of the informants held the view that tourists create impacts, but the severity depends on the purpose of their visit, the type of activities undertaken, and the longevity of their stay. A member of the focus group (Interview F) noted:

> The emphasis on potential sociocultural impacts is more relevant in some cases than others. When you have somebody who's been there for thirty days and he's in a hunting concession and is isolated from local communities, he doesn't really interact with locals except the guides and a couple of waiters. That is in contrast to the Peace Corps volunteers who live in the village two years. They get very close to the community, so there is a different potential impact regarding sociocultural affects. It's a continuum.

Informant B explained how they work locally to infuse codes of conduct throughout the tourism project:

> We'll work with managers of tourism businesses who we train. They go through a list of tourism best practices and match them with activities they are doing. Those best practices, such as boat drivers not dumping oil in waterways, get incorporated into each employee's checklist and job responsibilities. In that same course, a manager writes out a job description

for all their staff, developing checklists that will help them do their job, and those best practices are considered there. And for the enterprise as a whole, this responsible tourism policy is ideally developed to where they're actually looking at it as a whole. These are the operating principles that we follow to be sustainable, whether it's limiting the group size to ten or twelve people, employing only local people, or sourcing local products like food.

Much progress has been made by agencies' and NGO's working on multinational projects, but certainly there is more that can be done regarding ecotourism development in Africa. Much of the data show that key players in multinational agencies have adopted ecotourism principles, but some protocols are without formal guidelines and written policy. How these value systems are translated on the ground remains to be documented.

Conclusion

Ecotourism is still a major development tool of many multinational agencies (Duffy, 2013; Garland, 2008). Based on narratives from the sample, and despite contested progress (Bawa, 2013; Büscher, 2010; Igoe & Brockington, 2007), it appears that some of the critiques of ecotourism in past have been heeded. The summary of findings above addresses the first research question of this study 'What is the state of affairs regarding ecotourism development in Africa?' and while the six organisations presented here do not represent all organisations involved in ecotourism in Africa, they provide a snapshot of sentiments. The following section serves to respond to the second research question, 'What policies, protocols, and practices are in place to ensure that the projects remain true to ecotourism principles?'

Ownership should be local – While transgressions from multinational agencies continue (Goldman, 2009; Levine, 2002), some have adopted organisational values whereby local ownership, participation, and decision-making are paramount. The agencies in this study make it a priority to employ, consult, partner with, and train local African nationals (at all levels). The capacity-building efforts are based on principles of sustainability, but currently efforts are managed internally as new policy and protocols are in development. However, it is evident that many African nations are still reliant on foreign investment to fuel neoliberal conservation development (Slocum & Backman, 2011), which begs the question: do these agencies have an exit strategy?

Project activities should be transparent, documented and available – All of these agencies monitor the activities of their staff and partners. Five have transparent websites, detailing project goals, locations, action items, and strategies. Three provide tools and manuals on development on their website, and one provides results and lessons learnt from completed project cycles. The dissemination of this information, including the practice of leaving scientific data in-country, is helping to decentralise ecotourism and conservation development within a neoliberal paradigm (Jones & Murphree, 2004). In supporting a self-reliant conservation community that increases the direct involvement of stakeholders, multinational agencies are moving towards new levels of inclusion as development priorities evolve (Slocum & Backman, 2011).

Reliance on inclusive partnerships – Multinational agencies have learnt the value of empowering partners, including the development of international networks that bring expertise into the decision-making process. Schilcher (2007) argues that ecotourism, through its dependence on tourism infrastructure, brings communities into the neoliberal global economic system. But economic growth is invariably occurring either through the exploitation or through the protection of local resources. Capacity building appears to be a growing value system in conservation efforts that help provide valuable tools, processes, and skills training that support a sustainable system of economic advancement (Duffy, 2008). Additionally, through grant funding with local NGOs, the hiring of in-country scientists, and the inclusion of local communities, multinational agencies appear to be relinquishing power and allowing local organisations to be more actively involved in decision-making than in the past (Zebich-Knos, 2008). However, the levels of market-based approaches employed by multinational agencies are still being determined (Zerner, 2000).

Limitations to this study include its focus on DC-based organisations; different national perspectives would be most welcome in discovering a fuller picture of multinational agencies working in Africa. Also, the data represent only a snapshot in time for those who participated, and while lengths were taken to select the best representative, additional interviewees from each organisation might have broadened the narrative. Moreover, there are still areas to investigate. The perspective of various stakeholders on a particular ecotourism should be contrasted. Do the local guides and businesses see events similarly to the development agencies? To what extent are the protocols and policies of the agencies enacted on the ground? What issues are encountered by the African nationals working for foreign agencies? How do they perceive conservation efforts that are subject to capitalist market dynamics?

Neoliberalism involves incorporating marginalised communities into the global economic system. Multinational agencies in conservation are increasingly involved in facilitating neoliberalism through ecotourism development (Büscher, 2010). The results are still speculative. However, this article shows the mindset of conservation agencies and a concerted effort to include multiple stakeholders in the neoliberal outcomes of ecotourism development. Key players are becoming more aware of their responsibility to mitigate human interactions throughout Africa, rather than policing human behaviour at odds with conservation science (Dressler & Roth, 2011). Ecotourism offers new avenues of development (Nelson, 2004) and the 'global governance system' (Büscher, 2010) appears to be going through changes in value systems through an emphasis on ethical inclusion in the fight to sustain ecosystems, cultures, and lifestyles. It is argued that many of these ethical practices must be formalised into concrete policies and protocols in the near future to address the discrepancies and failures many researchers are still witnessing at the grassroots level in Africa (Bawa, 2013; Goldman, 2009; Levine, 2002; Nelson, 2012).

Acknowledgements

We thank the individuals who allowed us access to their organisational policies and processes. Their investment of time and their insights were invaluable.

Disclosure statement

No potential conflict of interest was reported by the authors.

References

Bawa, S. (2013). Autonomy and policy independence in Africa: A review of NGO development challenges. *Development in Practice, 23*(4), 526–536.

Benjaminsen, T. A., Goldman, M. J., Minwary, M. Y., & Maganga, F. P. (2013). Wildlife management in Tanzania: State control, rent seeking and community resistance. *Development and Change, 44*(5), 1087–1109.

Bernard, H. R., & Ryan, G. W. (Eds.). (2010). *Analyzing qualitative data: Systematic approaches.* Los Angeles: Sage.

Brown, F., & Hall, D. (2008). Tourism and development in the Global South: The issues. *Third World Quarterly, 29*(5), 839–849.

Büscher, B. (2008). Conservation, neoliberalism and social science: A critical reflection on the SCB 2007 Annual Meeting, South Africa. *Conservation Biology, 22*(2), 229–231.

Büscher, B. (2010). Derivative nature: Interrogating the value of conservation in 'Boundless Southern Africa'. *Third World Quarterly, 31*(2), 259–276.

Dressler, W., & Roth, R. (2011). The good, the bad and the contradictory: Neoliberal conservation governance in rural Southeast Asia. *Rural Development, 39*(5), 851–862.

Duffy, R. (2008). Neoliberalising nature: Global networks and ecotourism development in Madagascar. *Journal of Sustainable Tourism, 16*, 327–344.

Duffy, R. (2013). Interactive elephants: Nature, tourism and neoliberalism. *Annals of Tourism Research, 44*, 88–101.

Fletcher, R. (2009). Ecotourism discourse: Challenging the stakeholders theory. *Journal of Ecotourism, 8*(3), 269–285.

Garland, E. (2008). The elephant in the room: Confronting the colonial character of wildlife conservation in Africa. *African Studies Review, 51*(3), 51–74.

Goldman, M. (2009). Constructing connectivity: Conservation corridors and conservation politics in East African rangelands. *Annals of the Association of American Geographers, 99*(2), 335–359.

Honey, M. (2008). *Ecotourism and sustainable development: Who owns paradise?* (2nd ed.). Washington, DC: Island Press.

Igoe, J., & Brockington, H. (2007). Neoliberal conservation: A brief introduction. *Conservation and Society, 5*(4), 432–449.

Igoe, J., & Kelsall, T. (2005). Introduction: Between a rock and a hard place. In J. Igoe & T. Kelsall (Eds.), *African NGOs, donors, and the state: Between a rock and a hard place* (pp. 1–33). Durham, NC: Carolina Academic Press.

Jones, B. T., & Murphree, M. W. (2004). Community-based natural resource management as a conservation mechanism: Lessons and directions. In B. Child (Ed.), *Parks in transition: Biodiversity, rural development and the bottom line* (pp. 63–104). London: Earthscan.

Jones, C. (2012). Ecophilanthropy, neoliberal conservation, and the transformation of Chilean Patagonia's Chacabuco valley. *Oceania, 82*(3), 250–263.

Kimbu, A., & Ngoasong, M. (2013). Centralised decentralisation of tourism development: A network perspective. *Annals of Tourism Research, 40*, 235–259.

Lemos, C., & Agrawal, A. (2006). Environmental governance. *Annual Review of Environment and Resources, 31*, 297–325.

Levine, A. (2002). Convergence or convenience? International conservation NGOs and development assistance in Tanzania. *World Development, 30*(6), 1043–1055.

McAffee, K. (2012). The contradictory logic of global ecosystem services markets. *Development and Change, 43*(1), 105–131.

Nelson, F. (2004). *The evolution and impacts of community-based ecotourism in northern Tanzania.* IIED Drylands Programme Issue Paper 131, IIED, London, UK.

Nelson, F. (2012). Blessing or curse? The political economy of tourism development in Tanzania. *Journal of Sustainable Tourism, 20*(3), 359–375.

Ojeda, D. (2012). Green pretexts: Ecotourism, neoliberal conservation and land grabbing in Tayrona National Natural Park, Colombia. *Journal of Peasant Studies, 39*(2), 357–375.

Schilcher, D. (2007). Growth versus equity: The continuum of pro-poor tourism and neoliberal governance. *Current Issues in Tourism, 10*(2–3), 166–193.

Segi, S. (2014). Protecting or pilfering? Neoliberal conservationist marine protected areas in the experience of coastal Granada, the Philippines. *Human Ecology, 42*(4), 565–575.

Slocum, S. L., & Backman, K. (2011). Understanding government capacity in tourism development as a poverty alleviation tool: A case study of Tanzanian policy-makers. *Tourism Planning & Development, 8*(3), 281–296.

Slocum, S. L., & Kline, C. (2015). Chapter 3: Research as a forefront to tourism: Understanding conservation as a catalyst for ecotourism. In S. L. Slocum, C. Kline, & A. Holden (Eds.), *Scientific tourism: Researchers as travelers*. London: Routledge.

Willetts, P. (1996). *The conscience of the world: The influence of non-governmental organizations in the UN system*. Washington, DC: Brookings Institution; Christopher Hurst.

Zebich-Knos, M. (2008). Ecotourism, park systems, and environmental justice in Latin America. In D. V. Carruthers (Ed.), *Environmental justice in Latin America* (pp. 185–211). Boston: MIT Press.

Zerner, C. (2000). *People, plants, and justice: The politics of nature conservation*. New York, NY: Columbia University Press.

Analysing governance in tourism value chains to reshape the tourist bubble in developing countries: the case of cultural tourism in Uganda

Bright Adiyia[a], Arie Stoffelen[a], Britt Jennes[a], Dominique Vanneste[a] and Wilber Manyisa Ahebwa[b]

[a]Department of Earth and Environmental Sciences, University of Leuven (KU Leuven), Leuven, Belgium; [b]Department of Forestry, Biodiversity and Tourism, Makerere University, Kampala, Uganda

Several studies found larger benefits for communities when local stakeholders could participate in the tourism value chain by 'linking' their labour, products and services to the sector. However, the establishment of local linkages is difficult because of the complexity of the tourism system that consists of multi-sectoral and multi-scalar relationships. Moreover, in developing countries, empowered stakeholders tend to organise the tourism value chain vertically in which tourists are led in a spatially and socially confined trajectory in the destination, the so-called tourist bubble. This paper analyses the effect of governance in the tourism value chain on the establishment of local linkages to reshape the social and spatial boundaries of the tourist bubble in Uganda. Specifically, the possibilities of cultural tourism are explored as one particular way to reshape the bubble, that is centred on nature-based and ecotourism focuses. Results show that cultural activities can reshape the social boundaries of the bubble, while the catalyst role of cultural tourism developments is less successful in reshaping the spatial bubble boundaries. The national scale is pivotal to ensure that (1) local stakeholders are empowered to overcome existing barriers to enter and (2) international stakeholders are given incentives to reshape the bubble.

1. Introduction

Recent studies have provided evidence that linking labour, products and services of local communities in developing countries to the tourism sector, as described in the concept of local linkages, can provide a lever for sustainable regional development (Adiyia, Vanneste, Van Rompaey, & Ahebwa, 2014; Mitchell & Faal, 2008; Nyaupane & Poudel, 2011). However, the establishment of such linkages is not straightforward. The interplay between different scalar stakeholders from the public and the private sector as well as the civil society gives rise to a tourism value chain in which a multitude of stakeholders both compete and cooperate (Boyd & Butler, 1996; Bramwell & Meyer, 2007; Kaplinsky & Morris, 2000).

These multi-scalar and multi-sectoral characteristics of the tourism value chain generally result in power imbalances where each stakeholder tries to derive a larger share of value by gaining more power (Ford, Wang, & Vestal, 2012). This means that, when making an overall assessment of the regional development impacts of tourism, stakeholder interactions and power relations do not automatically fuel tourism development in a way that naturally leads to regional and/or local development (Kauppila, Saarinen, & Leinonen, 2009). Therefore, stakeholder interactions and power relations in tourism need to be actively managed, dealing with the multi-scalar and multi-sectoral characteristics of the value chain, in order to expand tourism to regional development by maintaining viability of the tourism value chain, and by maximising pro-poor aspects of tourism (Boyd & Butler, 1996; Kaplinsky & Morris, 2000).

In developing countries, the establishment of local linkages to the tourism value chain, and thus the poverty alleviation potential of the sector, is even more difficult because empowered stakeholders tend to organise the value chain vertically. This means that tourists are led from the airport to the main attractions and transported back to the airport, using a spatially and socially confined trajectory in the destination, the so-called tourist bubble (Cohen, 1972; Jaakson, 2004). When the tourist bubble is strongly delimited and tourists only rarely move outside this bubble, sustainable regional development is hampered by a dependency on the willingness of empowered stakeholders to link local labour, products and services to the value chain.

Therefore, as Van der Duim (2008) suggests, research into the governance of tourism value chain relations provides further insights into the role of tourism as an engine for sustainable regional development in developing countries. Hence, the aim of this paper is to study how tourism governance impacts the creation of local linkages within the tourism value chain, thereby influencing the regional development potential of tourism in developing countries by shaping the social and spatial delineation of the tourist bubble. Cultural activities are selected as a particular strategy to overcome limited linkages between tourism products and the local community. While nature-based tourism and ecotourism accents are dominant in most developing countries, establishment of linkages based on cultural activities and handicrafts is an additional strategy by which local communities can be involved and participate in the tourism value chain (Korutaro, Ahebwa, & Katongole, 2013; Mitchell & Faal, 2007).

The paper is organised as follows. Sections 2 and 3 elaborate the theoretical basis upon which the paper is hinged. It explains the role of governance in the tourism value chain as an engine to reshape the tourist bubble for sustainable regional development in the tourism–development nexus. Section 4 describes the research methods used for this study. Section 5 briefly presents the relevance of the case. Sections 6 and 7 present the results and discusses the implications of tourism governance on sustainable regional development. Finally, we conclude by giving recommendations for both policy and future research.

2.   Governance in tourism value chains

Tourism is a global industry that can provide a mechanism for wealth transfer from the rich to the poor (Spenceley & Meyer, 2012). However, people living nearby tourist attractions also bear disproportionate costs of tourism (Archabald & Naughton-treves, 2001). Value chain-based analyses (VCAs) are most suitable for tourism impact assessments on local households in developing countries (Meyer, 2009; Mitchell, 2012). VCAs are able to take most effects of tourism on the host economy into account, to assess the competitiveness of the tourism products and to focus on local economic development. In a tourism value chain, actors are interlinked and they collaborate to produce and distribute value for tourists (Song, Liu, & Chen, 2012). In its most basic form, the tourism value chain consists of the interrelations between 'nodes' formed by actors of tourism planning, primary suppliers, tourism intermediaries, and tourists (Romero & Tejada, 2011; Song et al., 2012).

The structure of these interactions creates experiential value that can be attained by tourists and a platform for local entrepreneurs and community stakeholders to link their labour, products and services to the international tourism system. (Re)configuration and coordination of these interrelations to provide local access to the tourism value chain are key in a sustainable tourism and development context. Governance of value chain relations should provide instruments to enhance democratic processes by aligning different stakeholder's capacities and aims, adjust the decision-making to specific contexts and overall goals, and provide means for practical progress (Bramwell & Lane, 2011).

2.1. *Implications of tourism planning for governance of the tourism value chain*

The governance process of tourism value chain relations, and hence the possibilities to create a more socially and spatially inclusive structure in the tourism value chain, is complicated by the multi-scalar and multi-sectoral characteristics of tourism. A functional governance situation should thus manage scalar processes and networked operations between a multitude of stakeholders that together shape the outcome of tourism development on lower scales (Hall, 2011; Milne & Ateljevic, 2001). In this process, the state is one of the key mediating stakeholders in the web of relations of tourism value chains as it has authority and justification to deal with issues of collective interests (Bramwell, 2010, 2011). States can do so by imposing requirements as well as incentives for tourism-related stakeholders to behave in a certain way (Bramwell, 2011).

Because of this central position of the state in the governance of the tourism value chain, the multi-level planning system of a country is a central factor in defining the structure of value chain relations (Romero & Tejada, 2011; Song et al., 2012), thereby having a key influence on the potential to enable or constrain the creation of local linkages. To optimise tourism impacts, tourism planning should be integrated in the overall development strategy, plans and contexts of a country or region (Bramwell & Lane, 2011; Kauppila et al., 2009; Timothy, 1998). Timothy (1998) points to four types of cooperation that need to be present to reach this integration in the planning system:

(1) cooperation between government agencies, reducing competition or mismatches between governmental departments;
(2) cooperation between levels of administration, dealing with the scalar structure of tourism planning responsibilities;
(3) cross-border cooperation between same-scale administrative units, dealing with potential cross-border resources and environmental, social and economic imbalances between areas;
(4) private and public sector cooperation, dealing with the diversity of tourism-related stakeholder groups.

To create an analytic benchmark, the requirements of integrative tourism planning as defined by Timothy (1998) can be interpreted by two dichotomies: internal versus external (within the public domain versus across public, private, voluntary domains and across territorial units) and horizontal versus vertical (on the same scale versus across scales) governance characteristics (Perkmann, 1999). When combined, they result in four spheres whose

Table 1. Spheres of multi-scalar and multi-sectoral tourism governance.

	Internal	External
Horizontal	Alignment and coordination of efforts between different policy domains (tourism, culture, economic development, spatial planning, …) on the same scale	Alignment and coordination of efforts between the public sector and private, community and voluntary sector stakeholders, potentially across territorial units, on the same scale
Vertical	(Multi)scalar configuration of tourism-related activities, responsibilities and strategies of governmental tourism management	Alignment and coordination of efforts between the public sector and private, community and voluntary sector stakeholders that operate on different spatial scales, territorial units and in different network connections

specific, contextual content shapes the governance system of the tourism value chain in specific places (Table 1).

Complicating factors can be added to this scheme. In developing countries, the control over natural resources and the crucial role of tourism planning and policy-making is generally regulated by the government or by government-led agencies, which tend to limit local involvement (Nelson, 2012). Yet, involvement of lower level governments is of vital importance to successfully implement tourism initiatives on the national scale to alleviate poverty (Jamal & Getz, 1995). Furthermore, the governance situation regularly empowers international stakeholders and dominant local elites to allow them to create barriers for local stakeholders to enter tourism markets or the decision-making arena (Duffy, 2006a, 2006b; Schilcher, 2008).

3. The tourist bubble

An important barrier for local stakeholders to enter tourism markets is the vertical organisation of the tourism value chain. In this structure, dominant international tour operators assemble individual components of the tourism product into a package product (Mosedale, 2006). This package turns into a travel experience in which tourists are led from the airport to the main attractions and back to the airport, creating a so-called tourist bubble (Carrier & Macleod, 2005; Cohen, 1972). The concept of the tourist bubble is built upon the 'environmental bubble' of Cohen (1972), used to express the touristic *Eigenwelt* that a tourist experiences during holidays (Cohen, 1972; Jaakson, 2004). The protective walls of the bubble cushion shocks for unfamiliar encounters and create a physical and psychological space 'in which a favourable version of local reality is presented to tourists' (van der Zee & Go, 2014, p. 5).

In the bubble, opportunities for local stakeholders to link labour, products and services to the tourism value chain are reduced. In other words, the possibility of creating local linkages, together with the degree or intensity of these linkages, generally depends on the strategies of empowered, often multinational tourism stakeholders of the tourism value chain that have a central position in the tourist bubble. Moreover, previous research showed that these bubbles create a spatial and social imbalance of tourism benefits inside the destination (Jaakson, 2004; Wilkinson, 1999). Judd (1999), studying the concept in an urban tourism context, suggested that 'tourist bubbles create islands of affluence that are sharply differentiated and segregated from the surrounding urban landscape' (Judd, 1999, p. 53). Hence, to overcome these spatial and social barriers, the structure of the tourism value chain needs to be governed in such a way that local stakeholders are empowered to create linkages to enter the tourism value chain (Cole, 2006; Sofield, 2003).

4. Research methods

To focus on governance in the tourism value chain and to find key actors and processes that control the tourist bubble, the various stakeholders, their roles and mutual relationships first need to be identified at different scales (Boyd & Butler, 1996; Gereffi, Humphrey, & Sturgeon, 2005; Mosedale, 2006). During fieldwork (July 2012–January 2013), 74 semi-structured in-depth interviews were conducted in Uganda ($n = 64$) as well as in Belgium and the Netherlands ($n = 10$) to grasp the role of various stakeholders on different scales in the Ugandan tourism sector and to identify their connection with the tourism value chain. In the data collection process, key stakeholders in the value chain were identified from a stakeholder list from Uganda Tourism Board (UTB) and from different tourism development plans, based on important positions in the stakeholders' model of Boyd and Butler (1996). This model, applied to ecotourism, shows that stakeholders on different scales have to be involved in the decision-making of tourism (Boyd & Butler, 1996). The respondents were selected by key informants who acted as a starting point for the snowball sampling technique. Interviews were undertaken with representatives from the private sector ($n = 46$), the public sector ($n = 12$), donor organisations ($n = 6$), national environmental groups ($n = 4$) and tourism interest groups ($n = 6$). Moreover, 7 focus group discussions with local communities were conducted in the area surrounding Kibale National Park (KNP) to triangulate the interview data on the impact of the tourism value chain at the destination scale. The interviews lasted between 30 minutes and more than two hours. All semi-structured interviews were recorded and transcribed, read and coded using NVivo® 10 to identify relevant themes. In addition to the interviews, secondary data and documents were collected and analysed.

5. Study area

Uganda is an emerging tourism destination in Sub-Saharan Africa, of which the local economy in rural areas is characterised by subsistence agriculture, high poverty levels and limited livelihood options (UBOS, 2013; Vermeiren, Adiyia, & Loopmans, 2013). The country was a very popular tourism destination during the 1960s and 1970s, but the growth of tourism abruptly ended with the reign of Idi Amin (Ahebwa, 2012; Ellis & Bahiigwa, 2003). Since tourism re-emerged in the early 1990s on the political agenda after a long period of instability, international tourist arrivals have annually increased to reach 1.2 million in 2013 (Ahebwa & Katongole, 2015; Ministry of Tourism, 2014; UBOS, 2013). In 2014, tourism was the top foreign exchange earner in the national economy, preceding the sectors of remittances and coffee in foreign exchange (World Travel & Tourism Council, 2014).

Tourism is used as a strategy by the Ugandan national government to alleviate poverty and develop rural areas. However, the sector is characterised by limited linkages between tourism and rural communities (Korutaro et al., 2013; National Planning Authority, 2010). The environs of KNP, located at 300 km west of Kampala (Figure 1), were selected for this study for multiple reasons; all related to the fact that KNP can be associated with a tourist bubble.

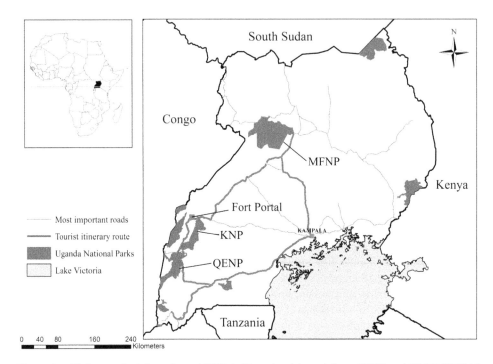

Figure 1. (Colour online) Location of KNP in Uganda. Adapted from IUCN and UNEP-WCMC (2015).

(1) Tourism in Uganda largely focuses on the western part of the country, as this region encloses most of the country's comparative advantages and tourism attractions. For example, the five most visited national parks are all situated in the (south) west of the country and contain 92% of all leisure tourists who visit a national park in Uganda (Weiss & Messerli, 2012).

(2) KNP has more than 10.000 visitors annually, and is listed fourth in the ranking of total visitor expenditures to national parks (8.2%) (Ahebwa & Katongole, 2015; UBOS, 2013). The development of asphalted roads ensures that each itinerary passes through Fort Portal (Figure 1). This major town adjacent to KNP has been earmarked as the 'tourism city' (Ministry of Tourism, 2013), since it is situated between the two most visited parks: Queen Elisabeth NP and Murchison Falls NP (Figure 1). As a result, the area provides a potential spatial hub of the tourism value chain where local linkages can be established (Adiyia et al., 2014).

(3) KNP has the protected status of a national park, although it does not have the exceptional status of UNESCO World Heritage. Therefore, it could be used as an interesting exemplary case for other national parks and protected areas inside tourist bubbles in Sub-Saharan Africa.

6. Tourism governance in Uganda

6.1. *Structure of the Ugandan tourism value chain*

On a national scale, the Ugandan tourism sector is horizontally managed by a complex network of stakeholders and institutions. This is led by the Ministry of Tourism, Wildlife and Heritage (MTWH) and six semi-autonomous parastatal institutions with different mandates that should provide an enabling and competitive environment for the private sector (International Trade Centre, 2011; National Planning Authority, 2010). The two most important are the Uganda Wildlife Authority (UWA), with a mandate for conservation and management of the national parks, and the UTB, in charge of destination marketing and product development (International Trade Centre, 2011; Korutaro et al., 2013). MTWH is linked with bilateral and multilateral donor organisations as well as NGOs. These organisations play a role in financing tourism and conservation projects on different scales and giving technical advice to MTWH and local stakeholders.

According to the National Development Plan, the private sector is supposed to develop the tourism value chain by investments in sub products on the destination scale, such as local accommodation, transport and catering (Korutaro et al., 2013; National Planning Authority, 2010). The private sector has organised itself per sub-segment into 10 associations[1] to increase communication and join forces in attaining more public sector support (National Planning Authority, 2010). These important stakeholders in the chain are summarised with their specific roles in Table 2.

Vertically, the main stakeholders in the tourism value chain are intermediaries such as global tour operators, offering sub products for different destinations as a wholesaler, or travel agencies, offering information on sub products as a retailer (Christian, Fernandez-Stark, Ahmed, & Gereffi, 2011; Romero & Tejada, 2011). Since the consumption of the tourism product is spatially fixed in the destination and international tourists are generally not familiar with travelling towards developing countries, tourists tend to purchase packages of individual sub products, such as air transfer, local accommodation and local transport, from tourism intermediaries (Mosedale, 2006; Song et al., 2012). In this process, nationally based tour operators, partly or fully owned by foreign investors, act as agents for global tour operators by coordinating in-country tours on the destination scale (Christian et al., 2011). They are vital in the chain since both international and domestic tourists can directly purchase sub products and package products with them (Christian et al., 2011).

Table 2. List of most important actors with corresponding functions.

Actors within the value chain	Function
MTWH	Regulation, control, planning and strategic development of tourism and natural and cultural heritage
UWA	Conservation, park management
UTB	Marketing and promotion, product development and quality assurance
Interest groups (AUTO, USAGA and UTA)	Representation of the private sector
Donor organisations (USAID, World Bank, UNDP, etc.)	Funding and technical advice
Environmental groups (national and international)	Research and interest delegation, possibly project funding, education
Local stakeholders (UCOTA)	Inactive or active local involvement

AUTO, Association of Ugandan Tour Operators: umbrella organisation for tour operator companies in Uganda; USAGA, Uganda Safari Guides Association: organisation for safari and bird guides in Uganda. UTA, Uganda Tourism Association: covering organisation for the whole private tourism industry. Sector-related organisations such as AUTO, USAGA, Uganda Hotel Owner's Association (UHOA) and The Uganda Association of Tourism Training Institutions (UATTI) are included. UCOTA, UGANDA Community Tourism Association: organisation with interests in community-based tourism.

On local scales, stakeholders are less influential in structuring the overall value chain relations, while their empowerment is key in the use of tourism for regional development purposes (Cole, 2006; Sofield, 2003). Figure 2 displays the simplified structure of the tourism value chain in Uganda, with various arrows portraying different types of relationships between the stakeholders.

6.2. *Governance complexities*

The horizontal and vertical structure of the tourism value chain shows important complexities in aligning internal and external governance connections. Within the public domain on the national scale, analysis of the most important tourism documents confirms functional overlaps between government-led bodies due to lack of communication and coordination mechanisms (Korutaro et al., 2013). Moreover, due to other prioritised economic sectors such as health, education and law and order, the government allocates insufficient resources to the tourism sector (tourism officer, MWTH, personal communication, August 28, 2012). This situation results in systematically understaffed and underfunded governmental tourism agencies (International Trade Centre, 2011; Weiss & Messerli, 2012). For example, in 2012, the government invested approximately US$4.5 million in the sector, corresponding to 0.13% of its total budget, while the sector provided more than US$2 billion to the national economy, corresponding to 8.8% of GDP (Weiss & Messerli, 2012). As a result of limited expertise and budget within UTB, the promotion of Uganda as a tourism destination is largely left to the private sector, such as national tour operators and lodge owners.

There is really a funding problem. People complain here, because we compare it with other countries like Kenya, Tanzania. (...) Rwanda is spending 5 million dollars for marketing. Tanzania had 8, Kenya has 28 million dollar. And they give us 300.000 dollar, which is not a lot. That is very important. Because if you make a plan, the plan is dependent on funding and the funding is not there yet. (Administrative manager, UTB)

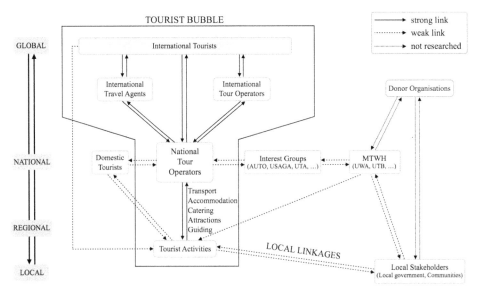

Figure 2.   Simplified structure of tourism value chain in Uganda.

It is my job to educate and re-educate my clients about the country as a whole, before I even get to the chance of selling them my services, my expertise, my intelligence, my vehicles, my drivers. I have to tell them about the lodges, the environment, the parks, etc. This cost is being borne by me at my own expense. Tour operators are spending own money on promoting Uganda. And that is not what is supposed to happen. (Foreign tour operator)

Hence, horizontal internal complexities importantly shape the content of horizontal external relations. Referring to the example of insufficient resource allocation, the public domain planned to install a VAT levy of 18% for the private domain to collect resources in order to increase governmental tourism resources to 1.8% of total government budget (National Planning Authority, 2010). However, the levy has been discarded on official request of AUTO, the association of tour operators, because the private sector does not want to take responsibility for additional resource collections (chairman AUTO, personal communication, August 22, 2012). In their latest Master Plan (2014–2024), funded by UNDP, MTWH acknowledges that current funding arrangements in the tourism sector 'are inadequate in relation to the responsibilities fulfilled' (Ministry of Tourism, 2014, p. 22). In this regard, the Master Plan proposes several financing strategies to address funding issues and mobilise investments funds from various resources.

To enhance communication and collaboration between different private tourism associations and to put forward and represent private sector interests towards the government (Weiss & Messerli, 2012), the Uganda Tourism Association (UTA) was founded as a private sector umbrella organisation. However, several respondents confirmed that the UTA is not effectively functioning for several reasons:

UTA is weak because there is an internal association rivalry. Where politics is, money is also, so some of the problems spring from resource locations. (. . .) You find that AUTO and UHOA do not like to subject themselves to the authority of the UTA. AUTO gets resources from the sale of gorilla permits. Now, UTA likes to control that, but AUTO says 'no, that is mine'. (Managing Director, UTB)

From 2014 onwards, UTA attempts to overcome this by developing a strategic plan. However, UTA still struggles with funding gaps as the organisation needs US$ 1.3 million to implement its strategic objectives in the coming five years (2014–2019) (Katongole & Ahebwa, 2014).

When analysing the vertical internal governance system, local tourism matters are handled by the local district government[2] in which tourism resources are located (Mackenzie, 2012b). However, due to the inexistence of local tourism departments, general district officers without any tourism background manage tourism issues in absence of a MTWH coordination mechanism, resulting in weakly addressed and implemented matters on a sub-national level (Korutaro et al., 2013; Weiss & Messerli, 2012). This problem of a lack of knowledge by tourism governmental officials is widespread and occurs even on the national level:

Our leaders have never studied tourism, they have no feeling for being in the tourism industry and they will never make a policy that is a committed to a pro-poor tourism development. (President USAGA)

Timothy (1998) showed that lower level governments are key in the successful implementation of tourism initiatives on the national scale. Several authors have addressed challenges of local-level governance around national parks in Uganda (Ahebwa, van der Duim, & Sandbrook, 2012; Mackenzie, 2012b). For example, a policy of tourism revenue sharing has been set up by UWA to compensate communities around national parks for the costs of tourism and conservation on their livelihoods (Mackenzie, 2012b). As a result, local governments are given 20% of park entrance fees to establish public utilities in communities, such as schools, health centres and road infrastructure (Ahebwa et al., 2012; Archabald & Naughton-treves, 2001; Mackenzie, 2012b). However, the outcome of these arrangements has achieved mixed success, insufficiently compensating and unequally distributing the surrounding communities (Archabald & Naughton-treves, 2001; Mackenzie, 2012a).

6.3. *The tourist bubble*

As demonstrated in Figure 2, nationally based tour operators have a central position in the value chain. They directly and indirectly manage in-country tours for both international and domestic tourists on the destination scale. Almost all nationally based tour operators in Uganda are located in Kampala or near Entebbe International Airport (Korutaro et al., 2013; Weiss & Messerli, 2012).

> We pick up the tourists at the airport and drop them off on their way back. Everything in between, we have organised it: gorilla permits, transportation, accommodation, special activities the client wants to do, meals, drinks, everything is included and planned in the offer. (Foreign tour operator)

The most successful nationally based tour operators in Uganda are partly or fully owned by foreign investors, attracted by an investment-friendly economic environment. Their position in the value chain is empowered in three different ways. First, global tour operators and travel agencies tend to prefer nationally based tour operators owned by foreign investors to tour operators by local investors, based on the assumption that they have a higher capacity to meet international service standards (Christian et al., 2011). Similarly, popular international travel guides list foreign-owned national tour operators as being more experienced and reliable (Briggs & Roberts, 2010). Second, these foreign tour operators tend to provide accommodation in own lodges in the national parks (Korutaro et al., 2013; lodge owner, personal communication, August 22, 2012), strengthening the creation of a tourist bubble with limited local linkages. Third, their position is empowered as the financial capital to back up their business allows their voices to be heard in UWA through representation in the AUTO. Local enterprises, interested to enter the value chain, perceive these conditions as barriers, resulting in an underrepresentation in AUTO and hence in the value chain.

> Local tour operators can also do business, but they need to register under AUTO. To register, you need to meet certain criteria. You need to have a specified number of guides who know international languages, trained staff and certified drivers with a well-maintained vehicle with a roof opening, nice seats, nice sitting windows, good mechanical condition and insurances in case of accidents. (Tourism officer, MTWH)

The above picture reflects a situation that increasingly empowers large tour operators in the sense that they socially and spatially shape the tourist bubble by controlling both tourist movements and their activities in the destination (Song et al., 2012). The strong position of tour operators results in a situation in which disempowered local stakeholders are depending on them for developing and marketing tourism products. This power imbalance socially and spatially fixes the boundaries of the tourist bubble, in which nationally based tour operators decide to what extent local stakeholders are able to link their products to the tourism value chain and, therefore, to what extent tourism contributes to poverty alleviation and sustainable regional development in terms of local linkages. Several respondents argue that the success of a local enterprise or activity depends on its proximity to the tourism circuit, confirming Jaakson (2004) who indicated the presence of a strong spatial core and a weak transition zone in the bubble:

> The guy (...) who has a farm over there may be beautiful, but is not along the road. Activities should be organised along the main routes between the national parks. And if they are well developed, tourists stay longer in Uganda. The longer you get them to stay in the country, the more money all of us get. (Foreign tour operator)

> Your activity has to be on the circuit. Because very few tour companies divert from the firmly set circuit. (International lodge owner)

It is clear that the international stakeholders need incentives to reshape the tourist bubble. Therefore, one should actively look for tools to facilitate the process of reshaping the bubble. Korutaro et al. (2013) list several strategies to reshape the bubble such as training and educating communities, investing in capacity building, linking communities to private sector, providing soft loans to enable communities starting tourism-related businesses and helping to organise these communities into associations to offer accommodation facilities or homestays. In summary, these strategies identify the barriers for entry for communities and suggest ways to enable them to be part of the tourism value chain. In their pursuance to actively promote tourism and stimulate poverty alleviation and regional development in remote areas, the Ugandan government puts cultural tourism development forward as a strategy to enlarge the existing product diversity (Ministry of Tourism, 2013; National Planning Authority, 2010).

7.   Cultural activities: a strategy to reshape the bubble?

Often, the perception lingers that international tourists in developing countries focus on the natural assets. Indeed, a number of high-end tourists travel to Uganda for primate tracking and wildlife safaris, but those tourists comprise a minority (5.5%) of total 1.2 million international arrivals (Ahebwa & Katongole, 2015; UBOS, 2013). The high-end tourists are important for the tourism sector as their average expenditure of US$3563 is significantly higher compared to other tourists visiting Uganda (Korutaro et al., 2013). Several respondents argue that, apart from this nature-based focus, there is a potential market for experiencing cultural activities in Uganda. Cultural tourism products in Uganda consist of traditional performances of music and dance, community walks, storytelling, homestays and handicrafts. This is confirmed by a UTB report displaying national tourism statistics in which travel purposes related to cultural tourism were estimated at 19% of international arrivals in 2012 (Korutaro et al., 2013).

  During our fieldwork, respondents confirmed the potential of cultural activities, especially for the large domestic market. However, governmental organisations in Uganda – similar to many other developing countries – place little emphasis on domestic tourism, even though first signs of change could be identified in the cooperation aims of MTWH and UTA (Katongole & Ahebwa, 2014; Ministry of Tourism, 2014).

> Cultural tourism is supposed to be a big area for many domestic tourists and tourists from our neighbouring countries, but it has been a largely neglected area. The product development has been focused on wildlife and not much on culture. Now, the overall domestic market is not

interested in going to track chimps. Even if you give them [domestic tourists] 1 million Shillings, they would spend it and not going to the national parks. (...) I think one of the main problems is that tourism is private sector driven. Some of those cultural attractions, no private sector can invest in them because they [private sector] do not make money from it. We think that the nature of tourism being private sector driven is a problem for this [cultural] development. (Tourism officer, MWTH)

Analysis shows that the few cultural activities that are offered for tourism are also located inside the tourist bubble. One example is an organised village walk near KNP's entrance. Part of the revenues of this village walk are distributed by a local organisation (Kibale Association for Rural and Environmental Development or KAFRED) in community projects, such as a secondary school, a health unit and a running water project (Nyakaana & Ahebwa, 2011; founding member KAFRED, personal communication, August 6, 2012). In addition, KAFRED allows a local women's group to sell handicrafts to tourists at their main offices; 90% of the handicraft revenues are transmitted to the individual household budgets and the remaining 10% goes to the maintenance of a nursery school, established by the women's group (managing director Bigodi's Women's Group, personal communication, August 8, 2012). It is interesting to notice that KAFRED managed to intrude into the value chain as a local stakeholder and reshape the tourist bubble. According to several respondents, KAFRED is able to successfully link their activities to the tourism value chain because of their strategic location next to KNP's entrance:

> KAFRED is successful because they are near a national park. Bigodi is next to Kibale National Park with the chimps, so everybody goes to Bigodi. In other places the local community was also interested and we tried to encourage it but no tourists came. (Local tour operator)

Tour operators partly or fully owned by foreign investors, on the one hand, and community-based organisations and tour operators owned by locals, on the other hand, acknowledge the importance of reshaping the bubble by cultural activities in the context of regional development. However, the former opines that developing cultural activities is non-profitable and, therefore, they can only be included on specific tourist demand. The latter state that cultural activities should be included in itineraries, stressing its large potential growing market due to a high diversity and relatively low cost.

> Our offer in cultural activities is limited, because the cultural and community aspects are more difficult to express and sell over the internet. (...) The level that they [tourists] want to be involved in local culture and communities depends on the clients themselves and we adjust the itinerary on demand. But the reason they come is predominantly for the gorillas and, unfortunately, there is more money to make out of gorillas. (Foreign tour operator)

> Why should I sell only gorilla trekking, over and over again? Uganda has much more, but you have to sell it as much more. (...) The element of culture should be more developed in a dynamic way. Now, 200 ladies in a village sell baskets, all doing the same thing. I mean, you see basket weaving everywhere. They should include tea products, candles, and bee products! Of course it has to do with the institutionalization. And are they underfunded? Yes! But who wants to put more money in it, if government is not doing anything? (Foreign tour operator)

> What we do after taking all those tourists to see the animals, to see everything, we always ask; what was your best activity here? And they answer: 'Oh, my visit to those people in the village or this visit to the cultural group is still in the memory.' So that shows if it is well marketed, if well packaged, it has a very big potential. (Local tour operator)

8. Discussion

Results indicate two main reasons why cultural activities are barely incorporated into the Ugandan tourism circuit as a tool to reshape the tourist bubble. First, MTWH creates barriers for local stakeholders, interested to expand the bubble and to enter the international tourism value chain, by further empowering the position of registered nationally based foreign-owned tour operators. Second, empowered private stakeholders are unwilling to include poorly developed, non-profitable tourism products in their itineraries. The Ugandan government has a clear role in this decision-making process since the potential of cultural tourism depends on destination marketing and product development. Analysis shows that MTWH fails in developing tourism and allocating resources to pro-poor strategies due to internal horizontal and vertical governance issues, caused by a lack of expertise and collaboration.

Furthermore, results confirm that it is too simplistic to blame the empowered position of profit-oriented international companies with little social conscience for hampering tourism development in developing countries (Erskine & Meyer, 2012; Meyer, 2013). Although foreign tour operators are empowered in the value chain because of an inherent advantage due to the international origin of leisure tourists in developing countries (Scheyvens, 2011), multi-scalar internal governance complexities undermine stable external governance mechanisms, such as public–private partnerships. These are necessary to establish local linkages in the value chain and to maximise the poverty alleviation potential of tourism on a local scale.

Provided meeting international standards and being profitable, cultural tourism developments are viable in the tourist bubble and function as a catalyst in creating linkages between local communities and the tourism value chain by increasing the degree of local inclusiveness. However, it is clear that cultural activities outside the tourist bubble are not viable, but result in unsuccessful attempts of local stakeholders to link with the tourism value chain. In other words, cultural activities are a potential tool to adjust the social boundaries of the tourist bubble, but it is much harder to reshape the spatial boundaries of the bubble (Figure 3). To spatially burst the bubble, existing multi-scalar internal governance complexities should be resolved to create stable external governance mechanisms. *Internally*, the government should clearly delineate the functional boundaries between the different government-led bodies and evaluate their functional capacities. Moreover, the government should further integrate tourism planning in local government structures and develop local tourism departments in which tourism issues are handled by qualified experts in the field. It is not sufficient to only allocate resources for tourism promotion without investing in (1) facilitating the linkage of local labour, products and services to the sector, (2) awareness building among local stakeholders to develop quality products and tap in the domestic tourism market and (3) road infrastructure as to create a physical accessible link with the value chain. Moreover, stable *external* governance mechanisms, such as public–private partnerships, could be built to improve the quality of tourism institutions, providing a robust human resources base needed to resolve existing skill and knowledge gaps among different government-led bodies.

Finally, the value chain needs to be governed in a way that local stakeholders are empowered to overcome existing barriers to enter such as a lack of financial investments, commercial experience and high responsibility levels (Christian, 2012; Schilcher, 2008). All measurements combined should allow increasing local empowerment in the tourism production system and facilitate to access to the tourism value chain as a supplier or as a complementary product provider, to break the tourist bubble by – socially and spatially – enlarging the product.

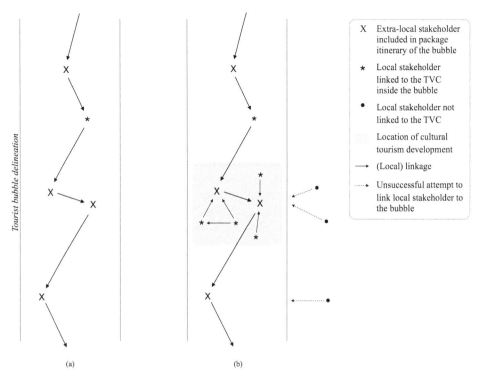

Figure 3.   Simplified structure of (a) the tourist bubble and (b) the role of cultural activities in the tourist bubble.

9.   Conclusion

In the presented study, key stakeholders were interviewed to assess the impact of govern-ance of tourism value chain relations on the spatial and social delineation of the tourist bubble in Uganda. This study focused on the structure of and problems related to govern-ance in the tourism value chain, as well as the possibilities of cultural activities to reshape the boundaries of the tourist bubble. Using an analytical benchmark to analyse governance characteristics, results show that tourism in Uganda is characterised by a field of tension between a weak institutional setting on one side and an uncoordinated and unregulated powerful private sector on the other. Multi-scalar internal governance complexities under-mine stability of external governance mechanisms, such as public–private partnerships and private sector coordination. As a result, the sector lacks ability to govern the value chain in a dynamic way to overcome imbalances in value chain relations and corresponding barriers for local stakeholders to enter the tourism value chain. This leads to a spatially and socially fixed delineation of the tourist bubble, hampering the establishment of local linkages and decreasing the regional development and poverty alleviation potential of tourism in rural areas.

Cultural activities can reshape the social boundaries of the bubble by functioning as a catalyst in the creation of linkages between local communities and the tourism value chain. However, the catalyst role of cultural tourism developments is limited in the sense that they are not able to reshape the spatial bubble boundaries, unless internal governance favours the construction of physical links. To burst the bubble, the national scale has a pivotal role in internally governing the value chain in a way that (1) local stakeholders are empowered to overcome existing barriers to enter and (2) international stakeholders are given incentives to reshape the bubble. In this argument, we acknowledge the central role of the state in the functioning and management of the overall tourism system and the integration of tourism in the overall planning system. This is in line with Bramwell (2011) who argues that the state does not only significantly influence governance for sustainable tourism and regional development when *strongly* organised but also when it is characterised by relative *absence* of a strong governing position. Investing in local linkages and awareness building, offering profitable cultural products of international standards, tapping in the domestic tourism market and including road infrastructure could be seen as opportunities to increase experiential value of tourism in Uganda and build on its regional development potential. Intangible cultural products have the advantage to be spatially widespread and, therefore, physical links are easier to establish than social links among the locals' awareness since social links require (1) awareness and a broader set of skills among the locals and (2) imagination and trust among the national and international tour operators.

Finally, the obstacles to sustainable tourism cannot be tackled with just one set of tools. Although it is clear that local linkages are one set of engines for regional development in developing countries, there is still a clear lack of academic research on complex development mechanisms of these linkages and their importance for local livelihoods of the rural poor.

Acknowledgements

We acknowledge the anonymous reviewers for their constructive feedback and suggestions. Moreover, we thank Prof. Nico Kotze for his critical comments and Egbert van der Zee for his input and advice. We are convinced that their feedback has improved the quality of the paper.

Disclosure statement

No potential conflict of interest was reported by the authors.

Notes

1. See Weiss & Messerli (2012) for an exhaustive list of associations.
2. The civil society is organised in a decentralised structure of five hierarchical council levels, in a declining hierarchical order: district, county, sub-county, village and parish levels (Mackenzie, 2012b).

References

Adiyia, B., Vanneste, D., Van Rompaey, A., & Ahebwa, W. (2014). Spatial analysis of tourism income distribution in the accommodation sector in western Uganda. *Tourism and Hospitality Research, 14*(1–2), 8–26.

Ahebwa, W. (2012). *Tourism, livelihoods and biodiversity conservation* (PhD thesis). Wageningen University, the Netherlands.

Ahebwa, W., van der Duim, R., & Sandbrook, C. (2012). Tourism revenue sharing policy at Bwindi Impenetrable National Park, Uganda: A policy arrangements approach. *Journal of Sustainable Tourism, 20*(3), 377–394.

Ahebwa, W., & Katongole, C. (2015). *Consultancy services to develop the tourism sector development plan 2015/16–2019/20*. Kampala: Celes International Limited.

Archabald, K., & Naughton-treves, L. (2001). Tourism revenue-sharing around national parks in Western Uganda?: Early efforts to identify and reward local communities. *Environmental Conservation, 8*(2), 135–149.

Boyd, S. W., & Butler, R. W. (1996). Managing ecotourism: An opportunity spectrum approach. *Tourism Management, 17*(8), 557–566.

Bramwell, B. (2010). Participative planning and governance for sustainable tourism. *Tourism Recreation Research, 35*(3), 239–249.

Bramwell, B. (2011). Governance, the state and sustainable tourism: A political economy approach. *Journal of Sustainable Tourism, 19*(4–5), 459–477.

Bramwell, B., & Lane, B. (2011). Critical research on the governance of tourism and sustainability. *Journal of Sustainable Tourism, 19*(4–5), 411–421.

Bramwell, B., & Meyer, D. (2007). Power and tourism policy relations in transition. *Annals of Tourism Research, 34*(3), 766–788.

Briggs, P., & Roberts, A. (2010). *Uganda*. Guilford, CT: Bradt Travel Guide.

Carrier, J. G., & Macleod, D. V. (2005). Bursting the bubble: The socio-cultural context of ecotourism. *Journal of the Royal Anthropological Institute, 11*(2), 315–334.

Christian, M. (2012). *Economic and social up (down) grading in tourism global production networks: Findings from Kenya and Uganda* (Working Paper No. 11). Capturing the Gains.

Christian, M., Fernandez-Stark, K., Ahmed, G., & Gereffi, G. (2011). *The tourism global value chain: Economic upgrading and workforce development*. Durham, NC: Center on Globalization, Governance & Competitiveness, Duke University.

Cohen, E. (1972). Toward a sociology of international tourism. *Social Research, 39*(1), 164–182.

Cole, S. (2006). Information and empowerment: The keys to achieving sustainable tourism. *Journal of Sustainable Tourism, 14*(6), 629–644.

Duffy, R. (2006a). Global environmental governance and the politics of ecotourism in Madagascar. *Journal of Ecotourism, 5*(1–2), 128–144.

Duffy, R. (2006b). The politics of ecotourism and the developing world. *Journal of Ecotourism, 5*(1–2), 1–6.

Ellis, F., & Bahiigwa, G. (2003). Livelihoods and rural poverty reduction in Uganda. *World Development, 31*(6), 997–1013.

Erskine, L. M., & Meyer, D. (2012). Influenced and influential: The role of tour operators and development organisations in tourism and poverty reduction in Ecuador. *Journal of Sustainable Tourism, 20*(3), 339–357.

Ford, R. C., Wang, Y., & Vestal, A. (2012). Power asymmetries in tourism distribution networks. *Annals of Tourism Research, 39*(2), 755–779.

Gereffi, G., Humphrey, J., & Sturgeon, T. (2005). The governance of global value chains. *Review of International Political Economy, 12*(1), 78–104.

Hall, C. M. (2011). Policy learning and policy failure in sustainable tourism governance: From first- and second-order to third-order change? *Journal of Sustainable Tourism, 19*(4–5), 649–671.

International Trade Centre. (2011). *Uganda tourism sector opportunity study: Inclusive tourism programme*. Author.

IUCN and UNEP-WCMC. (2015). *The world database on protected areas (WDPA)* [On-line]. Cambridge: UNEP-WCMC. Retrieved from www.protectedplanet.net

Jaakson, R. (2004). Beyond the tourist bubble? *Annals of Tourism Research, 31*(1), 44–60.

Jamal, T., & Getz, D. (1995). Collaboration theory and community tourism planning. *Annals of Tourism Research, 22*(1), 186–204.

Judd, D. R. (1999). Constructing the tourist bubble. In D. R. Judd & S. Fainstein (Eds.), *The tourist city* (pp. 35–53). New Haven, CT: Yale University Press.

Kaplinsky, R., & Morris, M. (2000). *A handbook for value chain research*. Ottawa: IDRC.

Katongole, C., & Ahebwa, W. (2014). *Uganda Tourism Association strategic plan 2014-2019*.

Kauppila, P., Saarinen, J., & Leinonen, R. (2009). Sustainable tourism planning and regional development in peripheries: A Nordic view. *Scandinavian Journal of Hospitality and Tourism, 9*(4), 424–435.

Korutaro, B., Ahebwa, W., & Katongole, C. (2013). *Provision of services for "a value chain analysis of the Ugandan tourism sector"*. United Nations Development Programme (UNDP).

Mackenzie, C. A. (2012a). Accruing benefit or loss from a protected area: Location matters. *Ecological Economics, 76*, 119–129.

Mackenzie, C. A. (2012b). Trenches like fences make good neighbours: Revenue sharing around Kibale National Park, Uganda. *Journal for Nature Conservation, 20*(2), 92–100.

Meyer, D. (2009). Pro-poor tourism: Is there actually much rhetoric? And, if so, whose? *Tourism Recreation Research, 34*(2), 197–199.

Meyer, D. (2013). Exploring the duality of structure and agency – the changing dependency paradigms of tourism development on the Swahili coast of Kenya and Zanzibar. *Current Issues in
Tourism*, *16*(7–8), 773–791.

Milne, S., & Ateljevic, I. (2001). Tourism, economic development and the global-local nexus: Theory
embracing complexity. *Tourism Geographies*, *3*(4), 369–393.

Ministry of Tourism. (2013). *Uganda Vision 2040: Accelerating Uganda's socioeconomic transformation*. Author.

Ministry of Tourism. (2014). *Uganda tourism development master plan 2014-2024* (pp. 1–168).
Author.

Mitchell, J. (2012). Value chain approaches to assessing the impact of tourism on low-income households in developing countries. *Journal of Sustainable Tourism*, *20*(3), 457–475.

Mitchell, J., & Faal, J. (2007). Holiday package tourism and the poor in the Gambia. *Development
Southern Africa*, *24*(3), 445–464.

Mitchell, J., & Faal, J. (2008). *The Gambian tourist value chain and prospects for pro-poor tourism*.
Overseas Development Institute.

Mosedale, J. (2006). Tourism commodity chains: Market entry and its effects on St Lucia. *Current
Issues in Tourism*, *9*(4), 436–458.

National Planning Authority. (2010). *National development plan (2010/11–2014/15)*. Author.

Nelson, F. (2012). Blessing or curse? The political economy of tourism development in Tanzania.
Journal of Sustainable Tourism, *20*(3), 359–375.

Nyakaana, J., & Ahebwa, M. W. (2011). Governance of community based tourism in Uganda: An
analysis of the Kibale association for rural and environmental development (KAFRED). In R.
Van der Duim, D. Meyer, J. Saarinen, & K. Zellmer (Eds.), *New alliances for tourism, conservation and development in Eastern and Southern Africa* (pp. 63–83). Delft: Eburon.

Nyaupane, G. P., & Poudel, S. (2011). Linkages among biodiversity, livelihood, and tourism. *Annals
of Tourism Research*, *38*(4), 1344–1366.

Perkmann, M. (1999). Building governance institutions across European borders. *Regional Studies*,
33(7), 657–667.

Romero, I., & Tejada, P. (2011). A multi-level approach to the study of production chains in the
tourism sector. *Tourism Management*, *32*(2), 297–306.

Scheyvens, R. (2011). *Tourism and poverty*. New York, NY: Routledge.

Schilcher, D. (2008). Growth versus equity?: The continuum of pro-poor tourism and neoliberal governance. *Current Issues in Tourism*, *10*(2–3), 166–193.

Sofield, T. H. B. (2003). *Empowerment for sustainable tourism development*. Bingley: Emerald
Group.

Song, H., Liu, J., & Chen, G. (2012). Tourism value chain governance: Review and prospects. *Journal
of Travel Research*, *52*(1), 15–28.

Spenceley, A., & Meyer, D. (2012). Tourism and poverty reduction?: Theory and practice in less economically developed countries. *Journal of Sustainable Tourism*, *20*(3), 297–317.

Timothy, D. J. (1998). Cooperative tourism planning in a developing destination. *Journal of
Sustainable Tourism*, *6*(1), 52–68.

UBOS. (2013). *2013 Statistical abstract* (p. 264). Author.

Van der Duim, V. R. (2008). Exploring pro-poor tourism research: The state of the art. In H. de Haan
& R. van der Duim (Eds.), *Landscape, leisure and tourism: Socio-spatial studies in experiences,
practices and policies* (pp. 179–196). Delft: Eburon.

Vermeiren, K., Adiyia, B., & Loopmans, M. (2013). Will urban farming survive the growth of African
cities: A case-study in Kampala (Uganda)? *Land Use Policy*, *35*, 40–49.

Weiss, B., & Messerli, H. (2012). *Uganda tourism sector situational assessment?: Tourism reawaken-
ing*. World Bank.

Wilkinson, P. F. (1999). Caribbean cruise tourism: Delusion? Illusion? *Tourism Geographies*, *1*(3),
261–282.

World Travel & Tourism Council. (2014). *Tourism is now the top foreign exchange earner in Uganda*.
Retrieved January 5, 2015, from http://www.wttc.org/global-news/articles/2014/oct/month-case-
study-uganda/

van der Zee, E., & Go, F. M. (2014). Analysing beyond the environmental bubble dichotomy: How
the 2010 World Cup case helped to bridge the host–guest gap. *Journal of Sport & Tourism*, *18*(3),
161–183.

Conservation tourism and landscape governance in Kenya: the interdependency of three conservation NGOs

Arjaan Pellis[a], Machiel Lamers[b] and René Van der Duim[a]

[a]Cultural Geography Group, Wageningen University, Wageningen, The Netherlands;
[b]Environmental Policy Group, Wageningen University, Wageningen, The Netherlands

Tourism plays an increasingly important role in the way non-governmental organisations govern landscapes, especially in decentralised conservation contexts in developing countries. In this paper, we examine the role of three key conservation organisations (the African Wildlife Foundation, the African Conservation Centre and the Northern Rangelands Trust) in landscape governance in Kenya. Our analysis of organisational strategies and practices between 2007 and 2013 demonstrates how conservation NGOs, as intermediators of various forms of conservation tourism, are subjected to multi-actor interdependencies. Our findings underpin the role of mismatching scale-making that not only hampers organisational objectives, but also contributes to a dynamic reshaping of conservation tourism landscapes. We illustrate our approach to landscape governance in the context of the Naibunga Conservancy Trust where multiple conservation NGOs are required to deal with overlapping and competing orderings.

1. Introduction

Landscapes matter to ecotourism. While wildlife and biodiversity have iconic status in Western representations and consumption of ecotourism (Cater, 2006; Echtner & Prasad, 2003; Ryan, Hughes, & Chirgwin, 2000), ecotourism would not survive for long without the habitat, scenery and other landscape qualities. In perpetuating ecotourism, multiple social actors interact in the context of dynamic natural processes in landscapes, leading to emerging alliances through which ecotourism in South and Eastern Africa is governed (van der Duim, Lamers, & van Wijk, 2015).

In Kenya's Arid and Semi-Arid Lands (ASALs), the institutional void – created by the inability of the Kenyan Wildlife Services to sufficiently address human–wildlife conflicts outside national parks – has incited innovative forms of ecotourism that progressively target biodiversity conservation and economic development since the 1990s (Lamers, Nthiga, van der Duim, & van Wijk, 2013). Such 'conservation tourism' is defined by Buckley (2010) as 'commercial tourism which makes an ecologically significant net positive contribution to the effective conservation of biological diversity' (p. 2). Conservation tourism has been introduced in communal landscapes through new partnership arrangements, resulting in numerous forms of land use and multiple interests of land owners, private enterprises, government agencies and non-governmental organisations (NGOs).

Not only do ASALs serve as a habitat for the majority of Kenya's wildlife (Zeppel, 2006), they also generate opportunities for conservation tourism next to other forms of human land use, such as livestock farming, agriculture, horticulture and nature conservation.

Conservation tourism in Kenya's ASALs has constantly changed through developments such as the eroding of group ranch structures (Kabubo-Mariara, 2006), the subdivision of land (Southgate, 2006), the growth of populations and poverty (Zeverijn & Osano, 2013), a ban on trophy hunting in Kenya (Zeppel, 2006), and a lack of formal governmental laws and policies to stimulate the increase of conservation tourism initiatives (Lamers, van der Duim, van Wijk, Nthiga, & Visseren-Hamakers, 2014). Since the 1990s, experimentation with conservation tourism in Kenya has resulted in the establishment of a market-based conservation landscape approach characterised by the emergence of approximately 250 nature-based tourism enterprises (van Wijk, van der Duim, Lamers, & Sumba, 2014). There is strikingly limited knowledge available about the role of conservation NGOs in shaping such conservation landscapes in Sub-Saharan Africa (Brockington & Scholfield, 2010), let alone the role of conservation tourism as a tool to integrate the often contradicting policy objectives of biodiversity conservation and economic development.

This article explores the role of three key conservation NGOs in developing conservation tourism in Kenya between 2007 and 2013: the African Wildlife Foundation (AWF), the Northern Rangelands Trust (NRT) and the African Conservation Centre (ACC). We commence with a brief introduction to landscape governance as a perspective to understand how multiple actors, orderings and related scales operate interdependently in landscapes. Next, we explain our research methods, introduce the organisations and describe how these organisations operate in targeted ASALs. We then empirically examine the role of these three organisations in the context of the Naibunga Conservancy Trust (NCT) in Northern Laikipia. We finally draw conclusions about the role of conservation NGOs in the governance of Kenya's ASALs.

2. Landscape governance

The concept of landscape is shared between different disciplines, leaving us no single and clear conceptual definition (Penker, 2009; Scott, 2011; Setten, 2006). Landscapes are basically 'open' constructions that depend on how and whether they become recognised through particular actor-networks (Callon, 1991; Fuchs, 2001). Landscapes represent temporary patchworks of various land tenure systems, vegetation types and land uses stitched together to 'appear' as a coherent whole (van Oosten, 2013), or as hybrid socioecological systems in which relations are made and unmade between natural and social systems (Görg, 2007; Gunderson & Holling, 2002). Landscapes should not be seen as essentially 'given' (Fuchs, 2001). Instead, one should 'take into account the plurality of landscape-comprehensions as well as the multiplicity and dichotomy of interests related to the landscape' (Görg, 2007, p. 960). There are endless ways in which landscapes become 'maintained, planned, developed and enhanced by countless environmental regulations, contracts with land owners, agri-environmental schemes, landscape and nature reserves' (Penker, 2009, p. 947). These underpin once more the fact that landscapes are not made by 'a single order', but by multiple orderings (Azcárate, 2006; Law, 2002).

A detailed study of the many organisations, actions, multiple orderings and mutual encounters in landscapes contributes to a complex and relational understanding of how tourism landscapes work (Johannesson, Ren, & van der Duim, 2015). The reconciliation of different interests becomes complex if we consider that these interests depend upon power and knowledge imbalances among actor-networks across different geographical, administrative or political scales (Giller et al., 2008; Rhodes, 2007), meaning that practices, decisions and negotiations elsewhere can have decisive effects upon local development: 'Place matters, but scale decides' (Swyngedouw, 1997, p. 144). The various scale dimensions are crucial in the negotiation of 'options and [ideally] work towards collective decisions about the organization of [...] space' (Henneman & Oosten, 2013, p. 1). However, political and administrative governance structures in developing countries seldom align with the spatial characteristics of landscapes (van Oosten, 2013).

In Kenya's ASALs, NGOs have taken a leading and mediating role in the meta-governance of novel policy interventions around conservation tourism by integrating conservation interests with the interests of international donors, private enterprises and local communities (Lamers, van der Duim, Nthiga, van Wijk, & Waterreus, 2015; van Wijk et al., 2014). Such integration has led to structural coupling of organisational and common goals where actors' strategies not only depend on 'previous steps, but also by the pattern of [other] actors and institutions that evolved over time' (van Assche, Beunen, & Duineveld, 2014, p. 30). Here we aim to understand how distinct practices of conservation tourism develop through interdependency and how different practices lead to contradictions that we likewise observe elsewhere in Eastern or Southern Africa (see also Ahebwa, van der Duim, & Sandbrook, 2012; van der Duim et al., 2015; Lamers et al., 2013; Pellis, Duineveld, & Wagner, 2015).

3. Methods

Our research focuses on, and is limited to, the role of three prominent yet different conservation organisations and their encounters in Kenya's conservation tourism landscape between 2007 and 2013. We explored organisational strategies, the extent to which these organisations have deployed tourism projects, and their on-the-ground experiences within the context of the NCT.

We collected primary and secondary data on conservation tourism projects that are part of wider and 'holistic' conservation programmes practised by the AWF, the NRT and the ACC. We also based our analysis upon funding proposals and progress reports from two consecutive funding rounds (2007–2011 and 2012–2013) made available by the Embassy of the Kingdom of the Netherlands in Nairobi (EKN), covering a total of six years of organisational progress. By means of 15 semi-structured and in-depth interviews, ranging between 1 and 2 hours, we initially explored how parastatal organisations, conservation organisations and donor organisations perceive tourism projects undertaken by AWF, NRT and ACC. To further understand and validate our findings, we explored how these organisations are part of a landscape governance of conservation tourism in Naibunga, Northern Laikipia. An additional six in-depth interviews focused on how various NGO strategies align and/or contradict and to what governance complexities this leads.

Verbatim transcripts of interviews were deductively analysed in KODANI, an MS Excel-based qualitative coding tool used for open, axial and selective coding (Boeije, 2009; Verschuren & Doorewaard, 2007). The NCT represents an illustrative case with respect to a broad range of landscape governance aspects, such as the multiple ways that conservation NGOs have deployed conservation tourism as part of their ongoing work in conservation, the ways in which natural and social interests across actors can possibly be bridged, and how encounters between interests and practices across administrative, ecological or project boundaries can become decisive processes. To guarantee the anonymity of interviewees, a coding scheme has been included in Table 1.

Table 1. Interview reference scheme.

Coding	Profile	Place and date
ACC-1	Executive Director at ACC	Nairobi, 24-02-2014
ACC-2	Natural Resource Management Specialists at ACC	Nairobi, 25-02-2014 and 27-10-2014
AWF-1	Conservation Enterprise Director at AWF	Nairobi, 24-02-2014 and 22-10-2014
AWF-2	Vice President Programme Design at AWF	Nairobi, 24-02-2014
AWF-3	Country Director Kenya at AWF	Nairobi, 04-03-2014
EKN-1	Deputy Permanent Representative at Royal Netherlands Embassy in Nairobi	Nairobi, 20-02-2014
LEW-1	Manager Lewa Wildlife Conservancy (telephone interview)	Nanyuki, 24-11-2011
LWF-1	Executive Director at LWF	Nanyuki, 25-11-2011 Nanyuki, 26-02-2014
LWF-2	Tourism officer at LWF	Nanyuki, 27-02-2014
NCT-1	Manager NCT	Kimanjo centre, Naibunga, 01-03-2012
NRT-1	Chief Executive Officer at NRC	Nairobi, 19-02-2014 and 23-04-2014
NRT-2	Community Development Manager & Grants Management Officer at NRC	Isiolo, 26-02-2014
NRT-3	Destination Marketing Experts hired by NRT to assess Samburu as a tourism destination	Nanyuki, 27-02-2014
NRT-4	Programmes Officer at NRC	Nanyuki, 22-11-2011
USA-1	Grant officer at USAID	Nairobi, 4-3-2014

Note: USAID, U.S. Agency for International Development.

To validate our overall analysis, a stakeholder workshop was organised on the 23rd of April 2014 in Nairobi, which brought together 17 representatives of the evaluated organisations and other relevant stakeholders in Kenya. This workshop mapped how various landscape initiatives become recognised in relation to conservation tourism.

4. Three conservation organisations

4.1. *African Wildlife Foundation*

The AWF is a large conservation NGO registered in the USA, with its headquarters in Nairobi, Kenya. Funding comes from a range of sources, including donations from individuals (e.g. online gifts, leadership gifts and legacy gifts), public sector donors, corporations and foundations. In the late 1990s, AWF began to offer advisory services to private sector parties and local communities to develop 'conservation enterprises', that is, commercial activities that generate economic benefits in ways that support the attainment of conservation objectives (Elliott & Sumba, 2011). Examples of such enterprises in the field of tourism include ecolodges, tented camps and cultural villages. By developing tourism conservation enterprises in biodiversity-rich areas, AWF hoped that income from tourism would be an incentive for landowners to protect wildlife (van Wijk et al., 2014). Between 2008 and 2013, AWF established 12 conservation enterprises in Kenya, of which 10 are exclusive tourism enterprises.

AWF has an extensive and African-wide experience in developing and brokering high-end ecolodges between communities which usually own the land and the enterprise, and private operators who run the lodge. Operators lease the land from the community and agree to transfer part of the revenues to a joint trust fund that distributes benefits to the community directly. AWF not only invests in the physical construction of conservation lodges, it also aims to support communities with getting a 'fair deal' with private investors (who generally take care of the interior decoration of the lodge or camp) and is regularly asked to intervene in governance issues.

The work of AWF in Kenya focuses on two priority landscapes, known in AWF terms as 'heartlands', that is, the Samburu (Laikipia and Samburu) and the Kilimanjaro (Amboseli) Heartland. Heartlands represent landscapes that hold rich biodiversity assets in private parks or dispersal areas within community land. In these landscapes, conservation efforts and investments are made in strategic areas with a high biodiversity potential (e.g. wildlife corridors).

4.2. *Northern Rangelands Trust*

NRT is an association of landowners in the northern rangelands of Kenya. A key concern of NRT is the establishment of conservancies that enable landowners to self-organise their land, provide security and conserve natural resources. NRT consists, at the time of writing, of 27 community conservancies representing beyond 31,000 square kilometres of land brought together under a trust and managed by communal land owners. To help communities achieve this mission, the Northern Rangelands Company (NRC), an associated not-for-profit company, runs the affairs of NRT. NRC operates 'like an industry association, […] acts to facilitate, train and raise money, introduces investors, but [does not] run any conservancies' (NRT-1). NRC does not identify itself as a typical conservation NGO. 'We don't operate anywhere; our mandate comes solely from the various member conservancies' (NRT-1). For the sake of clarity, we will refer to NRT when we speak of NRC practices here.

One of NRT's key interests is in diversifying livestock-dominated economies in the north. In 9 out of 27 conservancies, tourism has been introduced as a complementary form of income contributing to the running costs of conservancies. Tourism represents the largest share of commercial income for conservancies, next to (commercial) livestock and beadwork trading (see further Pellis, Anyango-van Zwieten, Waterreus, Lamers, & van der Duim, 2014). If a community conservancy desires to develop tourism, NRT provides assistance in establishing a partnership between the community and a private entrepreneur.

NRT has significantly expanded its geographical scale of operation from Samburu, Isiolo and Laikipia counties to the coast of Kenya. NRT sees itself as an example for communal landscape governance in Kenya: 'NRT is now widely seen as a model of how to support community conservancies. Its success has helped shape new government regulations on establishing, registering and managing community conservancies in Kenya' (2014).

4.3. *African Conservation Centre*

The ACC aims to conserve wildlife and its natural environment through the integration of scientific and indigenous knowledge to enhance community livelihoods and the development of local and regional institutions in Eastern Africa. ACC represents a conservation organisation that promotes 'community-based development as *the route* to conservation' (Brockington & Scholfield, 2010, p. 17; emphasis added).

ACC runs Tourism Support Programmes to 'support the development of resilient liveli-hoods to reduce vulnerability, enhance food security and alleviate poverty' (2012, p. 7). This involves the empowering of local communities by enabling them to sustainably manage, and benefit from, tourism activities, such as cultural villages, small-scale guest-houses or beadwork products. ACC has made a strong case of women's projects among Maasai communities, as ACC believes that women can play a crucial role in livelihood development and understanding of biodiversity threats (ACC-2).

ACC operates mostly in Amboseli, but has developed similar tourism projects in the South Rift, the Mara and Laikipia. Although ACC has invested substantial resources in the construction of new tourism enterprises in different parts of Kenya, its main role with regard to tourism development is in brokering partnerships at different levels (ACC-1).

5. Results

We commenced our analysis with a comparison of how these NGOs deploy conservation tourism by identifying crucial differences between organisational strategies, mandates and integration with (international) donor agendas (see Table 2 for an overview). Next, we will discuss to what extent these strategic differences and practices become practised in the NCT. In and around this conservation landscape, all three NGOs have played impor-tant roles in ordering tourism and conservation, raising questions on their joint ability to effectively learn and work towards common goals.

5.1. *Organisational strategies and mandates*

All three organisations take a different stance to conservation and tourism. AWF works internationally in priority landscapes and has a prominent business approach to biodiversity conservation (AWF-2). AWF operates simultaneously on different levels and projects throughout Kenya (and elsewhere in Africa), in contrast to 'local conservation organis-ations' that do not have the same means and expertise required for issues crosscutting Kenyan landscapes (AWF-1). Where biodiversity threats evolve over time, AWF has to constantly reassess where their resources are used most effectively (AWF-1). This approach can lead to a thin spread, high employee turnover across projects (USA-1), and possible decisions to withdraw from one area to another where biodiversity threats are becoming more acute (AWF-1).

ACC likewise operates through projects, yet distinguishes itself through small-scale community-based projects that prioritise 'people's development through community con-servation' (ACC-2). ACC's work concentrates on Maasai communities, particularly the empowerment of women. Women, according to ACC, are very much affected by land degradation as they 'understand what it means to walk long distances in search of water, fuel wood etc.' (ACC-2). Through tourism enterprises developed with ACC, women have become respected income earners and more influential in conservancy and group ranch decision-making. ACC coordinates partnerships with local communities and other NGOs, yet simultaneously invests profoundly in the construction of community-based (tourism) enterprises and local capacities to manage enterprises 'independently'. In the long term, ACC envisions itself as 'receding on a local level' to become a more inter-national organisation (ACC-2).

In contrast, NRT has a strong local mandate in supporting landowners in Northern Kenya, an area characterised by arid land, ongoing insecurity, and a need for coordinated

Table 2. Comparison of practices between AWF, NRT and ACC.

Organisation	AWF	NRT	ACC
General conservation mission	Conserving wildlife through enterprise	Resilient community conservancies	Enhancing livelihoods through community conservation
Tourism Approach	Conservation enterprises, fully operated by private operators	No tourism programme, only brokering for tourism enterprises, mostly run by private operators	Community-based/ owned Cultural tourism
Tourism Location	Amboseli and Laikipia	Samburu, Isiolo, Laikipia and recently the coast	Amboseli, Masaai Mara, Southrift Area and Laikipia
Tourism Market	International wildlife-based tourism	International wildlife-based tourism	Domestic and research tourism
Governance influence	Conflict resolution, PCPs and leading in national wildlife policy debate	Supporting conservancies through PCPs, leading in national conservancy development	Local trust and capacity building, regional ecosystem-based trust to support local initiatives
Donor support for tourism development	EKN (51%), USAID (27%), EU biodiversity fund (15%), Other (7%)	The Nature Conservancy (53%), EKN (19%), USAID (17%), Danida (7%), Other (4%)	EKN (83%), next to Ford Foundation (15%), Liz Clairebon Art Ottenburg Foundation (2%)
Livelihood effects of tourism	Communal benefit distribution, typically no individual income Tourism as an incentive through jobs and income for community projects to change people's behaviour towards biodiversity conservation	Wide span support of community resilience in conservancies. Strong focus on educational bursaries, improvement of local safety situation, communal pride and self-organisation	Income on household levels, especially through women empowerment. Individual dividends, community projects and educational bursaries (girls)
Relation to conservation	Securitisation of sensitive conservation projects (e.g. important corridors in heartlands), tourism income substantial due to size enterprise and limited land (potential to cover conservation costs)	Large-scale conservation of conservancy territory, tourism income relatively limited due to sheer size of conservancy territories	Through community conservation priority of community, livelihoods can be enhanced. Income for households, especially with women, is expected to improve community behaviour towards safeguarding biodiversity

and alternative natural resource use. NRT stresses a commercial and standardised approach to conservation tourism, yet prioritises resilience of land owners above biodiversity (NRT-1). If communities desire more tourism development, commercial livestock or oil extraction, it is up to local land owners to decide which strategy to take. NRT nevertheless promotes strict standardised community conservation in conservancies that they would like to see throughout Kenya. More recently, NRT tries to regulate incompatible practices across neighbouring conservancies (e.g. illegal grazing) by creating regional conservancy institutions that can help establish mega-conservancies (e.g. 'the greater Sera' or 'the greater Namunyak').

5.2. *Donor dependency*

The three organisations have received donor support for tourism initiatives from different sources. ACC received the majority of its tourism project funding from the Embassy of the Kingdom of the Netherlands in Nairobi (EKN) as, in the words of ACC, 'the Dutch are really big on livelihood enhancement' (ACC-1). AWF also received a large proportion of their budget from EKN, but depends on a broader portfolio of donor support, including USAID that typically appreciates 'market responsive enterprise development and sharing of profits within communities' (2014). AWF is currently experimenting with commercial private equity funding through a subsidiary of AWF called African Wildlife Capital (AWC). AWF expects AWC to generate more income for projects undertaken by AWF. This is required as state support for biodiversity conservation is expected to diminish (AWF-1/NRT-1/ACC-1). NRT depends likewise on a broad range of funding sources that include commercial and donor income. Support for tourism comes mainly from donors supporting NRT's ambition to make communities resilient and to improve the security situation in the north of Kenya. In general, the donor portfolios of all three organisations have become more diversified, but they continue to depend on the unconditional support of those donors who are willing to cover overhead costs, such as staff salaries and accommodation, involvement in national and regional policy-making, and brokering between communities and private entrepreneurs. These are indispensable in sustaining conservation tourism developments in Kenya's ASALs (see also Pellis et al., 2014). The various NGOs cannot finance their programmes without joint organisational initiatives (ACC-1/ AWF-1/LWF-1/USA-1). NGOs find this challenging as they 'are in competition for the donors and you may not want to be too open about what you're doing because it gives the other an advantage' (ACC-1). Donors on the other hand encourage NGOs to coordinate their activities in order to overcome unnecessary overlap and stimulate complementary work (USA-1/EKN-1).

6. Landscape governance of NCT

The NCT illustrates how the organisational strategies and practices of the three NGOs align and contradict in a wider landscape perspective. The NCT is situated in the Western Mukogodo Division of Laikipia, close to the border with Samburu and Isiolo counties where conservancies have become common practice in connection to the work of NRT. The NCT has secured 43,000 acres – out of a total surface of 243,000 acres – for biodiversity conservation by connecting group ranches and their ecosystems (LEW-1). The Masaai name 'Naibunga' is translated into 'connectedness' or 'collective responsibility'. NCT nevertheless includes multiple land-use orderings in an economy that is dominated by livestock. The 12,000 inhabitants depend upon scarce economic alternatives and are confronted with various risks, including recurring droughts (e.g. between 1997 and 2000 or in 2009 when large numbers of livestock died), diseases, scarce pastures, mismanagement in group ranches, high unemployment, banditry (Sumba, Warinwa, Lenaiyasa, & Muruthi, 2007) and neighbouring pastoralists trespassing territory in search of available water and good grazing land (Flintan & Puyo, 2012). Tourism, like bee keeping, is one of the few but promising land-use alternatives due to Naibunga's spectacular scenery and perceived wildlife viewing possibilities (NRT, 2015).

The NCT was initially founded in 2001–2003 with the support of AWF and the Laikipia Wildlife Forum (LWF), another regional membership-based conservation organisation operational within Laikipia. NCT currently 'connects' nine group ranches, namely Il Motiok, Musul, Nkiloriti, Koija, Tiemamut, Kijabe, Morupusi, Munishoi and Ilpolei (Figure 1). In the early stages of community conservation in this region, LWF worked on the involvement and capacity of communities to include tourism as a livelihood alternative, and continues to cover operational costs of the NCT through the NRT (LWF-1). AWF became involved by establishing Private-Community Partnerships (PCPs) for the Koija Starbeds in 2001 at the Koija group ranch, and the Sanctuary at Ol Lentille in 2007, involving Kijabe, Nkiloriti and Tiemamut group ranches (Lamers et al., 2014, 2015). Both enterprises offer exclusive lodging and experiences, targeting the high end of the market.

NRT became involved in Naibunga in 2007 due to ongoing insecurity in the region, an issue that NRT was already familiar with through its operations in adjacent Samburu conservancies. ACC, on the other hand, established a cultural village/resource centre named Twala Tenebo, which has contributed especially to women empowerment and community conservation in the Ilpolei and Munishoi group ranches (Southern part of the NCT) since 2006. Twala Tenebo focuses on small-scale community-based tourism activities and products and is the only tourism enterprise in the NCT without a private sector partner. The dissimilarities in scale and arrangement have resulted in large differences among the

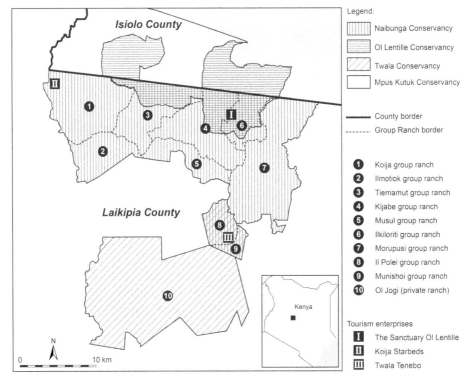

Figure 1.   Overlapping landscapes across NCT.

44

enterprises in the level of financial benefits generated, as well as the extent to which these benefits reach communities. We also acknowledge that more tourism enterprises have been developed within the territory of NCT, such as Lemartis Camp and Ewaso Cottages, which have not incorporated community development into their operations but do benefit from wildlife conservation projects undertaken by studied NGOs in the NCT.

NRT applies a strict standard for revenue distributions from commercial (tourism) income in affiliated conservancies, that is, 40% to support conservancy operational costs and 60% for community projects (NRT-3). Contributions to operational costs include wild-life scouts' salaries, vehicles and communication equipment, all of which aim to manage security and wildlife issues in relatively large territorial areas. In nearby NRT conservancies (e.g. Namunyak or West Gate), tourism enterprises already contribute substantially to these costs, at times up to 50%. According to NRT, Ol Lentille and Koija (both receive support from AWF) contribute nothing to Naibunga. This would have to change in the coming years according to NRT, but vested interests of investors and group ranches stand in the way. According to AWF, 'Koija and Ol Lentille [...] are paying local communities because the operators have concessions with the local communities. That was what was in existence when we set these up' (AWF-1). From the private enterprise perspective, it is impossible to contribute more to (other) institutional structures beyond the current partnerships as it is already difficult to break even (AWF-1), especially since the enterprises are experiencing low occupancy rates (Flintan & Puyo, 2012).

All nine group ranches are requested to support the operational costs of NCT by trans-ferring 20% of Group Ranch income, yet 'some group ranches are said to default on the payments' (NCT-1). Currently, the trust depends heavily on donor income, accounting for 70% of the conservancy's operational budget, in contrast to common practices of NRT and the desires of international donors towards being financially self-sustainable. USAID and EKN have repetitively emphasised such a need at the moment projects draw to an end. This places conservation tourism enterprises under pressure, considering the current contributions from tourism enterprises towards the NCT in the past decade.

In 2008, NRT temporarily abandoned its support for NCT (for a year) due to pol-itical conflicts among communities (Flintan & Puyo, 2012). Ongoing conflicts in this region are normally attributed to incompatible resource use intertwined with local pol-itical divisions (Muthiani, Njoka, Kinyua, & Gitau, 2011). This contrasts with formal representations of communities in the recently gazetted Wildlife Conservation and Management Act, a community is described here as 'a group of individuals or families who share a common heritage, interest, or stake in unidentifiable land, land based resources or benefits that may be derived there from' (Republic of Kenya, 2013). Issues about local benefit distributions arise again and again where 'it is [the chief's, chairman's or councillor's] children who are benefitting more from the bursaries than the rest of the community' (USA-1). Sumba et al. (2007) claim that these conflicts are part of 'a history of serious internal conflicts between sub-clans', and that these have already resulted in previous commercial failures, possibly harming the ongoing development of tourism.

Conflicts continue to part communities, whose first thought is 'who was claiming what' instead of 'what the message is' (LWF-3). Some communities have previously established partnerships with commercial enterprises, and this has likewise created vested interests. Such partnerships have 'clearly articulated roles, responsibilities and benefits and where necessary sealed this through legal contracts' (Sumba et al., 2007, p. 11) with the aim to avoid conflict. Previous agreements are nonetheless continuously re-evaluated by commu-nities (NCT-1, see also Muthiani et al., 2011), and this has already led to recurrent local conflict situations. For example, a long-running conflict between the chair of the Kijabe Conservation Trust and the private investor at Ol Lentille resulted in a dysfunctional trust (for three years) and required third-party mediation by AWF (Lamers et al., 2014; Muthiani et al., 2011). At the same time, the Ol Lentille financial arrangements become more complex as new collaborations with other neighbouring group ranches were formed to enlarge the conservation area from 4942 acres to 19,768 acres (Lamers et al., 2015). Currently Ol Lentille is negotiating the span of its own conservancy with communities (e.g. overlapping with Mpus Kutuk Conservancy in Isiolo County) who, according to Ol Lentille, have become convinced by Ol Lentille's way of 'community conservation in action' (2015). At the same time, the Il Polei and Munishoi group ranches, together with ACC and some nearby private ranches, are currently thinking of erecting another conservancy with the size of approximately 81,000 acres that temporarily is named 'Twala Conservancy', inspired by earlier community-based tourism practised in Twala Tenebo under the same leadership of ACC. Eventually, this new conservancy will collaborate with, or separate itself, from the NCT and other NRT practices (ACC-1).

7. Discussion

Our research shows that not only AWF, NRT and ACC, but also other organisations and pastoralist communities themselves are actively engaged in the landscape governance of Kenya's ASALs. It is in communal areas particularly – such as group ranches – that enterprises brokered by conservation NGOs, in collaboration with private sector parties and communities, have been able to create conservation areas and develop tourism. Without these third-party interventions, no tourism development would have been possible in Kenya's ASALs (Southgate, 2006), and without tourism, a great deal more donor support would be needed to financially sustain the very same landscapes in ways that conservation NGOs envision.

We have seen that although all three organisations are actively involved in developing tourism enterprises, their approaches and rationalities differ in terms of scale and scope. AWF and ACC work on local, regional and national levels, whereas NRT is (so far) more rooted in the north of Kenya (with exemption of recent support to conservancies at the Kenyan coast). AWF also works internationally by developing and supporting other conservation enterprises throughout Africa (2013), yet seems to lose its local grip, partly due to job rotations and lack of experienced staff and sufficient resources on the ground (Lamers et al., 2014).

The NCT case demonstrates that the three conservation organisations operate at multiple, partly overlapping, scales. By operating in this way, the three NGOs not only cross but also redefine administrative, ecological and political borders (Cash et al., 2006). The multi-actor and multi-level governance practices of the three conservation organisations in Kenya contribute to decision-making processes surpassing existing national or county administrative boundaries and create new assemblages of territory, authority and rights (Sassen, 2006), in this case institutional arrangements for conservation and development at alternating levels of group ranches, conservancies, ecosystem trusts or 'heartlands'. This multi-levelness not only discloses complex shifts in the relationship between state and society, but also between nature and society, reconciling ecological and economic interests (Görg, 2007). For example, we have seen how tourism enterprises connected to smaller scale arrangements do not currently contribute financially to larger scale arrangements of NCT. This reconciliation of ecological and economic interests is not only limited to local or regional conditions, but also involves processes and networks 'transcending the physical and political-administrative landscape boundaries, as landscapes are increasingly linked to the wider world of global and economic trends' (van Oosten, 2013, p. 661).

For example, the role of external donor support and control is still critical in sustaining conservation tourism in Kenya (Akama, 1999; Southgate, 2006). These international donors are increasingly demanding integration, forcing conservation organisations to collaborate even if this contradicts with their own practices (Mosse, 2004). Moreover, we found that conservation tourism discourses and practices are not simply given externally but are certainly also enacted in social encounters *in situ* (Johannesson et al., 2015; Tsing, 2005). Conservation organisations are forced to collaborate but they also compete for donor funding and available landscapes where their policies can become implemented. Likewise, communities play an important role in the dynamics of landscape governance. Not only do we find a heterogeneous set of local actors that contradict collective action (Agrawal & Gibson, 1999), we also acknowledge that the increased uptake of knowledge about conservation tourism increases communities' share of tourism opportunities, yet simultaneously enlarges possibilities of ongoing rivalry and conflict (Pellis et al., 2015; Southgate, 2006). The latter seem hard to overcome since local conservation tourism arrangements interdepend upon practices simultaneously taking place either through overlap or through effects generated elsewhere.

8. Conclusion

In this article, we examined the role of three conservation organisations (AWF, NRT and ACC) and the way they deploy conservation tourism as part of landscape governance in Kenya's ASALs.

Our analysis first demonstrated that the role of conservation NGOs in landscape governance is significant. While each organisation operates from a particular view on the tourism–conservation–development nexus, the organisations were forced to (re)define their mandate and geographical scale of operation when their practices interconnect. The three NGOs show interesting differences in organisational approaches, which translates into their scale of operation. Where AWF focuses their conservation efforts, such as tourism conservation enterprises in group ranches, on specific priority regions (i.e. 'heartlands'), NRT secures land for conservation through geographically stretched conservancies, and ACC develops small and community-based cultural tourism that prioritise local economic development. Tourism projects are furthermore integrated within discourses generating holistic conservation programmes of these organisations.

Second, experimentation with conservation tourism has contributed to changes at various administrative and political levels. Decentralisation of administrative control over ASALs has provided communities with more means to self-organise landscapes in cooperation with private organisations and NGOs. The growth and tensions at Ol Lentille or the development of a new conservancy by ACC illustrates the volatility of these boundaries. Moreover, the experimentation with conservation tourism results in shifting distributions of costs and benefits for conservation and livelihood at household, group ranch or conservancy levels, and the shifting scope of effects at different levels is continuously discussed and negotiated.

Third, the proliferation of different projects and partnerships at various levels of scale instigates the need for attuning activities in order to deal with mismatches and frictions of multiple conservation tourism strategies. Due to selective and recurrent scale-making practices, there is a constant risk that organisational approaches mismatch on the ground. Scale mismatches can lead to conflicts jeopardising organisational objectives, but can simultaneously work towards an integration of sector-wide objectives if organisations are open to inter-organisational learning.

Overall we conclude that the work of the three conservation NGOs has not only led to important contributions to landscape governance, community livelihoods and biodiversity conservation, but has also set the stage for ongoing experimentation with conservation tourism in Kenya. This article has shed light on the interaction and scale implications of the work of these organisations but offers plenty of scope for future research on conservation tourism initiatives in Kenya or elsewhere in the world.

Acknowledgements

Special thanks to Dr Rita Nthiga, Swen Waterreus, Nowella Anyango-van Zwieten and Annemiek Pas Schrijver for their collaboration, assistance and/or validation of empirical findings. The authors are grateful for the ongoing support and collaboration with AWF, ACC and NRT in providing access to valuable policy documents. And we wish to thank the three anonymous reviewers for their valuable recommendations that have helped to improve earlier versions of this paper.

Disclosure statement

No potential conflict of interest was reported by the authors.

References

ACC. (2012). *Sustainable Landscapes and Livelihood Programme – May 1, 2012 to December 31, 2012*. Nairobi.

Agrawal, A., & Gibson, C. C. (1999). Enchantment and disenchantment: The role of community in natural resource conservation. *World Development, 27*(4), 629–649.

Ahebwa, W. M., van der Duim, R., & Sandbrook, C. G. (2012). Private-community partnerships: Investigating a new approach to conservation and development in Uganda. *Conservation and Society, 10*(4), 305–317.

Akama, J. S. (1999). The evolution of tourism in Kenya. *Journal of Sustainable Tourism, 7*(1), 6–25. doi:10.1080/09669589908667324

van Assche, K., Beunen, R., & Duineveld, M. (2014). *Evolutionary governance theory: An introduction*. London: Springer.

AWF. (2013). Conservation lodges of Africa. Retrieved September 19, 2014, from http://www.awf.org/sites/default/files/media/Resources/Facts2026amp3B20Brochures/AWF_Conservation_Lodges_09102013-high_single_low.pdf

Azcárate, M. C. (2006). Between local and global, discourses and practices: Rethinking ecotourism development in Celestún (Yucatán, México). *Journal of Ecotourism, 5*(1–2), 97–111. doi:10.1080/14724040608668449

Boeije, H. R. (2009). *Analysis in qualitative research*. Los Angeles: Sage.

Brockington, D., & Scholfield, K. (2010). The work of conservation organisations in sub-Saharan Africa. *The Journal of Modern African Studies, 48*(01), 1–33.

Buckley, R. (2010). *Conservation tourism*. Wallingford: CABI.

Callon, M. (1991). Techno-economic networks and irreversibility. In J. Law (Ed.), *A sociology of monsters: Essays on power, technology and domination* (pp. 132–161). London: Routledge.

Cash, D. W., Adger, W. N., Berkes, F., Garden, P., Lebel, L., Olsson, P., ... Young, O. (2006). Scale and cross-scale dynamics: Governance and information in a multilevel world. *Ecology and Society, 11*(2), 8–100.

Cater, E. (2006). Ecotourism as a western construct. *Journal of Ecotourism, 5*(1–2), 23–39. doi:10.1080/14724040608668445 van der Duim, R., Lamers, M., & van Wijk, J. (2015). Novel institutional arrangements for tourism, conservation and development in Eastern and Southern Africa. In R. van der Duim, M. Lamers, & J. van Wijk (Eds.), *Institutional arrangements for conservation, development and tourism in Eastern and Southern Africa* (pp. 1–16). Dordrecht: Springer.

Echtner, C. M., & Prasad, P. (2003). The context of third world tourism marketing. *Annals of Tourism Research*, *30*(3), 660–682. doi:10.1016/S0160-7383(03)00045-8

Elliott, J., & Sumba, D. (2011). *Conservation enterprise: What works, where and for whom?* London: International Institute for Environment and Development.

Flintan, F., & Puyo, D. (2012). *Naibunga Conservancy Trust*. Naibunga Conservancy: NCT.

Fuchs, S. (2001). *Against essentialism: A theory of culture and society*. Cambridge, MA: Harvard University Press.

Giller, K. E., Leeuwis, C., Andersson, J. A., Andriesse, W., Brouwer, A., Frost, P., . . . Windmeijer, P. (2008). Competing claims on natural resources: What role for science? *Ecology and Society*, *13*(2), article no. 34. Retrieved from http://www.ecologyandsociety.org/vol13/iss2/art34/.

Görg, C. (2007). Landscape governance – the 'politics of scale' and the 'natural' conditions of places. *Geoforum*, *38*(5), 954–966. doi:10.1016/j.geoforum.2007.01.004

Gunderson, L. H., & Holling, C. (2002). *Panarchy: Understanding transformations in human and natural systems*. Washington, DC: Island Press.

Henneman, I., & Oosten, C. V. (2013). *Landscape governance as 'bricolage in practice' a case study from Indonesia*. Paper presented at the Capturing Critical Institutionalism workshop, King's College London, London.

Johannesson, G. T., Ren, C., & van der Duim, R. (2015). Tourism encounters, controversies and ontologies. In G. T. Johannesson, C. Ren, & R. van der Duim (Eds.), *Tourism encounters and controversies: Ontological politics of tourism development* (pp. 1–20). Surrey: Ashgate.

Kabubo-Mariara, J. (2006). *Land conservation in Kenya: The role of property rights*. African Economic Research Consortium.

Lamers, M., van der Duim, R., Nthiga, R., van Wijk, J., & Waterreus, S. (2015). Implementing tourism-conservation enterprises: A comparison of three lodges in Kenya. In R. van der Duim, M. Lamers, & J. van Wijk (Eds.), *Institutional arrangements for conservation, development and tourism in Eastern and Southern Africa – a dynamic perspective* (pp. 219–238). Dordrecht: Springer.

Lamers, M., van der Duim, R., van Wijk, J., Nthiga, R., & Visseren-Hamakers, I. J. (2014). Governing conservation tourism partnerships in Kenya. *Annals of Tourism Research*, *48*, 250–265.

Lamers, M., Nthiga, R., van der Duim, R., & van Wijk, J. (2013). Tourism–conservation enterprises as a land-use strategy in Kenya. *Tourism Geographies*, *16*(3), 474–489.

Law, J. (2002). *Aircraft stories: Decentering the object in technoscience*. Durham, NC: Duke University Press.

Mosse, D. (2004). Is good policy unimplementable? Reflections on the ethnography of aid policy and practice. *Development and Change*, *35*(4), 639–671.

Muthiani, E., Njoka, J., Kinyua, P., & Gitau, G. (2011). *Partnership challenges of community wildlife sanctuaries in Laikipia County, Kenya*. Paper presented at the KASAL Program Conference, Kenya Agricultural Research Institute Headquarters, Nairobi.

NRT. (2014). What is NRT. Retrieved October 15, 2014, from http://www.nrt-kenya.org/what-is-nrt/

NRT. (2015). Naibunga. Retrieved February 10, 2015, from http://www.nrt-kenya.org/naibunga/

Ol Lentille. (2015). The conservancy. Retrieved April 8, 2015, from http://www.ol-lentille.com/the-conservancy/

van Oosten, C. (2013). Restoring landscapes – governing place: A learning approach to forest landscape restoration. *Journal of Sustainable Forestry*, *32*(7), 659–676.

Pellis, A., Anyango-van Zwieten, N., Waterreus, S., Lamers, M., & van der Duim, R. (2014). *Tourism captured by the poor – evaluation of aid investments in the tourism sector of Kenya's ASALs*. Wageningen: Wageningen University.

Pellis, A., Duineveld, M., & Wagner, L. (2015). Conflicts forever. The path dependencies of tourism conflicts; the case of Anabeb Conservancy, Namibia. In G. T. Johannesson, C. Ren, & R. van der Duim (Eds.), *Tourism encounters and controversies: Ontological politics of tourism development* (pp. 115–138). Surrey: Ashgate.

Penker, M. (2009). Landscape governance for or by the local population? A property rights analysis in Austria. *Land Use Policy*, *26*(4), 947–953. doi:10.1016/j.landusepol.2008.11.007

Republic of Kenya. (2013). *The wildlife conservation and management act*. Nairobi: The National Council for Law Reporting with the Authority of the Attorney General.

Rhodes, R. A. W. (2007). Understanding governance: Ten years on. *Organization Studies*, *28*(8), 1243–1264. doi:10.1177/0170840607076586

Ryan, C., Hughes, K., & Chirgwin, S. (2000). The gaze, spectacle and ecotourism. *Annals of Tourism Research*, *27*(1), 148–163. doi:10.1016/S0160-7383(99)00061-4

Sassen, S. (2006). *Territory, authority, rights: From medieval to global assemblages*. Princeton, NJ: Princeton University Press.

Scott, A. (2011). Beyond the conventional: Meeting the challenges of landscape governance within the European landscape convention? *Journal of Environmental Management*, *92*(10), 2754–2762.

Setten, G. (2006). Fusion or exclusion? Reflections on conceptual practices of landscape and place in human geography. *Norsk Geografisk Tidsskrift – Norwegian Journal of Geography*, *60*(01), 32–45.

Southgate, C. R. (2006). Ecotourism in Kenya: The vulnerability of communities. *Journal of Ecotourism*, *5*(1–2), 80–96.

Sumba, D., Warinwa, F., Lenaiyasa, P., & Muruthi, P. (2007). *The Koija Starbeds® Ecolodge: A Case Study of a Conservation Enterprise in Kenya* (AWF Working Papers). AWF.

Swyngedouw, E. (1997). Neither global nor local: 'Glocalization' and the politics of scale. In K. R. Cox (Ed.), *Spaces of globalization: Reasserting the power of the local* (pp. 137–166). New York, NY: The Guilford Press.

Tsing, A. L. (2005). *Friction: An ethnography of global connection*. Princeton, NJ: Princeton University Press.

USAID (2014). What we do – sustainable tourism. Retrieved October 20, 2014, from http://www.usaid.gov/content/global-climate-change/sustainable-tourism.

Verschuren, P. J. M., & Doorewaard, H. (2007). *Het ontwerpen van een onderzoek*. Den Haag: Lemma.

van Wijk, J., van der Duim, R., Lamers, M., & Sumba, D. (2014). The emergence of institutional innovations in tourism: The evolution of the African Wildlife Foundation's tourism conservation enterprises. *Journal of Sustainable Tourism*, *23*(1), 104–125.

Zeppel, H. D. (2006). *Indigenous ecotourism: Sustainable development and management*. Wallingford: CABI.

Zeverijn, A., & Osano, P. (2013). *'Frontiers and challenges' – high level evaluation of EKN funded interventions in the arid and semi-arid lands of Kenya: A report to the Embassy of the Kingdom of the Netherlands*. Nairobi: Zeverijn.

Good governance strategies for sustainable ecotourism in Tanzania

Liliane Pasape[a], Wineaster Anderson[b] and George Lindi[b]

[a]School of Business Studies and Humanities, Nelson Mandela African Institution of Science and Technology, Arusha, Tanzania; [b]Department of Marketing, University of Dar es Salaam, Dar es Salaam, Tanzania

AbstractThis article assesses the role of good governance strategies in sustaining ecotourism. Using a qualitative method through exploratory research design, 18 good governance strategies that promote sustainable ecotourism were identified. Thereafter, a specific stakeholder survey ($n = 250$) was conducted in the eastern and northern tourist circuits in Tanzania. Through the discrete choice binary logit model, relationships between the identified strategies and specified ecotourism sustainability indicators were analysed by looking for the strategies that are more associated with each indicator. The findings show that sustainability of ecotourism in the country is mainly jeopardised by inadequate transparency, poor accountability practices and weak integration mechanisms between ecotourism operations and the country's development plans. As a result, poor governance has led to unproductive planning, inefficiencies and mismanagement of ecotourism resources. The study concluded by recommending accountability, transparency and integration between economic activities in order to ensure that ecotourism meets the needs of both current and future generations.

Introduction

Despite the great need for sustainable ecotourism, many of its activities have been unsustainable partly due to what McKercher (2003) expressed as the fierce competition that ecotourism resources face from local residents and tourism activities. This has raised concern as to how best various communities can be incorporated and governed and contribute to sustainable ecotourism. This study, therefore, looked at the sustainability of ecotourism from the perspective of the stakeholders and their role in ensuring good governance.

It is common practice that people around the world travel for different reasons such as recreation, leisure or business, and this is regarded as tourism. However, not all types of tourism ensure the future needs of both tourists and the local community, and so tourism can be categorised as either unsustainable or sustainable tourism. The current study is very interested in sustainable tourism because it benefits the majority of the people involved in it, now and in the future. According to Agheorghiesei and Bedrule-Grigoruta (2007), the development of sustainable tourism meets the needs of tourists, tourism companies and host destinations, while at the same time protecting the environment and, where possible, increasing employment opportunities in the future. It is conceived that this would lead to resource management that would help meet social, economic and aesthetic needs, while at the same time preserving cultural integrity and essential ecological processes, as well as leading to healthier lives.

Ecotourism is part of sustainable tourism which is made up of cultural, rural and natural tourism. Cultural tourism encourages people to visit cultural attractions away from their normal place of residence in order to gain new information and experiences to satisfy their cultural needs. Rural tourism takes place where rural locations are the main attraction and is based on accommodation services, complemented by additional facilities, which adhere to the principles of sustainable development. On the other hand, natural tourism refers to ecologically sustainable tourism with a primary focus on experiencing natural areas (Anderson, 2009). Ecotourism is the fastest growing sector of the global tourism industry, which primarily focuses on experiencing natural areas and fosters environmental and cultural understanding, appreciation and conservation (Roberts & Thanos, 2003). In view of that, ecotourism has been recognised as one of the vital tools for fostering sustainable development around the world, particularly in developing countries, Tanzania being one of them. The International Ecotourism Society (2004) defines ecotourism as responsible travel to natural areas that conserves the environment and sustains the well-being of the local people.

In Tanzania, the Ministry of Natural Resources and Tourism (1999) stipulates that the country seeks to develop tourism which is culturally and socially responsible, ecologically friendly, environmentally sustainable and economically viable, as well as to market Tanzania as a tourist destination for adventure safaris, wildlife viewing, a variety of cultures and beaches. In an effort to secure its success, those priorities were incorporated in the country's Integrated Tourism Master Plan (2002) in the five primary areas of awareness creation in the source markets through expanding tourist products, securing a more competitive position, maximising the necessary service skills and establishing the necessary structures and controls to underpin tourism development.

Most inbound tourists to Tanzania come for ecotourism attractions, as it is estimated that at least 90% of tourists follow nature-based tourism (Anderson, 2010; Pasape, Anderson, & Lindi, 2013). According to Anderson (2009), for an attraction to be regarded as ecotourism-oriented it should primarily involve the natural environment, with associated cultural elements constituting secondary components. Tanzania ranks second in the world for its natural resources as it has approximately 14 national parks, 33 game reserves, 44 game-controlled areas, 1 conservation area and 2 marine parks. Furthermore, Tanzania is the only country in the world which has allocated more than 25% of its total area to national wildlife parks and protected areas compared with the world average of 4% (Anderson & Saidi, 2011; Honey, 2008).

Tourism contributes around 18% of the country's GDP with the earnings from tourism in 2013 topping US$1.88 billion, up from US$1.7 billion in 2012 and US$1.45 billion in 2011 (Anderson, 2014). According to Pasape, Anderson, and Lindi (2014) and Anderson (2014), the substantial contribution of tourism to the social and economic development of the country has resulted from its biodiversity and cultural assets. Exposing visitors to culture and traditions provides an opportunity for tourists to see, understand and appreciate other cultures. Ecotourism is also benefiting locals through the sale of various items such as handicrafts and agricultural produces, thereby encouraging local people to support conservation efforts (Loibooki, 2010).

Despite progress in the research of governance in many other fields such as corporate management (Cornforth, 2001; Michael, 2002), development (Rocha Menocal, 2011), politics (Forest & Wild, 2010) and social transformation (Khan, 2004), there is still a sub-stantial research gap to be filled in the ecotourism sector. Bessa and Faria (2006) identified two basic actions in relation to governance, which may also be considered in the promotion of sustainable ecotourism. These are the facilitation of political dialogue to prevent conflicts between different actors, and the strengthening of institutional capacities. Also, Faria, Bessa, and Tonet (2009) concluded that, while the notion of governance suggests directions for research in terms of investigating the interaction between state and non-state actors, at least at the normative level (e.g. democratic or good governance forms), appropriate and applicable models are still lacking for developing countries. Thus, this study addresses the gap from the stakeholders' perspective.

Thus, the objective of this study is to determine the role of good governance in terms of transparency, accountability and integration in ensuring sustainable ecotourism in Tanzania. To achieve the desired objectives, the rest of the article is organised as follows. The litera-ture review comes before the research methods, followed by the findings and finally the conclusion.

Literature review

The concepts of governance and good governance

Governance is an old phenomenon which represents decisions that define expectations, grant power or verify performance in a society. It also relates to steady management and consistent policies and procedures which enhance the making and implementation of good decisions which are useful to a particular society or organisation. Various definitions of governance have been put forward by a number of authors. For instance, UNESCAP (2009) defines governance as the process by which decisions are made and implemented (or not implemented). Usually, governance involves institutions, authority structures and even collaboration in allocating resources and coordinating or controlling activities in society or the economy (Empter & Josef-Janning 2003). Likewise, governance is the exer-cise of political, economic or administrative power to manage a country's resources, affairs and societal problems. It comprises the mechanisms, processes and institutions through which citizens and groups articulate their interests, exercise their obligations and mediate their differences (Australian Government Overseas Aid Program [AuAID], 2000; World Bank, 1991).

Despite the fact that there is no single or exhaustive definition of good governance, various sources of literature depict that there are key attributes or characteristics, which differentiate between good and bad governance. AuAID (2000) pointed out that good gov-ernance involves competent management of national resources and affairs in a manner that is open, transparent, accountable, equitable and responsive to people's needs. Most of the time good governance is linked to an ideal democratic process in which the voiceless are heard, the powerless are empowered, the disadvantaged get a fair share and all stakeholders are in a win-win situation. It ensures that corruption is minimised, the views of minorities are taken into account and the voice of vulnerable groups is heard when decisions are made (Pokharel, 2004).

However, UNESCAP (2004) revealed that the main aim of good governance is to ensure that organisations achieve their goals and produce valuable results. In so doing, good governance can operate in different ways, such as centralised governance in the form of government regulations, which comprises the top-down approach taken by the national centralised agency with clear bureaucratic procedures, or decentralised governance in the form of local agencies acting autonomously through networks and public–private partnerships or through cooperation with community organisations. These forms of governance depend on the level of heterogeneity of the desired public goods, the level of externality and the presence of economies of scale. Based on UNESCAP (2009), good governance is believed to comprise six key principles, namely:

(1) Purpose and outcomes clearly visible,
(2) Functions and roles clearly defined,
(3) Values reflected in stakeholders' behaviour,
(4) Taking decisions and justifying them,
(5) Developing capacity and capability and
(6) Engaging all the stakeholders.

The Asian Alliance for Good Forest Governance (2002) identified a similar set of good governance principles known as: participation; equity; balanced power relations; recognition/legitimacy of rights; clear roles and responsibilities; transparency; accountability; democracy and decentralisation. Having all characteristics of good governance in one society is an ideal situation, but society should aim, through broad–based consensus-building, to ensure that there is transparency, accountability, participation and predictability (UNDP, 1997). Transparency is a major requirement of good governance. It means, for instance, that the enforcement of decisions taken abides by rules and regulations. It also means that information is freely available and directly accessible to those who will be affected by such decisions and their enforcement (ADB, 1999).

Likewise, based on Graham, Amos and Plumptre (2003) accountability means that decision-makers in the government, the private sector and civil society organisations are accountable to the public and institutional stakeholders. Generally, accountability differs depending on the type of organisation and whether decisions are made internally or externally. With regard to participation, UNESCAP (2009) argued that the involvement of both men and women is a key to good governance. Involvement could be either direct or through legitimate intermediate institutions or representatives. It is important to point out that representative democracy does not necessarily mean that the concerns of the most vulnerable in society would be taken into consideration when decisions are made. Participants need to be informed and organised. This means freedom of association and expression on the one hand and an organised civil society on the other.

For a number of years good governance has been linked to the political dimensions of countries. However, good governance is now becoming an increasingly important issue with respect to protected areas, partly because of the growing number of international agreements and conventions such as the World Heritage Convention, Convention on Biological Diversity, the Ramsar Convention on Wetlands of International Significance and UNESCO's Man in the Biosphere Programme (Graham et al., 2003). In view of that, various models of good governance have been developed, for example the one by Governance International (2009) that provides a new framework for policy-makers, public managers and community leaders who want to improve the governance capacity of their organisation by bringing together the three main elements of governance, which are multiple stakeholders, political and social values and policy outcomes. It focuses on improving the quality of life, trust and other important social values in addition to efficiency, effectiveness and economy.

The relevance of this model to the current study is that it appreciates the fact that multiple stakeholders are needed for good governance, which supports the overall objective of the study on assessment of stakeholders' strategies for ensuring sustainable ecotourism. Moreover, it is a catalyst for change as it activates citizens and other stakeholders and mobilises new resources in the form of volunteering and fund-raising (see Figure 1). The model also offers a flexible framework which can be used by organisations to assess how well they manage governance issues and also as a tool for obtaining stakeholders' perceptions to improve partnership working.

Methodology

This study adapted both the quantitative and qualitative research design. Although the quantitative approach was the core of the design as statistics were used to arrive at the study's conclusion, the qualitative approach was used after completion of the quantitative research (sequential design). The aims of the qualitative research was to gain an in-depth understanding of the subject matter and investigate the sampled respondents' attitude towards the assessed issues in order to generalise and verify the results. Therefore, the mixed research design was used so that the results from one method were complemented by the results from the other to aid clarification and interpretation (also depicted by Brannen, 2005; Bryman, 1988; Cresswell, 1995; Creswell and Vicki, 2007; Driscoll, Yeboah, Salib, & Rupert 2007).

The sampled population comprised 250 tourism stakeholders located in 8 regions in Tanzania, namely, Dar es Salaam, Coast, Morogoro, Tanga and Zanzibar (forming tourism's

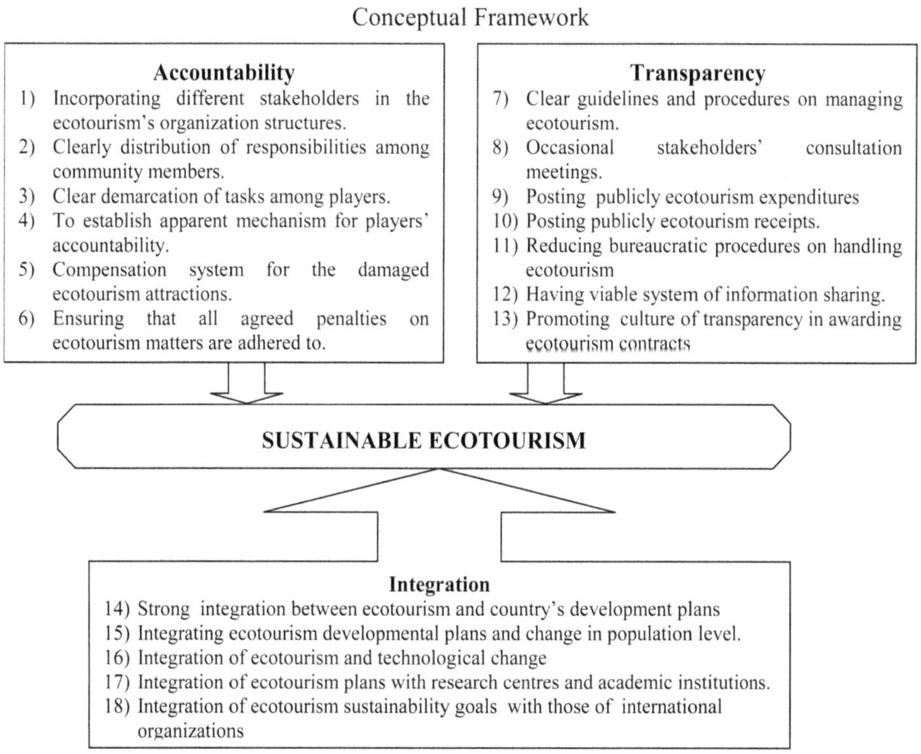

Conceptual Framework

Accountability
1) Incorporating different stakeholders in the ecotourism's organization structures.
2) Clearly distribution of responsibilities among community members.
3) Clear demarcation of tasks among players.
4) To establish apparent mechanism for players' accountability.
5) Compensation system for the damaged ecotourism attractions.
6) Ensuring that all agreed penalties on ecotourism matters are adhered to.

Transparency
7) Clear guidelines and procedures on managing ecotourism.
8) Occasional stakeholders' consultation meetings.
9) Posting publicly ecotourism expenditures
10) Posting publicly ecotourism receipts.
11) Reducing bureaucratic procedures on handling ecotourism
12) Having viable system of information sharing.
13) Promoting culture of transparency in awarding ecotourism contracts

SUSTAINABLE ECOTOURISM

Integration
14) Strong integration between ecotourism and country's development plans
15) Integrating ecotourism developmental plans and change in population level.
16) Integration of ecotourism and technological change
17) Integration of ecotourism plans with research centres and academic institutions.
18) Integration of ecotourism sustainability goals with those of international organizations

Figure 1. Conceptual framework.
Source: Designed by this study.

eastern circuit) and Kilimanjaro, Arusha and Manyara (forming tourism's northern circuit). The main reason for choosing these two circuits was that Tanzania is rich in ecotourism attractions and most cultural and natural tourism takes place in those areas. The distribution of respondents was 60% in the northern circuit and 40% in the eastern circuit, because there are more ecotourism activities in the former than in the latter circuit.

Since the population from which the sample was drawn did not constitute a homogeneous group, the selection of respondents was aided by stratified sampling. The respondents were stratified into several strata based on their role and level of involvement in ecotourism. Through this, the percentage and number of respondents for each stratum were obtained (Table 1). Following formation of the desired strata, the respondents required for each stratum were chosen through random sampling and given a questionnaire to complete. Thus, local community members were greatly involved (20%), followed by non-government officers (NGOs) (12%) due to their involvement in collaboration and empowerment, and local government officers (10%) who daily govern and monitor the use of ecotourism resources in their respective locality. In addition, 8% comprised central government officers, community-based organisations (CBOs), researchers and hotel and tour operators due to their involvement in the process in terms of policy, governance, information sharing, capacity building and support. The lowest percent (4–6) comprised government organisations, academicians and transporters due to their lowest involvement.

Specifically, the collection of data involved the use of a structured questionnaire to collect primary data after communicating with the respondents beforehand to ensure the smooth collection of data. The questionnaire with nine closed questions was in three sections; the first part (containing five questions) sought to obtain demographic details of the respondents, such as their gender, age, location in the tourism circuits, education level and role in ecotourism.

The second part comprising questions six, seven and eight sought to assess respondents' understanding of good governance practices, such as: 'how do you rate the importance of allowing private players to manage ecotourism on behalf of the community and government?', 'how do you rate the importance of delegating resources and power to the community and other stakeholders in the management of ecotourism in Tanzania?' and 'how do

Table 1. Sample framework.

Respondent category	Planned respondents (%)	Planned respondents (number)	Actual respondents (number)
• Local community members	20	50	51
• Central government officers	8	20	21
• Local government officers	10	25	26
• Community- based organisations	8	20	20
• Non-government organisations	12	30	30
• Government organisations	6	15	12
• Researchers	8	20	18
• Academicians from public institutions	4	10	12
• Academicians from private institutions	4	10	08
• Hotel and restaurant workers	8	20	20
• Tour operators	8	20	20
• Transporters	4	10	12
Total	100	250	250

you rate the importance of integrating ecotourism in other sectors for its sustainability in Tanzania?'.

The third part which had only 1 question consisted of 18 statements (Table 2) that sought to assess the linkage between good governance strategies (through the 3 items of transparency, accountability and integration) and sustainable ecotourism. The respondents were asked to indicate whether they agreed or disagreed with each of the statements according to their experience, knowledge and understanding of governance of ecotourism. In all those nine questions respondents' opinions were recorded and coded in the form of a five-point Likert scale of 'totally agree' 1, 'agree' 2, 'neither agree nor disagree' 3, 'disagree' 4 and 'totally disagree' 5 so as to collect the specific views of the respondents. During data analysis, those responses were further grouped into two of '1 = agree' (for options 1 and 2) and '2 = disagree' (for options 3, 4 and 5), hence qualifying it to be a binary discrete choice model, which requires it to have (0, 1) options for responses, as recommended by Pallant (2007).

In addition, appropriate and relevant secondary data were collected from various online and physical sources. These data were used to supplement the primary data and provide background information on the study, to enhance the assessment of previous and current trends in ecotourism and to show the existing linkages and networks in Tanzania's ecotourism. Therefore there was no analysis of the secondary data.

The study pre-tested the questionnaire, used the findings from previous similar studies, and conducted factor analysis and Cronbach's alpha analysis to ensure the validity and reliability of the research. To ensure the good response of non-English speakers, the questionnaire was translated into Kiswahili and so respondents had the option of using either the English or Swahili version.

The statistical package for social sciences (SPSS) aided the process of estimating the degree of agreement on the influence of the 3 variables of transparency (statements 1–7), accountability (statements 8–13) and integration (statements 14–18) on sustainable

Table 2. Good governance strategy.

Some strategies of good governance as summarised from the empirical literature
(1) Clear guidelines and procedures for managing ecotourism
(2) Occasional stakeholders' consultation meetings
(3) Posting publicly ecotourism expenditure
(4) Posting publicly ecotourism receipts
(5) Reducing bureaucratic procedures for handling ecotourism
(6) Having a viable system of information sharing
(7) Promoting a culture of transparency in awarding ecotourism contracts
(8) Incorporating different stakeholders in ecotourism's organisational structure
(9) Clear distribution of responsibilities among community members
(10) Clear demarcation of tasks among players
(11) Establishing a mechanism to ensure players' accountability
(12) Compensation scheme for damaged ecotourism attractions
(13) Ensuring that all agreed penalties on ecotourism matters are adhered to
(14) Ensuring ecotourism is integrated in the country's development plans
(15) Linking ecotourism developmental plans with a change in the population level
(16) Linking ecotourism with technological change
(17) Linking ecotourism plans with research centres and academic institutions
(18) Integrating ecotourism sustainability goals in those of international organisations

ecotourism, using the discrete choice model as follows:

$$P(\text{AGREE} = i) = \exp(xi\beta) / 1 + \exp(xi\beta), \qquad (1)$$

where : $xi\beta = \beta_0 + \beta_1 \text{trans} + \beta_2 \text{accou} + \beta_3 \text{integ} + \sum_j^i \beta_j z_{ij}$.

From the above model, AGREE_I denotes that the nth individual agrees ($\text{AGREE}_i = 1$) or does not agree ($\text{AGREE}_i = 0$) with the good governance strategies, z_{ij} denotes the dummy variables, and β_1 and β_2 denote the regression coefficients. The above model was used to predict the factors that influence respondents' decisions on the given choices. Those factors were the respondents' age, sex, education level, residence and role in the tourism industry. To interpret the model, the following variables were selected as a reference group: male respondents aged between 36 and 35, resident in Kilimanjaro, educated to the level of college certificate and local community members. The reason for choosing the discrete choice model is because it permits assessment of the factors determining respondents' decisions on a given set of stakeholder strategies for ensuring sustainable ecotourism in Tanzania. Likewise, the study adopted the logit form because it is the most widely used discrete choice model which also fits the study's assumption that unobserved factors are uncorrelated with alternatives. Logit analysis was also employed because all the predictors are categorical.

Findings

Respondents' characteristics

The sample population comprised those living in the northern and eastern tourist circuits of Tanzania. The population in the two circuits is made up of a variety of cultures and traditions. For instance, despite the fact that Dar es Salaam and Coast regions contain the majority of coastal tribes, such as the 'wazaramo','wakwere' and 'wandengereko', they host people from almost every tribe and region of the country due to their social and economic development, which is more advanced than in other regions. This circuit is rich in cultural attractions with the exception of Morogoro, which has a few natural attractions, such as Mikumi and Ruaha National Parks, etc. Both the northern and eastern circuits have various educational institutions ranging from primary schools to universities, and so residents have the opportunity to go to school, although the number of educated people in specific regions varies, depending on educational awareness, economic level, cultural issues and related reasons.

The study findings revealed that the sample population comprised 65.2% of males and 34.8% of females, and more males were found in the northern circuit (62.6%) than in the eastern circuit (37.4%). With regard to female respondents, the percentages were 55.2 and 44.8 for the northern and eastern circuits, respectively. The majority of respondents (30.8%) were between 36 and 46 years old, but approximately 60% of the respondents were aged between 26 and 46, possibly because the majority of the workforce in Tanzania who participate actively in different ecotourism activities fall into those age ranges. The findings also revealed that 60% and 40% of the respondents were found in the northern and eastern tourism circuit, respectively, due to the fact that more ecotourism activities take place in the northern circuit than in the eastern circuit, as evidenced in the Ministry of Natural Resources and Tourism (2009).

Furthermore, the level of education of the respondents varied substantially in that 34.4% had reached an advanced level of secondary education while those with a first degree formed the majority of 51.2%. The respondents possessing a Master's or PhD formed the lowest group (14.2%). As regards their role, the majority were local community members comprising 20.4%, and 18.8% of the respondents were government officials working in various departments dealing with tourism in the country. The respondents from non-governmental, community-based and governmental organisations comprised 12, 8 and 4.8%, respectively.

A further 7.2% of the respondents were researchers, 8% were academicians in various institutions and 20.8% were service providers, who comprised tour operators, transporters and workers in hotels and restaurants. Community members represented the major group of ecotourism stakeholders as found by Navruzov (2000), who stated that the word community is widely used with varying meanings, but the most important are individuals, social groups, non-governmental organisations and CBOs and the local population. The respondents' characteristics are summarised in Table 3.

Good governance

In an effort to ascertain the status of good governance and what contributes to it as far as ecotourism is concerned, the study assessed the three general strategies for ensuring good governance, which are the management of ecotourism by both the public and private sector, delegation of power and resources to stakeholders and their integration for sustainable ecotourism as follows:

Public–private partnerships for sustainable ecotourism

The study findings show that an uneven proportion of stakeholders from the public and private sectors are involved in the management of ecotourism. While 71.6% of the

Table 3.   Respondents' characteristics.

SN	Variable	$N = 250$ (%)
1.	*Gender*	
	Male	65.2
	Female	34.8
2.	*Age*	
	< 25 years	9.6
	26–35	28.4
	36–45	30.8
	46–55	24.0
	> 55 years	7.0
3.	*Residency*	
	Eastern tourist circuit (Dar es Salaam, Morogoro, Pwani, Tanga and Zanzibar)	40.0
	Northern tourist circuit (Arusha, Kilimanjaro, Manyara, Tanga)	60.0
4.	*Education*	
	≤ primary education	8.8
	Secondary school education	26.4
	Vocational education	35.6
	University bachelor's degree	15.6
	Master's and PhD education	13.6
5.	*Occupation*	
	Local community member (unemployed)	10.8
	Employees in non-governmental organisations	20.0
	Employees in governmental organisations	23.6
	Academics and/or researchers	15.0
	Tourism providers (tour operator, hotel and restaurants, transporters, etc.)	20.8

respondents agreed that the management of ecotourism by both the public and private sectors has a higher chance of making ecotourism sustainable, 28.4% had a negative opinion on that issue. Community participation is vital for the success of any ecotourism project since every active meeting enables local residents to have the final say in what their community needs and wants (Wood, 2002). Without active participation and the equal distribution of profits, any ecotourism project is destined to fail because the residents will not care enough or know enough about it.

However, the 28.4% who disagreed with collective management might be because some local communities do not trust private actors. Whenever the issue of private players is brought up, they always think of those foreigners who take advantage of them and benefit more. Therefore, the study findings depict the great need for ecotourism to be managed by both the public and private sectors, although the following key policy lessons must be emphasised. First, good governance at the local, regional and national levels is central to ensuring conservation and rural development through community-based ecotourism. Second, policy-makers and local communities need to work together to prevent outside organisations taking over local resources and ecotourism revenue, and policy-makers need to help local people to realise and maintain their right to control and manage natural resources (Nelson, 2004).

Although these issues have not yet been fully resolved, the current study observed that the Tanzanian government has made an effort to address them. For example, it created the national Tourism Facilitation Committee in 2000, whose objective is to increase cooperation and the involvement of stakeholders in policy matters that are related to the tourism development. The committee of about 50 members meets quarterly and the convenor is the Permanent Secretary of the Ministry of Natural Resources and Tourism. The committee comprises members of public and private institutions that are closely related to tourism, including bankers, transport, communication and immigration officials, the police, foreign affairs officials, and personnel from local authorities, tourism agencies and a number of private sector organisations involved in hospitality and tourism. One of the achievements of the committee has been to increase awareness of the importance of tourism to the national economy and some communication barriers between different organisations have been removed.

Delegation of resources and power to the community for ecotourism management

In most cases, delegation refers to the handing over of resources and power to organisations outside regular bureaucratic structures, such as public corporations, development agencies or non-governmental organisations (World Bank, 1983). The report shows that some state agencies do not protect the local population and so the rate of communities claiming the right to manage and govern wildlife increases day after day. In view of that, governments are assigning a formal participatory, monitoring or enforcement role to local users. In spite of that, many of them are being criticised today for having produced results far below expectations (Agrawal & Kent, 2006). A more fundamental challenge for developing indigenous ecotourism in a sustainable manner is to identify who should be involved in policy-making and making decisions about ecotourism development, or who should direct, control and decide the goals, processes and desired outcomes of development plans. The respondents had different opinions on the decision to delegate resources and power to the community and other stakeholders in an effort to ensure the sustainability of ecotourism in Tanzania. Whilst respondents with a positive opinion formed 66.8%, those with a negative opinion comprised 33.2%.

The need to delegate resources and power to the community and other stakeholders was also supported by Colton and Harris (2007), Cole (2006) and Timothy (2007), who argued that one of the key solutions to the problem of ecotourism development in indigenous communities is to transfer political and social powers to these communities to enable them to exert greater control over development projects and so control their own destiny. Additionally, Cotthem (2007) reveals that good governance at the local, regional and national levels is central to ensuring conservation and rural development through community-based ecotourism. Because of this, the decentralisation and delegation of power is crucial. It reduces the need for co-ordination as the centralised structure transfers to lower levels of government those functions it cannot manage effectively (Roy & Tisdell, 1998). The same authors depicted that decentralisation of power can facilitate the empowerment of people.

Integrating ecotourism in other sectors for its sustainability in Tanzania

The literature shows that there is potential for integrated and community-driven ecotourism to increase the likelihood of fiscal, ecological and institutional sustainability by granting communities more options. In Tanzania, for instance, ecotourism has been integrated in the education system in such a way that college degrees and diplomas are now offered in tourism and the hospitality profession. Likewise, ecotourism is linked to infrastructure development which aids the construction and improvement of hotels, particularly of different levels at ecotourism sites. The integration of ecotourism in education is expected to contribute substantially to the promotion of ecotourism as a sustainable form of tourism development because it can raise awareness of the importance of culture and ecological conservation (Duffy, 2002; Higham, 2007). Apart from education, it is high time that ecotourism is linked with other sectors for community development.

The potential benefits of the tourism industry to the development of local economic sectors through local linkages have been acknowledged (McBain, 2007) and in order to realise the positive impact of the tourism sector on reducing poverty, it is necessary to create a strong linkage with other economic sectors, particularly the agricultural sector, despite many barriers (Anderson & Juma, 2011). Moreover, ecotourism has been integrated in Tanzanian government policies, such as the National Tourism Policy (1999), Wildlife Policy, Land Policies and many more. From the study's output, the majority of the respondents (80.8%) agreed on the need to link ecotourism with other sectors as one good governance practice for the sustainability of ecotourism, whilst only 19.2% of the respondents disagreed.

Good governance strategies for ensuring sustainable ecotourism

The study also assessed the impact of good governance strategies, specifically through transparency, accountability and integration, for ensuring sustainable ecotourism in Tanzania. The following were the results.

Transparency

Transparency in ecotourism can be related to all decisions taken by stakeholders in and outside the sector, as well as their enforcement in a manner that abides by the rules and regulations of a particular society and internationally accepted practices. This will in turn make the relevant information readily accessible and available to all the parties concerned. The study findings on the transparency aspect revealed that, although the respondents had different opinions on the proposed strategies, most of them agreed on the need to have clear guidelines and procedures for managing ecotourism (82.4%), followed by cutting down on bureaucracy when dealing with ecotourism matters (82%) and ensuring that stakeholders' consultation meetings are held occasionally (80%). Despite these findings, the extent of disagreement with the proposed transparency strategies ranged from 17.6% to 22.2%, with promoting a culture of transparency when awarding ecotourism contracts being the one most disagreed with (see Table 4).

The output also shows that transparency strategies were correctly classified with 79.2% of the cases on the lower side and 82.4% on the higher side. With the exception of publicly posting ecotourism expenditure, all seven proposed transparency strategies positively influence good governance and the sustainability of ecotourism. It is, therefore, asserted that for ecotourism to be sustainable from the governance point of view, the transparency of stakeholders and partners has to be seen. Also, emphasis should be placed on ensuring that stakeholders follow clear guidelines and procedures for managing ecotourism, particularly those involved in public/private partnerships. Also, occasional consultative meetings of stakeholders must be held so as to plan, report on and assess new and ongoing projects.

Transparency has to be extended to the point that the key players publicly post ecotourism's relevant expenditure and receipts when deemed necessary. These meetings and financial transparency will avoid any unnecessary misunderstanding between players and encourage commitment. The authorities have to ensure that there is a viable system of information sharing among stakeholders and the bureaucracy involved in dealing with ecotourism matters is reduced. Also, a culture of transparency when awarding ecotourism contracts has to be promoted and different stakeholders need to be incorporated in ecotourism's organisational structure at various levels.

Table 4. Transparency strategies for sustainable ecotourism.

Transparency strategies	Agree (%)	Disagree (%)	β	Significance
(1) Clear guidelines and procedures for managing ecotourism	82.4	17.6	0.2	.08 residence .1 role
(2) Occasional stakeholders' consultation meetings	79.2	20.8	0.6	.01 residence .09 education .07 role
(3) Posting publicly ecotourism expenditure	80.4	19.6	−0.3	.02 residence .04 education
(4) Posting publicly ecotourism receipts	79.2	20.8	0.21	.02 residence .03 role
(5) Reducing bureaucracy when dealing with ecotourism	82	18	0.99	.01 residence
(6) Having a viable system of information sharing	79.6	20.4	0.69	.09 residence
(7) Promoting a culture of transparency when awarding ecotourism contracts	78.8	22.2	0.38	.00 residence .01 role

Source: Obtained from the study's data analysis.

Accountability

In most cases, accountability refers to the intention and ability of particular people involved in society or projects to give an account of their ongoing or future plans and activities and their expenditure and revenue to their colleagues, the general public or authorities so that they can be held accountable if things go wrong. This was found to be crucial for the management, development and sustainability of ecotourism in the country. The findings from the binary logit regression (Table 5) show small variations in the value of the coefficient of determination, in that the model was explained by values of less than 50% (Cox and Snell R Square) and between 21% and 80% (Negelkerke R Square) of the variance. This implies that statistically the most explained strategies, which were explained more in the study's model, were incorporating different stakeholders in ecotourism's organisational structure, emphasising the compensation scheme for damaged ecotourism attractions and ensuring that all agreed penalties on ecotourism matters are adhered to.

Despite the fact that all 6 accountability strategies positively influenced the good governance and sustainability of ecotourism, they were also correctly classified in over 72% of the cases. Over 80% of the respondents were in agreement that efforts should be made to ensure that a compensation scheme for damaged ecotourism attractions is effectively adhered to together with all agreed penalties. Other accountability strategies recommended by the respondents are a clear distribution of responsibilities among community members and a clear demarcation of tasks among the players so that nobody can take advantage of anything and everyone needs to know the scope of his/her duties and responsibilities.

Integration

The integration of tourism in other sectors is not a new phenomenon. For instance, Ashley, Goodwin and Roe (2002) cited in Anderson and Juma (2011) showed that when tourism and the agriculture sector are integrated, they benefit from each other's activities. There is substantial statistical evidence of the need for a strong link between ecotourism activities

Table 5. Accountability strategies for sustainable ecotourism.

Accountability Strategies	Agree (%)	Disagree (%)	β	Significance
(1) Incorporating different stakeholders in ecotourism's organisational structure	77.6	22.4	0.12	.04 gender .07 age .01 residency .07 education .02 role
(2) Clear distribution of responsibilities among community members	74	16	0.40	.07 gender .08 age .01 residence
(3) Clear demarcation of tasks among players	72.4	27.6	0.14	.01 residence .09 role
(4) To establish an apparent mechanism for players' accountability	75.2	24.8	0.39	-
(5) Compensation scheme for damaged ecotourism attractions	84.8	15.2	1.08	.07 age .00 residence
(6) Ensuring that all agreed penalties on ecotourism matters are adhered to	80	20	0.76	.09 residence

Source: Obtained from the study's data analysis.

and the country's development plans. To some extent this gives an opportunity for the planned activities to be funded and successfully taken care of in the ongoing development plans. The success and development of ecotourism depend on well-built and managed linkages between ecotourism-related activities and various developmental agencies.

The key issues for effective integration comprise population level and technological advancement, research centres and academic institutions as well as related international organisations. Lee (2010) argued that, in order to conserve the global ecosystem, it is important to integrate ecotourism in ecosystem conservation. This will lead to a balance between conservation and local development. It will also improve local residents' awareness and facilitate their participation in conservation and ecotourism. The output of the binary logit regression shows that, with the exception of integrating ecotourism plans in research centres and academic institutions, all other integration strategies positively influence the sustainability of ecotourism as evidenced by their coefficient of determination values (Table 6).

Estimating logit models

All 18 logit models that deliver the estimated probability of agreement with each of the proposed good governance strategies for ensuring sustainable ecotourism were estimated to ascertain the attributes relating to each strategy. Table 7 presents a summary of each model's results in the form of signs either positive (+) or negative (−) expressing the effect of the predictors on the dependent variables due to the fact that it is not possible and unrealistic for the estimated values to interpret the direct effect of each independent variable on the probability of agreement with the study models. Hence, the positive sign (+) expresses the increasing probability of agreement whilst the negative sign (−) articulates the decreasing probability of agreement with transparency, accountability and integration with respect to the reference groups.

Specific findings depicted that all seven transparency strategies in the good governance group contribute significantly to the sustainability of ecotourism, In addition, the findings reveal the cry of society for the system to be more transparent in terms of guidelines,

Table 6. Integration strategies for sustainable ecotourism.

Integration strategies	Agree (%)	Disagree (%)	β	Significance
(1) Integrating ecotourism in the country's development plans	76.4	23.6	1.06	.06 age .01 residence .07 education .09 role
(2) Integrating ecotourism in change in the population level	76	24	1.89	.03 age .01 residence .06 education .04 role
(3) Integrating ecotourism in technological change	74.8	25.2	0.10	.01 residence
(4) Integrating ecotourism plans in research centres and academic institutions	66.4	33.6	−1.4	.00 residence .06 role
(5) Integrating ecotourism sustainability goals in those of international organisations	81.2	18.8	0.91	.08 age .08 role

Source: Obtained from the study's data analysis.

Table 7. Categorical estimation of good governance strategies for ensuring sustainable ecotourism.

Respondents' characteristics	Good governance strategies																				
	Transparent										Accountability						Integration				
	1	2	3	A	B	C	D	E	F	G	H	I	J	K	L	M	N	O	P	Q	R
Gender																					
1. Female					+	+															−
Age																					
1. < 25 years	−																+	+			
2. Between 25 and 35 years	−								+												
3. Between 46 and 56 years		+																+			
4. > 55 years	−																				
Residency																					
1. Dar es Salaam				+	+	+										+		+		+	
2. Pwani			+	+																	
3. Morogoro			+			+			+	+	+	+	+	+		+	+	+	+	+	
4. Zanzibar																					
5. Tanga	+		+	+	+	+			+					+							
6. Arusha		+	+												+		+	+			
7. Manyara	+	+		+	+	+	+										+	+	+	+	
Education																					
1. Un educated					+																
2. Primary education																		+			
3. Form four					+																
4. Form six																					
5. College diploma																		+			
6. First degree			+																		
7. Master's	−																				
8. Doctor of Philosophy	−																				
Occupation																					
1. Central government officer							−					+					+				
2. Local government officer													+							+	

(*Continued*)

Table 7.   Continued.

Respondents' characteristics	\multicolumn{21}{c}{Good governance strategies}

| | \multicolumn{7}{c}{Transparent} | \multicolumn{6}{c}{Accountability} | \multicolumn{5}{c}{Integration} |

Respondents' characteristics	1	2	3	A	B	C	D	E	F	G	H	I	J	K	L	M	N	O	P	Q	R
3. Community- based organisation member				+																	
4. Non- governmental organisation member																					
5. Governmental organisation member														+							
6. Researcher																					
7. Academician in private institution				+											+						
8. Academician in public institution				+																	
9. Tour operator																					
10. Hotel and restaurants		+																		+	
11. Transporter																		+			−

Source: Obtained from the study's data analysis.
Note: '+' denotes increasing probability of AGREEMENT with stakeholders' collaboration strategy and '−' denotes decreasing probability of AGREEMENT with stakeholders' collaboration strategy.

procedures, occasional meetings, information sharing and award of contracts. In the case of accountability strategies all of them were reported to contribute significantly to sustainable ecotourism, except strategy number four 'establishment of an apparent mechanism for eco-tourism players' accountability'. Apart from that, strategy number one 'incorporating different stakeholders in ecotourism's organisational structure' was highly significant and explained by all five factors. As in the transparency strategies, all five strategies with respect to integrating ecotourism in the country's development plans, population changes, research centres and international agenda contribute significantly to the sustain-ability of ecotourism.

Moreover, the general findings of the estimated logit models depict that the probability of agreement with the selected good governance strategies increases with respondents' resi-dence (both in the northern and eastern tourism circuits), age, occupation and education. The specific findings with regard to the six proposed strategies with respect to transparency established that being a female respondent increases the likelihood of agreement with strat-egies numbers 2 and 3 on 'occasional stakeholders' consultation meetings' and 'posting publicly ecotourism expenditure'. This might be due to the argument that, since it is not so common for females in rural areas to attend meetings and gatherings where useful infor-mation is issued and shared because of cultural and traditional reasons, there is a greater chance of them demanding special meetings or a system such as notice boards or other means, which will enable them to receive relevant information.

As regards age, the degree of agreement with strategy 6 on 'having a viable system of information sharing' increases with those aged 26–35, because this group comprises people active in society who are involved in various economic activities relating to ecotourism, and so they are more likely to demand that they are adequately informed so that they can make an informed decision when deemed necessary. Additionally, with the exception of Zanzibar, all other respondents residing in the eastern tourism circuit were increasingly more likely to agree with strategies 2 and 3 on 'occasional stakeholders' consultation meetings' and 'posting publicly ecotourism expenditure'.

Moreover, while the likelihood of agreement with strategy 6 of 'having a viable system of information sharing' increases when respondents reside in Morogoro and Manyara, the probability of agreement with strategy 7 on 'promoting a culture of transparency when awarding ecotourism contracts' increases when they reside in Coast region. The findings were somewhat different when logits were estimated on accountability strategies, as for instance being male or female had no influence on the probability of agreement on any of the study's six strategies. The same applied to the age of respondents. However, as regards residence, the likelihood of agreement with strategy 13 increases when respondents reside in Dar es Salaam. Additionally, residing in Morogoro increases the probability of agreement with all the accountability strategies with the exception of 12 and 13 on ensuring adherence to the compensation scheme for damaged ecotourism attractions and all agreed penalties on ecotourism matters.

With respect to integration strategies of good governance, the findings reveal that gender and education level of the respondents had no influence on either agreement or dis-agreement with all strategies. Regarding the other dimensions respondents who were under 25 were increasingly more likely to agree with strategies 14, 15 and 18 pertaining to 'inte-grating ecotourism in the country's development plan', 'change in population level' and 'goals of related international organizations'. This is because the age group, also known as generation 'y', has experienced a lot of technological reforms, globalisation and multi-disciplinarity of issues worldwide as opposed to the older generation which has not. Additionally, the results show that residing in Dar es Salam, Morogoro, Manyara and Arusha increases the probability of agreement with strategies 14, 15, 16, 17 and 18. This is probably because these regions experience a greater number of tourists than other regions, and so the need to integrate ecotourism in other sectors, national development plans, population level and technological advancement is more relevant to them.

In summary, the study's findings on good governance of ecotourism are supported by Sama (2011), who argues that 'common-pool resources can be owned and managed by governmental institutions as public goods, by firms or individuals as private goods or can be left free as open access resources'. Therefore, the best solution for ensuring sustainable ecotourism would be to support local institutions to collectively manage the common-pool resources. The main purpose would be to control and prevent the two problems of exclusion and subtraction. To be successful, the monitoring of subsistence communities must be associated with conservation and utilisation rules established to govern the commons, as well as with sanctions imposed on lawbreakers. If not properly managed, unrestrained ecotourism risks bringing unequal economic benefits not only to foreign firms, but also to a few members of the community, thereby altering cultural traditions and values and triggering potential conflicts and corruption.

Conclusion

This study's assessment of the role of good governance strategies for ensuring the sustainability of ecotourism focused on the three key aspects of transparency, accountability and integration. With respect to policy-makers, although there are potential opportunities for the growth of ecotourism in Tanzania, the results indicate that there is a need to produce clear operational guidelines on the distribution of responsibilities, to reduce unnecessary bureaucracy and to strengthen the linkages between ecotourism activities and the country's development plans, research findings and societal needs. All these will guarantee good governance of ecotourism. Almost 80% of the respondents stressed the need to strengthen the penalties for those damaging ecotourism attractions, which shows that the majority of them are unhappy with how the authorities handle these cases. This means that more ways, approaches and regulations are needed to deal with these issues.

As regards academicians, the majority of tourists or investors are unlikely to engage in any ecotourism activities unless there are effective strategies for ensuring transparency and accountability, and the lack of integration of ecotourism activities in the country's development plans, research findings and societal needs undermines the sustainability of ecotourism. In view of that, once linkages are established by all stakeholders (mostly academia/ researchers, the government and society) through planning, implementation, monitoring and evaluation, then ecotourism activities are more likely to be successful. Academicians through their research and other activities are obliged to recommend the best and most sustainable models for the linkages and other good governance practices.

Concerning practitioners in the field, at the moment a number of organisations in both the public and private sectors are involved in ecotourism through planning, promoting, educating, advocacy or training stakeholders. Pasape et al. (2013) also suggested public/private partnerships in six key areas of infrastructure development, building the capacity of the community, information and communication, research and development and management of projects. Ecotourism stakeholders differ in terms of education, skills or finances and so one cannot expect similar effectiveness or efficiency in their operations, which means that guidelines, demarcation and regulations are needed. The Tanzania Commission for Tourism needs to ensure that all its members are guided and directed accordingly.

To ensure that stakeholders and the general public become part and parcel of the sustainability effort, the study recommends that representatives of all key stakeholders should be involved in doing a needs analysis, and planning, managing and coordinating ecotourism-related activities and projects at all levels. Regarding academics and research, although the study's findings contribute substantially to widening the literature and body of knowledge on the good governance of ecotourism stakeholders, further research needs to be conducted on how best ecotourism can be integrated in the country's development plans and research findings as well as incorporating society's needs. A study on the level and extent of transparency in ecotourism programmes is also required to ensure the necessary confidentiality of information and to make stakeholders aware of what is going on and of planned future activities.

Furthermore, as regards policy-makers and decision-makers, every effort should be made to ensure that there are good governance practices through transparency, accountability and integration of activities in most ecotourism programmes, especially those involving local communities, not only to ensure that the laws and guidelines are adhered to, but also to ensure that the community is willing to support a sustainable ecotourism project. All in all, Roy and Tisdell (1998) argued that the possibility of good governance depends on institutional structures and the economic resources available to it. In some cases centralised governance structures are inefficient and in others decentralised structures turn out to be inadequate.

Disclosure statement

No potential conflict of interest was reported by the authors.

References

Agheorghiesei, D., & Bedrule-Grigoruta, M. (2007). *Sustainable tourism in Romania: Tendencies, Opportunities and threats.* Tourism in the New Millennium, June 18–20. Social Science Electronic Publishing. Retrieved from SSRN: http://ssrn.com/abstract=982329

Agrawal, A., & Kent, K. (2006). *Poverty, development, and biodiversity conservation: Shooting in the dark?* (Working paper number 26). New York, NY: Wildlife Conservation Society (WCS) Institute.

Anderson, W. (2009). Promoting ecotourism through networks: Case studies in the Balearic Islands. *Journal of Ecotourism, 8*(1), 51–69.

Anderson, W. (2010). *Marketing of domestic tourism in Tanzania.* Dar es Salaam: Dar es Salaam University Press.

Anderson, W. (2014). Cultural tourism and poverty alleviation in the rural Kilimanjaro, Tanzania. *Journal of Tourism and Cultural Change, 12*(2), 1–17.

Anderson, W., & Juma, S. (2011). Linkages at tourism destinations: Challenges in Zanzibar. *ARA Journal of Tourism Research, 3*(1), 27–41.

Anderson, W., & Saidi, S. A. (2011). Internationalization and poverty alleviation: Practical evidence from Amani butterfly project in Tanzania. *Journal of Poverty Alleviation and International Development, 2*(2), 17–45.

Ashley, C., Goodwin, H., & Roe, D. (2002). *Pro-poor tourism strategies: Expanding opportunities for the poor.* Pro-poor Briefing No. 1, Overseas Development Institute. International Institute for Environment and Development (IIED), Centre for Responsible Tourism, London. Retrieved June 2, 2011, from www.propoortourism.infor/library.html

Asian Development Bank. (1999). *Governance: Sound development management.* Manila: Asian Development Bank.

Australian Government Overseas Aid Program. (2000). *Good governance: Guiding principles for implementation.* Canberra: Australian Agency for International Development.

Bessa, L. F., & Faria, S. C (2006). *Governança ambiental: Aspectos conceituais*, Texto Didático: *Série Planejamento e Gestão Ambiental* 8, 6–15. Brasília: Universa.

Brannen, J. (2005). Mixing methods: The entry of qualitative and quantitative approaches into the research process. *International Journal of Social Research Methodology, 8*, 173–184.

Bryman, A. (1988). *Quantity and quality in social research*. London: Unwin Hyman.

Cole, S. (2006). Cultural tourism, community participation and empowerment. In M. Smith & M. Robinson (Eds.), *Cultural tourism in a changing world: Politics, participation and (re) presentation* (pp. 89–103). Great Britain: Channel View Publications.

Colton, J., & Harris, S. (2007). Indigenous ecotourism's role in community development: The case of the Lennon Island first nation. In R. Butler & T. Hinch (Eds.), *Tourism and indigenous peoples: Issues and Implications* (pp. 220–233). Oxford: Elsevier.

Cornforth, C. (2001). What makes boards effective? An examination of the relationship between board inputs, structures, processes and effectiveness in non-profit organisations. *Corporate Governance: An International Review, 9*(3), 217–227.

Cotthem, W. (2007). *Does community-based ecotourism really benefit rural people in Tanzania?* Retrieved April 27, 2012 from http://www.id21.org/rural/r1fn1g1.html

Cresswell, J. W. (1995). *Research design: Qualitative and quantitative approaches*. Newbury Park, CA: Sage Publications.

Creswell, J. W., & Vicki, P. C. (2007). *Designing and conducting mixed methods research*. Newbury Park, CA: Sage Publications.

Driscoll, D. L, Yeboah, A., Salib, P., & Rupert, D. J (2007). Merging qualitative and quantitative data in mixed methods research: How to and why not. *Ecological and Environmental Anthropology, 3* (1), 19–28.

Duffy, R. (2002). *A trip too far: Ecotourism, politics and exploitation*. London: Earthscan Publications.

Empter, S., & Janning, J. (2009). Sustainable governance indicators 2009 – An introduction. In B. Stiftung (Ed.), *Sustainable governance indicators policy performance and executive capacity in the OECD* (p. 15). Gütersloh: Verlag Bertelsmann Stiftung.

Faria. S. C, Bessa, L. F., & Tonet, H. C. (2009). A theoretical approach to urban environmental governance in times of change. *Management of Environmental Quality: An International Journal, 20*(6), 638–648.

Forest, M., & Wild, L. (2010). *Support to political parties: a missing piece of the governance puzzle*. London: Overseas Development Institute.

Governance International. (2009). *Good Governance Model*. Retrieved August 10, 2009, from http://www.govint.org/english/model.html, Retrieved May 17, 2012, from http://www.tnrf.org/resources, Retrieved May 13, 2012, from http://www.tanzaniatravelcompany.com/c_tourism.htm

Graham, J., Amos, B., & Plumptre, T. (2003). *Governance principles for protect areas in 21st century*. Durban: UICN.

Higham, J. (2007). Ecotourism: Competing and conflicting schools of thought. In J. Higham (Ed.), *Critical issues in ecotourism: Understanding a complex tourism phenomenon* (pp. 1–20). London: Elsevier.

Honey, M. (2008). *Ecotourism and sustainable development: Who owns paradise?* (2nd ed.). Washington, DC: Island Press. p. 551.

Khan, M. H. (2004). *State formation in Palestine: viability and governance during a social transformation*, Vol. 2 of Political economy of the Middle East and North Africa, Routledge.

Lee, Y. (2010). *Ecotourism management triangle: A future direction for international cooperation*. Seoul: Korean Tourism Research Institute.

Loibooki, B. (2010). *The role of Tanzanian national parks in ecotourism*. Retrieved from www.nric.net/tourism/sidebar/Role_TANAPA.pdf

McBain, H. (2007). *Caribbean tourism and agriculture: Linking to enhance development and competitiveness*. Economic Commission for Latin America and the Caribbean (ECLAC), Study and Perspective Series – The Caribbean No. 2.

McKercher, B. (2003, November 5–9). *Sustainable tourism development – Guiding principles for planning and management*. Presentation to the National Seminar on Sustainable tourism Development, Bishkek, Kyrgyzstan.

Michael, A. (2002). Into the fire: Boards and executive transitions. *Non-profit Management and Leadership, 12*(4), 341–351.

Ministry of Natural Resources and Tourism (1999). *National Tourism Policy.* Dar es Salaam: Tanzania Government Printer.

Ministry of Tourism and Natural Resources. (2009). Retrieved June 10, 2009, from www.mtnr.or.tz

Navruzov, Y. (2000). *The category Gromada in Modern Lexicon of Public Administration: Actual Problems of Public Administration.* DB UAPA Research Papers, No. 1, 134–145.

Nelson, F. (2004). *The evolution and impacts of community-based ecotourism in northern Tanzania* (Paper No. 131). London: International Institute for Environment and Development.

Pallant, J. (2007). *SPSS survival manual: A step by step guide to data analysis using SPSS for Windows* (3rd ed.). Mc Graw Hill: Open University Press.

Pasape, L., Anderson, W., & Lindi, G. (2013). Towards sustainable ecotourism through stakeholder collaboration in Tanzania. *Journal of Tourism Research and Hospitality, 2*(1), 1–14.

Pasape, L., Anderson, W., & Lindi, G. (2014). Sustaining ecotourism in Tanzania through community empowerment. *Journal of Tourism Research/Revista De Investigación En Turismo, 7*, 7–25.

Pokharel, R (2004). *Handouts on good governance in community forestry*, for M.Sc. forestry students. Retrieved from http://www.forestrynepal.org/images/thesis/BSc_MUpadhyay.pdf

Roberts, T., & Thanos. N. D. (2003). *Trouble in paradise: Globalization and environmental crises in Latin America.* New York, NY : Routledge.

Rocha Menocal, A. (2011). *Analyzing the relationship between democracy and development.* London: Overseas Development Institute.

Roy, K., & Tisdell, C. A. (1998). Good governance in sustainable development: The impact of institutions. *International Journal of Social Economics, 25*(6/7/8), 1310–1325.

Sama, D. (2011). *The relationship between common management and ecotourism development: tragedy or triumph of the commons? A law and economics answer.* A paper prepared for the chair of economic analysis of property law (Prof. Dr Boudewijn Bouckaert), at the European Master in Law and Economics, Centre for Advanced Studies in Law and Economics, Ghent University, Belgium.

The International Ecotourism Society [TIES], (2004). *Definition and principles of ecotourism.* Retrieved from http://www.ecotourism.org

Timothy, D. J. (2007). Empowerment and stakeholders' participation in tourism destination communities. In A. Church & T. Cole (Ed.), *Tourism, power and space* (pp. 199–216). London: Routledge.

United National Development Program (1997). Governance *for Sustainable Human Development.* Retrieved from www.undp.org

UNESCAP (2004). *Human settlements: What is good governance.* Retrieved from http://www.unescap.org

United Nations Economic and Social Commission for Asia and the Pacific (UNESCAP) (2009). *What is good governance.* Retrieved from http://www.unescap.org/pdd/prs/projectactivities/ongoing/gg/governance.asp

Wood, M. (2002). *Ecotourism: Principles, practices and policies for sustainability.* Paris: UN.

World Bank. (1983). *World development report.* New York: Oxford University Press.

World Bank. (1991). *World development report.* New York, NY: Oxford University Press.

Community-based ecotourism: a collaborative partnerships perspective

Moren Tibabo Stone

Okavango Research Institute, University of Botswana, Maun, Botswana

Collaboration is a key principle in community-based tourism approaches in most developing countries. This paper assesses how community-based ecotourism is perceived in terms of community participation and empowerment. Data were collected through semi-structured interviews and secondary sources. Collaborative partnerships underpinnings are adopted to guide the research. Results suggest that participation in ecotourism brings mixed results on biodiversity conservation and community livelihoods due to the involvement of multiple stakeholders in the design, planning, and implementation of ecotourism projects. Due to the diversity of stakeholders, the empowerment of communities using ecotourism is complex. Nonetheless, while the study may be perceived as having attained mixed results, the case study offers a progressive example of how stakeholders approach to natural resource management are evolving. Ecotourism development in Botswana still needs improvement; more considerations have to be given to *in situ* settings. The Chobe Enclave Community Trust, a community living adjacent to Chobe National Park in Botswana, provides the context on which this study's discussion focuses.

Introduction

The legacy of ecotourism has dominated community-based ecotourism (CBE) narratives over the last two decades. In recent years, there has been greater recognition that the outcomes of these trials do not happen automatically but instead need to be planned, resourced, and led by a range of partners (Weaver, 2011). In academic and practitioners' congresses, there have been debates over which strategies and tactics are the most useful in ensuring that beneficiaries of tourism dealings are considered in advance, during delivery, and in the period beyond (Chalip, 2006). Increasingly, collaborations and partnerships between communities, businesses, non-profit, funding and development agencies are being championed as powerful strategies (Bramwell & Lane, 2000; Bramwell & Sharman, 1999) to adopt in order to achieve a vision otherwise not possible when independent, and rural community entities work alone (Villiers, 2011) to achieve CBE benefits. CBE is 'a practice of tourism where the local community has a significant control over, and participation in its development and management, and a major percentage of the benefits stay within the community' (WWF, 2001, p. 43). Ideally CBE enterprises are run by one or more defined communities, or as joint venture partnerships with the private sector. Their aim is to ensure equitable community participation, the sustainable use of natural resources, and improvements in communities' standards of living (Rozemeijer, 2001).

CBE development has been credited with the potential to positively change communities' perceptions on the use of natural and cultural resources (Mbaiwa, 2011; Mbaiwa, Stronza, & Kreuter, 2011; Stone, 2013). On the other hand, there is contestation over the value of CBE development and its impacts on the people and places affected by its delivery (Almeyda, Broadbent, Wyman, & Durham, 2010; Kruger, 2005).

Given the amplified cognizance about the prominence of host communities and environmental responsibility in tourism, CBE has expanded its attractiveness as a scheme for social appropriation and environmental safeguarding (TIES, 2006). At present, CBE platforms are *in situ* in various countries across Africa, Latin America, and Asia (Baktygulov & Raeva, 2010).

CBE as a sustainable tourism development

The advent of sustainable tourism can be regarded as a rejoinder to theoretical reinforcements of sustainable development (WCED, 1987). However, sustainable tourism arguments have prolonged further than scrutinising tourism impacts, to offering strides, which could be engaged by the industry (Bramwell & Lane, 1993; Inskeep, 1991) to realise sustainable tourism development. Sustainable tourism does not merely endeavour to address economic and environmental conservation concerns, but also issues of power and equity in society (Crick, 1989; Urry, 1990). While available writings delineate sustainable tourism in manifold, by and large, sustainable tourism denotes tourism that can sustain its feasibility for an indeterminate period of time (Tosun, 2001) and 'does not degrade or alter the human and physical environment in which it exists' (Butler, 1993, p. 29). In order to achieve sustainable tourism, numerous approaches to tourism development have been explored. For example, community participation, ownership, and empowerment through the rubric of community-based natural resources management (CBNRM) are considered vital strides in that tourism development is sustainable in host destinations.

CBNRM practices encompass resident communities determining how best to protect and utilise the natural resources on their communal land (Taylor, 2002). The inadequacy of top-down approaches to conservation ('fortress conservation') led many countries to involve communities in conservation management (Swatuk, 2005).

In Botswana, several communities living in wildlife-rich areas have adopted CBNRM (Stone & Rogerson, 2011). The assumption CBNRM makes is that a community will manage natural resources better once it realises the benefits accrued from them (Mbaiwa, 2011). Botswana's CBNRM focuses on three domains: conservation, rural development, democracy and/or good governance (Zuze, 2006). When focused on conservation, it is concerned with the wise and sustainable use of the resources. As a rural development strategy, CBRNM promotes income generation or improved livelihoods; and when focused on democracy and/or good governance, CBRNM involves the devolution of authority from central government to communities (Zuze, 2006). In Botswana, CBNRM projects are run as ecotourism enterprises.

Although there are many controversies over an exact definition of ecotourism, many experts in ecotourism assert that ecotourism should have low impact on nature, with a goal to benefit both conservation and the well-being of local communities (Guangming et al., 2008; Lindberg, Enriquez, & Sproule, 1996, Weaver, 2011). Another controversy surrounds ecotourism activities, especially whether consumptive tourism activities such as sport or trophy hunting should be embraced (Moufakkir & Burns, 2012). However, the many definitions of community participation and empowerment through ecotourism promote either interpersonal or contextual elements and define it either as an outcome or a process (Laverack, 2001).What these definitions have in common is their focus on a level of control, community ownership, and the importance of community livelihoods derivation (Tosun, 2005; United Nations World Tourism Organization, 2011; WTO, 2002; WWF, 2001).

Ecotourism and consumptive tourism

The consumptive nature of ecotourism through wildlife hunting has increasingly become part of conservation arguments and policies. It is promoted as a low-impact sustainable use approach, adding value to natural resources (Hofer, 2002; Novelli & Humavindu, 2005). Yet, this practice remains debatable, being the focus of vigorous discussion between key interest groups, such as conservationists, animal welfare lobbyists, hunter associations, NGOs, as well as governments (Novelli, Barnes, & Humavindu, 2006). The controversy is premised on contradictory positions. While some believe that the consumptive use of individual animals for the sake of the population, the species, the ecosystem, is ethically acceptable, others vehemently oppose the killing of animals for personal satisfaction (Hofer, 2002). Criticisms have been directed towards initiatives such as CBNRM and CAMPFIRE projects in Botswana and Zimbabwe, respectively, which are promoted as ecotourism ventures that place emphasis on trophy hunting (Novelli et al., 2006). On a positive note, the resultant devolution of community ownership realised through ecotourism schemes has generally been considered as sound practice for wildlife management (Smith & Duffy, 2003).

Arguments that ecotourism is a non-consumptive practice have been better received than those supporting consumptive forms, such as sport or trophy hunting tourism (Novelli et al., 2006). Contributing to the debate, Hoenegaard (1994) argues that as long as ecotourism consumptive undertakings are low-volume, high-value activities that bring high-value benefits and are part of conservation and policies strategies, they should strive. Supporting the consumptive nature of ecotourism, Butler (1991) argues that an ecotourism project must be consistent with positive environmental ethics, should not denigrate the resources, must benefit the resource, and should have an expectation of gratification measured in appreciation and education. In espousing this debate, the researcher adopts Milner-Gulland and Bennett's (2003) argument that the problem can only be tackled by looking at wider economic and institutional contexts within which such hunting occurs since the successful conservation of hunted wildlife requires collaboration at all scales, involving local people, resource extraction companies, governments, and scientists.

Ecotourism and CBNRM

The CBNRM approach integrates ecotourism philosophy in many ways by addressing some of the core pillars of ecotourism. CBNRM-like ecotourism is an incentive-based conservation philosophy that links the conservation of natural resources with rural development (Swatuk, 2005). The two concepts emphasise the devolvement of management decisions from centralised governments to local land users (Mbaiwa, 2015), recognise the autonomy of community as an institution, proprietorship and tenurial rights, rights to make the rules and viable mechanisms to enforce them, and ongoing incentives in the form of benefits that exceed costs (Bromley, 1992). Central to the concepts of CBNRM and ecotourism are the theories and assumptions underlying the political decentralisation of natural resources management that imply a process of redistribution of power and the transfer of responsibilities from central governments to rural communities (Boggs, 2000). Both CBNRM and ecotourism paradigms are thus reforms of conventional 'protectionist conservation philosophies' and 'top-down' approaches and promote 'bottom-up' approaches that involve all affected stakeholders (Stone, 2015). In this respect, CBNRM and ecotourism are perceived as having the potential to stimulate rural development and a change in local communities' attitudes towards sustainable natural resource utilisation.

Despite the promotion of community participation and empowerment through ecotourism and CBNRM projects, the meaning and reception of community participation and empowerment through ecotourism from the community's perspective is little understood. Warburton (1998) argues that true active participation or empowerment has received little attention in the ecotourism development literature. In the same vein, Laverack (2001) posits that for the realisation of sustainable tourism, community empowerment is regarded as a central component to community development and yet making this concept operational in a programme context remains elusive.

In an endeavour to bridge this oversight, this paper adopts collaborative partnerships underpinnings to assess how CBE is perceived in terms of community participation and empowerment as well as how ecotourism has transformed community livelihoods and biodiversity conservation.

The theory of collaboration and partnerships

One of the vital subjects in the debate on sustainable development addresses the question of what institutional arrangements are the most promising in advancing the process of progressive transformation (Glasbergen, 2007). One such approach is the formation of collaborative partnerships with the endeavour to solve societal problems. Thus, organisational scholars have hyped collaborative partnerships as a useful and necessary instrument for problem-solving within a problem realm (e.g. Gray, 1989, Selin & Beason, 1991). Problem realms are contexts in which the central issues cannot be controlled or governed by individual actors behaving independently (Gray, 2007). Collaboration involves relationships between stakeholders when such stakeholders interact with each other in relation to a common issue of interest (Bramwell & Lane, 2000). The term collaborative partnership in this paper adopts Bramwell and Lane's (2000) definition which states collaboration 'is used to describe interactions between parties based on at least some agreed rules or norms, intended to address a common issue' (p. 1). In a diversified community setting, each stakeholder controls resources, such as knowledge, expertise, and capital, but on its own it is unlikely to possess all the resources necessary to achieve its objectives and to plan effectively for its future in relation to a significant development project (Jamal & Stronza, 2009). The stakeholders' interdependence means that there are potential mutual or collective benefits from stakeholders collaborating with each other (Selin & Beason, 1991). Stakeholders may work together if they consider that the probability of realising their goals and creating new opportunities in a problem domain are greater by performing jointly rather than acting alone (Czernek, 2013). A variety of terms are used to describe different collaborative and partnership arrangements in the tourism development literature. These include coalitions, forums, alliances, task forces, community–private partnerships, community–private agreements, joint venture partnerships, and public–private partnerships (Bramwell & Lane, 2000; Jamal & Stronza, 2009; Jones, 2002; Rozemeijer, 2001).

The fragmented nature of tourism development has long been recognised as one of the root problems of tourism planning. The means of overcoming the fragmentation problems have also been long highlighted (Jamal & Stronza, 2009). Nevertheless, Bramwell and Lane (2000) caution that the definition of collaborative partnerships makes no assumptions about which stakeholders will participate, how much power they may have, how representative they may be, or about the total number of stakeholders involved. Collaborative partnerships can help to avoid or reconcile the long-term costs of adversarial conflicts between interest groups (Mbaiwa et al., 2011).

In summary, Bramwell and Lane (2000) identified potential benefits of collaborative partnerships in tourism planning as follows:

- There may be involvement by a range of stakeholders, all of whom are affected by the multiple issues of tourism development and may be well placed to introduce change and improvement.
- Decision-making power and control may diffuse to the multiple stakeholders.
- The involvement of several stakeholders may increase the social acceptance of policies, so that implementation and enforcement may be easier to effect.
- More constructive and less adversarial attitudes might result as a consequence of working together.

Nevertheless, although there are positive potential benefits of collaborative partnerships in tourism planning and development, there are also potential challenges: these may include:

- Setting them up simply as 'window dressing' to avoid tackling real problems head-on with all interests.
- Actors may not be disposed to reduce their own power or to work together with unfamiliar partners or previous adversaries.
- Those stakeholders with less power may be excluded from the process of collaborative working or may have less influence on the process.
- The complexity of engaging diverse stakeholders in policy-making makes it difficult to involve them all equally.
- The power of some partnerships may be too great, leading to the creation of cartels (Bramwell & Lane, 2000).

In view of this discussion, Hall (1996) argues that collaborative partnerships methodologies in tourism planning have the potential to take in a wide set of stakeholders, escalate political participation and social equality, and contribute to more sustainable forms of tourism. Contrary to this, Hall (1996) cautions that collaborative arrangements may not be satisfactorily inclusive in nature.

This paper is therefore informed by the above-mentioned theoretical underpinnings to assess the potential for collaborative partnership efforts and contributions to the objectives of sustainable tourism development.

Study area

The Chobe Enclave Conservation Trust (CECT) is a community-based organisation located in the Chobe District, Botswana. Five villages of Mabele, Kavimba, Kachikau, Satau, and Parakarungu share the project. The villages, as illustrated in Figure 1, are located on a belt that runs along the Chobe Basin forming an enclave. The villages are located within two

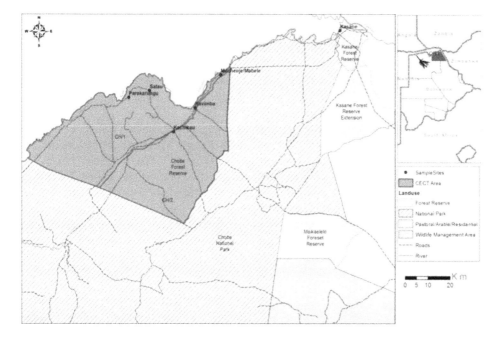

Figure 1. (Colour online) Study area.
Source: (Stone, 2013).

controlled hunting areas: CH1 and CH2 where photographic and hunting tourism are practised, respectively.

The estimated population of the enclave community is 4128 (Kachikau: 1356,
Kavimba: 549, Mabele: 773, Parakarungu: 845, and Satau: 605) (Botswana, 2011). The
CECT community has a mixed economy based on three main domains: subsistence livestock rearing, crop production, and tourism employment. The CECT cattle population is
estimated at around 9000 (Stone, 2013). The local soil is dry, sandy, and has poor crop
yields mainly due to the arid desert environment.

CECT is run by a board of trustees elected from each participating village. There are 15
board members; 2 members are elected from each village by the general membership. Fur
thermore by virtue of their positions, village chiefs are ex officio members. The board is
elected for a term of three years in office. The board works closely with all the village development committees (VDCs), which are responsible for the development of villages. Thus,
income generated by CECT is allocated to VDCs to decide on which village developments
to undertake.

Methods

Due to the exploratory nature of this study, this paper is guided by qualitative research
methods. A case study approach is adopted. Case studies require a problem that seeks a holistic understanding of the situation using inductive logic (Patton, 1990). CECT was selected
as a case study because it was the first CBE project in the country and has been adopted as
the model for implementing CBE elsewhere in Botswana. It is thus an enlightening site to
study in order to understand the nature and dynamics of collaborative community participation and empowerment.

Primary and secondary data sources were used. Primary data included individual semi-structured interviews with village chiefs, CECT board members, VDC members, key government officers, and household heads, or individuals 18 years and older, where household heads were not present. Interviews took place between the months of May and August 2013. As reasoned by Kvale (1996), interviews were chosen because they allow ' ... an interchange of views between two people on a topic of mutual interest' and allow 'human interaction for knowledge production' (p. 14).

A household list from CECT was used to randomly pick household interviewees. Forty-one respondents were interviewed: 23 men and 18 women. The number of interviews was guided by the attainment of theoretical saturation (Patton, 1990). Government officials' interviewees included those from the Departments of Police, Land Board, Wildlife & National Parks (DWNP), Tourism (DoT), Botswana Tourism Organisation (BTO), and Crop and Animal Production. Government officials were selected to represent related government offices actively involved in tourism, conservation, and livelihood improvement planning. To accelerate the data collection process, interviews were audio-recorded with the permission from respondents. Where interviewees were not comfortable with their voices being recorded, shorthand entries were performed.

An interview technique referred to as funnelling was adopted (Patton, 1990). This involved starting the interview process by asking broad questions on the community's perceptions on ecotourism, livelihoods, and conservation, followed by more specific inquiries about particular positions. Some questions asked included: What does ecotourism represent to you? What changes in your lifestyle have been facilitated by your participation in ecotourism? Who were involved in the commencement of ecotourism development? To safeguard the trustworthiness of data, procedures were undertaken to seek clarification and explanations during and immediately after the interviews, as recommended by Harrison, MacGibbon, and Morton (2001).

Secondary data sources used include published research articles, CECT, and government reports. These were used to establish how CECT was formed.

Data analysis

Data analysis was guided by the adoption of an analytical procedure that is based on techniques proposed by extant interpretive studies (Miles & Huberman, 1994). The first steps entailed transcribing the data and translating it from *Setswana* (the local language) to English. Since the researcher is fluent in both languages, it made the interview and translation process much easier. As suggested by Denzin and Lincoln (2000), transcripts were first read several times to get a sense of the data. In the process, a defined codebook with detailed descriptions of each code category was developed after a few transcripts had been coded to help to consistently and systematically code all transcripts. Each transcript was systematically analysed with the goal of understanding participants' overall perceptions and contextual meanings. This process aided a better understanding of the community's construction and views on ecotourism development.

Next, a modified grounded theory analysis approach (Padgett, 2008) was employed. The analytic procedure predominantly entailed a holistic content perspective whereby the researcher explored the central meaning of participant narratives (Lieblich, Tuval-Mashiach, & Zilber, 1998). Subsequent steps involved carefully reading the transcripts to code different segments of each transcript with a certain theme. The idea was to become grounded in the data and to allow understandings to emerge from the close study of texts (Glasser & Strauss, 1967). This process of coding was guided by Miles and Huberman

(1994), and involved the identification of words, phrases, sentences, or paragraphs that conveyed a particular message relating to the community's perceptions. All transcripts as well as field notes were coded thematically.

Theme development followed. This was facilitated by the memo technique, a widely used method for recording relations among themes (Bernard, 2006). Finally, group-like codes, treated as common themes, were then categorised into narrower, more specific codes.

This paper offers an evaluation of CECT's experience; it does not attempt to make generalisation of any kind.

Results

Dawn of CBE

The commencement of collaboration and partnerships through CBE is traced back to several meetings held in 1989 to find ways to mitigate human–wildlife conflicts and promote community benefits through wildlife utilisation. The government's willingness to promote CBE through CBNRM is interpreted as turning the existing problem into an opportunity for both the economy and the promotion of biodiversity conservation. CECT villages, NGOs – the Chobe Wildlife Trust (CWT), Kalahari Conservation Society, World Wildlife Fund (WWF), African Wildlife Foundation (AWF), and donors – and USAID were involved in the formation of collaborations and partnerships. The government of Botswana's involvement was mainly in the provision of policy guidelines. Due to the community's deficiency in technical expertise, community mobilisation, and wildlife utilisation, collaborative efforts were initiated to compensate for this shortfall. NGOs involvement entailed mobilising and capacitating the community as well as sourcing funds from external donors. To appreciate this development, a community member stated:

> We are what we are today because everybody from government offices, NGOs, donors participated . . . even ourselves as CECT community. . . . everyone is a winner today. (a Satau female resident, aged 39)

The commencement of the collaborative partnership process started in 1991, when a team of exterior advisors from the government's NRMP, financed by USAID, began working with the DWNP to assist the government in the implementation of CBE activities. The DWNP/NRMP team began a series of consultative meetings, first at district level, then with chiefs, headmen and VDCs, and then the general membership. Consequently, the WWF and CWT co-jointly drafted a proposal supporting the community, highlighting issues like limited funding and a need for technical assistance and capacity building to make CBE work. Nevertheless, villagers were suspicious about the collaborative partnership initiative, especially the involvement of some of the NGO stakeholders, particularly CWT, whose interests were seen as favouring wildlife resources at the expense of communities. Due to a lack of consensus on what CWT would support, the DWNP director asked CWT to suspend its involvement and interest in the project in 1991 (Jones, 2000). This development of mistrust affected the acceleration of the project, especially on community organisation and capacity building. Building a collaborative partnership requires facilitators' capacity to ensure the assimilation of tourism stakeholders' heterogeneity and diverse viewpoints. The process of community consultation, mobilisation, and capacity building took five years due to the community's suspicions on other stakeholders' interests. Eventually, without thorough facilitation on capacity building and mobilisation, in 1993, CECT was granted its first wildlife hunting quota. Due to the lack of business skills to manage the quota, CECT opted to sell its quota to the private sector. A hunting quota was granted due to the growing populations of certain wildlife species as well as the damage they caused to the community's property.

Community participation

There seem to be two opposing insights on issues of the success brought about by the collaborative partnerships through CBE. On the one hand, through collaborations sought from different stakeholders, the CECT community formed a formal institution to lead community participation in tourism development. The creation of this new institution indicates the devolution of power from the central government to community level. Results indicate that the community is now participating in tourism and can now decide on what to do with funds generated from CBE. For example, every year when the income generated from CBE is ready for distribution, each village holds a meeting to propose projects for funding. In 2008, for instance, the community bought five tractors with trailers and ploughing equipment to boost agriculture. Two general shops were also built to provide services to the community. Before the tractors and general shops, the community used hands and cows as draught powers and travelled more than 100 km to the town of Kasane to access shops. To appreciate this development, one participant stated:

> Tourism has brought us tractors and shops, I was unable to use my hands to plow and travelling long distances to access shops in Kasane, I can now plow and we have shops in Kavimba. (a Kavimba female resident, aged 59)

Furthermore, in 2009 CECT funded three mechanised corn grinding mill projects, one cement brick moulding project, and bought five large size tents with chairs for the community to use during weddings and funeral ceremonies. For funeral ceremonies, tents are used free of charge. However, for weddings, members have to hire them, thereby generating more funds for CECT.

To evaluate the performance of CECT, an annual general meeting is held where the board reports back to general members. This development has improved transparency and accountability issues. Furthermore, it has esteemed CECT's governance and role as a business entity. According to DWNP and DoT officials, the formation of CECT has brought Chobe National Park management closer to the community since the community is now regarded as a key stakeholder. Results indicate that before participation in CBE, there was hostility between the DWNP and community members because the community felt it was denied access to its land and resources. This was a result of lack of trust, consultations, networking, and harmony between stakeholders. The lack of trust was not only between the government and community, but also within and among villagers themselves. Community members reported each other to government agencies in cases of poaching and wildfires detonations. As a result, some community members were considered whistle-blowers, and the DWNP was accused of using 'divide and rule' tactics among CECT community. A change in community attitudes and the development of trust is illustrated by one respondent who indicated:

> Before we participated in tourism, we never attended meetings called by the DWNP to discuss wildlife and related issues ... we did not benefit from wildlife but rather we lost our property to it, without any form of compensation, ... such meetings are attended in large numbers nowadays as we have developed interest in wildlife management. (a Kachikau male resident, aged 43)

Participation in CBE has led to a shift in thinking on conservation and development efforts. The government proactively facilitated the CBE development process through the development of policy frameworks. Highlighted legislative changes of significance include the Conservation Policy of 1989, National Tourism Policy (1990), Ecotourism Policy (2002), and the CBNRM Policy (2007), which all call for community inclusion in conservation and development. Despite these, implementation is often a problem.

Indications of lack of coherent collaborative partnership arrangements still exist. For instance, there is still a perception of limited restructuring of power and control among interested and affected stakeholders. For example, some community members still perceive that decision-making powers lie with government-controlled departments such as the DoT, DWNP, and BTO. More specifically, the BTO still has the power to select, develop, and bring to marketable standards any tourism product from CECT, while the DWNP unilaterally decides the species and numbers to allocate to communities as hunting quota. Some segments of community members therefore perceive that the authority on natural resource management remains with the same institutions, and accountability ultimately still lies with the central government. To illustrate this variation, one community member said:

> If you truly own resources like a plowing field, a cow or a goat would it be appropriate for an outsider to come and give you instructions on what to do with them? I would ask the outsider whose property this is. But with our wildlife we cannot wholly decide what to do with it, the government does it for us. (a Mabele male resident, aged 56)

This arrangement is prone to conflict of interest and yields tensions between the community and government agencies. The prevailing circumstances are therefore viewed as a lack of trust by the government to grant communities full natural resources management custodianship. This could be in line with Bramwell and Lane's (2000) view that collaborative partnership may be set up simply as 'window dressing' to avoid tackling real problems head-on with all interested parties.

Although the community has the power to decide on what to do with funds from their CBE, the collaborative partnership did not tilt government–community power relations.

Economic participation

An analysis of CECT's economic participation as a result of collaborative partnerships indicates positive outcomes. Due to the lack of human and financial capitals to invest in ecotourism ventures, the community collaboratively opted for a joint venture agreement (JVA) and partnerships with private safari companies. In the context of Botswana, a JVA refers to 'business arrangements between a private company and a rural community for the commercial utilization of an area's natural resources; be it game, land or culture' (Gujadhur, 2001, p. 15). To this end, CECT has collaborative contractual agreements and partnerships with three private safari companies on hunting and photographic tourism, a camping site, and Ngoma Lodge. Figure 2 summarises revenue generated due to these collaborative agreements and partnerships. In addition to the hunting safari collaborative agreements, the community also gets a portion of game meat from each kill by professional hunters: an arrangement meant to mitigate community wildlife poaching. JVAs provide the community with revenue, employment, and game meat/food. Nevertheless, at the beginning of 2014, the government decided to stop safari hunting based on indications that wild animals populations were dwindling. Its ban will affect collaborative measures in place as communities will have to change their tourism products.

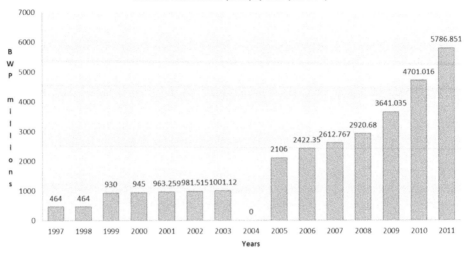

Figure 2. Revenue generated by CECT from 1997 to 2011.
Note: US$1 = BWP 8.98 as on 8 September 2014.
(Source: Stone, 2013).

With assistance from donors (i.e. USAID and AWF), CECT was awarded a grant and also contributed US$1.77 million towards the construction of Ngoma Lodge, the private partner contributed an equivalent amount. Through this partnership, employment for 36 people was created. The private partner provides professional human capital in business planning and operations, hospitality management, and marketing. The goal is to transfer skills to community members so that they can eventually take over when the partnership agreement ends.

The trickling-down effects of CBE have led to increasingly expanding subsistence arable farming due to investments generated from ecotourism. These have a potential to escalate existing human–wildlife conflicts. Farming has been mechanised, some crop fields have been fenced, and pesticides, fertilisers, and modern practices like row planting are used. An interview with a DWNP official indicates that the introduction of ecotourism was meant to ultimately replace subsistence agriculture. However, communities believe that solely depending on ecotourism is too risky, especially in the event that a shock or stress occurs, thus revenue generated from ecotourism has been used to boost agriculture. One community member indicated:

> We cannot just abandon farming because now we have tourism; we still need to be convinced that tourism can support us, and truly is a livelihood option we can rely on. (a Kavimba female resident, aged 46)

Figure 2 indicates that the revenue generated has been increasing annually, except in 2004, a drought year, when there was no wildlife quota allocated due to low wildlife numbers. Between the years 2005 and 2011, revenue generated was high. Some was reinvested in projects discussed above; however, the bulk of the money is saved in the community's bank account. During the data collection period, further discussions on what to use the money for were ongoing.

Employment opportunities have been created too. One CECT board member linked employment creation to the reduction in the dependence on veldt products. To illustrate this point he noted that:

> In our area who cannot appreciate the value of tourism? Most households have someone working in tourism establishments ... people are now employed, there is no time for them to hunt and gather. (a Parakarungu male CECT board member, aged 41)

The same view was shared by one VDC member, who noted that:

> Before we participated in tourism, we used to hunt and collect a lot of veld products to supplement the food we got from subsistence agriculture ... through waged employment from tourism, we are able to buy better food to feed ourselves. (a Kachikau female VDC member, aged 28)

These comments indicate that individuals employed in tourism establishments no longer prioritise participating in traditional activities that have a direct impact on natural resources. The community is now economically enabled to use the money made from tourism.

Results also indicate that although collaborations and partnership engagements have brought positive changes, ecotourism has generated inequalities among community members. Ecotourism is thus perceives as bringing about fiscal imbalances within the community. For those who are directly employed, there is a clear difference in terms of lifestyle changes. Some have built better houses, bought bicycles, clothes, connected electricity, and bought communication gadgets like radios, cell phones, and televisions. Figure 3 illustrates the changes in terms of housing, connection to electricity and satellite dishes for television and better pit latrine toilets.

Results therefore indicate that collaborative partnerships in ecotourism bring mixed results: both economic empowerment and disparities. Limitations include the inability to employ the whole community.

(a)

(b)

Figure 3. (Colour online) Housing transformation. (a) The house is better than the mud and reeds structure located in front and is connected to an overhead electricity cable and a television satellite dish, (b) shows an improved pit latrine, beside it, it is a cloth structure that was used before as a pit latrine.
(Source: Stone, 2013).

Ecotourism beneficiaries versus non-beneficiaries

In assessing how the community perceives ecotourism benefits, results are also mixed. On the one hand, CECT board members, VDC members, and those who are directly employed in tourism establishments are happy with the new arrangement and how it has transformed their lives. For instance, arable farmers recognise the importance of the new mechanised farming arrangement that has relieved them from labour intensive. On the other hand, some farmers blame collaborative arrangements for the failure to lessen the impacts of property damage by wild animals. Rather, they blame ecotourism for increasing the number of wildlife, leading to the exacerbation of crop damage and livestock predation. Some felt that wildlife is now accustomed to people due to increased human–wildlife confrontations. Some farmers reported elephants damage their livestock water points. Diseases, especially on foot and mouth, which are prevalent in the area are attributed to the African buffalo.

Due to competition between ecotourism and agriculture, some farmers find it difficult to recognise ecotourism collaborative and partnership arrangements as community empowering ventures. Equally, farmers highlighted that like ecotourism issues, agricultural constraints should be addressed collaboratively. Some farmers considered themselves disempowered as they are disillusioned and frustrated. This is in variance with Ladkin and Bertramini's (2002) argument that collaborative processes overcome power imbalances just by involving all the stakeholders in a process that meets their needs. Subsequently, where collaborative CBE supplements existing livelihood activities, it is seen as an alternative livelihood development strategy. However, where it is seen as competing with existing livelihoods it is regarded as a disempowering venture.

Ecotourism multi-stakeholders: managing competing interests and conflicts

Due to the involvement of multiple stakeholders, there are different perceptions on who should benefit from generated benefits (i.e. individuals, households, or community) and on how benefits should trickle down to beneficiaries. Indications of empowerment through collaborative efforts are shown by some members of the CECT management believing that as trustees they are already empowered to manage the trust on behalf of the larger community. Some believe that the ultimate target for empowerment should be the 'community' and/or households. CECT management strongly believes in terms of income distribution the community should be the main beneficiary, hence the use of VDCs. Another common shared understanding was the appreciation of tractors that help CECT farmers to till their fields. This is something they considered empowering as tractors can be used by all, thereby promoting community solidarity. However, crop damages caused by wildlife bring costs and lead to the community's loss of self-sufficiency in food production and security.

However, other respondents also assess benefits of CBE at an individual level. They ask, how am I going to benefit? This segment of respondents felt that if there is nothing in it for them as individuals, they would rather not invest in such interventions. This finding diverges from the collaborative partnership philosophy, as CBE does not contribute equally across community. Logically, collaboration efforts should empower all levels of community: individuals, households, and community. The findings here emphasise the diverse and heterogeneous nature of a 'community'. Thus, collaborative partnership efforts empower and disempower certain segments of the community at the same time. While the collaborative partnership approach is conceptually distinct, in practice it also yields unintended consequences. This is explained by the fact that CBE development involves multiple stakeholders and/or heterogeneous communities. As a consequence, this leads to competing interests and conflicts that need to be managed. The diverse community itself often has fundamentally different values, constructions, and understandings of what is at stake and how tourism and conservation problems can be addressed (Lewicki, Gray, & Elliot, 2003).

Discussion and conclusion

Overall, though community collaborative partnership is a useful and necessary mechanism for organising stakeholders for ecotourism development, CBE at CECT is not uniformly perceived within the community. Results indicate perceptions on community collaborative partnership are a function of how CBE affects people's livelihoods. One functioning problem of CBE is the supposition that collaborative partnerships efforts can reconcile diverse stakeholders' viewpoints, contested settings, and community heterogeneity. Thus, in Botswana, CBE has been motivated by a single model approach of grouping villages to become a 'community', irrespective of local variations. Consequently, as alluded by Arntzen et al. (2003), the one-fit-all-model approach can easily become coercive and ignore important local factors. For instance, the term community-based may sound neutral and suggest an integrated community order, and this case proves it is a complex, overlapping, and disjunctive approach. As reasoned by Gusfield (1975), this verifies the insight that a community is not merely geographical but has relational, emotional, different interests, and psychological dimensions involving interpersonal relationships. CBE may sound to be germane in promoting a win–win situation in community development and biodiversity conservation; however, it may not always bring intended consequences as it is not neutral, but practised on contested environments.

As results indicate, collaboration and partnerships through CBE is a subjective, malleable entity, and can easily misrepresent community's interests. Of importance to note, CBE is intended to reconcile development and conservation, but is undertaken by a diverse set of stakeholders, representing stakeholders' wide-ranging intents. Immediate stakeholders are community members with diverse opinions, interests, and aspirations. Other stakeholders are donors, international organisations, NGOs, and regulatory agencies. The effects of different social actors representing a wider community are different interests. It is important to note the role power plays in collaboration efforts. At the CECT project, collaborative stakeholders did not have the same power especially on the wildlife quota allocation. Swift and Levin (1987) also recognise the implication of power and indicate power is principal to the concept of community participation and empowerment. Therefore, collaboration and partnership models transcend hierarchical, patriarchal, coercive, or violent conceptualisations of power (Gerschick, Israel, & Checkoway, 1990). They also challenge the assumption that power is a zero-sum commodity. That is, increasing the power of one community or individual implies decreasing the power of another (Bartunek & Keys, 1982). For example, donor agencies are powerful entities as they have templates that dictate how money should be spent, regardless of local variations that may exist. In critical reviews of major international funding institutions, it has been suggested that such global agencies' agenda to support poor people is not done for altruistic reasons but to serve their interests as promoters of globalisation from below (Brecher, Costello, & Smith, 2000). The stakeholders' conceptual differences of what constitutes CBE as a 'vehicle' of community development and conservation are downplayed in favour of reaching a common goal. Due to the diverse structural nature of CBE, what is to be developed and conserved, the inclusiveness of stakeholders' opinions, and the array of goals become very wide-ranging and difficult to accomplish equitably. Nevertheless, collaborative partnerships arrangements complement local communities' access to capital, management, and marketing skills to invest in and benefit from the tourism sector. Even though collaborative partnerships augment community deficits, there is still a need to provide training to local people to enable them to develop skills and expertise they require to participate more in the tourism business (Shoo & Songorwa, 2013), if communities are to graduate and become full custodians of their tourism enterprises.

In view of these discussions, theoretically, CBE sounds like a noble idea; however, others view it as an example of a community development 'imposter' driven by economic imperatives and a neo-liberal agenda, purported to further exploit local communities (e.g. Blackstock, 2005). Nonetheless, while CECT may be interpreted as having attained mixed CBE success, the case study offers a progressive example of how stakeholders' approach to natural resource management is evolving. Yet, CBE at CECT still needs improvement.

Contingent on this paper's results, we can conclude that the structural design of CBE at CECT may not in itself guarantee the achievement of rural development and environmental conservation. Thus, and as a way forward, it is necessary to carefully balance local diverse viewpoints with strategic community participation intervention objectives. As a key finding, the substantial variation in the various roles and levels of community livelihoods make it difficult to define how CBE empowers community. The government as a key collaborative partner is perceived as residing with the power to decide on community wildlife quota allocation unilaterally, mistrusting the community's ability to manage wildlife resources. This is in line with Bramwell and Sharman's (1999) conclusion that the most important challenge is building trust between the actors and recognising that there is a shared problem. The government's action represents a serious weakness in the machinery of collaboration efforts in dealing with tourism in its coordination with other stakeholders. Therefore, structures initiated to promote CBE must be sensitive and informed by *in situ* circumstances.

This paper therefore recommends that conservation/development planners need to have multiple 'lenses' in their repertoire, in order to capture the varied peoples and situations within which they work. It is important that all stakeholders' needs and aspirations are taken into consideration. If this is jeopardised, community resentment can occur and the intended goals of CBE will not be realised. Collaborative partnership was vital in forming CECT as a new village institution that coordinates CBE activities. An institution is considered important and effective when people realise its benefits, when it is ready to listen to, discuss, and make decisions in consultation with people and when it is capable of providing the right solutions to their problems (Shoo & Songorwa, 2013). Only then can CBE live up to its full potential.

To conclude, whereas some authors emphasise the potential of CBE collaborative efforts to promote the well-being of both local people and their environments (Hoenegaard, 1994), others are cautious about these assumptions and call for the critical acceptance of CBE as a form of community development (e.g. Cater & Lowman, 1994; Ziffer, 1989). In the light of this debate, and drawing on the CECT case study, the employment of collaborative partnerships demonstrates that the degree of community participation and empowerment differs in a community. For instance, CECT board members, VDCs, and people working in the tourism establishment felt positive about their participation and felt empowered by CBE. Other segments of community, for example, farmers, felt disempowered as they felt they did not benefit sufficiently from tourism. In view of this development, Gray (2007) cautions that assembling an array of collaborative stakeholders may enhance partnerships' success in the long run; however, key players who are not benefiting or are excluded may try to block implementation agreements. Therefore, we can conclude that CBE development empowers communities unequally. As argued by Bramwell and Lane (2000), the complexity of engaging diverse stakeholders in projects makes it difficult to involve them all equally. This is so because tourism planning as contended by Hedlunda, Marella, and Gärlingb (2012) can be seen as a complex process, where the various choices influence and depend on each other, hence influencing stakeholders' perception in differing ways. Thus, Cusick, McClure, and Cox's (2010) argument that the tourism sector appears to be interested in expanding the opportunities for ecotourism because this market has economic potential, yet, its role is still marginal despite the rhetoric of support from the industry and state agencies. Nevertheless, Ladkin and Bertramini (2002) posit that it is only through a process of shared information and decision-making with all the stakeholders involved ecotourism planning can evolve with minimal negative impacts. To a certain extent this case study indicates a success story in view of its achievements. As suggested by Kiss (2004), CBE projects that create a bit of local employment or help to conserve natural resources can be regarded as success stories or disappointments, depending on what they set out to achieve.

This study's limitation is on the use of cross-sectional data. Sequences of action and social change over time can be analysed better using longitudinal studies.

Disclosure statement

No potential conflict of interest was reported by the author.

Reference

Almeyda, A., Broadbent, E., Wyman, M., & Durham, H. (2010). Ecotourism impacts in the Nicoya Peninsula, Costa Rica. *International Journal of Tourism Research*, *12*(6), 803–819.

Arntzen, J., Molokomme, D., Terry, E., Moleele, N., Tshosa, O., & Mazambani, D. (2003). *Final report of the review of community-based natural resource review in Botswana*. Report by the Centre for Applied Research for the National CBNRM Forum, Gaborone.

Baktygulov, S., & Raeva, D. (2010). *Creating value for all: Community-based tourism*. GIM Case Study No. B058. New York, NY: United Nations Development Programme.

Bartunek, J., & Keys, C. (1982). *Power equalization in schools through organizational development*. London. Sage.

Bernard, H. (2006). *Handbook of methods in cultural anthropology*. Walnut Creek, CA: Altamira Press.

Blackstock, K. (2005). A critical look at community based tourism. *Community Development Journal*, *40*, 39–49.

Boggs, L. (2000). Community power, participation, conflict and development choice: Community wildlife conservation in the Okavango Region of northern Botswana (Discussion paper No. 17). Maun: IIED.

Botswana. (2011). *Botswana population & housing census*. Gaborone: Government Printers.

Bramwell, B., & Lane, B. (1993). Sustainable tourism: An evolving global approach. *Journal of Sustainable Tourism*, *1*(1), 1–5.

Bramwell, B., & Lane, B. (2000). Collaboration and partnerships in tourism planning. In B. Bramwell & B. Lane (Eds.), *Tourism collaboration and partnerships: Politics, practice and sustainability* (pp. 1–19). Clevedon: Channel View.

Bramwell, B., & Sharman, A. (1999). Collaboration in local tourism policy-making. *Annals of Tourism Research*, *26*(2), 392–415.

Brecher, J., Costello, T., & Smith, B. (2000). *Globalization from below: The power of solidarity*. Boston, MA: South End Press.

Bromley, D. (1992). *Making the commons work*. San Francisco, CA: Institute for Contemporary Studies.

Butler, R. W. (1991). Tourism, Environment, and sustainable development. *Environmental Conservation, 18*(3), 201–209.

Butler, R. W. (1993). Tourism—an evolutionary perspective. In J. G. Nelson, R. W. Butler, & G. Wall (Eds.), *Tourism and sustainable development* (pp. 26–44). Waterloo, Ontario: University of Waterloo (Department of Geography Publication 37).

Cater, E., & Lowman, G. (Eds.). (1994). *Ecotourism: A sustainable option?* Chichester: Wiley.

Crick, M. (1989). Representations of international tourism in the social sciences. *Annual Review of Anthropology, 18*, 307–344.

Cusick, J., McClure, B., & Cox, L. (2010). Representations of ecotourism in the Hawaiian Islands: A content analysis of local media. *Journal of Ecotourism, 9*(1), 21–35.

Czernek, K. (2013). Determinants of cooperation in a tourist region. *Annals of Tourism Research, 40*, 83–104.

Denzin, N., & Lincoln, Y. S. (2000). *Handbook of qualitative research* (2nd ed.). Thousand Oaks, CA: Sage.

Gerschick, T., Israel, B., & Checkoway, B. (1990). *Means of empowerment in individuals, organizations, and communities*. Ann Arbor, MI: Program on Conflict Management Alternatives, University of Michigan.

Glasbergen, P. (2007). Setting the scene: The partnership paradigm in the making. In P. Glasbergen, F. Biermann, & P. J. Mol (Eds.), *Partnerships, governance and sustainable development* (pp. 29–48). Northampton, MA: Edward Elgar.

Glasser, B. G., & Strauss, A. L. (1967). *The discovery of grounded theory: Strategies for qualitative research*. Chicago, IL: Aldine.

Gray, B. (1989). *Collaborating: Finding common ground for multiparty problems*. San Francisco, CA: Jossey-Bass.

Gray, B. (2007). The process of partnership construction: Anticipating obstacles and enhancing the likelihood of successful partnerships for sustainable development. In P. Glasbergen, F. Biermann, & P. J. Mol (Eds.) *Partnerships, governance and sustainable development* (pp. 29–48). Northampton, MA: Edward Elgar.

Guangming, H., Xiaodong, C., Wei, L., Scott, B. Shiqiang, Z., Lily, Y., & Jianguo, L. (2008). Distribution of economic benefits from eco-tourism: A case study of Wolong nature reserve for giant pandas in China. *Journal of Environmental Management, 42*, 1017–1025.

Gujadhur, T. (2001). *Organisations and their approaches in community based natural resource management in Botswana, Namibia, Zambia and Zimbabwe*. Gaborone: SNV/IUCN CBNRM Support Programme.

Gusfield, R. (1975). *The community: A critical response*. New York, NY: Harper Colophon.

Hall, C. M. (1996). *Introduction to tourism in Australia: Impacts, planning and development*. Melbourne: Addison, Wesley and Longman.

Harrison, J., MacGibbon, L., & Morton, M. (2001). Regimes of trustworthiness in qualitative research: The rigors of reciprocity. *Qualitative Inquiry, 7*(3), 323–345.

Hedlunda, T., Marella, A., & Gärlingb, T. (2012). The mediating effect of value orientation on the relationship between socio-demographic factors and environmental concern in Swedish tourists' vacation choices. *Journal of Ecotourism, 11*(1), 16–33.

Hoenegaard, G. (1994). Ecotourism: A status report and conceptual framework. *Journal of Tourism Studies, 5*(2), 24–35.

Hofer, D. (2002). *The Lion's share of the hunt. Trophy hunting and conservation: a review of the Eurasian tourist hunting market and trophy trade under CITES*. Brussels: Traffic

Inskeep, E. (1991). *Tourism planning: An integrated and sustainable development approach*. New York, NY: Van Nostrand Reinhold.

Jamal, T., & Stronza, A. (2009). Collaboration theory and tourism practice in protected areas: Stakeholders, structuring and sustainability. *Journal of Sustainable Tourism, 17*(2), 169–189.

Jones, B. (2000). *CBNRM in Botswana: Review of the tender assessment process for community controlled hunting areas*. Washington, DC: Chemonics International.

Jones, B. (2002). *Chobe Enclave, Botswana – Lessons learnt from a CBNRM project 1993–2002*. Gaborone: IUCN/SNV CBNRM Support Programme.

Kiss, A. (2004). Is community-based ecotourism a use of biodiversity conservation funds? *Trends in Ecology and Evolution, 19*(5), 232–237.

Kruger, O. (2005). The role of ecotourism in conservation: Panacea or Pandora's Box? *Biodiversity and Conservation*, *14*, 579–600.

Kvale, D. (1996). *Interviews*. London: Sage.

Ladkin, A., & Bertramini, A. (2002). Collaborative tourism planning: A case study of Cusco, Peru. *Current Issues in Tourism*, *5*(2), 71–93.

Laverack, G. (2001). An identification and interpretation of the organizational aspects of community empowerment. *Community Development Journal*, *36*(2), 134–145.

Lewicki, R., Gray, B., & Elliot, M. (2003). *Making sense of intractable environmental conflicts: Concepts and cases*. Washington, DC: Island Press.

Lieblich, A., Tuval-Mashiach, R., & Zilber, T. (1998). *Narrative research: Reading, analysis and interpretation*. Newbury Park, CA: Sage.

Lindberg, K., Enriquez, J., & Sproule, K. (1996). Eco-tourism questioned case studies from Belize. *Annals of Tourism Research*, *23*(3), 543–562.

Mbaiwa, J. E. (2011). The effects of tourism development on the sustainable utilisation of natural resources in the Okavango Delta, Botswana. *Current Issues in Tourism*, *14*(3), 251–273.

Mbaiwa, J. E. (2015). Community-based natural resource management in Botswana. In R. Van der Duim, M. Lamers, & J. Wijk (Eds.), *Institutional arrangements for conservation, development and tourism in Eastern and Southern Africa* (pp. 59–80). New York, NY: Springer.

Mbaiwa, J. E., Stronza, A., & Kreuter, U. (2011). From collaboration to conservation: Insights from the Okavango Delta, Botswana. *Society and Natural Resources*, *24*(4), 400–411.

Miles, M., & Huberman, A. (1994). *Qualitative data analysis*. Thousand Oaks, CA: Sage.

Milner-Gulland, E., & Bennett, E. (2003). Wild meat: The bigger picture. *Trends in Ecology and Evolution*, *18*(7), 351–357.

Moufakkir, O., & Burns, P. M. (2012). *Controversies in tourism*. Cambridge, MA: CAB.

Novelli, M., Barnes, J., & Humavindu, M. (2006). The other side of the ecotourism coin: Consumptive tourism in Southern Africa. *Journal of Ecotourism*, *5*(1)2, 62–79.

Novelli, M., & Humavindu, M. N. (2005). Wildlife use vs local gain: Trophy hunting in Namibia. In M. Novalli (Ed.), *Contemporary issues, trends & cases* (pp. 171–182). Wallington: Heinemann.

Padgett, D. K. (2008). *Qualitative methods in social work research*. Thousand Oaks, CA: Sage.

Patton, M. (1990). *Qualitative evaluation and research methods*. Beverly Hills, CA: Sage.

Rozemeijer, N. (2001). *Community-based tourism in Botswana: The SNV experience in three community-tourism projects*. Botswana: SNV/IUCN CBNRM Support Programme.

Selin, S., & Beason, K. (1991). Inter-organizational relations in tourism. *Annals of Tourism Research*, *18*(4), 639–652.

Shoo, R., & Songorwa, A. (2013). Contribution of ecotourism to nature conservation and improvement of livelihoods around Amani nature reserve, Tanzania. *Journal of Ecotourism*, *12*(2), 75–89.

Smith, M., & Duffy, R. (2003). *The ethics of tourism development*. London: Routledge.

Stone, M. T. (2013). *Protected areas, tourism and rural community livelihoods in Botswana* (Unpublished Ph.D. dissertation). Arizona State University, Phoenix, Arizona.

Stone, M. T. (2015). Community empowerment through community-based tourism: the case of Chobe Enclave Conservation Trust in Botswana. In R. Van der Duim, M. Lamers, & J. Wijk (Eds.), *Institutional arrangements for conservation, development and tourism in Eastern and Southern Africa* (pp. 81–100). New York, NY: Springer.

Stone, M. T., & Rogerson, C. M. (2011). Community-based natural resource management and tourism: Nata bird sanctuary, Botswana. *Tourism Review International*, *15*(2), 159–169.

Swatuk, L. (2005). From project to context: Community-based natural resources management in Botswana. *Global Environmental Politics*, *5*(3), 95–124.

Swift, C., & Levin, G. (1987). Empowerment: An emerging mental health technology. *J PrimPrev*, *8*, 71–94.

Taylor, M. (2002). Comparative analysis of CBNRM movements in Southern Africa, Botswana. *Journal of Applied Behavior Sciences*, *18*, 171–183.

TIES. (2006). Community based ecotourism: Best practice stories and resources. Digital traveler and Asia Pacific Newsletter.

Tosun, C. (2001). Challenges of sustainable tourism development in the developing world: The case of Turkey. *Tourism Management*, *22*, 289–303.

Tosun, C. (2005). Stages in emergence of participatory tourism development process in developing countries. *Geoforum*, *36*(3), 333–352.

United Nations World Tourism Organization. (2011). *Indicators of sustainable development for tourism destinations: A guidebook*. Madrid: UNWTO.

Urry, J. (1990). *Tourist Gaze: Leisure and travel in contemporary societies*. London: Sage.

Villiers, J. (2011). *Strategic alliances between communities with special reference to the twinning of South African provinces, cities and towns with international partners* (Unpublished dissertation). Business Management and Administration, University of Stellenbosch.

Warburton, D. (1998). A passive dialogue: Community and sustainable development. In D. Warburton (Ed.), *Community and sustainable development* (pp. 2–19). London: Earthscan.

WCED. (1987). *Our common future*. Tokyo: World Commission on Environment and Development.

Weaver, D. (2011). Celestial ecotourism: New horizons in nature-based tourism. *Journal of Ecotourism, 10*(1), 38–45.

WTO. (2002). *Tourism and poverty reduction*. Madrid: WTO.

WWF. (2001). *Guidelines for community-based ecotourism development*. Gland, Switzerland: WWF International.

Ziffer, K. (1989). *Ecotourism: The uneasy alliance*. Washington DC: Conservation International.

Zuze, C. (2006, October 23–24). *Conservation education vs community based natural resources management*, DWNP, community extension and outreach division workshop, Gaborone.

Community agency and entrepreneurship in ecotourism planning and development in the Great Limpopo Transfrontier Conservation Area

Chaka Chirozva[a,b]

[a]Department of Environmental Science, Bindura University of Science Education, Bindura, Zimbabwe; [b]School of Environmental Sciences, Charles Sturt University, Albury, NSW, Australia

In much of southern Africa, ecotourism has been widely acknowledged as critical for enhancing livelihoods of communities living outside protected areas. Several studies highlight the potential of tourism as a mechanism for driving rural economies in Africa. Using the case of the Great Limpopo Transfrontier Park shared among Zimbabwe, South Africa, and Mozambique, this paper demonstrates how communities are engaging in ecotourism entrepreneurship. A decade after the emergence of transfrontier parks in the region, no studies have explored how new and vibrant assemblages of individuals and community actors tap the potential of ecotourism. This study is based on 57 semi-structured interviews with participants drawn from four wards in southeast Zimbabwe. In addition, a netnography (online ethnography) of a Facebook page administered by a local community trust promoting ecotourism was undertaken. Findings demonstrate that innovative community leaders imagine, embrace, and exploit ecotourism opportunities that arise from their proximity to transfrontier parks. More specifically, this study characterises these entrepreneurs, their local and extra-local connections, how they actively engage in social networking to promote cultural tourism and development of a visible ecotourism product. This paper contributes to the understudied aspect of social entrepreneurship in ecotourism planning within transfrontier conservation areas.

Introduction

Tourism is one of the fastest growing industries in the world and ecotourism is the fastest growing component of that industry (Dowling & Fennell, 2003; Fennell, 2015; Gössling, 1999, 2000). Notwithstanding the lack of consensus among scholars as evidenced by a voluminous definitional discourse (Donohoe & Needham, 2006), ecotourism continues to attract academic, political, and industry support globally. To show this prominence, the United Nations declared 2002 as the International Year of Ecotourism (Weaver & Lawton, 2007). Ecotourism covers travelling to often remote places to either experience their culture or for adventure and emphasises activities that are economically sustainable and promote local control (Honey, 1999). In most developing countries, ecotourism is widely championed by governments as important for socio-economic development (Garrod, 2003; Weaver & Lawton, 2007). In southern Africa, new opportunities for establishing transfrontier conservation areas (TFCAs) have rekindled debates on the contribution that ecotourism can play in reducing poverty (van Amerom & Büscher, 2005; Ferreira, 2006; Spenceley, 2008, 2006). TFCAs are conservation areas that cross the frontiers of two or more countries and are intended to address the transnational nature of the environment (Katerere, Hill, & Moyo, 2001). Despite their popularity in southern Africa, TFCAs have proven to be very controversial as a conservation policy because of their failure to deliver on socio-economic imperatives (van Amerom & Büscher, 2005; Duffy, 2006; Ramutsindela, 2007). Notwithstanding this, ecotourism continues to be eulogised as an opportunity for poor communities to generate income and wide development benefits (Duffy, 2006; McNeely, 1993, 1994). Within TFCAs, there is a very specific form of ecotourism that is widely promoted: community-based ecotourism. Proponents of newly established TFCAs draw inspiration from community-based natural resource management programmes that devolved responsibilities to communities for managing resources occurring on their lands (Jones, 1999; Murphree, 2001; Taylor, 2009).

Several studies paint a pessimistic outlook about livelihood gains for communities living in and adjacent to TFCAs (Dzingirai, 2004; Ferreira, 2004; Hughes, 2005). Baseline reports conducted in the first decade of TFCA implementation show little potential for tourism as there was no significant infrastructure in place (Spenceley, Dzingirai, & Tangawamira, 2008; Suich, Busch, & Barbancho, 2005). More recently, several critiques have emerged on contribution of TFCAs to biodiversity conservation and livelihoods of communities living at the edge of these areas (Andersson, de Garine-Wichatitsky, Cumming, Dzingirai, & Giller, 2013; Büscher, 2013; Quinn, Broberg, & Freimund, 2012). One argument which has been advanced by many scholars is that TFCAs render communities living in and adjacent to them invisible. This paper argues that communities affected by TFCAs are not just mere subjects of the state or conservation programmes but they (intentionally) use and construct their own subjectivity. Communities mobilise ethnicity as a means to reassert their position and claim place in broader governance processes. Second, and once visibility is achieved, communities begin to appropriate spaces and articulate particular discourses which are not intended at completely challenging the expansion of TFCAs but more at reworking how they can live with new realities. This paper argues that one avenue they engage in such reworking is through social entrepreneurship in ecotourism planning and development. Building on the literature on social configuration of entrepreneurship (Alsos, Ljunggren, & Pettersen, 2003; Grande, Madsen, & Borch, 2011) and production of space by Lefebvre (1991), the paper argues communities' entrepreneurial intentions and behaviours can be construed as a form of 'spatial appropriation'. Both individuals and communities capture and appropriate meanings of symbolised TFCAs space and incorporate them within their own identity as entrepreneurs. Community leaders are not only concerned with modifying their space to serve the needs and aspirations of local people, but they situate such practices in broader debates on empowering marginalised ethnic groups.

In what follows, the paper first outlines key conceptual and theoretical framework and then introduces the methodology. The paper then presents research findings focusing on characteristics of entrepreneurs, nature of ecotourism product on offer and extra-local stakeholder linkages and collaboration. The last section offers a discussion and conclusion.

A review of conceptual and theoretical issues

Entrepreneurs and entrepreneurship

A review of the literature on the definitions of entrepreneurs and entrepreneurship shows much diversity. The topic is inherently complex and multidisciplinary making it difficult to offer a comprehensive overview (Gartner, 1989). However, a starting point can be to explore and characterise the intentions of individuals who seek to start new business enterprises (Krueger & Brazeal, 1994; Zhao, Seibert, & Hills, 2005); their intentions to own a business enterprise (Kickul & Gundry, 2002) or become self-employed (Douglas & Shepherd, 2002; Van Gelderen, Brand, van Praag, Bodewes, Poutsma, & Van Gils, 2008). This means that it is the state of mind which directs and guides entrepreneurs towards the planning, development, and implementation of new business enterprises (Roxas, Cayoca-Panizales, & de Jesus, 2008). Such a formulation echoes Reitan's (1997) perspective which specifies that there is need to identify and explore how potential entrepreneurs recognise an opportunity and study their entrepreneurial intention. According to Reitan (1997), a potential entrepreneur is a person who perceives an opportunity and/or intends to start a new venture, but has not (yet) taken any steps regarding venture start-up. This is critical since opportunity recognition and entrepreneurship intentions are key characteristics of potential entrepreneurs, which make them distinct within a particular population. Similarly, Bruyat and Julien (2001) observe that '[an] entrepreneur is the individual responsible for the process of creating new value (an innovation and/or a new organization) – in other words, the individual without whom the new value would not be created' (p. 169). Within the behavioural research domain, entrepreneurial intentions are the most often expressed and studied antecedent of new enterprise creation (Ferreira, Raposo, Rodrigues, Dinis, & do Paço, 2012; Krueger & Carsrud, 1993). As will be shown, this concept of entrepreneurial intentions is used at both individual and group/community levels to show the propensity to engage in, plan for, and develop ecotourism enterprises.

Community tourism entrepreneurship research could benefit by drawing on this construct of entrepreneurship intentions. This is especially true in TFCAs where community-based ecotourism enterprises have long gestation periods. As Krueger, Reilly, and Carsrud (2000) observe, entrepreneurial intentions are a best predictor of planned behaviour 'when the behaviour in question is rare, hard to observe, or involves unpredictable time lags' (p. 411). For this reason, the concept of entrepreneur is not exclusively limited to innovating individual (or groups) who have already developed an ongoing business activity where none existed before. As Bygrave (1989) formulates, 'entrepreneurship is a process of becoming rather than a state of being', a formulation that is encompassing to include even emerging ideas as with community trusts established in the Great Limpopo Transfrontier Conservation Area (GLTFCA).

Research on entrepreneurship must examine how, by whom, and with what effects opportunities to create future goods and services are discovered, evaluated, and exploited (Venkataraman, 1997). Ecotourism entrepreneurship research should explore the sources of opportunities; the processes of discovery, evaluation, and exploitation of opportunities; and the set of individuals who discover, evaluate, and exploit them (Venkataraman, 1997). This study draws theoretical insights from three strands to entrepreneurship research, namely rural sociology perspective (RSP), opportunity perspective (OP), and resource-based view (RBV) (Alsos et al., 2003; Grande et al., 2011). To summarise, the OP to entrepreneurship focuses on business opportunities as the main source of entrepreneurial activities and an important trigger of new business ventures, while the RBV focuses on how unique resource endowments within a particular environment are presumed as a driver of entrepreneurial activities. The RSP is widely applied in research focusing on strategies taken by predominantly agricultural households. In this perspective, households diversify or engage in pluriactivity to explore new business opportunities (Alsos et al., 2003). These three perspectives provide important constructs for exploring how individuals and communities, in the course of time, perceive or exploit emerging opportunities based on internal and external variables (Krueger & Carsrud, 1993). Decisions to start new ventures are made through perceptions or the cognitive map of the person involved and therefore are intimately linked to sense making (Weick, 1979). With these constructs in mind, it is important to turn to theoretical issues on the production of space.

Henri Lefebvre: spatial appropriation

Space is not merely a natural phenomenon but is produced and manipulated by human beings for specific purposes (Kipfer, Saberi, & Wieditz, 2013; Merrifield, 1993). For example, spaces such as churches, classrooms or prisons are constructed to represent specific aspects of a material culture. What is apparent is that space is produced, experienced, interpreted, and negotiated by human agents in quite specific ways. Space is a product of human behaviour. While space is created, mediated, and defined by human agents; it also creates, defines, and mediates how human agents behave in specific places (Lefebvre, 1991). The implementation of TFCAs results in a transformation of landscapes through acts such as fencing or gazettal of wildlife corridors. Apart from producing 'transfrontier parks', 'conservation areas', or 'wildlife corridors' as objects of governance, the implementation of TFCAs also results in the emergence of human subjectivities – particular kinds of people with different visions and beliefs of how particular spaces can and should be used. This paper uses Lefebvre's work on production of space as a theoretical heuristic for studying the interaction between how communities use particular spaces within the GLTFCA prefecture. Lefebvre envisioned three moments to the production of space. In simple terms, the first is *perceived space*, which refers to everyday or common-sensical perceptions of space. This aspect of spatialisation (perceived space) is primarily concerned and reliant on the visual. Within conservation, this comprises physical interventions that change the materiality of the environment, such as fencing; and how humans appropriate fences that are erected. The second, *conceived space* is theoretical space promulgated and employed by professionals such as cartographers and planners. At the centre of this space are particular ways of representing phenomena such as signs, jargon, codifications, and objectified representations used and produced by these agents. The third, *lived space* is space dwelled in and experienced by human actors (Lefebvre, 1991; Shields, 2011). Lived space includes dominated and appropriated spaces. Dominated space is the space that is transformed and mediated by technology and practice to fulfil the interests of its master. When space is appropriated, it is used to serve the needs and visions of those seeking to use it.

This paper argues that communities appropriate TFCAs and render them understandable through various spatial practices. It could thus be suggested that any enterprise that emerge within GLTFCA 'is at once *work* and *product* – a materialization of "social being"' (Lefebvre, 1991, pp. 101–102, emphasis in original). Two cognate components of appropriation are worth elaborating: physical and mental. On the one hand, physical appropriation involves the actual occupation and control of physical space (such as Sengwe–Tshipise Wilderness Corridor (STWC), Sengwe Wildlife Strip, among others) and targeting it for community-based ecotourism enterprises. On the other hand, mental appropriation occurs when individuals and community groups deploy their cognitive capabilities to control space. This includes imaginations of what the Great Limpopo Trans-frontier Park (GLTP) as a spatial unit would mean and expectations of how relations can and should be structured, both in the short and long terms. For mental appropriation, individuals do not necessarily have to be physically present in a specific spatial area; it is their angle of vision that structures their thoughts and how they relate to particular spaces. It is suggested that entrepreneurial intentions and behaviours are thus a product of how individuals and communities dominate and appropriate space.

Materials and methods

Description of study area

This research was carried out in two districts which fall within the GLTFCA (see Figure 1). Data were collected in four wards located in southeast Zimbabwe, an area which forms a constituent component of the GLTFCA (see Figure 2). Three of these wards, namely

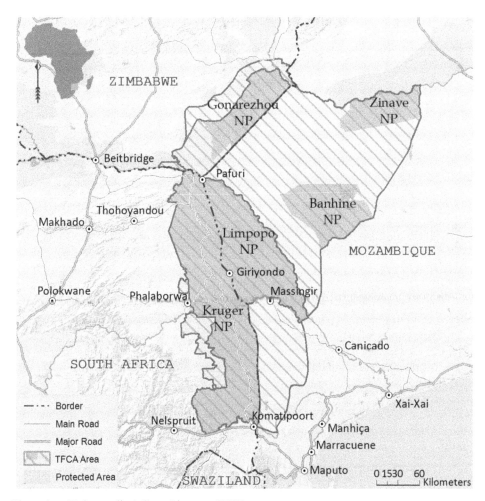

Figure 1.   (Colour online) Great Limpopo TFCA.
Source: Map produced by Peace Parks Foundation, www.peaceparks.org for work in the facilitation of transfrontier conservation.

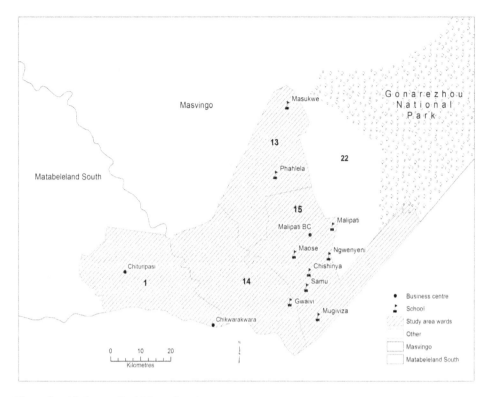

Figure 2. (Colour online) Map of study area.
© [Deanna Duffy]. Reproduced by permission of Deanna Duffy of the Spatial Data Analysis Network (SPAN), Charles Sturt University

Pahlela (ward 13), Sengwe (ward 14), Malipati (ward 15) are in the Chiredzi district, while one ward (Chikwarakwara ward 1) is in the Beitbridge district. For local government purposes, a ward is an administrative and management unit comprising about four to six villages. Three wards lie in proximity to Gonarezhou National Park (GNP) and one lies on the banks of Limpopo River and is adjacent to Kruger National Park. Generally, all four wards are in proximity to STWC, which links GNP and Kruger National Park and stretches from ward 15 in Chiredzi, up to Chikwarakwara and Tshipise in Beitbridge. The STWC was established as part of the 2002 Treaty signed to establish the GLTP. In both districts, the Communal Areas Management Programme for Indigenous Resources (CAMPFIRE) provides significant revenue for community development (Child, 1993). This region is generally characterised by low and unreliable rainfall in terms of onset, timing, and duration and thus experiences recurrent droughts. Contemporary livelihoods include livestock production with dry land cropping limited to drought-resistant crops such as sorghum and millet. Timber and non-timber forest products are also harvested by most communities adjacent to GNP (Mutenje, Ortmann, Ferrer, & Darroch, 2010).

Research methods

Data were collected using a two-phase research design and triangulation of collection methods. Data collection for the first phase occurred between September and December of

96

2013, while that for the second phase took place between May and July of 2014. Given the dynamic and discontinuous nature of entrepreneurial activities and processes, qualitative methods were deemed suitable (Hofer & Bygrave, 1992; Steyaert, 1997). Primary methods for data collection included semi-structured interviews, document analysis, and net-nography (online ethnography). Qualitative data were gathered from 57 participants across 4 wards using a semi-structured interview instrument. The interview guide, taking approximately 1 hour to finish, included questions on (a) general knowledge about the GLTP; (b) knowledge about community ecotourism sites; (c) entrepreneurial intentions and behaviours over time; (d) challenges and obstacles faced; and (e) links with other actors promoting eco-tourism. All interviews were conducted at interviewees' residence prior to appointment or other locations of their choice such as shopping centres and schools. Participants included traditional leaders, community trust leaders, and ordinary villagers. These participants were selected using purposive and snowball sampling to ensure that the interviewees could speak to the questions and reflect on their experiences about having an idea and begin-ning to establish an ecotourism enterprise (Hofer & Bygrave, 1992). As others highlight in entrepreneurial studies, attention should focus on interviewing those participants who had been directly involved in creating new value (like a new organisation or business model) (Bruyat & Julien, 2001). Apart from those leading the process of establishing ecotourism enterprises, ordinary community members were interviewed as they had taken part in com-munity forums on planning and development of ecotourism enterprises.

In addition to interviews, narrative drives (Jerneck & Olsson, 2013) were also con-ducted with selected community trust leaders to gather their spatial knowledge on tourist attractions. During these drives, open-ended questions were used to gather their views as much as possible using conversational style in order to minimise leading questions. For example, community trust leaders where asked 'If you look at ecotourism site X, describe how you see that progressing in the future? What are you currently doing about the site?' For accuracy, with consent from study participants, all interviews were first digitally recorded and then transcribed using 'literacization' techniques (Bucholtz, 2000), a process of transcription that privileges written over oral discourse features of language. Notes were also taken during some of the interviews to assist with probing questions and after the interview to enhance data richness. Using a combination of thematic analysis (Miles & Huberman, 1994) and process tracing (Venesson, 2008), data were analysed for types of entrepreneurs, their visions, extra-local linkages, and current and future initiatives. Document analysis was also conducted for project and policy documents such as the Inte-grated Tourism and Business Development Plan for the GLTP, Sengwe–Tshipise Local Development Plan and GNP Management Plan.

During the second phase of research, netnography was conducted (Kozinets, 2002). Netnography involves adapting traditional ethnography to study cultures and communities in social network sites (such as Facebook, MySpace, and Instagram) that afford users an opportunity to create personal profiles, virtually meet, communicate, and develop relation-ships with other users whom they might or might not be familiar with in the real world (Boyd & Ellison, 2007; Kozinets, 2002). Netnography is less time consuming and provides rich data without researcher interference (O'Reilly, Rahinel, Foster, & Patterson, 2007). Netnography is suitable for exploratory research on emerging novel phenomena such as the present focus on entrepreneurial intentions and behaviours in ecotourism planning and development. Permission was first sought to review user-generated content (e.g. photo-graphs, 'shares', 'comments', and 'likes') from a Facebook Group Page run by Gaza Trust (GT), a community NGO established to promote ecotourism and cultural tourism in the GLTFCA. Thematic analysis was then conducted on all user-generated content to identify themes with substantive significance across and within study participants (Floersch, Long-hofer, Kranke, & Townsend, 2010; Miles & Huberman, 1994).

Results

An analysis of each of the data sources (semi-structured interviews, documents, and netno-graphy) revealed a number of key themes based on individuals and community trust leaders' entrepreneurial intentions and behaviours and how they seek to appropriate space. Results suggest that communities living outside the Sengwe–Tshipise Wilderness Corridor are in continuous attempts to modify their space to exploit opportunities in the GLTFCA. Based on both theoretical and participant constructs, several themes were con-densed into common characteristics of emerging entrepreneurs; planning and development of community-based ecotourism enterprises; nature of ecotourism product on offer, and extra-local stakeholder linkages and collaboration. Each is considered in turn with selected quotes presented to illustrate key findings.

Characteristics of emerging entrepreneurs

To assess entrepreneurial intentions, study participants were interviewed on their likeli-hood of establishing community-based tourism enterprises and specifically asked on what they were doing to show such intentions. Based on different motivations, sources of entrepreneurial ideas and broader objectives, three types of entrepreneurs emerged. A common thread for all types of entrepreneurs is that they mentioned that they were 'dreamers', more interested in capturing opportunities presented by their proximity to the GLTP. When asked on what they were actually doing to fulfil their intentions and dreams, a majority of interviewees revealed that they were 'still exploring' and 'looking at the other side' with only a few, especially leaders from community trusts insisting 'they had already taken collective risk'. This resonates with the definition of entrepreneur adopted for this research. Entrepreneurship was not limited to those instances where only a new venture has been already created. The first group comprised farmers practising pluriactivity where they continue with dry land cropping but simul-taneously expand into ecotourism. A majority of interviewees in this category mentioned that opportunities for diversifying livelihoods exist especially with increased tourism traffic in the GLTFCA. This, most interviewees insisted, will generate demand for certain agricultural produce that they can grow on irrigation plots and community gardens. A second group of entrepreneurs is the 'resource-exploiting entrepreneur'. This group, which produces crafts and other artefacts for tourist consumption, comprised women from the Sengwe Vamanani Crafts Association, a group that was set with assist-ance from an NGO called Southern Alliance for Indigenous Resources. In several inter-views, the low entry costs to establish craft-based tourism enterprises were articulated. One woman summed up this perspective:

> Products can be made from readily available *ilala*. Before, we had a very strong women's group and we now think there is need to rekindle the activities in view of the opportunities presented by the GLTP. This does not require a lot of resources at all on our part. This means we just have to increase our efforts. A number of women welcome our group initiative. There is power in numbers.

In addition, some individual entrepreneurs mentioned the drive within the community to commercialise naturally occurring veldt products such as Marula Tree (*Scelerocarya birrea*) and buffalo thorn (*Ziziphus mucronata*). A third and more prominent group comprised 'portfolio entrepreneurs', whose intentions are to commence particular ventures and lead community trusts for developing ecotourism and promoting local culture. To this end, three community trusts that were established, namely GT, Malipati Development Trust (MDT), and Mateke Trust (MT). In examining their perceptions and intentions to become entrepreneurs, community trust members were asked to comment on the desirability and feasibility of establishing community-based ecotourism enterprises. By listening to their narratives and networks in which locals are involved, it became apparent that they are engaged in a complex hierarchy of articulations meant to promote visibility of ecotourism and culture. For example, during interviews, leaders of the MDT mentioned that establishing joint ventures was not only desirable but also feasible. They mainly draw upon experiences from other areas where joint venture arrangements are in place. One senior member of the MDT summarised the situation:

> So it is a question of courting these operators. They [Wilderness Safaris] are running a similar arrangement across the Limpopo River with our neighbours in the Makuleke Contractual Park. I know there could be local possibilities to engage but our local guys said they would be more interested in working in Chiredzi North. So we approached these guys and they sent representatives to explore a potential site inside GNP. It is promising.

Common among leaders interviewed was 'the need to make a difference in their community'. After several community meetings, some leaders have mobilised cultural and political capital to pursue broader community interest in setting up new enterprises. For example, MDT applied for and was granted permission to lease one site to establish tourism lodge and campsite inside the GNP by the Parks and Wildlife Management Authority. However, as the chairman of MDT indicated, holding out the offer letter, the annual lease fees of $25,000 per year are prohibitive and can only be met if they secure assistance from a private sector operator. Although the details of the proposed joint venture were still sketchy, the official was adamant that ecotourism was not only more environmentally appealing, but it was also set to be have higher returns on investment in the long term. He mentioned that the revenue derived from safari hunting under CAMPFIRE could be used to underwrite the development of lodges at the prime site inside GNP:

> We are sitting on a diamond mine in Sengwe. When the officials from Wilderness Safaris visited, they were very excited. We can get excellent returns if we pursue a joint venture agreement with them. We can certainly achieve this if we take a hard look at some of our local revenue streams, such as hunting in both Sengwe 1 and 2. If all people see as I do, we can achieve a lot.

This quote shows that there is a profound sense of hope among the leaders about opportunities that come with fully participating and engaging in ecotourism. Village leaders treasured the organisational and networking skills of community trust leaders. For example, commenting on the role of MDT in promoting visibility of ecotourism in the area, following the hosting of the Shangaan Cultural Festival in July 2013, one village head said:

> That is when you realise that there are proactive leaders in your midst with potential that you always underestimated. When the 19 tourists crossed into Zimbabwe from South Africa using one point on the Limpopo River, then we [community] said, surely this whole GLTP is a reality. It was really an eye opener because before they were talking of linking parks but now we see the ideas coming to fruition.

This sentiment was further echoed in an interview with one woman who commented:

> We were involved in hosting of the Shangaan Cultural festival, which sort of made us feel and believe that ecotourism can really be experienced. As the idea of linking communities in and promoting tourism has been said before, this was something that we thought was a starting point. And now everybody assumes that the GLTP is indeed real; this is a community initiative. We are doing something ourselves as locals with no outside support.

Many villagers revealed that there is a compelling need within the entire community to work towards collectively improving livelihoods through establishing ecotourism enterprises. The MDT has been active in promoting ecotourism and culture in ward 15 and GT has been predominantly working in the entire southeast Lowveld. This sometimes resulted in clashes and conflicts over who should represent community interests. As one villager said:

> Now there is a sense of belonging. We now respect and trust each other's initiatives. We are singing from the same hymnbook. At first we did not want to join hands with them [Gaza Trust]. But then we realised we are doing the same thing. We are united more by what binds us as a region. They are also promoting the culture of the Shangaan. So each time there is something even in Chiredzi, they invite us. If we have something as well we call them, our dance groups take part in some of the fairs organised by Gaza Trust. You can achieve something if you have that spirit of cooperation.

Most villagers interviewed attested to the need for communities to be responsible for the nature, scope, and direction of their region's ecotourism future. One villager at Chikwarakwara summed up this position in this way:

> The ecotourism ventures will help the region. They spur growth in other areas like having improved access roads and communication. Once you understand you have the resource ... scenic attractions, immediately you know that these things are possible. We became more confident after visiting the Mahenye Community in Chipinge district. The Mahenye people run joint venture with the private sector [River Lodges of Africa], and we were saying to ourselves, if we could have some arrangement like that.

Interviews with traditional leaders, councillors, and community trust leaders revealed that community leaders had in one way or another assumed responsibility for the planning and development of the area. Such responsibility is often demonstrated at stakeholder workshops where these leaders openly challenge the status quo. For example, during one interview with a former councillor for ward 15, this view was expressed:

> I have attended a number of council meetings. Initially these issues were not discussed. It was just about the Park, just about excluding us. Now things have changed. We have managed to lobby for recognition as an area, this is our land and we should ultimately be responsible for determining where the prime tourists go. I appreciate that we are now seen differently.

Similarly, these leaders spoke of how they persuaded many locals to accept the sites for ecotourism lodges and chalets.

Planning and development of community-based ecotourism enterprises

One way communities are appropriating and dominating space is through planning to establish community-based ecotourism enterprises. Most of the tourist lodges and chalets are set to be developed in and around the STWC. According to the Sengwe–Tshipise Local

Development Plan, this area will not be under cultivation and its wilderness value will be enhanced through a link to the Sengwe Wildlife Strip. This is a strip of land parallel to the Limpopo River to be used for wildlife and development of tourist accommodation. Interviewees also imagined that if a crossing point is fully developed, it would provide a tourist border crossing point linking the Kruger to the Sengwe Wildlife Strip, a development that could allow tourists from the Kruger to visit Sengwe en route to GNP. As an important component of people's spatial images, particular spaces are marked as unique and communities even ignore or silence particular uses of landscapes so as to sell a certain image. For example, most interviewees maintained that the unique wilderness area and culture would attract tourists who are interested in experiencing the 'other side' of GNP. In one interview, a member of the MDT mentioned that it is important for communities to organise the development of new enterprises:

> As leaders our responsibility is develop the product and integrate culture as part of our offering. We have a very rich cultural resource that will attract tourists to visit chalets outside the GNP. As a community, we are taking this as an opportunity, the way we see these places is now different. We have to get the best. This means we have to lead in setting up these ventures and leave this to the younger generation so that they continue to see the benefits. For example, our dance groups participate at cultural fairs.

In addition, most interviewees perceived that the uniqueness of tourist spots such as the Manjinji Pan Sanctuary was critical for positioning the tourist product. In one interview, the idea of creating network of ecotourism lodges and chalets was echoed: 'I think this is possible as the pan is already visible, so creating something around it will help in positioning our chalets. We can even establish chalets for use by tourists with interests in fishing and bird viewing'. Currently, there are six potential sites for ecotourism that have been identified. In this regard, space is dominated by boundaries that are specifically set and places that are signified as critical for the development of chalets and ecotourism lodges (see Figure 3). During interviews, most participants revealed that these ecotourism lodges could be established and offered as part of a broader tourism experience. One villager summed up the view of the majority, stating:

> The good thing is that we will own the lodges. Although the tourist flows into GNP are erratic, a starting point is once we own chalets; these could be part of tourist route in the GLTFCA. If we have a couple of tourists staying for a night, it means we pocket the dollars. We see this as an opportunity to own lodges, chalets and craft centres that will benefit the entire community.

A netnographic analysis of content of GT Facebook page shows that group members have a passion and determination to promote the visibility of ecotourism and their cultural offering. This is characterised in the following member post:

> Combined regional festivals like the Great Limpopo Cultural Festival (Zimbabwe, South Africa and Mozambique) must celebrate such historical links and provide information about the links to the public.

And another member posted a statement that read:

> We shall be taking the culture of Vatsonga and Hlengweni to the Mapungubwe Heritage Tour Celebrations (Vhembe carnival) in South Africa, Malamulele Stadium as from the 1- 5th of October 2013.

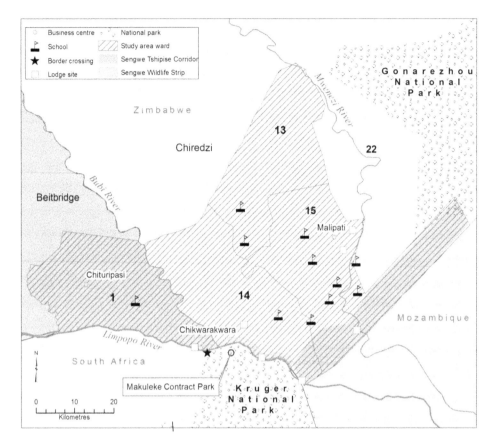

Figure 3.   (Colour online) Map showing Sengwe–Tshipise corridor and potential sites for lodges and chalets.
© [Deanna Duffy]. Reproduced by permission of Deanna Duffy of the Spatial Data Analysis Network (SPAN), Charles Sturt University

Similarly, during community meetings and stakeholders' workshops, community leaders appropriate space and engage in spatial practices to generate a particular tourist image and obtain sympathy. This was expressed earlier at stakeholders' workshops. In reviewing meeting documents, it seems that tourism operators also discussed support for the community to be given an opportunity to lease sites. In meetings of meetings, one prominent private ecotourism operator made the following remark:

> There are two major opportunities that need to be explored: One inside the park and one outside. Inside the park there are opportunities for joint ventures between parks, the private sector and neighbouring communities; through the lease of prime sites for tourist lodges ...
> I would suggest that local communities must be given the opportunity to be involved in the prime sites because without this involvement, they will become a source of conflict in the future.

From interviews, it emerged that communities are vigorously asserting their place and position in TFCA debates. On several occasions, during interviews, it was common for villagers to mention particular terminologies that are used in governing the TFCA space and functions that have emerged. For example, terms such as 'wildlife strip', 'viewing platforms', 'bird viewing', and 'crossing points' were frequently mentioned as part of broader attempts to sanitise landscapes and prepare them for tourist consumption. To show the extent of these spatial practices, two local schools (Samu and Malipati Secondary) now have bird watching clubs that are responsible for conducting a bird inventory. In an interview with the Chairman of the MDT, these bird-watching clubs would help establish a local inventory which can be corroborated by outside experts. Similarly, at other fora such as community meetings, particular terms are increasingly appropriated intended at signifying both control and knowledge of what happens in the GLTP. The importance of linking the protected areas can be best demonstrated by a public performance of a poem called 'Bhundula lesvihari' in the local Shangaan language, which means wildlife corridors. This poem is performed with passion and determination at most community gatherings to show an image where wildlife movements are signified as critical for the GLTFCA. It could be suggested that apart from targeting specific sites for setting up ecotourism enterprises, communities also actively imagine and appropriate and rework particular terms used by TFCA planners. What we witness in practice is the utilisation of spaces within and outside the STWC in an attempt to maximise returns that can be secured from ecotourism.

Extra-local linkages

Data from interviews and netnography show that entrepreneurs are engaged in cross-border cooperation and cross-border networking. As part of socio-spatial practices, they imagine a borderless region where areas such as Sengwe–Tshipise Wilderness Corridor and Sengwe Wildlife Strip are presented as part of a tourism region. Most community members interviewed maintained that a 'borderless region' was beneficial to tourism development. Historically, these communities had cultural and social ties with other communities across the border, especially in South Africa. In one interview, one traditional leader expressed this view:

> We are committed to supporting efforts for improving links between countries. We enjoy strong historical and cultural links with our neighbours and believe this is a rallying point for tourists. We share a common language; some people have two homes, one here and another across the Limpopo. Even now, because of this shared and rich cultural heritage, our young people, more like their forefathers, continue to marry and engage in customary practices across the border.

As part of networking, some entrepreneurs now transcend national boundaries to explore opportunities for attracting private capital for joint ventures in South Africa. For instance, in one interview, a senior member of MDT mentioned:

> I went to Wilderness Safaris to explain our business model. We want to attract investment so we can have a partnership. One thing we have been discussing as a community is we cannot go it alone. We can go one mile but we need someone who takes us for two miles.

The success of Wilderness Safaris in the Makuleke region is widely seen as a model that communities in Sengwe and Tshipise seek to emulate. Similarly, an analysis of postings on the GT Facebook page shows that community trust members have established strong links with communities outside Zimbabwe to promote ecotourism and cultural tourism. Photographs are posted marking occasions in which some of the members participated in cultural fairs including different stakeholders in the GLTFCA. By sometimes 'showing without telling' (Zhao, Grasmuck, & Martin, 2008), the intention is to make certain implicit identity claims aimed at generating desired impressions on their viewers especially in terms of the depth and extent of their cultural capital. For example, with a photo showing some participants at one carnival, a posting by one member on the page read:

> The Mapungubwe heritage route tour celebrations gave us the opportunity to learn much about our African culture especially the San and Khoi.

Photographs of groups of cultural dancers are then presented and other participants make comments, likes, and shares all intended at rekindling cultural and heritage routes. To date, most activities have focused on establishing links between cultural groups in South Africa and Zimbabwe. GT seeks to conduct cultural fairs in Mozambique. To increase local participation, their Facebook page posts details of past and upcoming events on cultural fairs and events.

Discussion

The aim of this study was to explore and describe the role of social entrepreneurship in ecotourism planning and development in the GLTFCA. As noted in previous studies, the planning and development of tourism can be successful by adopting a 'people-centric' approach, in which the voices of local communities are heard and decisions relating to the type, scale, and rate of tourism development informed by their input (Matthews, 1978; Murphy, 2012). Notwithstanding inherent community heterogeneity within the study area, results suggest that most villagers and especially community trust leaders in all four wards exhibit clear entrepreneurial intentions and behaviours to exploit opportunities offered by living in proximity to the GLTP. By interrogating the different spatial practices and imaginations of individuals, this paper offers a process perspective on a very important component of ecotourism enterprise creation in the GLTFCA. Based on theoretical constructs from Alsos et al. (2003), three groups of entrepreneurs emerged from condensing the intentions, time invested, creativity, and risk-taking capability of participants from all four wards. In all cases, most community members interviewed exhibited traits of visionaries, who are guided by either realistic or imagined visions within the GLTFCA, to initiate, plan for, and seek to develop new ecotourism enterprises. Communities are engaging in spatial practices that result in restructuring of their landscapes. As Filion (2004) highlights, it is those entrepreneurs who learn from their environment who can learn and reflect on their environment and be successful. This is a trait displayed especially among the portfolio entrepreneurs – leaders of community trusts who inspire the whole community with entrenched visions, moving from self-satisfaction to a collective drive to empower marginalised ethnic groups in the GLTFCA. At both theoretical and practical levels, individual/community intentions and behaviours are consistent with Degeorge and Fayolle's (2011) model to explain entrepreneurial new value creation process. All entrepreneurial behaviours are planned and as such are a constitute component of spatial appropriation in the GLTFCA. As Degeorge and Fayolle argue, focusing attention on intentions is critical for explaining not only the emergence and development of the entrepreneurial process, but also triggers to new venture creation. What is clear from these intentions is that communities in all four wards seek to create particular types of ecotourism enterprises; they coordinate such activities to enhance their prosperity and livelihoods in the long term.

The development of ecotourism requires a multi-stakeholder approach and community participation will be critical for the success of any planned enterprises. This observation is echoed in other studies where communities are involved in planning of sites for ecotourism in TFCAs such as the Kgalagadi Transfrontier Park (Moswete, Thapa, & Child, 2011). Community trusts are innovative and engage in a complex hierarchy of articulations to promote ecotourism and culture. Most information on cultural events is shared via social media platforms on Facebook. This has allowed GT to connect with relatively young followers to promote a particular ethnic identity. It seems that entrepreneurship success will be influenced more by this emerging culture of embracing opportunities; the cultural influence of these communities will depend on their political clout; how they embrace opportunities and organisational capacity of communities living in the borderlands (Brunet-Jailly, 2005). It is often those who are labelled culturally marginalised who are more likely to be innovative to exploit opportunities for entrepreneurship driven by ecotourism and culture. Following Van den Berghe (1980), community trust members are 'entrepreneurs in exoticism', wishing to facilitate tourist consumption of Xitsonga, Shangaan, and other cultures in the GLTFCA. They seek to sell a particular exotic culture.

Although not all communities are involved in the selling of culture, there is a distinct group of community leaders who, even though from a position of relative marginal socio-economic status are set to participate in creation of new value. It is clear that ecotourism has resulted in local innovation and entrepreneurship which may subsequently have a multiplier effect on the local economy and encourage the development of even more new enterprises (Ashley & Haysom, 2006; Meyer, 2010). Community-based ecotourism enterprises that are created form part of broader narratives that communities deploy to appropriate space in the GLTFCA. Through particular mindscapes and perceptual images (Newman & Paasi, 1998), influential individuals and leaders of community trusts are engaged in networks and increasingly deploy new spatial images and terms to describe their desires and efforts in a way that also connect with international conservation community discourses on TFCAs.

While it is commendable that portfolio entrepreneurs emerged from the community itself, there are occasional conflicts. Proactive entrepreneurs, who seize opportunities and set up community trusts are often a catalyst for friction and power struggles and may even be perceived to be challenging the status quo (Butler & Hinch, 1996). In this case study, leaders of community trusts seem to be working closely with traditional leaders. Representatives of traditional leaders attended look-and-learn visits to other ecotourism sites in the region and argued that community-based enterprises can be part of a regional tourism route delivering cultural heritage. As the GLTFCA is primarily about opening national borders to enhance tourist traffic within the region, cultural products, and heritage routes proposed by locals can form an important component of regional tourist routes. As one official in the Beitbridge district mentioned, such clustering of activities can be 'observed in the Tuli Circle, where Wilderness Safaris coordinates an annual cycling event for biking tourists called "Tour de Tuli"'. Briedenhann and Wickens (2004) note that clustering of activities and attractions enhances cooperation and partnerships between communities in local and neighbouring regions and serves as a vehicle for the stimulation of economic development. Even in the absence of significant community-run infrastructure, the entrepreneurship process encourages regional interplay as well as a regional identity, which are sometimes presented as healthy components of economic development (Kline, Hao, Alderman, Kleckley, & Gray, 2014).

As an emerging land use, community-based ecotourism may be incompatible with already existing land uses such as safari hunting. For example, while communities mentioned that it is desirable to promote the development of ecotourism, others maintained that safari hunting was inconsistent and incompatible with the wilderness image of the

STWC. Despite such resentment, most community trust members and traditional leaders insisted that these two (safari hunting and photographic tourism) could be complementary. This position is consistent with other studies that maintain that CAMPFIRE should aim at coupling wildlife revenue with other income-generating projects resulting in a diversified portfolio that improves community livelihoods (Poshiwa, Groeneveld, Heitkonig, Prins, & van Ierland, 2013).

Conclusion

This study intended to investigate the role of community agency in ecotourism entrepreneurship, given the numerous opportunities and promises around the GLTFCA. The ambition of this research was to argue that through reading how communities engage in particular spatial practices, it is possible to shed light on the role of agency in ecotourism planning and development. Based on the theoretical constructs of entrepreneurial intentions and behaviours and insights from Lefebvre on spatial appropriation, results suggest that communities have dominated and controlled space within the GLTFCA. They do this by targeting sites for ecotourism lodges and chalets; collaborating with the private sector, and promoting culture and ecotourism in to enhance visibility. Arguments presented here are different from those in the literature that seem to emphasise lack of tangible benefits and as such do not pay attention emerging forms of organisation in social entrepreneurship. It is by explicating the entrepreneurial intentions and behaviours of communities that we can begin to understand the relative contribution of locals in planning and development of ecotourism in the GLTFCA. Limiting to only those instances where actual ventures are fully operational, this paper argues, is narrow and risks missing the social transformation that is occurring as part of spatial appropriation. By focusing on how and in what ways individuals and communities are appropriating space, the study extends debates on community agency in ecotourism entrepreneurship.

Disclosure statement
No potential conflict of interest was reported by the author.

References
Alsos, G. A., Ljunggren, E., & Pettersen, L. T. (2003). Farm-based entrepreneurs: What triggers the start-up of new business activities? *Journal of Small Business and Enterprise Development, 10*(4), 435–443.
van Amerom, M., & Büscher, B. (2005). Peace parks in southern Africa: Bringers of an African Renaissance? *Journal of Modern African Studies, 43*(2), 159–182.
Andersson, J. A., de Garine-Wichatitsky, M., Cumming, D. H. M., Dzingirai, V., & Giller, K. E. (Eds.). (2013). *Transfrontier conservation areas: People living on the edge.* London: Routledge.
Ashley, C., & Haysom, G. (2006). From philanthropy to a different way of doing business: Strategies and challenges in integrating pro-poor approaches into tourism business. *Development Southern Africa, 23*(2), 265–280.
Boyd, D., & Ellison, N. (2007). Social network sites: Definition, history, and scholarship. *Journal of Computer-Mediated Communication, 13*(1), 210–230.
Briedenhann, J., & Wickens, E. (2004). Tourism routes as a tool for the economic development of rural areas – Vibrant hope or impossible dream? *Tourism Management, 25*(1), 71–79.
Brunet-Jailly, E. (2005). Theorizing borders: An interdisciplinary perspective. *Geopolitics, 10*(4), 633–649.
Bruyat, C., & Julien, P.-A. (2001). Defining the field of research in entrepreneurship. *Journal of Business Venturing, 16*(2), 165–180.

Bucholtz, M. (2000). The politics of transcription. *Journal of Pragmatics*, *32*(10), 1439–1465.

Büscher, B. (2013). *Transforming the frontier: 'Peace Parks' and the politics of neoliberal conservation in southern Africa*. Durham, NC: Duke University Press.

Butler, R., & Hinch, T. (1996). *Tourism and indigenous peoples*. London: Routledge.

Bygrave, W. (1989). The entrepreneurship paradigm: A philosophical look at its research methodologies. *Entrepreneurship Theory and Practice*, *14*(1), 7–26.

Child, B. (1993). Zimbabwe's CAMPFIRE programme: Using the high value of wildlife recreation to revolutionize natural resource management in communal areas. *The Commonwealth Forestry Review*, *72*(4), 284–296.

Degeorge, J.-M., & Fayolle, A. (2011). The entrepreneurial process trigger: A modelling attempt in the French context. *Journal of Small Business and Enterprise Development*, *18*(2), 251–277.

Donohoe, H. M., & Needham, R. D. (2006). Ecotourism: The evolving contemporary definition. *Journal of Ecotourism*, *5*(3), 192–210.

Douglas, E. J., & Shepherd, D. A. (2002). Self-employment as a career choice: Attitudes, entrepreneurial intentions, and utility maximization. *Entrepreneurship Theory and Practice*, *26*(3), 81–90.

Dowling, R. K., & Fennell, D. A. (2003). The context of ecotourism policy and planning. In D. A. Fennell & R. K. Dowling (Eds.), *Ecotourism policy and planning* (pp. 1–20). Oxon: CABI.

Duffy, R. (2006). The potential and pitfalls of global environmental governance: The politics of trans-frontier conservation areas in southern Africa. *Political Geography*, *25*(1), 89–112.

Dzingirai, V. (2004). *Disenfranchisement at large: Transfrontier zones, conservation and local livelihoods*. Harare: IUCN ROSA.

Fennell, D. A. (2015). *Ecotourism* (4th ed.). London: Routledge.

Ferreira, J. J., Raposo, M. L., Rodrigues, R. G., Dinis, A., & do Paço, A. (2012). A model of entrepreneurial intention: An application of the psychological and behavioral approaches. *Journal of Small Business and Enterprise Development*, *19*(3), 424–440.

Ferreira, S. (2004). Problems associated with tourism development in southern Africa: The case of transfrontier conservation areas. *GeoJournal*, *60*(3), 301–310.

Ferreira, S. L. A. (2006). Communities and transfrontier parks in the Southern African Development Community: The case of Limpopo National Park, Mozambique. *South African Geographical Journal*, *88*(2), 166–176.

Filion, L. J. (2004). Operators and visionaries: Differences in the entrepreneurial and managerial systems of two types of entrepreneurs. *International Journal of Entrepreneurship and Small Business*, *1*(1), 35–55.

Floersch, J., Longhofer, J. L., Kranke, D., & Townsend, L. (2010). Integrating thematic, grounded theory and narrative analysis: A case study of adolescent psychotropic treatment. *Qualitative Social Work*, *9*(3), 407–425.

Garrod, B. (2003). Local participation in the planning and management of ecotourism: A revised model approach. *Journal of Ecotourism*, *2*(1), 33–53.

Gartner, W. B. (1989). Some suggestions for research on entrepreneurial traits and characteristics. *Entrepreneurship: Theory & Practice*, *14*(1), 27–37.

Gössling, S. (1999). Ecotourism: A means to safeguard biodiversity and ecosystem functions? *Ecological Economics*, *29*(2), 303–320.

Gössling, S. (2000). Tourism – Sustainable development option? *Environmental Conservation*, *27*(3), 223–224.

Grande, J., Madsen, E. L., & Borch, O. J. (2011). The relationship between resources, entrepreneurial orientation and performance in farm-based ventures. *Entrepreneurship & Regional Development*, *23*(3–4), 89–111.

Hofer, C. W., & Bygrave, W. D. (1992). Researching entrepreneurship. *Entrepreneurship Theory and Practice*, *16*(3), 91–100.

Honey, M. (1999). *Ecotourism and sustainable development: Who owns paradise?* Washington, DC: Island Press.

Hughes, D. M. (2005). Third nature: Making space and time in the Great Limpopo Conservation Area. *Cultural Anthropology*, *20*(2), 157–184.

Jerneck, A., & Olsson, L. (2013). More than trees! Understanding the agroforestry adoption gap in subsistence agriculture: Insights from narrative walks in Kenya. *Journal of Rural Studies*, *32*, 114–125.

Jones, B. T. B. (1999). Policy lessons from the evolution of a community-based approach to wildlife management, Kunene Region, Namibia. *Journal of International Development*, *11*(2), 295–304.

Katerere, Y., Hill, L., & Moyo, S. (2001). *A critique of transboundary natural resources management (TNRM) in southern Africa*. Harare: International Union for Conservation of Nature and Natural Resources/Regional Office of Southern Africa (IUCN/ROSA).

Kickul, J., & Gundry, L. (2002). Prospecting for strategic advantage: The proactive entrepreneurial personality and small firm innovation. *Journal of Small Business Management, 40*(2), 85–97.

Kipfer, S., Saberi, P., & Wieditz, T. (2013). Henri Lefebvre: Debates and controversies. *Progress in Human Geography, 37*(1), 115–134.

Kline, C., Hao, H., Alderman, D., Kleckley, J. W., & Gray, S. (2014). A spatial analysis of tourism, entrepreneurship and the entrepreneurial ecosystem in North Carolina, USA. *Tourism Planning & Development, 11*(3), 305–316.

Kozinets, R. V. (2002). The field behind the screen: Using netnography for marketing research in online communities. *Journal of Marketing Research, 39*(1), 61–72.

Krueger, N. F., & Brazeal, D. V. (1994). Entrepreneurial potential and potential entrepreneurs. *Entrepreneurship Theory and Practice, 18*, 91–91.

Krueger, N. F., & Carsrud, A. L. (1993). Entrepreneurial intentions: Applying the theory of planned behaviour. *Entrepreneurship & Regional Development, 5*(4), 315–330.

Krueger, N. F., Reilly, M. D., & Carsrud, A. L. (2000). Competing models of entrepreneurial intentions. *Journal of Business Venturing, 15*(5), 411–432.

Lefebvre, H. (1991). *The production of space*. Oxford, MA: Blackwell.

Matthews, H. (1978). *International tourism: A political and social analysis*. Cambridge, MA: Schenkman.

McNeely, J. A. (1993). Conservation and development: How protected natural areas can contribute to local communities. In A. H. Westing (Ed.), *Transfrontier reserves for peace and nature: A contribution to human security* (pp. 49–58). Nairobi: United Nations Environment Programme.

McNeely, J. A. (1994). Protected areas for the 21st century: Working to provide benefits to society. *Biodiversity and Conservation, 3*(5), 390–405.

Merrifield, A. (1993). Place and space: A Lefebvrian reconciliation. *Transactions of the Institute of British Geographers, 18*(4), 516–531.

Meyer, D. (2010). Pro-poor tourism: Can tourism contribute to poverty reduction in less economically developed countries? In S. Cole & N. Morgan (Eds.), *Tourism and inequality: Problems and prospects* (pp. 164–182). London: CABI.

Miles, M. B., & Huberman, A. M. (1994). *An expanded sourcebook: Qualitative data analysis* (2nd ed.). Thousand Oaks, CA: Sage.

Moswete, N. N., Thapa, B., & Child, B. (2011). Attitudes and opinions of local and national public sector stakeholders towards Kgalagadi Transfrontier Park, Botswana. *International Journal of Sustainable Development & World Ecology, 19*(1), 67–80.

Murphree, M. W. (2001). Community, council & client: A case study in ecotourism development from Mahenye, Zimbabwe. In M. W. Murphree & D. Hulme (Eds.), *African wildlife and livelihoods: The promise and performance of community conservation* (pp. 177–194). London: James Currey.

Murphy, P. E. (2012). *Tourism: A community approach*. London: Routledge.

Mutenje, M., Ortmann, G., Ferrer, S., & Darroch, M. (2010). Rural livelihood diversity to manage economic shocks: Evidence from south-east Zimbabwe. *Agrekon, 49*(3), 338–357.

Newman, D., & Paasi, A. (1998). Fences and neighbours in the postmodern world: Boundary narratives in political geography. *Progress in Human Geography, 22*(2), 186–207.

O'Reilly, N. J., Rahinel, R., Foster, M. K., & Patterson, M. (2007). Connecting in megaclasses: The netnographic advantage. *Journal of Marketing Education, 29*(1), 69–84.

Poshiwa, X., Groeneveld, R., Heitkonig, I., Prins, H., & van Ierland, E. C. (2013). Reducing rural households' annual income fluctuations due to rainfall variation through diversification of wildlife use: Portfolio theory in a case study of south eastern Zimbabwe. *Tropical Conservation Science, 6*(2), 201–220.

Quinn, S. M., Broberg, L., & Freimund, W. (Eds.). (2012). *Parks, peace and partnership: Global initiatives in transboundary conservation*. Calgary: University of Calgary Press.

Ramutsindela, M. (2007). *Transfrontier conservation in Africa: At the confluence of capital, politics and nature*. Wallingford: CABI.

Reitan, B. (1997, June 21–24). *Where do we learn that entrepreneurship is feasible, desirable and/or profitable? A look at the processes leading to entrepreneurial potential*. Paper read at United States Association for Small Business and Entrepreneurship Annual National Conference, San Francisco, CA.

Roxas, B. G., Cayoca-Panizales, R., & de Jesus, R. M. (2008). Entrepreneurial knowledge and its effects on entrepreneurial intentions: Development of a conceptual framework. *Asia-Pacific Social Science Review, 8*(2), 61–77.

Shields, R. (2011). Henri Lefebvre. In P. Hubbard & R. Kitchin (Eds.), *Key thinkers on space and place* (pp. 279–285). Thousand Oaks, CA: Sage.

Spenceley, A. (2006). Tourism in the Great Limpopo Transfrontier Park. *Development Southern Africa, 23*(5), 649–667.

Spenceley, A. (2008). Requirements for sustainable nature-based tourism in transfrontier conservation areas: A southern African Delphi Consultation. *Tourism Geographies, 10*(3), 285–311.

Spenceley, A., Dzingirai, P., & Tangawamira, Z. (2008). *Economic impacts of transfrontier conservation areas: Tourism in the Greater Limpopo Transfrontier Conservation Area*. Johannesburg: Report to IUCN SASUSG.

Steyaert, C. (1997). A qualitative methodology for process studies of entrepreneurship: Creating local knowledge through stories. *International Studies of Management & Organization, 27*(3), 13–33.

Suich, H., Busch, J., & Barbancho, N. (2005). *Economic impacts of transfrontier conservation areas: Baseline of tourism in the Kavango–Zambezi TFCA* (Paper Number 4). Conservation International.

Taylor, R. (2009). Community based natural resource management in Zimbabwe: The experience of CAMPFIRE. *Biodiversity and Conservation, 18*(10), 2563–2583.

Van den Berghe, P. L. (1980). Tourism as ethnic relations: A case study of Cuzco, Peru. *Ethnic and Racial Studies, 3*(4), 375–392.

Van Gelderen, M., Brand, M., van Praag, M., Bodewes, W., Poutsma, E., & Van Gils, A. (2008). Explaining entrepreneurial intentions by means of the theory of planned behaviour. *Career Development International, 13*(6), 538–559.

Venesson, P. (2008). Case studies and process tracing: Theories and practices. In D. Della Porta & M. Keating (Eds.), *Approaches and methodologies in the social sciences: A pluralist perspective* (pp. 223–240). Cambridge, MA: Cambridge University Press.

Venkataraman, S. (1997). The distinctive domain of entrepreneurship research. In J. Katz & R. Brockhaus (Eds.), *Advances in entrepreneurship, firm emergence and growth* (pp. 119–138). Greenwich, CT: JAI Press.

Weaver, D. B., & Lawton, L. J. (2007). Twenty years on: The state of contemporary ecotourism research. *Tourism Management, 28*(5), 1168–1179.

Weick, K. E. (1979). *The social psychology of organising* (2nd ed.). Reading, MA: Addison-Wesley.

Zhao, H., Seibert, S. E., & Hills, G. E. (2005). The mediating role of self-efficacy in the development of entrepreneurial intentions. *Journal of Applied Psychology, 90*(6), 1265–1272.

Zhao, S., Grasmuck, S., & Martin, J. (2008). Identity construction on Facebook: Digital empowerment in anchored relationships. *Computers in Human Behavior, 24*(5), 1816–1836.

Ecotourism in Botswana: 30 years later

Joseph E. Mbaiwa[a,b]

[a]Okavango Research Institute, University of Botswana, Maun, Botswana; [b]Faculty of Management, School of Tourism & Hospitality, University of Johannesburg, Johannesburg, South Africa

Thirty years ago, conservationists, host communities, academics, and tourism practitioners perceived ecotourism as a panacea to conservation and poverty problems in tourism destination areas, especially in developing countries. This paper, therefore, analyses the performance of ecotourism as a tool designed to achieve improved livelihoods and conservation in the Okavango Delta, Botswana. The concept of ecotourism is debated and the context used in this paper is explained. Secondary data from published and unpublished sources on ecotourism in Botswana and the Okavango Delta are used. Primary data were collected through informal interviews with key stakeholders to update secondary data. Results indicate that in its 30 years of existence in the Okavango Delta, ecotourism had mixed results. That is, it succeeded in some areas and failed in others. Where ecotourism succeeded, it generated economic benefits such as income and employment opportunities, leading to positive attitudes of residents towards ecotourism and conservation. Where ecotourism failed, the lack of entrepreneurship, and managerial and marketing skills of local communities are cited as some of the key factors contributing to the failure of projects. Despite the failure of particular projects, this paper argues that ecotourism has proved to be a tool that can be used to achieve improved livelihoods and conservation. However, this depends on the socio-economic and political dynamics of host communities in a specific ecotourism destination area.

1. Introduction

The degradation of biodiversity resources and poverty are challenges that remain a global sore in the twenty-first century. However, 30 years ago, ecotourism became a buzzword among environmental conservation groups, tourism practitioners, and academia. Ecotourism was seen as a remedy for the protection of nature and a solution to environmental conservation problems that affect the world (Mbaiwa, 2008). Ecotourism was believed to be able to achieve conservation mainly because of the assumption that it has the potential to generate income that can be ploughed back into biodiversity conservation. Scholars (Davis & Tisdell, 1998; Hoyt, 1996; Krüger, 2005; Leader-Williams, 2002) argue that the overall potential of ecotourism to generate revenue for conservation is enormous. This argument is confirmed by Groombridge (1992) and Cater (1994) who estimated that annual growth rates of ecotourism in the 1990s were twice as high as the overall 6% global tourism growth rate. Goodwin (1996) predicted the amount of revenue created by ecotourism and environmentally sensitive tourism to be 50 billion and 300 billion US$ in 2000. This demonstrates that scholars and practitioners are convinced that ecotourism can provide an alternative form of economic development that ensures biodiversity conservation through the generation of revenue that can be ploughed back to conservation.

In the 1990s, ecotourism was also assumed to result in the development of environmentally friendly visitors in nature-based tourism destinations. Ecotourists were assumed to be educated individuals who easily become aware of the need to promote biodiversity conservation and improve rural livelihoods in host destinations. Krüger (2005), Chi and Luzar (1998), Wearing and Neil (1999), Boo (1991), and Wight (1996) note that ecotourists are highly educated and earn higher incomes. This results in them having a higher willingness to spend money in the destination country. Wearing and Neil (1999) argue that psychographic characteristics of ecotourists include the possession of an environmental ethic and a willingness not to degrade the resource. In this regard, there is a huge potential for ecotourism to raise not only revenues for conservation, but also awareness among people who often support conservation schemes after an ecotourism experience (Krüger, 2005; Wearing & Neil, 1999). Ecotourism was thus designed as a means to achieve conservation when considering the existence of environmentally friendly and educated visitors, revenue generation that is ploughed back to conservation, and environmentally friendly small-scale tourism infrastructure (Mbaiwa, 2008).

The evolution and adoption of ecotourism across the globe, especially in developing countries, in the last 30 years raises several questions about its achievements. That is, how much has been achieved by ecotourism, particularly its goals of improved livelihoods and conservation in host tourism destinations. Krüger (2005) rhetorically asks whether ecotourism contributes towards conservation of threatened species and habitats or is it just a marketing ploy of the tourism industry. It is also important to ask whether ecotourism contributes to improved livelihoods in host destinations. These questions about the performance of ecotourism are also relevant for ecotourism development in Botswana. Botswana is faced with environmental challenges that threaten its biodiversity, especially in wetland areas located on the northern parts of the country. The Department of Environmental Affairs (2008) highlights that environmental concerns in Botswana include the growing pressure on water resources; the degradation of rangeland pasture resources; the depletion of wood resources; the overuse or exploitation of some rangeland products; pollution of air, water, soil, and vegetation resources; and wildlife depletion. Tourism, especially mass tourism, is one of the key nature-based tourism activities that threaten environmental conservation in Botswana (Darkoh & Mbaiwa, 2014; Mbaiwa, 2003). It is from this perspective that ecotourism in Botswana is analysed to determine whether it has made significant contribution to biodiversity conservation and improved livelihoods in the last 30 years.

Ecotourism in Botswana is carried out largely in the northern parts of the country, especially in the Okavango and Chobe regions. These areas are endowed with a variety of wildlife species and scenic beauty. The Okavango Delta is a renowned international wildlife-based tourism site, Wetland of International Importance and Ramsar Site since 1997, and the 1000th World Heritage Site from June 2014. Though a rich international tourism destination, poverty in the Okavango Delta is very high (CSO, 2008). As a result, the threat of biodiversity conservation in the wetland is equally very high partly due to poverty problems (Darkoh & Mbaiwa, 2014). Poverty has created conditions for over-harvesting of natural resources by the local people in the Okavango Delta (Mbaiwa, 2008). From the 1990s, Botswana adopted the ecotourism approach to address challenges of natural resource degradation and livelihoods in tourism destination areas such as the Okavango Delta. However, the performance of ecotourism in Botswana particularly in the

Okavango Delta since its adoption 30 years ago is not adequately analysed. The objective of this paper, therefore, is to analyse the performance of ecotourism as a tool designed to achieve improved livelihoods and conservation in the Okavango Delta, Botswana.

2.   Definition and origins of ecotourism

The context and a common understanding of what ecotourism means are needed before any analysis about its performance is made. In terms of definition, ecotourism as a concept is surrounded by confusion (Bjork, 2000). The concept of ecotourism lacks an agreed definition (Boo, 1990; Goodwin, 1996; Wearing & Neil, 1999). Different researchers and practitioners define and apply the concept of ecotourism differently. As such, between 1993 and 1994, over 30 definitions of ecotourism were created and marketed (Dowling, 2000). Ecotourism is, therefore, a fuzzy concept defined and named in many different ways (Bjork, 2000; Valentine, 1993) by researchers, conservationists, and tourism practitioners.

Despite the many definitions of ecotourism, some of the commonly used definitions include those by the International Ecotourism Society (TIES) which defines ecotourism as 'responsible travel to natural areas that conserves the environment and improves the well-being of local people' (Honey, 2008, p. 33). Ceballos-Lascurain (1996, p. 20) defines ecotourism as:

> travelling to relatively undisturbed or uncontaminated natural areas with the specific objective of studying, admiring, and enjoying the scenery and its wild plants and animals, as well as any existing cultural manifestations (both past and present) found in these areas.

Loon and Polakow (2001) relate ecotourism to a hotel or accommodation facility and hence define an ecotourism operation simply as a hotel situated in natural areas. According to Wearing and Neil (1999), ecotourism is defined as a form of nature-based tourism, contributing towards both socio-economic and environmental benefits, burst into the scientific and later public consciousness in the 1990s. The popularity of the term ecotourism from the 1990s made it to be considered one of conservation biology's hottest 'buzzwords' (Aylward, Allen, Echeverria, & Tosi, 1996).

The global interest in ecotourism is attributed to the rise of sustainability or the concept of sustainable development in 1987 (Krüger, 2005). The concept of sustainable development became popular after the publication of the Brundtland Report in 1987, also known as the World Commission on Environment and Development (WCED). According to WCED (1987, p. 43), sustainable development is defined as development designed to 'meet the needs of the present without compromising the ability of future generations to meet their own needs'. The Brundtland Report in 1987 argues for sustainable development and conservation of natural resources (Krüger, 2005). Previously, there was a global dilemma of conserving nature while achieving short-term economic gains to satisfy the needs of the people. Many countries, especially developing countries, faced this seemingly unbalanced development approach (McNeely, Miller, Reid, Mittermeier, & Werner, 1990; Myers, Mittermeier, Mittermeier, da Fonseca, & Kent, 2000). Failure to balance economic development and conservation contributed to global resource decline. Conservationists termed areas of rich biodiversity and also threatened with resource decline as 'biodiversity hotspots' (Jepson & Canney, 2001; Mittermeier, Myers, & Mittermeier, 2000; Orme et al., 2005). Some biodiversity hotspots are leading international tourism destination areas. For examples, the World Wildlife Federation notes that the Galapagos, which is a popular ecotourism destination, is experiencing the following:

Human population growth, invader species and commercial fishing threaten to destroy the fragile ecological balance in the world famous Galapagos islands ... Although 97% of the island's land area has National Park status, the population of the Galapagos islands has more than doubled in the last 10 years, mainly due to migration from the Ecuadorian mainland. With this migration, many foreign plant and animal species are being introduced. Their estimated numbers have grown from about 77 in 1971 to more than 260 today.

The idea of ecotourism thus came at an era when the degradation of biodiversity and natural resources was high and intervention critical. From the 1990s, ecotourism became an alternative approach to adopt if sustainability in biodiversity conservation and livelihoods in host regions was to be achieved. Ecotourism was viewed as a panacea for the protection of nature (Burnie, 1994; Gössling, 1999; Gurung & De Coursey, 1994; Place, 1991; Ruschmann, 1992; Stiles & Clark, 1989). This is because ecotourism generates much-needed foreign currency, both locally and nationally, while at the same time providing a strong incentive to manage nature's strongholds in a way that would conserve them (Krüger, 2005).

Ecotourism has its own critics, particularly in achieving its goals of biodiversity conservation and improved rural livelihoods. Scholars (Cater, 1994; King & Stewart, 1996; Wall, 1997; Wheeller, 1992) argue that tourism of any kind is always a threat to protected areas, this includes ecotourism. Durbin and Ratrimoarisaona (1996) argue that the revenues created by ecotourism are too small to support conservation on a larger scale. In this regard, ecotourism may never make any significant contribution to biodiversity conservation. Although there are many different definitions and critics of ecotourism across the globe, the theme that runs across most of the definitions and arguments is that which describes ecotourism as nature-based tourism that includes an educational component, promotes the socio-economic well-being of local people, and is managed on a sustainable basis (Mbaiwa, 2008). Its popularity since the 1990s resulted in many governments particularly in developing countries adopting policies and strategies that support ecotourism in nature-based tourism destination areas. Botswana adopted the National Ecotourism Strategy (NES) of 2002 to strengthen local participation in ecotourism and biodiversity conservation. The NES aims at contributing actively to environmental conservation; involves local communities in tourism planning, development, and operation and contributes to their well-being; and promotes nature-based tourists who are environmentally friendly (Department of Tourism, 2002). This therefore makes it appropriate to analyse the performance of ecotourism as a tool designed to achieve improved livelihoods and conservation in Botswana in its 30 years of implementation in the country.

3.   The Okavango Delta

The Okavango Delta is located in north-western part of Botswana (Figure 1). The Delta is formed by the inflow of the Okavango River, whose two main tributaries (the Cuito and Cubango Rivers) originate in the Angolan Highlands. The Okavango River flows across Namibia's Caprivi Strip and finally drains in the north-west of Botswana, forming a wetland known as the Okavango Delta.

The Okavango Delta is characterised by a conical and triangular-shaped alluvial fan and covers an area of about $16,000 \text{ km}^2$ (Tlou, 1985). The geological formation of the Okavango Delta is a result of the active uplift (upwelling) associated with the African Superswell (Gumbricht & McCarthy, 2002). The upwelling caused the flow of the Okavango River to split into several channels that form many islands, lakes, and lagoons. The Okavango River and its Delta sustain life in an otherwise inhospitable environment. The Okavango Delta is an oasis in what would otherwise be semi-desert. It is characterised by large amounts of open water and grasslands, which sustain human life and a variety of

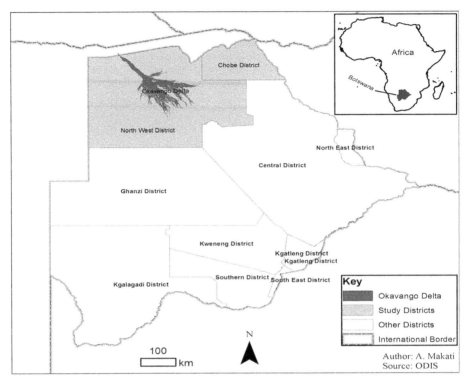

Figure 1. Map of the Okavango Delta.
Source: Mbaiwa (2008).

flora and fauna. The Okavango Delta was named a Wetland of International Importance and Ramsar Site in 1997 and United Nations Education Scientific & Cultural Organizations 1000th World Heritage Site in 2014.

The Okavango Delta is a major source of livelihoods for the rural communities who have lived in the area for hundreds of years. Over 95% of the 150,000 people who live in the Okavango Delta directly or indirectly rely on natural resources found in the wetland to sustain their livelihoods (CSO, 2011). Due to its rich wildlife diversity, wilderness nature, permanent water resources, rich grasslands, and forests, the Okavango Delta has become a key international tourism destination in Botswana. Factors such as human activities like tourism and agro-pastoralism as well as climate change make the Okavango Delta one of the most threatened of all ecosystems in Botswana (Darkoh & Mbaiwa, 2014). The Okavango Delta, therefore, is a suitable site to analyse the performance of ecotourism.

4. Methodology

This paper used several methods for data collection and analysis: firstly, personal observation, interaction with key people in ecotourism which includes those in government, private sector, and local communities in the Okavango Delta. The author of this paper has also been living and working for over 20 years at the Okavango Research Institute (ORI), University of Botswana. The ORI is devoted to research on the physical and human environment of the Okavango Delta which includes ecotourism development.

Research by this author has focused on tourism development, rural livelihoods, and biodiversity conservation.

Secondly, secondary data were collected from different published and unpublished sources on ecotourism development. Secondary data sources consisted of articles and reports on tourism development in Botswana, particularly those about the Okavango Delta. These include government policy documents, consultancy reports, community-based tourism, and related cultural and wildlife-based tourism reports. Particular consultancy reports used include 'The Status of CBNRM in Botswana up to 2010' and 'The Status of CBNRM in Botswana 2010–2012' prepared by this author for the World Wide Fund. Information derived from these sources includes the evolution and performance of ecotourism in Botswana. Particular attention is paid to the success, failures, and challenges of ecotourism in the Okavango Delta. The data collected provided the basis for analysing the performance of ecotourism development in Botswana.

This paper is largely qualitative in nature. As a result, content or thematic analysis was used to analyse data collected. Thematic analysis involved data reduction into themes and patterns reported. Leininger (1985, p. 60) argues that in thematic analysis, themes are identified by 'bringing together components or fragments of ideas or experiences, which often are meaningless when viewed alone'. The themes that emerge from informants' stories are pieced together to form a compressive picture of their collective experience (Aronson, 1994). Qualitative data collected from secondary sources about ecotourism in the Okavango Delta were also summarised into themes and patterns. This provided an analysis about the performance of ecotourism in the Okavango Delta in the last 30 years. Finally, the limited quantitative data collected were analysed and it involved the production and interpretation of frequencies and tables that describe ecotourism development in Botswana.

5. Results and discussion

Ecotourism in the Okavango Delta has mixed results; that is, some ecotourism projects have collapsed while others have succeeded (Mbaiwa, 2011). The performance of ecotourism in the Okavango Delta is discussed as follows.

5.1. *Community trusts and ecotourism*

As a government prerequisite to participate in ecotourism, communities in the Okavango Delta formed institutions known as Community Trusts. Trusts are formed by communities in order to benefit from natural resources through ecotourism in their local areas (Department of Wildlife and National Parks [DWNP], 1999). Community Trusts implement ecotourism projects on behalf of their communities. The basic aim of a Community Trust is to utilise natural resources (e.g. wildlife) through ecotourism development in their local environment to generate jobs, revenues, and meat for the benefit of community members. Community Trusts are registered legal entities, and are formed in accordance with the laws of Botswana to represent community interests and implement their management decisions in natural resources use. Membership of Community Trusts includes all people who have resided in the respective village for more than five years and are adults of over 18 years (Mbaiwa, 2002; Rozeimejer & van der Jagt, 2000).

The operations of Community Trusts are guided by constitutions which specify, *inter alia*, the memberships and duties of the trusts, powers of the Boards of Trustees, nature of meetings, and resource governance and sanctions of the trusts (Mbaiwa, 2008).

Community Trusts are headed by a Board of Trustees which is considered to be the supreme governing body in each Community Trust. The Board of Trustees is composed of 10 members in most Community Trusts. The Board of Trustees conducts and manages all the affairs of the Trust on behalf of its members. These affairs include signing of legal documents such as leases and contracts with safari companies and maintaining a close contact with the Trust's lawyers. It also keeps Trust records, financial accounts, and reports, and presents them to the general membership at annual general meetings. As a result of its important role, the Board of Trustees is the focal point for important decision-making regarding benefit distribution, business deals with partners, and agreements with support agencies such as donors and non-governmental organisations. The Board of Trustees acts as an intermediary between the government, non-governmental organisations, and their communities on local participation in ecotourism and conservation.

The Board of Trustees is essentially responsible for identifying and putting before the general membership issues that the Board may deem necessary for the furtherance of eco-tourism in their community area. It is also the Board's primary responsibility to implement decisions of the Trust made by the general membership regarding the use of the Trust's property and funds. It is the Board that handles all the ecotourism business aspects of the Trust including applying for permits and licences, as may be required from time to time. At the end of each financial year, the Board is expected to produce and announce to the general membership progress reports and audited financial reports. The financials usually include Trust income and expenditure for the previous year, surplus or deficit resulting from those finances, and lastly a proposed budget for the coming financial year.

The existence of local institutions such as Community Trust makes it possible for collective action in biodiversity conservation and ecotourism development by communities. Local communities make regulations about resource harvesting and monitoring in their respective concession areas. For example, Mbaiwa (2008) notes that communities at Khwai, Sankoyo, and Mababe have agreed among themselves that thatching grass should be harvested when it is dry in the winter season and after it has released seeds. The Trusts work with the village chief to declare the harvesting period at a public gathering known as a *Kgotla*, where dates and the amount of grass to be harvested are prescribed. These conservation regulations are observed by all community members and enforced by community employed 'community resource rangers' known as Community Escort Guides. Those who fail to observe rules agreed upon by the community have their membership and benefits from ecotourism suspended until such a time that the community is satisfied that the culprits have redeemed themselves. Ecotourism in this sense provides the opportunity upon which rules and norms are adopted by local people to achieve effective collective action, monitoring and sanctioning behaviour for those who fail to conform to agreed rules. Ecotourism has therefore enhanced community political capital, in that local communities are now able to make rules and local regulations on natural resource management which previously did not exist. Collective action on resource use through eco-tourism shows that where local institutions exist and are respected within a community, there is likelihood that conservation practices will be observed by all community members provided they derive significant benefits from such resources.

5.2. *Popularity of ecotourism in rural villages*

There is an overwhelming support for ecotourism in rural villages in Botswana and in the Okavango Delta. In 2012, a total of 105 ecotourism registered organisations, and 123 villages with a total population of 283,123 people were found to be involved in ecotourism projects in Botswana (Mbaiwa, 2013). Ecotourism is supported due to the assumption that it will contribute to poverty alleviation in villages (Mbaiwa, 2013). Similarly, in 2006, more than 150 villages in 10 districts/provinces with more than 135,000 people or 10% of Botswana's population were directly involved in ecotourism projects (Schuster, 2007).

In 2012, 105 ecotourism registered Community Trust were actively operating as viable entities, generating revenue, receiving benefits, managing natural resources, or distributing their benefits within the community (Mbaiwa, 2013). The Okavango Delta has about 27% of all the ecotourism projects in Botswana (Mbaiwa, 2013). Most of these ecotourism projects focus on wildlife-based tourism activities. There are several cultural activities such as dug-out canoe (*mekoro*) safaris along the various channels of the Okavango River and cultural lodges and campsites such as Santawani and Shanderika cultural village owned by Sankoyo community (Mbaiwa, 2008). This suggests that rural communities in Botswana perceive ecotourism as an alternative livelihood strategy that can improve their lives. Most of the ecotourism are wildlife based and operating in the Okavango Delta and the Chobe regions (Mbaiwa, 2013).

5.3. *Employment opportunities*

Ecotourism is associated with the creation of employment opportunities and improving rural livelihoods in the Okavango Delta. Between 2011 and 2012, a total of 610 people were employed in 14 ecotourism organisations in the Okavango Delta (Mbaiwa, 2013). Arntzen et al. (2003) note that in 2003 roughly 600 people were employed in ecotourism projects in the Okavango Delta. In 2009, Johnson (2009) notes that a total of 629 people were employed in ecotourism projects in the Delta. In Botswana, ecotourism projects employed 8800 people in 2006 (Schuster, 2007). This shows the importance of ecotourism in the creation of employment opportunities in rural areas.

A significant number of people were employed in ecotourism projects between the 1990s and 2007 in Sankoyo, Khwai, and Mababe villages (Mbaiwa & Stronza, 2010). Mbaiwa and Stronza (2010) note that in Sankoyo, the number of people employed in ecotourism increased from 51 people in 1997 to 105 in 2007. In Mababe, the number increased from 52 in 2000 to 66 people in 2007. In Khwai, the number increased from 5 people in 2000 to 74 people in 2007. This represented a total of 22.8% of people employed in Mababe, 21% in Khwai, and 28% in Sankoyo. Mbaiwa and Stronza argue that these percentages are very high considering the numbers of elderly people, school-going children (under 18 years), and sick and expectant mothers in the villages. In 2007, Manager of Eco tourism projects at Mababe rhetorically remarked, 'Go to Mababe right now and you will find zero unemployment. You will only find old people and children in the village. All the young and strong people are out in camps working'. This indicates that ecotourism is an important economic activity that provides employment opportunities in the Okavango Delta. However, most of the jobs are semi-skilled and involve positions where local people work as cooks, cleaners, storekeepers, and escort guides (Mbaiwa & Stronza, 2010).

The creation of jobs in ecotourism contributes to rural poverty alleviation in the Okavango Delta. Economies and governments around the world aim at full employment for their labour force, likewise ecotourism in the Okavango Delta aims at maximising employment opportunities and improving the rural economy. Local community members employed in ecotourism enterprises financially support their families, thereby raising households' standards of living. Mbaiwa and Stronza (2010) note that households use funds from their wages and salaries from ecotourism employment for various household needs. These include buying food, building houses, buying toiletries and clothes, financially supporting their parents, and helping meet expenses associated with school for children. Some save the income they derive from tourism in the bank for future uses, such as paying dowry, paying school fees, and for household emergencies. Ecotourism therefore has positive aspects on the rural livelihoods in the Okavango Delta.

5.4. *Financial benefits from ecotourism*

In the Okavango Delta, ecotourism revenue is generated from activities such as trophy hunting, photographic tourism activities (game drives, accommodation, food and beverages, etc.), *mokoro* (dug-out canoe) safaris, camping, land rentals, craft production, walking safaris, veld production, meat sales, and other activities such as vehicle hire and donation (Mbaiwa, 2012; Mbaiwa & Stronza, 2010). This income is distributed to individuals, households, and community projects. As shown in Table 1, at a national level, a total of BWP 106,070,219 was generated through various ecotourism activities in the period 2006–2012 (Mbaiwa, 2013).

Over 80% of the ecotourism projects in Botswana are located in the Okavango Delta (Mbaiwa, 2013). An analysis of the total revenue generated by ecotourism projects only in the Okavango Delta between 2010 and 2012 reveals that there has been an increase in total revenue in this period. For example, P16,030,056 was generated in 2010, P13,743,688 in 2011, and P6,360,981 in 2012 (Mbaiwa, 2013). These results suggest that ecotourism generates money for communities. As a result, ecotourism is an economic activity that cannot be ignored in rural communities like in the Okavango Delta.

Although there are arguments that safari hunting is not an ecotourism activity, in Botswana until January 2014 it was undertaken as an ecotourism activity. Trophy hunting generates more income than photographic tourism in Botswana. Between 2006 and 2009, trophy hunting generated P33,041,127, while photographic tourism generated only P4,399,900 (Johnson, 2009). Safari hunting was carried by most of the ecotourism projects in Okavango, resulting in huge amounts of revenue accruing to communities. Safari hunting was carried out after annual aerial surveys were conducted to determine the number of animals to be hunted (Mbaiwa, 2004). In this regard, sustainability was achieved in keeping proper numbers in the veld.

5.4.1. *The use of revenue from ecotourism*

Individuals use revenue generated from ecotourism for different purposes. Income from ecotourism subsequently ends up in households in the form of dividends (Arntzen, 2003;

Table 1.   Revenue from ecotourism projects 2006–2012.

Year	Amount in BWP[a]
2006	8,390,606
2007	16,268,289
2008	16,189,183
2009	11,638,464
2010	18,066,213
2011/2012	35,517,534[b]
Totals	106,070,219

[a]1 US$ = BWP 9.4, 2015 exchange rates.
[b]Data collected from the Department of Wildlife & National Parks did not separate income for 2011 and 2012, hence are reported as provided.
Source: Mbaiwa (2013) and Johnson (2009).

Schuster, 2007). Between 1996 and 2001, each household in Sankoyo village was paid P200; this sum increased to P250 in 2002, P300 in 2003, and P500 in the years 2004, 2005, and 2006 (Schuster, 2007). This income is distributed to each household every October or November. The distribution of income to the various households is an important aspect in improving rural livelihoods and income diversification, in that villagers are able to diversify their existing revenue base.

Some successful communities involved in ecotourism have expanded their tourism business and diversified into other ecotourism projects. For example, Sankoyo has established a 16-bed safari lodge known as Santawani Lodge, a cultural tourism centre called Shandrika where tourists can view the cultural activities and way of life of the people of Sankoyo, and a campsite known as Kazikini (Mbaiwa, 2004). All the communities involved in ecotourism in the Okavango Delta (e.g. Sankoyo, Mababe, Khwai, Seronga, Ditshiping, Daunara, Xaxaba, Gudigwa, Beetsha, Eretsha, and Gunitsoga) use revenue generated from ecotourism to provide social services and develop community development projects. As such, these communities have invested a certain percentage of their funds in physical development projects and into assets that are made accessible to most people in their villages. Most communities involved in ecotourism in the Okavango Delta operate grocery and bottle stores in their villages, own vehicles, have built their own offices, and have access to radios and computers (Arntzen et al., 2003; Mbaiwa, 2008; Schuster, 2007).

Assets owned by the community are bought using communal funds generated from ecotourism enterprises. Schuster (2007) argues that even though vehicles bought by ecotourism projects are meant for business, they are also used for personal reasons such as moving them from one village to the other. Community members can also hire these vehicles to transport their goods. This is yet another important aspect of rural development since most of the villages involved in ecotourism are located in remote areas which are very difficult to access. The availability of transportation due to ecotourism has increased accessibility of these remote villages to big regional towns like Maun. The introduction of television sets, modern computer technology, Internet, and radios in remote villages involved in ecotourism is also an important aspect of rural development that keeps people informed on the latest developments in Botswana and the rest of the world. Ecotourism can therefore be described as an approach that can promote economic development in rural areas of Botswana.

5.5. *Funding social services*

Ecotourism revenue in the Okavango Delta funds several social services. Some services funded include the construction of houses for the needy and orphans, community microcredit schemes, funeral assistance, and the provision of scholarships (Arntzen et al., 2003; Arntzen, Buzwani, Setlhogile, Kgathi, & Motsolapheko, 2007; Mbaiwa, 2013). In relation to micro loan schemes, all community members in respective villages can apply for this loan scheme. There is a committee set up to review the loan applications and make recommendations to the Board. In addition, allowances are paid monthly to elderly and disabled persons. The amount given to household members may vary from year to year depending on the number of the elderly and the disabled. This payment is made twice a year. In 2006, about P110,000 was set aside for the payment of this pension to 36 people; each person received P3055,00 in Sankoyo village (Mbaiwa & Stronza, 2010).

Funeral assistance of P3000 is provided to households that lose a member who is over 16 years; P1000 is given to households that lose members less than the age of 16. At Sankoyo, the total expenditure on funeral assistance was P11,000 in 2002 and increased to P9000,00 in 2005. Villages involved in ecotourism also have funeral policy covers for all community members. The funeral policy cover results in the provision of a casket, transporting the corpse to the burial site, and expenses for food to be eaten during the funeral and time of mourning which usually takes seven days. Ecotourism revenue is used to pay monthly installments at Botswana Life Insurance Company in respective villages.

Water supply and distribution in most rural villages in the Okavango Delta is a challenge. As a result, some of the communities involved in ecotourism have decided to use income generated from ecotourism to make provisions for water supply through boreholes. Mbaiwa and Stronza (2010) note that in 2007, Sankoyo funded the provision of water to 56 out of the 76 households in the village and Mababe funded water for 30 out of the 54 households in the village. The other remarkable social service funded by ecotourism funds in villages is housing, especially for the needy and elderly. In Sankoyo, ecotourism funds led to the construction of 7 houses for the poor; in Khwai 18 were built; 10 were built in Mababe for the elderly and the poor (Mbaiwa & Stronza, 2010). Ecotourism funds also pay a monthly allowance of P200 to orphans and P500 to the elderly twice a year at Sankoyo, Mababe, and Khwai (Mbaiwa & Stronza, 2010). Mbaiwa and Stronza also report that Sankoyo sponsored 14 students to study catering, professional guiding, bookkeeping, and computer studies. Mababe sponsored 20 students and by 2007 Khwai used P250,000 to sponsor 30 students to study tourism-related courses. For the period 2011/2012, Khwai spent P11,000 per death in the village, P100,000 on scholarships, P75,000 on sports, and P91,000 for household dividends (Mbaiwa & Stronza, 2010). Ecotourism therefore has economic benefits to communities in the Okavango Delta. Schuster (2007) argues that ecotourism has transformed some rural communities in the Okavango Delta from being beggars who live on donor agencies and Botswana Government hand-outs into productive communities that are moving towards achieving sustainable livelihoods. Poverty in ecotourism villages was reported to have been high (i.e. 60% of households lived under poverty datum line in the Okavango) before the introduction of ecotourism (CSO, 2008; Mbaiwa, 2005). This changed with the introduction of ecotourism in the Okavango Delta as some households derived socio-economic benefits such as income and employment which improved their livelihoods (Mbaiwa & Stronza, 2010). However, the lack of a mechanism by communities to fairly distribute ecotourism benefits to all households results in some households remaining in poverty despite the fact that their villages derive significant benefits from ecotourism.

5.6.   *Access to land for ecotourism development*

Access to land for ecotourism development is one of the major benefits that remote communities in Botswana have achieved since the 1990s. Before the 1990s, people living in the Okavango Delta did not have access to land for ecotourism development. The Wildlife Conservation Policy of 1986 and Tourism Policy of 1990 laid the foundation for ecotourism development in Botswana. The two policies call for increased opportunities for local communities to benefit from wildlife and natural resources through tourism development (Mbaiwa, 2004). Through the Wildlife Conservation Policy of 1986, land in wildlife areas was subdivided into concession areas for tourism development, while the Tourism Policy of 1990 allows local communities to participate in ecotourism projects (Mbaiwa, 2004). Local communities involved in ecotourism in the Okavango Delta lease concession areas where they build ecolodges and campsites, and carry out ecotourism activities. The zoning of wildlife areas for ecotourism purposes indicates a partial return of custodianship and stewardship of natural resources to local communities. Studies (Bolaane, 2004;

Mbaiwa, 2002) have shown that local people were displaced from resource areas in the Okavango Delta. Access to land by rural communities can be described as local empowerment to natural resource use. The empowerment of local people has the potential to improve rural livelihoods and promote sustainable natural resource use.

5.7. *Ecotourism and conservation*

The introduction of ecotourism has resulted in a reduction in poaching incidents in ecotourism areas as compared to that in non-ecotourism areas (Mbaiwa, Stronza, & Kreuter, 2011). The motivation in the adoption of ecotourism in the Okavango Delta was driven by factors such as the threat of species extinction due to the over-utilisation of resources especially wildlife through poaching, the inability of the state to protect its declining wildlife resources, land-use conflicts between rural communities living in resource areas and resource managers, especially wildlife managers, and the need to link conservation and development (Mbaiwa, 2004). Economic and social benefits contribute to the reduction in poaching levels in ecotourism areas when compared to non-ecotourism areas (Mbaiwa, 2008). For example, almost 17 years after the first ecotourism project began, the DWNP records indicate that illegal hunting decreased throughout the Okavango Delta. That is, recorded incidents of illegal hunting declined from a high of 23 in 1998 to 5 in 2006 (Mbaiwa et al., 2011).

Before ecotourism was adopted in the Okavango Delta, local attitudes were negative towards wildlife conservation. For example, a study by Mbaiwa (1999) covering the villages of Khwai, Sankoyo, and Mababe showed that in 1998, a total of 71.6% of the households derived no benefits from tourism; hence, their attitudes towards tourism were negative. Local people also felt they had no role in resource management and hence could not benefit from it. Similarly, a total of 93.7% of the households in these three villages noted that they had no role in wildlife management and hence saw no need to conserve wildlife resources in their area. Almost a decade later in 2007, a study by Mbaiwa (2008) indicates that the introduction of ecotourism in the Okavango Delta resulted in the reversal of these negative attitudes towards wildlife conservation to become positive. Mbaiwa revealed that attitudes towards tourism and wildlife conservation in the three villages of Khwai, Mababe, and Sankoyo had drastically changed to positive. For example, a total of 94.4% supported tourism in the Okavango Delta, 96.7% noted that they would be happy if a household member works in tourism, while 90% supported wildlife based tourism as a key land-use option in the area. Arntzen et al. (2003) and Mbaiwa (2004) argue that economic benefits from ecotourism and access to land use for ecotourism purposes have resulted in the development of positive attitudes by indigenous communities towards wildlife conservation.

Reduction in poaching is an important aspect of wildlife conservation in the Okavango Delta. Arntzen et al. (2003) argue that even though animal species such as buffalo, lechwe, hippo, and sitatunga are still on decline, there is stability and even an increase in some species. For example, species such as steenbok, impala, and elephant populations have increased by 5% in the last decade (Arntzen et al., 2003). The low rates in wildlife poaching in ecotourism areas show that when local communities begin to derive economic benefits from ecotourism and natural resources in their area, they start putting value on natural resources and use such resources sustainably.

The national government requires ecotourism projects to incorporate biodiversity conservation goals in their constitutions. Communities are also required to produce management plans in which they specify how conservation will be achieved in their ecotourism areas. Communities are also required to provide an annual report on how conservation was achieved in their areas in that particular year. In order to meet conservation objectives in their areas, communities appoint community escort guides to ensure conservation ideals in their areas. Escort guides patrol ecotourism areas and enforce agreed-upon community regulations on environmental management. Schuster (2007) notes that by 2006, 14 Trusts in the Okavango Delta had a total of 111 escort guides to control poaching and ensure compliance with hunting regulations. Escort guides have proved effective in ensuring that poaching is reduced in their respective areas. The effectiveness of escort guides and their desire to conserve resources in their ecotourism areas is demonstrated by their numerous patrols in respective concession areas. Escort guides act like wardens in their respective areas and ensure that rules and regulations aimed at conserving natural resources are observed. This indicates the role communities play in natural resource conservation in their ecotourism areas.

6. Challenges of ecotourism in Botswana

Ecotourism in the Okavango Delta competes with a predominately foreign-owned and well-developed tourism industry described as enclave tourism (Mbaiwa, 2005). These forms of tourism compete for the same natural resources, particularly land, wildlife, and scenic beauty of the area. Enclave tourism and ecotourism also compete for the same clientele who mostly come from developed countries (Mbaiwa, 2005). Foreign-owned companies operating in the Okavango Delta have the needed entrepreneurial skills such as marketing in developed countries where most tourists originate. They also have the management skills and technological know-how which are not readily available among local ecotourism communities. In addition, foreign-owned companies have strong financial capital to establish tourism projects, while local communities lack the necessary funds to compete with them. In this respect, enclave tourism renders ecotourism facilities less attractive when compared with those owned by foreign companies. Ecotourism, therefore, generates less financial benefits when compared with enclave tourism in the Okavango Delta.

Local communities also lack the necessary negotiating business skills when making partnership deals with foreign safari companies. As a result, in most cases local groups get cheated and end up signing partnership deals they do not understand (Mbaiwa, 2008). The lack of entrepreneurship skills has resulted in most communities opting to sub-lease their ecotourism concession areas to foreign safari companies. In areas where there are joint venture partnership between local communities and a tourism company, the expectation by the Government of Botswana is that there would be a transfer of entrepreneurship and management skills from safari operators to the local people (DWNP, 1999). However, the joint venture partnership system is very weak and there has been no significant transfer of entrepreneurial and managerial skills between safari hunting operators and Trusts (Mbaiwa, 2002). This shows that there is no real collaboration and learning between safari companies and communities. This is a major challenge for communities involved in ecotourism in the Okavango Delta.

The misappropriation and mismanagement of ecotourism funds by some individuals especially those in Boards of Trustees is another challenge in the Okavango Delta (Mbaiwa, 2007). For example, in 2000, DWNP (2000, p. 4) noted there was a misappropriation of funds amounting to P12,500 by some members of the Okavango Kopano Mokoro Community Trust in the Okavango Delta. In Khwai village, the Board of Trustees misappropriated about P400,000 between 2002 and 2003. This money was unaccounted for following the audit conducted by Meyer and Associates (Potts, 2003). Potts (2003, p. 4) notes that Khwai board members do not follow proper financial or accounting procedures. He notes that the Khwai Board

> does not have a business or annual work plan-no proper budgeting was done and hence no control over trust finances. Money was just spent in a willy-nilly and haphazard fashion resulting in there being no receipts, supporting documents or paper to follow.

The misuse and poor management of trust funds by the Khwai Board is a reflection of what happens in most ecotourism projects in the Okavango Delta.

There is no mechanism for the fair distribution of benefits derived from ecotourism in most villages in the Okavango Delta (Mbaiwa, 2008). This problem threatens the sustainability of ecotourism projects in the Okavango Delta. The poor distribution of benefits is a result of the poor co-ordination between the ecotourism leadership and the rest of the general membership (Mbaiwa, 2004). For example, at Seronga village, the Board of Trustees is accused of communicating poorly with the wider community (DWNP, 2000). Members accuse the Board of Trustees for running the trusts without much participation of other community members, hence disparities in benefit sharing (Rozemeijer & van der Jagt, 2000). Only the emerging elite who are at the helm of ecotourism management may be benefiting from ecotourism, the majority of community members derive little or no benefits. The distribution of benefits is probably the most crucial component of ecotourism development in the Okavango Delta. It has become a stumbling block for the success of ecotourism as it generates internal conflicts in ecotourism communities. This does not suggest that all ecotourism projects are failing to fairly distribute benefits to members, some particularly Sankoyo are reported to be successful in communicating and distributing benefits to its members (Arntzen et al., 2003).

The ban on safari hunting in January 2014 has affected ecotourism development in the Okavango Delta. A report on ecotourism projects in the Okavango Delta indicates that in 2014, ecotourism projects lost a total of P7 million and 200 jobs due to the hunting ban (Kgamanyane, 2014). Specifically, Mababe had its income drop from P3.5 million to P500,000 – in addition 30 jobs were lost; Sankoyo's income dropped from P3.5 million to P1.8 million, experiencing 35 job losses; Okavango Kopano Mokoro Community Trust's income fell from P4.8 million to P2.5 million and about 40 people lost their jobs. Seronga, Gudigwa, Phuduhudu, and Xaixai projects experienced job losses totaling about 80 jobs (Kgamanyane, 2014). At the time of the ban, Johnson (2009) argued that a possible consequence of the ban on safari hunting tourism could be that communities that have become accustomed to receiving and selling hunting quotas to professional hunting outfitters for large sums of money will not have any sources of income. The ban on safari hunting tourism has resulted in the reduction of income and the loss of jobs and community projects. As such, communities might not be obliged to support ecotourism and wildlife conservation anymore. This therefore is likely to reverse the gains and achievements ecotourism has achieved in the last 30 years in the Okavango Delta.

7. Conclusion

Ecotourism in the Okavango Delta has mixed results, that is, some ecotourism projects succeeded while others collapsed. Ecotourism projects that have succeeded have improved livelihoods in respective villages due to economic benefits that accrue to local communities. These benefits include the creation of employment opportunities, income generation, provision of social services like water reticulation, availability of game meat, scholarships for students in hospitability courses, acquisition of tourism business skills and the establishment of facilities like recreation halls and sponsorships for local sporting activities. Livelihoods were worse off and poverty was higher before ecotourism in some of the villages in the Okavango Delta (Mbaiwa & Stronza, 2010). However, increased benefits from ecotourism have improved the quality of life in remote villages. Ecotourism can, therefore be described as a tool that can be used to achieve improved livelihoods in the Okavango Delta.

Ecotourism in the Okavango Delta also faces several challenges such as the lack of skills in entrepreneurship in tourism development, misappropriation of funds, and the lack of re-investment of funds generated from ecotourism and completion from enclave tourism. In its 30 years of existence in the Okavango Delta, ecotourism has not been able to develop local skills particularly in marketing, management, professional guiding, and apprenticeship. Ecotourism projects rely on foreign skills for marketing and management. Therefore, skill development by local communities needs priority. Joint venture partnerships appear to be a viable option to pursue by communities until such a time when they are equipped with the necessary entrepreneurial skills and capabilities to manage ecotourism enterprises on their own. In this regard, local empowerment particularly training on entrepreneurship and managerial skills in the tourism business should be given priority if ecotourism is to achieve its goals of sustainable livelihoods and conservation of the Okavango Delta.

Prior to the adoption of ecotourism in the Okavango Delta, local communities had negative attitudes towards tourism and conservation. Communities had hostile attitudes towards wildlife and tourism agencies (Mbaiwa, 1999). This was because they did not have a role in resource management, nor were they deriving any economic benefits from natural resources in their local area (Mbaiwa, 1999). However, in areas where ecotourism is implemented, negative attitudes are changing. In the Okavango Delta, ecotourism has been established to meet Ostrom (1990) and Bromley (1992)'s principles of common property resource management, which are the autonomy and recognition of the community as an institution; proprietorship and tenurial rights; rights to make the rules and viable mechanisms to enforce them; and ongoing incentives in the form of benefits that exceed costs. Meeting these principles may be factors that explain the changing positive attitudes of communities towards ecotourism and conservation.

The success of ecotourism in villages such as Khwai, Sankoyo, and Mababe suggests that conservation in the Okavango Delta is achievable with communities at the forefront. As a result of ecotourism benefits, local communities are eager to promote biodiversity conservation in the Okavango Delta (Mbaiwa, 2008). This confirms claims by Mwenya, Lewis, and Kaweche (1991) whose research in Zambia's ecotourism projects argued that successful wildlife conservation is an issue of 'who owns wildlife' and 'who should manage it'. If people view wildlife resources as 'theirs', they realise the benefits of 'owning' wildlife resources, and understand that wildlife management needs to be a partnership between them and the government. This results in communities conserving wildlife species in their areas. Communities in the Okavango Delta recognise that natural resources around them are theirs and they feel obliged to conserve these resources, while at the same time deriving benefits from them through ecotourism development. A similar study by Stronza (2008) in three Amazon countries (Ecuador, Peru, and Bolivia) indicates that ecotourism can be an incentive for conservation, especially when it triggers positive economic change in a community. Stronza argues that ecotourism introduces many changes to communities. Some of the positive changes include opportunities by communities to gain skills and leadership, heightened self-esteem, expanded networks of support, and better organisational capacity in ecotourism development. Stronza (2008) further argues that communities as owners and managers of ecotourism projects note that substantial community involvement fosters greater levels of trust, leadership, and organisation, thus expanding social capital which results in improved livelihoods, and this acts as an incentive for conservation. In Zimbabwe, Child, Jones, Mazambani, Mlalazi, and Moinuddin (2003) argue that environmental benefits of community participation in ecotourism include an increase in wildlife population in areas reserved for ecotourism. Child *et al.* argue that wildlife populations increased by about 50%, with elephants doubling from 4000 to 8000 in ecotourism areas. Child and others thus conclude by noting that when local communities derive economic benefits from ecotourism in their area, they begin putting a higher economic value on natural resources around them and become obliged to conserve such resources.

Finally, if ecotourism has improved livelihoods and biodiversity conservation in parts of the Okavango Delta, this contradicts arguments by scholars (Brandon, 1998; Oates, 1999; Terborgh, 1999) who largely studied in the Americas, and their results argue against community conservation and development programmes and contend that such programmes fail to achieve conservation and livelihood goals. These critics of community programmes call for the return to authoritarian and centralised forms of resource management. However, the contribution of ecotourism to conservation and livelihoods in the Okavango Delta indicates that arguments against community conservation and development programmes might be misleading. Ecotourism perspectives from Zambia (Mwenya et al., 1991) and Amazon (Stronza, 2008) and Zimbabwe (Child et al., 2003) seem to suggest that it is erroneous to pick one failed ecotourism project anywhere in the world and then generalise and conclude that community conservation and development programmes are failing to achieve conservation and livelihoods, as is the case with scholars such as Brandon (1998), Oates (1999), and Terborgh (1999) noted above. Wilshusen, Brechin, Fortwangler, and West (2002) also dismissed arguments that call for government authoritarian practices in resource management because they are made in isolation of the political, social, and economic factors in particular areas and particular projects. Therefore, the case of the Okavango Delta suggests that ecotourism can be an effective tool to achieve conservation and improved livelihoods.

Acknowledgements

I would like to thank all the various participants consulted in the course of the various fieldwork conducted.

Disclosure statement

No potential conflict of interest was reported by the author.

Funding

I would like to thank the Okavango Research Institute, University of Botswana, for funding various research projects which resulted in the production of this manuscript.

References

Arntzen, J., Buzwani, B., Setlhogile, T., Kgathi, D. L. & Motsolapheko, M. K. (2007). *Community-based resource management, rural livelihoods and environmental sustainability* (Unpublished Report). Centre for Applied Research, Gaborone.

Arntzen, J., Molokomme, K., Tshosa, O., Moleele, N., Mazambani, D., & Terry, B. (2003). *Review of CBNRM in Botswana*. Gaborone: Applied Research Unit.

Arntzen, J. W. (2003). *An economic view on wildlife management areas in Botswana* (CBNRM Support Programme Occasional Paper No. 10). Gaborone.

Aronson, J. (1994). A pragmatic view of thematic analysis. *The Qualitative Report, 2*(1), 1–3.

Aylward, B., Allen, K., Echeverria, J., & Tosi, J. (1996). Sustainable ecotourism in Costa Rica: The monteverde cloud forest preserve. *Biodiversity and Conservation, 5*, 315–343.

Bjork, P. (2000). Ecotourism from a conceptual perspective, an extended definition of a unique tourism form. *International Journal of Tourism Research, 2*, 189–202.

Bolaane, M. (2004). The impact of game reserve policy on the river BaSarwa/Bushmen of Botswana. *Social Policy and Administration, 38*(4), 399–417.

Boo, E. (1990). *Ecotourism: The potentials and pitfalls* (Vol. 1 and 2), Washington, DC: World Wildlife Fund.

Boo, E. (1991). Planning for ecotourism. *Parks, 2*, 4–8.

Brandon, K. (1998). Perils to parks: The social context of threats. In K. Redford, K. Brandon, & S. Sanderson (Eds.), *Parks in peril: People, politics, and protected areas* (pp. 415–439). Washington, DC: The Nature Conservancy and Island Press.

Bromley, D. (1992). *Making the commons work*. San Francisco, CA: Institute for Contemporary Studies.

Burnie, D. (1994). Ecotourists to paradise. *New Scientist, 1942*, 23–27.

Cater, E. (1994). Ecotourism in the third world – Problems and prospects for sustainability. In E. Cater & G. Lowman (Eds.), *Ecotourism: A sustainable option?* (pp. 69–86). Chichester: John Wiley & Sons.

Ceballos-Lascurain, H. (1996). *Tourism, ecotourism, and protected areas: The state of nature-based tourism around the world and guidelines for its development*. Cambridge: IUCN.

Central Statistic Office (CSO). (2008). *Poverty map of Botswana*. Gaborone: Ministry of Finance and Development Planning.

Central Statistic Office (CSO). (2011). *Population and housing census of 2011*. Gaborone: Ministry of Finance and Development Planning.

Chi, Y., & Luzar, E. J. (1998). An economic analysis of non-consumptive wildlife recreation expenditures. *Louisiana Rural Economist, 60*, 8–11.

Child, B., Jones, B., Mazambani, M., Mlalazi, A., & Moinuddin, H. (2003). *Final evaluation report: Zimbabwe natural resources management program-USAID/Zimbabwe*. Harare: USAID.

Darkoh, M. B. K., & Mbaiwa, J. E. (2014). Okavango Delta – A Kalahari Oasis under environmental threats. *Journal of Biodiversity & Endangered Species, 2*(2), 4. Retrieved from http://dx.doi.org/10.4172/2332-2543.1000138

Davis, D., & Tisdell, C. A. (1998). Tourist levies and willingness to pay for a whale shark experience. *Tourism Economics, 5*(2), 161–174.

Department of Environmental Affairs (DEA). (2008). *Okavango Delta Management Plan of 2008*. Gaborone: Author, Ministry of Environment, Wildlife and Tourism, Government Printer.

Department of Tourism. (2002). *Botswana national ecotourism strategy of 2002*. Gaborone: Author, Government Printer.

Department of Wildlife and National Parks (DWNP). (1999). *Joint venture guidelines*. Gaborone: Author.

Department of Wildlife and National Parks (DWNP). (2000). *CBNRM progress report for 2000*. Gaborone: Author.

Dowling, R. K. (2000). Developing ecotourism into the millennium. *International Journal of Tourism Research, 2*, 203–208.

Durbin, J. C., & Ratrimoarisaona, S. N. (1996). Can tourism make a major contribution to the conservation of protected areas in Madagascar? *Biodiversity and Conservation, 5*, 345–353.

Goodwin, H. (1996). In pursuit of ecotourism. *Biodiversity and Conservation, 5*, 277–291.

Gössling, S. (1999). Ecotourism: A means to safeguard biodiversity and ecosystem functions? *Ecological Economics, 29*, 303–320.

Groombridge, B. (1992). *Global biodiversity*. London: Chapman & Hall.

Gumbricht, T., & McCarthy, T. S. (2002, December 4–8). Hierarchical processes and patterns sustaining the Okavango: An integrated perspective for policy and management. In T. Bernard, K. Mosepele, & L. Ramberg (Eds.), *Environmental monitoring of tropical wetlands, proceedings of a conference in Maun, Botswana*. (pp. 181–195). Maun: Harry Oppenheimer Okavango Research Centre.

Gurung, C. P., & De Coursey, M. (1994). The Annapurna conservation area project: A pioneering example of sustainable tourism? In E. Cater & G. Lowman (Eds.), *Ecotourism: A sustainable option?* (pp. 177–194). Chichester: John Wiley & Sons.

Hoyt, E. (1996). Whale watching: A global overview of the industry's rapid growth and some implications and suggestions for Australia. In K. Colgan, S. Prasser, & A. Jeffery (Eds.), *Encounters with whales, 1995 proceedings* (pp. 31–36). Canberra: Australian Nature Conservation Agency.

Honey, M. (2008). *Ecotourism and sustainable development: Who owns paradise?* (2nd ed.). Washington, DC: Island Press.

Jepson, P., & Canney, S. (2001). Biodiversity hotspots: Hot for what? *Global Ecology and Biogeography, 10*, 225–227.

Johnson, S. (2009). *State of CBNRM report 2009* (Botswana National CBNRM Forum). Gaborone, Botswana.

Kgamanyane, J. (2014, December 22). Hunting ban causes 200 job losses. *The Weekendpost.*

King, D. A., & Stewart, W. P. (1996). Ecotourism and commodification: Protecting people and places. *Biodiversity and Conservation, 5*, 293–305.

Krüger, O. (2005). The role of ecotourism in conservation: Panacea or pandora's box? *Biodiversity and Conservation, 14*, 579–600.

Leader-Williams, N. (2002). Animal conservation, carbon and sustainability. *Philosophical Transactions of the Royal Society of London Series A: Mathematical, Physical and Engineering Sciences, 360*, 1787–1806.

Leininger, M. M. (1985). Ethnography and ethnonursing: Models and modes of qualitative data analysis. In M. M. Leininger (Ed.), *Qualitative research in nursing* (pp. 33–72). Orlando, FL: Grune & Stratton.

Loon, R. M., & Polakow, D. (2001). Ecotourism ventures: Rags or riches? *Annals of Tourism Research, 28*(3), 892–907.

Mbaiwa, J. E. (1999). *Prospects for sustainable wildlife resource utilization and management in Botswana: A case study of east Ngamiland District* (M.Sc. thesis). Department of Environmental Science, University of Botswana, Gaborone.

Mbaiwa, J. E. (2002, July 2002). *The socio-economic and environmental impacts of tourism development in the Okavango Delta, Botswana: A baseline study* (144 pp.). Maun: Harry Oppenhiemer Okavango Research Centre.

Mbaiwa, J. E. (2003). The socio-economic and environmental impacts of tourism development on the Okavango Delta, north-western Botswana. *Journal of Arid Environments, 54*(2), 447–468.

Mbaiwa, J. E. (2004). The success and sustainability of community-based natural resource management in the Okavango Delta, Botswana. *South African Geographical Journal, 86*(1), 44–53.

Mbaiwa, J. E. (2005). Enclave tourism and its socio-economic impacts in the Okavango Delta, Botswana. *Tourism Management, 26*(2), 157–172.

Mbaiwa, J. E. (2007). The success and sustainability of consumptive wildlife tourism in Africa. In: B. Lovelock (Ed.), *Tourism and the consumption of wildlife: Hunting, shooting and sport fishing* (pp. 141–154). London: Routledge.

Mbaiwa, J. E. (2008). The realities of ecotourism impacts in Botswana. In: A. Spancency (Ed.), *Responsible tourism: Critical issues for conservation and development* (pp. 205–224). London: Earthscan.

Mbaiwa, J. E. (2011). Changes on traditional livelihood activities and lifestyles caused by tourism development in the Okavango Delta, Botswana. *Tourism Management, 32*(5), 1050–1060.

Mbaiwa, J. E. (2012). *CBNRM status report of 2010–12*. Gaborone: Kalahari Conservation Society.

Mbaiwa, J. E. (2013). *CBNRM status report of 2012/13*. Gaborone: Kalahari Conservation Society.

Mbaiwa, J. E., & Stronza, A. L. (2010). The effects of tourism development on rural livelihoods in the Okavango Delta, Botswana. *Journal of Sustainable Tourism, 18*(5), 635–656.

Mbaiwa, J. E., Stronza, A. L., & Kreuter, U. P. (2011). From collaboration to conservation: Insights from the Okavango Delta, Botswana. *Society and Natural Resources, 24*(4), 400–411.

McNeely, J. A., Miller, K. R., Reid, W. V., Mittermeier, R. A., & Werner T. B. (1990). *Conserving the world's biological diversity.* Washington, DC: World Bank.

Mittermeier, R., Myers, N., & Mittermeier, C. G. (2000). *Hotspots: Earth's biologically richest and most endangered terrestrial ecoregions.* Washington, DC: Conservation International.

Mwenya, A. N., Lewis, D. M., & Kaweche, G. B. (1991). *Policy, background and future: National parks and wildlife services, new administrative management design for game management areas.* Lusuka: United States Agency for International Development.

Myers, N., Mittermeier, R. A., Mittermeier, C. G., da Fonseca, G. A. B., & Kent, J. (2000). Biodiversity hotspots for conservation priorities. *Nature, 403*, 853–858.

Oates, J. (1999). *Myth and reality in the rainforest: How conservation strategies are failing West Africa*. Berkeley: University of California Press.

Orme, C. D. L., Davies, R. G., Burgess, M., Eigenbrod, F., Pickup, N., Olson, V. A., ... Owens, P. F. (2005). Global hotspots of species richness are not congruent with endemism or threat. *Nature, 436*, 1016–1019.

Ostrom, E. (1990). *Governing the commons: The evolution of institutions for collective action*. New York, NY: Cambridge University Press.

Place, S. E. (1991). Nature tourism and rural development in Tortuguero. *Annals of Tourism Research, 18*, 186–201.

Potts, F. (2003). *Khwai development trust – A short case study* (11 pp.). Maun: Eco-tourism Support Services.

Rozemeijer, N., & Van der Jagt, C. (2000). *Community based natural resource management in Botswana: How community based is community based natural resource management in Botswana* (Occasional Paper Series). Gaborone: IUCN/SNV CBNRM Support Programme.

Ruschmann, D. V. D. M. (1992). Ecological tourism in Brazil. *Tourism Management, 13*, 125–128.

Schuster, B. (2007). *Proceedings of the 4th national CBNRM conference in Botswana and the CBNRM status report*, November 20–23, 2006. Gaborone: IUCN Botswana.

Stiles, G. F., & Clark, D. A. (1989). Conservation of tropical rain forest birds: A case study from Costa Rica. *American Birds, 43*(3), 420–428.

Stronza, A. (2008). Through a new mirror: Reflections on tourism and identity in the Amazon. *Human Organization, 67*(3), 244–257.

Terborgh, J. (1999). *Requiem for nature*. Washington, DC: Island Press.

Tlou, T. (1985). *History of Ngamiland: 1750–1906: The formation of an African state*. Gaborone: Macmillan.

Valentine, P. (1993). Ecotourism and nature conservation. A definition with some recent developments in Micronesia. *Tourism Management, 14*(2), 107–115.

Wall, G. (1997). Is ecotourism sustainable? *Environmental Management, 21*, 483–491.

Wearing, S., & Neil, J. (1999). *Ecotourism: Impacts, potentials and possibilities*. Oxford: Butterworth Heinemann.

Wheeller, B. (1992). Is progressive tourism appropriate? *Tourism Management, 13*, 104–105.

Wight, P. (1996). North American ecotourists: Market profile and trip characteristics. *Journal of Travel Research, 34*, 2–10.

Wilshusen, P. R., Brechin, S. R., Fortwangler, C. L., & West, P. C. (2002). Reinventing a square wheel: Critique of a resurgent "protection paradigm" in international biodiversity conservation. *Society Natural Resources, 15*, 17–40.

World Commission on Environment and Development (WCED). (1987). *Our common future*. Oxford: Oxford University Press.

Ecotourism implementation in the Kakum Conservation Area, Ghana: administrative framework and local community experiences

Patrick Brandful Cobbinah, Rosemary Black and Rik Thwaites

School of Environmental Sciences, Institute for Land Water and Society, Charles Sturt University, Albury, NSW, Australia

In principle ecotourism should support environmental conservation and local development; however, achieving success in delivering on frequently competing objectives of conservation and development has often proven difficult in many ecotourism destinations in Africa. This paper focuses on the implementation of ecotourism in the Kakum Conservation Area (KCA), the most popular ecotourism destination in Ghana. It examines the current administrative framework for implementing ecotourism, and the involvement and experiences of ecotourism by communities around the KCA. A case study research method was adopted using in-depth interviews with local residents and relevant park and non-governmental organisation agency staff. Findings indicate that the implementation of ecotourism is not recognised by the park officials as a process requiring negotiation between stakeholders with different agendas. Thus, the current ecotourism administrative framework does not acknowledge community involvement and participation as relevant to the implementation of ecotourism in the KCA which has generated mixed experiences among the local residents.

Introduction

Research has shown that ecotourism is one of the necessary and important strategies for delivering both environmental conservation and socio-economic development outcomes in host destinations in Africa (Cobbinah, Black, & Thwaites, 2013; Spenceley & Snyman, 2012). However, past and recent experiences generate concerns about the lack of explicit attention devoted to understanding the process of implementing ecotourism. While some scholars have taken up this issue from a theoretical perspective (Donohoe & Needham, 2006; Ross & Wall, 1999), it appears that many important questions and obstacles persist. For example in Africa, very little attention has been given to understanding the administrative framework for implementing ecotourism especially in protected areas that would help to focus efforts on achieving a balance between environmental conservation and local development. Likewise, there has been only limited research on the operationalisation of the theoretical objectives of ecotourism in host communities (Coria & Calfucura, 2012; Stone & Wall, 2004).

This paper responds to calls from many authors (Coria & Calfucura, 2012; Donohoe & Needham, 2006; Ross & Wall, 1999) for further research into the implementation of eco-tourism in developing countries. Focusing on Africa, the paper examines the process of implementing ecotourism in the Kakum Conservation Area (KCA), the most popular eco-tourism destination in Ghana. The first part of the paper evaluates the existing administrative framework – that is, the management structure – used for implementing ecotourism in the KCA. The authors acknowledge previous studies that have described the ecotourism administrative framework in the KCA (Appiah-Opoku, 2004, 2011). Unfortunately, none of these studies analysed the implications of the existing administrative framework on sustainable implementation of ecotourism in the KCA, in terms of responding to local development needs and meeting environmental conservation targets. This paper therefore describes and analyses the administrative framework in terms of its ramifications on sustainable implementation of ecotourism. The paper then examines how host communities are involved in ecotourism implementation in the KCA and finally explores their experiences regarding the process of implementing ecotourism in the KCA.

Ecotourism activities aimed at stimulating local development and managing the natural environment present some challenges to both policy-makers and stakeholders. According to The International Ecotourism Society (TIES) (2013), ecotourism is defined as responsible travel to natural areas which seeks to conserve the environment and sustain the well-being of the local communities. By its very nature, ecotourism is a complex activity to implement and manage because it often involves competing goals of environmental conservation and local development, and multiple stakeholders (Courvisanos & Jain, 2006; Ezaki & Bricker, 2012; Weaver, 2001). Ecotourism implementation requires a framework that engages with the multiple actors and agencies to deliver widespread outcomes to meet the goals of conservation and development. Worldwide, there are claims of ecotourism activities that have led to improved livelihoods of host communities by reducing poverty levels, stimulating growth and empowering local people (Chhetri & Lama, 2012; Epler Wood, 2002; Scheyvens, 1999).

Unfortunately, Cattarinch (2001) argues that in many cases, ecotourism activities in developing countries tend to favour only one of ecotourism's goals, environmental conservation, which tends to inadvertently exclude other goals (e.g. local development) leading to unintended and often unwelcome consequences such as increased deprivation in host communities. In other cases, host communities especially in Africa have experienced continuous neglect and lack of involvement in ecotourism activities that have reduced their interest in ecotourism (Bediako, 2000; Charnley, 2005). In such situations, the future of ecotourism becomes uncertain as its multiple goals of conserving the environment and promoting local development are put at risk.

Ecotourism in Africa should not be regarded as simply an environmental conservation strategy, because it often affects the livelihoods of individuals, lifestyle of communities and operations of businesses. For example, ecotourism in Africa largely occurs in protected areas and directly influences the livelihoods of host communities dependent on natural resources (Akyeampong, 2011; Asiedu, 2002; Cobbinah, 2015; Cobbinah, Black, & Thwaites, 2015). Thus, ecotourism as an activity must contend with multiple, conflicting and frequently poorly understood sociocultural values and spatio-temporal concerns of host communities, which are necessary in conserving the environment and stimulating local development. Regrettably, Bediako (2000) observes that ecotourism activities occurring in protected areas across Africa are often politically motivated and initiated, and do not provide opportunities for addressing local development challenges such as unemployment.

Since the popularity of ecotourism in the 1980s, research has indicated a mismatch between the theoretical objectives of ecotourism as reported in the literature and its implementation on the ground (Coria & Calfucura, 2012; Stone & Wall, 2004). A number of host communities in Africa remain in poverty partly due to poor implementation of ecotourism leading to leakage of returns and limited involvement of host communities (Charnley, 2005; Lindberg & Enriquez, 1994). According to Donohoe and Needham (2006), if ecotourism activities are not designed to respond to the concept's theoretical objectives of involving the local community, and delivering environmental and socio-economic benefits, they may jeopardise 'the natural environment upon which such experience directly depends, the natural ethics upon which the activity is conceptualised and the legitimacy of the ecotourism industry' (p. 193). In such situations, it will be difficult to realise the multiple goals of environmental conservation and local development in Africa. The purpose of this paper is to contribute to understanding the process of ecotourism implementation in Africa using a case study in Ghana.

Literature review

Importance of ecotourism to developing countries: Why implementation remains a challenge?

The ecotourism literature continues to evolve, with a steady shift from the importance placed on the environmental conservation objective only (Ceballos-Lascurain, 1987), to achieving sustainable development, in relation to environmental conservation, social inclusion and economic development (Baral, 2013; Donohoe & Needham, 2006; Fennell, 2008; Honey, 2008; Scheyvens, 1999; Spenceley & Snyman, 2012). According to Honey (1999), ecotourism has been hailed globally as a strategy for achieving the multiple goals of conservation and local development in poor countries, especially in Africa for a number of reasons. First, ecotourism generates direct employment for unskilled, semi-skilled and skilled labour (Coria & Calfucura, 2012; Spenceley & Snyman, 2012). Many people, especially those in host communities, may be employed in direct ecotourism projects, as boat drivers, waiters, tour guides and hospitality staff in hotels. For example, a study by United Nations Environment Programme (UNEP) (2001) revealed that over 40% of local people in the vicinity of Hol Chan Marine Reserve in Belize benefit from ecotourism economically.

Second, research (Chhetri & Lama, 2012; Pradhan, 2001) has shown that ecotourism projects empower the disadvantaged in society, such as women and young people, by opening economic and management roles for them, ranging from income generating activities to decision-making. For example, in the Annapurna Conservation Area in Nepal, women have been employed in ecotourism activities (Pradhan, 2001). Pradhan (2001) indicates that the occupational involvement of local women in ecotourism has been exemplary and has become a source of inspiration for several villages across Nepal. In addition, Chhetri and Lama (2012), using the successful operation of '3 Sisters Adventure Trekking' in Nepal, claim that ecotourism has contributed to women's empowerment through training and mentoring of village women to become trekking professionals.

Third, other scholars (Kruger, 2005; Scheyvens, 1999) have reported that ecotourism is more likely to lead to stewardship of natural resources when locals gain some measure of control, and share equitably in the benefits of ecotourism. This, according to Kruger (2005) and Scheyvens (1999), is fundamental to conservation efforts, since participation by host communities remains central to conservation and a key to ecotourism success (Courvisanos

& Jain, 2006). An analysis by Stronza and Gordillo (2008) further indicates that, in some cases, ecotourism can promote local ownership and management of resources, which can lead to new learning and greater cohesion in host communities. Examples in Africa include Rwanda's mountain gorillas (Honey, 1999) and the Communal Areas Management Programme for Indigenous Resources (CAMPFIRE) in Zimbabwe (Frost & Bond, 2008).

Despite these potential benefits, some previous studies (Landell-Mills & Porras, 2002; Sarrasin, 2013; Stone & Wall, 2004) have raised a number of concerns about the negative effects of ecotourism in host communities. The first concern is the limited socio-economic benefits to host communities (Sarrasin, 2013; Stone & Wall, 2004). While the literature acknowledges the potential multiple economic returns of ecotourism (Stronza & Gordillo, 2008), the United Nations World Tourism Organisation (UNWTO) (2002) explains that the benefits are often inadequate to offset the negative effects such as limited engagement of host communities. As a result, few communities have realised significant benefits, often due to limited stakeholder involvement and lack of programme evaluation (Landell-Mills & Porras, 2002). In Africa, the Ngorongoro Conservation Area in Tanzania is an example where the Maasai community has received limited benefits from ecotourism, owing to a lack of policy direction and weak institutions (Charnley, 2005).

The second concern is that ecotourism in protected areas can generate negative environmental effects when it is poorly implemented, including pollution, depletion of natural resources, and through the physical impacts of ecotourism development and the activities of tourists (Roberts & Thanos, 2003; World Wildlife Federation, 2001). Such negative effects may damage the vegetation cover, and result in the general destruction of the natural environment (Farrell & Marion, 2002; Ormsby & Mannie, 2006).

Drawing from the above discussion, it is true that, in a variety of contexts, ecotourism can indeed deliver widespread benefits in terms of environmental conservation and local development. Moreover, these reported benefits can quite easily be spread to multiple stakeholders, including conservation agencies and host communities. However, ecotourism research in developing countries particularly Africa has often raised a number of concerns, including leakage of ecotourism returns, environmental degradation and limited involvement of host communities, which mainly revolve around poor implementation. In these situations, it is difficult for host communities to experience the full benefits of ecotourism as espoused in its theoretical objectives. In evaluations of ecotourism activities in Africa, it is often common for researchers to emphasise the contributions and limitations of ecotourism to poverty reduction, environmental conservation or local development. However, this understanding of ecotourism based on its contributions and limitations often ignores the process of ecotourism implementation. It is therefore important to understand the process of delivering the ecotourism experience in order to appreciate the kind of outcomes being experienced. This paper addresses this issue by examining the process of implementing ecotourism in the KCA in Ghana, and the experiences of host communities.

Ecotourism in Ghana

With its location in West Africa within the tropical region, Ghana shares boundaries with Cote d'Ivoire to the west, Togo to the east, Burkina Faso to the north and to the south by the Gulf of Guinea. As illustrated in Figure 1, Ghana is endowed with diverse ecotourism resources, including national parks, historical sites and game reserves (Akyeampong, 2011; Asiedu, 2002; Cobbinah, 2015; Cobbinah et al., 2015; Tamakloe, 2000), which are mostly found in rural areas and many remain undeveloped.

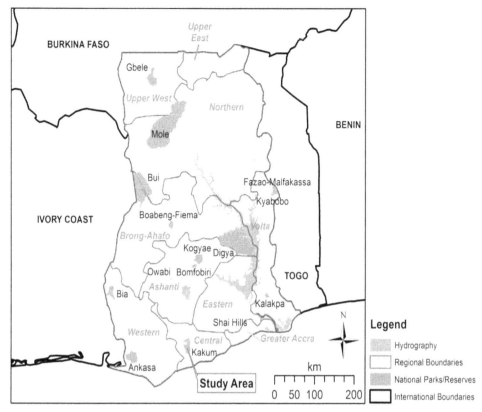

Figure 1. (Colour online) Major ecotourism attractions in Ghana.
Source: Charles Sturt University Spatial Analysis Unit (2013).

While it is worth noting that these ecotourism resources present an opportunity to advance environmental conservation and local development initiatives in host destinations, recent research has identified multiple challenges facing Ghana's ecotourism sector including limited recognition of ecotourism as a sustainable local development tool, and inadequate community involvement (Akyeampong, 2011; Akyeampong & Asiedu, 2008; Asiedu, 2002; Bediako, 2000). According to Bediako (2000), the ecotourism sector is accorded low priority in the national development framework, particularly by the Ghana Wildlife Division (GWD), the agency in charge of managing natural areas in Ghana. Some of the resulting and well-established outcomes of limited commitment to ecotourism development are the poor quality and inadequate provision of tourist services and infrastructure and lack of environmental interpretation (Akyeampong & Asiedu, 2008; Asiedu, 2002). The low commitment to destination development in rural communities, in Asiedu's (2002) view, means that ecotourism has not achieved its potential to promote local development. Asiedu (2002) asserts that the development of these ecotourism destinations and associated tourism activity has the potential to spread direct and indirect benefits across the country, which could result in improvements in the living conditions of host communities.

In many cases, a widespread recognition of ecotourism in protected areas in Ghana as government initiated and owned has limited the involvement and participation of host communities. According to Bediako (2000), this has often resulted in community disillusionment over limited involvement in, and outcomes of ecotourism activities. Previous studies (Asiedu, 1998; Haligah, 1998) indicate that the resulting community disillusionment frequently tends to threaten environmental conservation efforts because of negative conservation behaviours such as poaching, illegal logging and apathy on the part of local people that often arise. This problem of limited involvement of host communities and its associated community disillusionment in Ghana put at risk the theoretical objectives of ecotourism and can lead to local disinterest among the host communities (Asiedu, 2002).

Study location and methods

Characteristics of case study location

The KCA, covering a land area of 360 km^2, is located about 30 km north of Ghana's Central Regional capital, Cape Coast (Cobbinah, 2015; Cobbinah et al., 2015). The KCA is endowed with faunal diversity with mammals such as elephants and potto; species of primates such as black and white colobus; reptiles such as dwarf crocodile; and a total of 266 bird species and about 405 species of butterflies (International Union for Conservation of Nature [IUCN], 2010). In 1992, the KCA was legally gazetted as a national park and resource reserve by the Wildlife Reserves Regulations (Ll 1525) under the administrative jurisdiction of the GWD. The KCA was established to protect the watersheds of the Kakum River and other rivers which supply the water needs of Cape Coast and surrounding communities (IUCN, 2010), and to restore and maintain the integrity of the rapidly diminishing rainforest reserve (Appiah-Opoku, 2011; Conservation International [CI], 1998).

With the assistance of Conservation International (CI) non-governmental organisation (NGO), ecotourism was introduced in 1995 to facilitate the management of the KCA and support local development (1998). Ecotourism development started with the construction of a canopy walkway in the western part of the KCA by the Government of Ghana and the CI in 1995 and the establishment of a tree platform in the eastern part of the KCA by the GWD in 2000. Since the introduction of ecotourism, tourist visitation to the canopy walkway in the KCA has increased over the past decade (Table 1).

Table 1.   Tourist visitation to the KCA canopy walkway (2000–2012).

Year	Domestic tourists	International tourists	Total visitation
2000	34,350	15,410	49,760
2001	35,825	19,201	55,026
2002	54,198	16,917	71,115
2003	36,874	16,597	53,471
2004	44,962	17,866	62,828
2005	45,292	18,697	63,989
2006	67,949	40,385	108,334
2007	80,771	31,538	112,309
2008	87,418	34,301	121,719
2009	117,686	33,198	150,884
2010	118,385	36,752	155,137
2011	129,747	29,009	157,610
2012	141,477	29,656	171,133

Source: GHCT Records, February 2014.

Other community ecotourism attractions, such as a craft village, the traditional bamboo orchestra, the bee-keeping centre and the monkey sanctuary, have developed outside the reserve to leverage off the KCA in-park developments. Unlike the attractions in the KCA, tourist visitation data for the community attractions are poor due to limited and intermittent tourist visitation. For the purpose of this research, attractions located in the KCA and the community are referred to as KCA ecotourism and community ecotourism, respectively.

Research methods

A case study method was used for the research. This method presents a comprehensive understanding and an in-depth analysis of a contemporary phenomenon being investigated, and allows for the collection of data from multiple sources (Babbie, 2007; Yegidis & Weinbach, 2009; Yin, 2002). The primary technique of data collection used in this research included semi-structured interviews ($n = 6$ interviewees), in-depth interviews ($n = 20$ interviewees), secondary data analysis and participant observations. Data collection was carried out at community and institutional levels in two phases focusing on relevant agencies and individuals related to the research.

At the institutional level, semi-structured interviews were used to collect background information on ecotourism, with representatives of six agencies: GWD responsible for the management of the KCA; Ghana Heritage Conservation Trust (GHCT) responsible for ecotourism activities in the KCA; CI who were key contributors to the design and development of ecotourism facilities in the KCA; Ghana Tourism Authority (GTA) responsible for tourism policy implementation and product marketing; Department of Hospitality and Tourism Management (DHTM) of the University of Cape Coast (UCC), a key contributor to tourism research in the KCA; and the Central Region Development Commission (CEDECOM), in charge of the socio-economic and physical development of the Central Region of Ghana. The interviews were conducted in English and lasted between 45 and 120 minutes depending on the agency officials' interest, knowledge and experience with ecotourism.

At the community level, although the KCA has over 100 communities bordering it (Dei, 2000), only communities with ecotourism attractions (Akyeampong, 2011), and located within the range of 1–10 km around the Conservation Area (Appiah-Opoku, 2011), were considered for this paper. As a result, two communities, namely Abrafo and Mesomagor, were selected as case study areas to provide a diversity of experience in relation to ecotourism. As presented in Table 2, Abrafo community provides major corridor to the KCA, and has a number of ecotourism attractions, while Mesomagor community has a community-based ecotourism attraction and also serves as the eastern entry to the KCA.

Figure 2 shows the location of the case study communities.

Consultation with community leaders was held during the introductory visit to the case study communities which presented an opportunity for the community leaders to update the

Table 2. Reasons for the selection of case study communities.

Case study communities	Reason for selection
Abrafo	Major entry to the KCA canopy walkway, and the location of the craft village, bee-keeping centre and monkey sanctuary
Mesomagor	Eastern entry to the tree platform in the KCA, and the availability of the traditional bamboo orchestra attraction

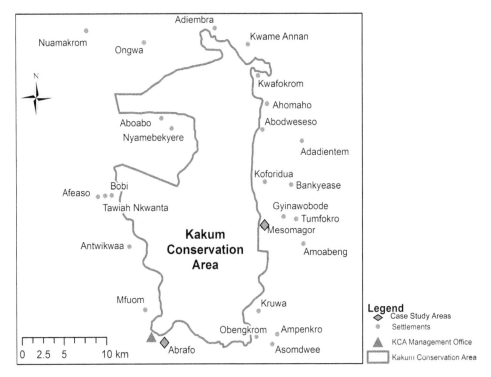

Figure 2.   (Colour online) Location of case study communities.
Source: Adapted from Appiah-Opoku (2011).

researchers about the state of their community's development and response to ecotourism. Following consultation with community leaders which led to the identification of those involved in, and concerned about, ecotourism in the communities, in-depth interviews were conducted with 10 residents from each of the 2 communities. The selection was based on their understanding and experiences with ecotourism projects and socio-economic conditions (Table 3) using a purposive sampling method (Guarte & Barrios, 2006). Given that one of the researchers is a native of the study region, the interviews were conducted in a local language (Fanti) and translated into English, and lasted between 60 and 120 minutes depending on the knowledge, experience and interest of the respondents. Interview findings were further compared with the findings from the agency semi-structured interviews. For instance, the findings from the community in-depth interviews informed the design of the agency semi-structured interviews, and the selection of relevant agencies to be involved in the research. This ensured the involvement of agencies with adequate understanding and knowledge of ecotourism in the KCA.

Two field trips were conducted to collect the primary data. The first in April to July 2012 sought to gather a broad range of data from the communities and agencies on ecotourism and its influence in the host communities. Following the analysis of these data, a confirmatory field work was undertaken in February to March 2014 which sought further explanation of ecotourism implementation, and addressed gaps and inconsistencies that had occurred during the initial data analysis. The results from the first field research process were presented to the agencies, while the local residents were engaged in informal community meetings in each of the two case study communities. The presentation to the six

Table 3. Socio-economic characteristics of community respondents.

Community	Sample (20)		Education (%)				Occupation (%)					Average monthly income (GH¢)
	Male	Female	N	P	JH	SH	KCA	CE	A	SOB	U	
Abrafo	5	5	34	12	31	23	6	11	51	18	14	126
Mesomagor	6	4	39	54	5	2	4	19	70	2	5	62

Notes: N, Never; P, primary level; JH, junior high school level; SH, senior high school level; KCA, ecotourism in the KCA; CE, community ecotourism; A, agriculture; SOB, self-owned business; U, unemployed.
Source: Field Survey, April to July 2012.

relevant agencies lasted for 60 minutes followed by a discussion. The agency representatives sought clarification on some of the findings, which further allowed the researchers to probe for explanations. All six agency representatives attended the presentation at the UCC, in addition to some tourism academics from UCC. Again, the agency representatives were guaranteed confidentiality for the data provided for this research.

The average time for the community meetings was two hours, which allowed the local people to ask questions on, and provide further explanations to major issues raised during the first field visit in 2012. About 15–25 local residents from each of the two case study communities participated in the community meetings. The researchers reiterated the confidentiality of the data provided by the community residents for this research. The confirmatory research was very useful, as it strengthened the results and ensured the research process was robust. In addition to the primary data, secondary data such as tourist visitation records and the KCA management plan were collected from various agencies involved in ecotourism in the KCA.

Interview transcripts and secondary data were analysed through an inductive and deductive coding process (Rubin & Rubin, 2005), facilitated by the use of the NVIVO 10 programme. Codes and categories were developed based on the interview transcripts. Guided by the inconsistencies that might arise in the analysis process (Bryman & Burgess, 1994), relationships were established by merging and refining codes and categories into more conceptual categories based on common relationships. This process ensured that the research participants' perceptions and experiences of ecotourism were reflected in the final categories.

Results

Framework for implementing ecotourism in the KCA

Although previous studies on ecotourism in the KCA have described the administrative framework for implementing ecotourism (Appiah-Opoku, 2004, 2011), they failed to analyse the implications of the existing framework on the sustainable development of ecotourism in terms of engaging with local communities and supporting conservation efforts. This section describes and analyses the ecotourism framework, in terms of its usefulness in achieving sustainable implementation of ecotourism in the KCA, and other ecotourism destinations in Africa.

A review of GWD and GHCT ecotourism documents reveals a clearly defined administrative framework for implementing ecotourism in the KCA. The framework has two components: a day-to-day management component and a marketing component. The GWD and the GHCT are responsible for the day-to-day management component. The

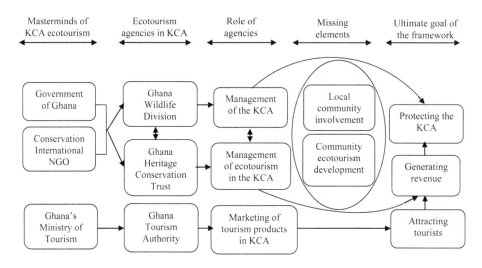

Figure 3.   Ecotourism administrative framework in the KCA.

GWD is responsible for managing the KCA, while the GHCT, a non-profit NGO, estab-lished by the CI manages ecotourism in the KCA on behalf of the Government of Ghana to generate funds for the management of the KCA. The GHCT has, thus, been collaborating with the GWD to manage the KCA, and are locally referred to as 'park officials'. Both the GWD and the GHCT are accountable to the Government of Ghana, while the GHCT further reports to the CI. Figure 3 shows the ecotourism framework with missing elements in the KCA.

The marketing component of the ecotourism administrative framework is undertaken by the GTA. A review of GTA documents (e.g. development plans) indicates that ecotourism marketing forms part of the role of the GTA under Ghana's Ministry of Tourism, but does not have a local/district level office. As a consequence, although ecotourism attractions in the KCA are marketed to both domestic and international tourists by the GTA, the agency is not involved in the day-to-day management of ecotourism in the KCA. In addition, although Ghana's Ministry of Tourism is responsible for the overarching ecotourism policy for protected areas in Ghana and the development of community tourism attractions, agency interviews show that there is a lack of a cohesive plan to ensure that the attraction of the KCA is linked to developing community ecotourism opportunities and resources. Responsibilities in relation to ecotourism development in the KCA appear to be fragmented among a number of agencies, and there is no one agency responsible for implementing eco-tourism as a whole. While this may not be a challenge in some African countries such as South Africa, agency interview results revealed that this situation has negatively affected ecotourism implementation in the KCA, and other destinations in Ghana such as the Mole National Park. For example, the agencies (GTA, GHCT and GWD) involved in eco-tourism implementation in Ghana particularly in the KCA operate under different govern-ment ministries with different interests and agendas. This, in the view of the DHTM official, prevents the realisation of the multiple goals of ecotourism:

> ... All tourism sites in Ghana have different administrative structures with different roles and under different ministries, which is wrong. There are vested interests and those vested interests have mother responsibilities, which the agencies are keen in achieving ... Given that some of

the agencies don't have tourism as a core function [e.g. GWD], for them tourism is not a priority .... (DHTM, February 2014)

The apparent responsibility vacuum in relation to ecotourism implementation in the KCA and many destinations in Ghana has resulted in a lack of local/district planning process to link the attractions in the KCA to the community ecotourism attractions at the perimeter of the Conservation Area. In many cases, the agency interviewees perceived ecotourism activities as only occurring in the KCA, and thus they are the responsibility of the GWD and not the host communities; however, the GWD does not have tourism as a core business. Ultimately, what often goes unrealised in the KCA ecotourism administrative framework is the lack of involvement of host communities and other stakeholders such as academics, which is a sign of failure of ecotourism implementation. For this reason, Segbefia (2008) has advocated that, for ecotourism implementation and all other forms of tourism in Ghana to be meaningful and successful, it should involve the local communities, and provide a platform for tourists to engage more with them and experience their culture. In this sense, the process of implementing ecotourism may deliver benefits to the local communities, ensure intercultural experiences and stimulate local support towards conservation.

In addition, the international community such as the United Nations (UN) has argued that tourism development, particularly in developing countries, cannot be detached from the environment and the host communities and their cultural experiences (2003). Regrettably, a common perception and recognition by both the agencies and the host communities is that the KCA is a national facility rather than a locally managed facility that seems to account for the exclusion of host communities in ecotourism implementation:

> ... Kakum is not a community-based ecotourism project. Kakum has a national and international recognition because of national government support and increasing international research and interests ... it is therefore difficult for the local communities to be directly involved in ecotourism implementation .... (GHCT, May 2012)

One key finding of this research is that the ecotourism implementation framework in Ghana particularly in the KCA is problematic and does not promote sustainable implementation of ecotourism, despite its acceptance and use over the past decades (Appiah-Opoku, 2004, 2011). Regardless of these implementation challenges, the above quote gives an indication that some local people are employed in ecotourism in the KCA. The next section examines the characteristics of those involved in ecotourism.

Ecotourism implementation: local community involvement

Within the two case study communities, interview results show that an individual's involvement in ecotourism is largely determined by his/her attitude towards, perception of, and the benefits derived from ecotourism in the KCA. This reflects a common trend in many ecotourism destinations in Africa such as the Rwanda's mountain gorilla (Honey, 1999) and Zimbabwe's CAMPFIRE (Frost & Bond, 2008). As a result, job opportunities appear to be one of the most important economic benefits of ecotourism. Thus, community and agency interviewees were asked to outline and explain the conditions or requirements for involving/employing people in the KCA (canopy walkway and tree platform) and community (bamboo orchestra, bee-keeping centre, monkey sanctuary and craft village) ecotourism projects.

Community and agency interviews reveal that the requirements for working in ecotourism activities in the KCA and at the community level are different. The GHCT official explained that the minimum condition for working in the KCA canopy walkway is a basic school certificate, although some workers (e.g. cleaners) are employed without any qualification. However, as illustrated in Table 3, many of the local people in these communities are illiterate and do not have this level of education. As a result, although ecotourism in the KCA requires only a limited number of employees (40), those employed are not only from the host communities but also from other parts of the Central Region. Moreover, the lack of qualifications among community members around the KCA has become an impediment to assuming supervisory positions for the few local people employed:

> ... We have few of our workers from Cape Coast and other places ... the problem with the communities around the park is that many of those who come seeking for jobs, have never been to school. And you know what we do here it's all about interacting with tourists, how can such people be able to communicate or explain things to tourists? (GHCT, May 2012)

Whilst the park officials (GWD and GHCT) explained the conditions, and the difficulty in engaging more local people, findings from the community meetings during the confirmatory research phase revealed that the residents are unhappy with the situation, especially with the small numbers of local people employed:

> ... Just consider the number of communities around the park, so if you employ 20 people, what have you done? (Abrafo community meeting, February 2014)

In contrast, although there appear to be no specific qualifications or requirements for working in community ecotourism, community interview results show that participation is mainly dependent on an individual's interest and commitment. For example, Mesomagor residents explained that the only requirement for joining the traditional bamboo orchestra is an interest in the orchestra, and a personal commitment to the group. Nonetheless, community interviews show that only indigenes of Mesomagor are involved, and are mainly youth (20–49 years). The leader of the orchestra commented that:

> ... It is true that this group is made up of about 25 local people, but that doesn't mean it belongs to the members or the leader. This cultural group is for the community ... those who are willing to join especially the young ones are always welcome .... (Mesomagor 2, June 2012)

In the Abrafo community, residents reported that there are no specific requirements for engaging people in community ecotourism. However, agency interviews reveal that attempts have been made by the Government of Ghana and other development partners to provide support for local residents who lost their livelihoods as a result of the gazettal of the KCA:

> ... If you take the craft village in Abrafo, the purpose was to engage community people who are jobless partly because of the park .... (CEDECOM, July 2012)

Agency and community interviews identify no specific political, social or economic factors characterising those involved in ecotourism, both in the KCA and at the community level. As discussed earlier in this section, involvement of people in ecotourism activities is based on individuals' education and willingness. The GHCT official said that:

... If it's about job, there is nothing like your political affiliation or your status in your community, if you qualify and there is room, we will employ you . . . . (GHCT, May 2012)

Overall, analysis of community and agency interviews shows that basing involvement in community ecotourism on an individual's willingness rather than educational qualifications seems to have encouraged the participation of more local people. In contrast, the illiteracy rate in the host communities, coupled with the small numbers of employees required in ecotourism, appears to be limiting more local people from being employed in the KCA ecotourism. With different requirements regarding ecotourism employment in the KCA and at the community level, it is important to understand the local communities' experiences with the implementation of ecotourism. These are presented in the next section.

Ecotourism implementation: experiences of the local residents

Abrafo community's experience with ecotourism implementation

Abrafo residents reported that the canopy walkway in the KCA provides employment for local people as tour guides and cleaners, and also creates opportunities for the community to engage with tourists who visit the facility:

> ... We [Abrafo] are happy having the canopy walkway close to our community ... Some of our people work there and also some of the tourists visit our community so we get the opportunity to interact with, and sell some of our farm produce to them . . . . (Abrafo 2, April 2012)

In addition, interviews with Abrafo residents identified the craft village, the bee-keeping centre and the Frami monkey sanctuary as attractions in the Abrafo vicinity. Residents indicated that the craft village has provided jobs for some local people, who have received training in creative skills (e.g. bead making):

> ... In this community, one of the few job opportunities you can talk about is the craft village. It is at this place that you will see men and women who are skilled in craft work. They are involved in all sorts of products which provide them with income . . . . (Abrafo 3, April 2012)

However, discussions with some craft village workers identified several factors challenging the activities of the craft village, including low patronage of products by tourists because of poor marketing in terms of tourist knowledge of the existence of the craft village in Abrafo. Other interviewees also explained that some tourists do not patronise crafts made out of wood because of the negative impact on deforestation. One worker explained that:

> ... Less than 5 percent of the tourists who visit the canopy walkway come here, we don't have a good market. We used to produce so many assorted products here but now, only few workers are in the village because of low patronage. This is really affecting our activities and we want government to support us . . . . (Abrafo 9, April 2012)

The above quote suggests that the craft village is barely functional and the workers expect the government to help them revive the craft village. However, agency interviews show that the low patronage is a result of the weak relationship and lack of collaboration between the park officials and the craft village. As a consequence, despite the opportunities the craft village provides, regarding jobs and training of local people in creative skills, residents expressed mixed feelings regarding their experience with the facility because of the low patronage and its dysfunctional state. In contrast to the experiences with the craft village,

Abrafo interviewees (seven out of ten) identified strong community connection to the bee-keeping centre because of its dual role: supporting the development of the local community and sustaining environmental conservation:

> ... We have some people from this community who work there ... Also, the activities of the bee-centre don't disturb us and the environment in any way ... . (Abrafo 7, April 2012)

This perspective was reinforced by the majority of agency representatives (five out of six), who identified a number of training programmes (e.g. farm management practices) organised by the bee-keeping centre for the local farmers and agricultural extension officers, to improve their agricultural productivity, while conserving the environment. It would appear that Abrafo residents have developed a strong connection to the bee-keeping facility, despite the small number of tourists it attracts, possibly because of the benefits (e.g. training) the facility provides to the local community. However, the residents do not have any connection with the monkey sanctuary because of its foreign (European) ownership and management, as well as the employment of few residents. Some Abrafo interviewees (four out of ten) were unhappy with the European dishes (e.g. sandwiches) which are served at the restaurant instead of local food. As explained by an Abrafo interviewee, in his view, this situation does not promote local culture and development:

> ... Because they [European owners] are here to make profit from their investment, they do what will benefit them not the local people ... Can you imagine that the foods that are served at the restaurant are European? You will go there and they will serve you sandwiches and other food from Holland. How do you expect the local farmers to benefit from such a facility? (Abrafo 4, April 2012)

However, further clarification from the agencies (e.g. GHCT and DHTM) reveals that the activities of the monkey sanctuary are mainly influenced by the operational capacity of the facility and the demand by tourists. The GHCT official said that:

> ... If the community complain about few people being employed there [Frami monkey sanctuary], we understand, even ecotourism in the KCA employs just a few people ... But that's the number of people the facility can employ at a time, if there is a possibility of future expansion, they will employ more local people. The fact that it is owned by foreigners doesn't mean they will intentionally employ few local people when their capacity to operate requires more ... We should also understand that the facility serves tourists with different tastes and preferences ... so they will serve food or drinks that the tourists want ... . (GHCT, May 2012)

Mesomagor community's experience with ecotourism implementation

In Mesomagor, the community interview data identify the tree platform in the KCA and the traditional bamboo orchestra as the major ecotourism attractions. As explained earlier, the tree platform was established in 2000 by the GWD and has since developed as an important destination for tourists in the Kakum region, especially at the eastern part of the KCA. Describing the relevance of the tree platform to the Mesomagor community, local residents (six out of ten) said that it has become a symbol that reminds the community of its commitment to support the conservation of the KCA:

> ... For us in this community, the tree platform always makes us renew our commitment to protect the park because it supports the development of our traditional bamboo orchestra and provides jobs for some of our people ... . (Mesomagor 5, June 2012)

142

The above quote suggests a strong community connection to this ecotourism experience. Discussions with the local community further revealed that a tour to the tree platform is regarded by Mesomagor residents as an educational and enjoyable expedition for both tourists and the local tour guides. Some residents (four out of ten) indicated that local tour guides teach tourists about the variety of plant species, their uses and relevance in traditional medicine, as well as tracking wildlife in the KCA. As a result, there is a strong local connection to the tree platform in Mesomagor, as it reinforces their cultural values and knowledge.

In addition, Mesomagor residents indicated that the traditional bamboo orchestra entertains tourists who visit the tree platform with traditional music, ensuring they enjoy their stay, while they learn about the traditions of the community:

> ... Our cultural group makes tourists who visit here happy and creates a platform for us to teach the tourists about our traditions .... (Mesomagor 1, June 2012)

The DHTM official also emphasised the significance of the traditional bamboo orchestra, and the strong community connection to it, and further described it as a 'perfect model of community-based ecotourism':

> ... Mesomagor is the only success story of a community-based ecotourism ... Their bamboo orchestra serves as an important attraction for tourists who visit the tree platform ... Every community member, whether directly involved or not, is proud of the group. It's a legacy that binds the community together ... Should you visit there now, everyone will be talking about the bamboo orchestra ... that's the kind of love the community has developed towards the bamboo orchestra. Because of that all the benefits also stay in the community .... (DHTM, June 2012)

Comparing ecotourism experiences in Abrafo and Mesomagor

Analysis of the community interviews shows stark differences between Abrafo and Mesomagor residents' views regarding their experiences with ecotourism implementation in and outside the KCA. The above findings show that all ecotourism attractions within the vicinity of the Abrafo community were either introduced by the Government of Ghana (e.g. craft village), NGOs (e.g. canopy walkway) or private investors (e.g. monkey sanctuary). Despite the existence of local cultural attractions such as festivals in the Abrafo community, they have not been developed into ecotourism attractions. Findings from the Abrafo interviews indicate that the residents lack confidence in initiating, planning and developing local ecotourism attractions:

> ... We are all poor in this community. How can we invest in tourism when we don't have money to take care of our families? The government should help us to develop our attractions so that many tourists can visit us .... (Abrafo 1, April 2012)

Abrafo residents have a strong connection to and positive experience with the bee-keeping centre, because the facility employs local people and provides support and opportunities to the community. However, they expressed mixed reactions regarding their experience with the craft village, possibly because it is locally owned and they lack the confidence to take planning and management decisions, as they expect the government to be supporting them. Abrafo residents may lack this confidence, but the confirmatory research phase found that collaboration remains a key challenge to ecotourism development in Abrafo particularly the dysfunctional craft village. Findings from Abrafo community meetings and agency presentations show that the lack of collaboration between the park officials and the community ecotourism facilities such as the craft village and the bee-keeping centre has resulted in low tourist visitation to the community attractions, despite increasing tourist numbers to the canopy walkway. Thus, although the Abrafo community remains a major point of entry into the KCA and has many community ecotourism attractions compared to Mesomagor, residents expressed concerns with the limited socio-economic benefit of ecotourism to the community.

On the other hand, Mesomagor residents have capitalised on the presence of tourist visits to the tree platform in the KCA by developing the traditional bamboo orchestra without any government support. An examination of the Mesomagor interviews shows that key factors underlying the success of ecotourism have been the availability of a guest house constructed with the support of an NGO, and committed and supportive community residents. As reported by Mesomagor residents, the strong community connection to, and greater experience with ecotourism are due to a number of factors including the recognition of the traditional bamboo orchestra as a symbol of unity, the employment and income opportunities, the collaboration between the park officials and community in managing the tree platform, and the community pride derived from delivering these ecotourism products as a result of their interactions with tourists. Thus, ecotourism, particularly the traditional bamboo orchestra, is highly valued by Mesomagor residents, compared to the situation in Abrafo.

In essence, the experience of the Mesomagor community in relation to ecotourism implementation has shown that ecotourism in itself does not necessarily deliver positive experiences, but requires careful planning, management and collaboration. The communities around the KCA and other parts of Ghana and Africa can take advantage of opportunities available to them to develop ecotourism attractions without necessarily depending on the government. The success of ecotourism in Mesomagor is mainly contingent on the community's initiative and commitment, strong leadership of the bamboo orchestra and collaboration with the park officials. The Mesomagor experience provides some lessons for successful ecotourism implementation especially for the agencies. The results suggest that community involvement, collaboration and engagement are key to ecotourism implementation.

Discussion and conclusion

This research demonstrates that administrative framework for implementing ecotourism remains key to the success of ecotourism especially in protected areas. In the context of the KCA, the ecotourism administrative framework is flawed, as it fails to recognise ecotourism implementation as a process that centres on the participation of the various stakeholders especially host communities. As a result, the framework does not recognise the importance of community involvement and participation in ecotourism implementation in the KCA particularly the canopy walkway. However, previous research (Drumm & Moore, 2002; Petrovska, Reckoski, & Reckoska, 2009) has emphasised the importance of stakeholder engagement in ecotourism implementation. For example, Drumm and Moore (2002) argued that a key to the success of ecotourism planning and implementation is the establishment of strong relationships among stakeholders, to ensure that multiple ecotourism goals relating to environmental conservation and local development are met. It is in recognition of the relevance of local community involvement that the UN (2003) indicated that the planning and implementation of ecotourism, and all other forms of tourism development, cannot be separated from the host communities and their cultural experiences.

Regrettably, this understanding does not appear to exist among agencies in the KCA, as community involvement and collaboration are not recognised by the park officials and NGOs as relevant to ecotourism implementation in the KCA especially the canopy walkway. As presented in Figure 3, the ecotourism administrative framework in the KCA shows that park officials and NGOs operating in the region of the KCA are adopting the term ecotourism as a means to promote environmental conservation and generate revenue but under the banner of promoting ecotourism as a sustainable local development strategy. As a result, there is poor collaboration between the park officials and the host communities particularly Abrafo, in terms of developing community ecotourism attractions. In addition, it would seem from the interview results that while the majority of these agencies (e.g. CI and GWD) have the agenda of conservation at heart, the government through the GHCT has a revenue generation agenda. For example, CI and GWD are recognised globally and nationally, respectively, as conservation-focused agencies and are therefore pursuing ecotourism because it can deliver environmental conservation benefits. They therefore do not necessarily recognise and pursue the agenda of ecotourism as a sustainable development model that responds to the needs of host communities. This finding supports Bediako's (2000) claim that ecotourism in Ghana is accorded low priority by the GWD, possibly because ecotourism is not a primary interest of the agency.

This research has demonstrated that implementation of ecotourism considerably depends on strong administrative framework that responds to the needs of multiple stakeholders to achieve multiple socio-economic and environmental conservation outcomes. Ecotourism implementation cannot be regarded as a homogenous process but rather as a complex political process of negotiations between different interest groups seeking to influence the outcome to achieve their agendas. Thus, implementation of ecotourism in Ghana and Africa in general cannot be considered as an objective or altruistic enterprise.

Despite the poor administrative framework for implementing ecotourism in the KCA, the findings have shown that some local people are involved in ecotourism both in and outside the KCA. While the condition for involving people in ecotourism in the KCA is a minimum of a basic school education, community ecotourism requires individual willingness. Although the park officials claimed that illiteracy among the local communities has affected the number of people employed in the KCA ecotourism particularly the canopy walkway, Abrafo interviewees were unhappy with the situation reporting that the park officials do not consider local development as a priority in ecotourism implementation. However, Mesomagor residents, recognising the tourism potential of the KCA, have developed their culture as an ecotourism attraction, and further developed positive relations with the park officials in managing tourist visitation to the tree platform. The commitment of the Mesomagor residents, and the pride they derive from delivering this tourist experience, underlies the success of ecotourism implementation in this community.

The Mesomagor community's experience supports the theory that effective ecotourism implementation can generate employment opportunities, encourage interactions between tourists and local people and afford a deeper intercultural experience. Therefore, the experience of the Mesomagor community, in terms of engaging with, and benefiting from the process of ecotourism implementation in the KCA, could be replicated in the other communities around the KCA and other ecotourism destinations in Ghana and other African countries, so that ecotourism may deliver widespread benefits in terms of environmental conservation and local development. However, the role of park officials, in terms of reforming the KCA ecotourism administrative framework by involving local communities, remains central to ensuring effective ecotourism implementation. The involvement of community representatives in ecotourism in the KCA may lead to a reflection of local ideas in ecotourism implementation and increase awareness among local communities in relation to supporting environmental conservation and maximising tourism potential of the KCA by linking community attractions to the KCA ecotourism facility.

Acknowledgements

This paper forms part of a Ph.D. research with funding from a PhD Writing-Up Award from the Charles Sturt University, Australia. The authors acknowledge the contribution of Mr Simon McDonald for providing the maps used in this article. We honour the contributions of the anonymous referees of this journal for their insightful and constructive comments.

Disclosure statement

No potential conflict of interest was reported by the authors.

Funding

This paper was funded by PhD Writing-Up Award from the Charles Sturt University, Australia. The authors are grateful to Charles Sturt University for the award.

References

Akyeampong, O. A. (2011). Pro-poor tourism: Residents' expectations, experiences and perceptions in the Kakum National Park area of Ghana. *Sustainable Tourism, 19*(2), 197–213.

Akyeampong, O. A., & Asiedu, A. B. (Eds.). (2008). *Tourism in Ghana, a modern synthesis*. Accra: Assemblies of God Literature Centre Limited.

Appiah-Opoku, S. (2004). Rethinking ecotourism: The case of Kakum National Park in Ghana. *African Geographical Review, 23*, 49–63.

Appiah-Opoku, S. (2011). Using protected areas as a tool for biodiversity conservation and ecotourism: A case study of Kakum National Park in Ghana. *Society and Natural Resources, 24*(5), 500–510.

Asiedu, A. B. (1998). An overview of issues in domestic tourism promotion in Ghana. *Legon Journal of Humanities, 11*, 67–84.

Asiedu, A. B. (2002). Making ecotourism more supportive of rural development in Ghana. *West African Journal of Applied Ecology, 3*, 1–16.

Babbie, E. (2007). *The practice of social research* (11th ed.). Belmont, CA: Thomson Higher Education.

Baral, N. (2013). Evaluation and resilience of ecotourism in the Annapurna Conservation Area, Nepal. *Environmental Conservation, FirstView*, 1–9. doi:10.1017/S0376892913000350

Bediako, V. J. (2000). *Sustainable ecotourism development in Ghana: A case study of the Kakum National Park* (MPhil thesis). Department of Geography, Norwegian University of Science and Technology, Trondheim, Norway.

Bryman, A., & Burgess, R. (1994). *Analysing qualitative data*. London: Routledge.

Cattarinch, X. (2001). *Pro-poor tourism initiatives in developing countries: Analysis of secondary case studies*. London: Overseas Development Institute, International Institute for Environment and Development (IIED) and Centre for Responsible Tourism.

Ceballos-Lascurain, H. (1987). The future of ecotourism. *Mexico Journal, January*, 13–14.

Charles Sturt University Spatial Analysis Unit. (2013). *Major ecotourism attractions in Ghana*. Albury: Charles Sturt University.

Charnley, S. (2005). From nature tourism to ecotourism? The case of the Ngorongoro conservation area, Tanzania. *Human Organisation, 64*(1), 75–88.

Chhetri, L., & Lama, W. B. (2012). Breaking gender barriers: A market-based approach to women's empowerment through tourism. In K. S., Bricker, R., Black, & S. Cottrell (Eds.), *Sustainable tourism and the millennium development goals: Effecting positive change* (pp. 115–126). Burlington, MA: Jones & Bartlett Learning.

CI. (1998). *Creating solutions for the 21st century: Annual report.* Washington, DC: Conservation International NGO.

Cobbinah, P. B. (2015). Local attitudes towards natural resources management in rural Ghana. *Management of Environmental Quality: An International Journal, 26*(3), 423–436. doi:10. 1108/MEQ-04-2014-0061

Cobbinah, P. B., Black, R., & Thwaites, R. (2013). Tourism planning in developing countries: Review of concepts and sustainability issues. *International Journal of Social, Education, Economics & Management Engineering, 7*(4), 468–475.

Cobbinah, P. B., Black, R., & Thwaites, R. (2015). Biodiversity conservation and livelihoods in rural Ghana: Impacts and coping strategies. *Environmental Development.* doi:10.1016/j.envdev.2015. 04.006

Coria, J., & Calfucura, E. (2012). Ecotourism and the development of indigenous communities: The good, the bad and the ugly. *Ecological Economics, 73*, 47–55.

Courvisanos, J., & Jain, A. (2006). A framework for sustainable ecotourism: Application to Costa Rica. *Tourism and Hospitality Planning & Development, 3*(2), 131–142.

Dei, L. A. (2000). Community participation in tourism in Africa. In P. U. C. Dieke (Ed.), *The political economy of tourism development in Africa* (pp. 285–295), New York, NY: Cognizant Communication.

Donohoe, H. M., & Needham, R. D. (2006). Ecotourism: The evolving contemporary definition. *Journal of Ecotourism, 5*(3), 192–210.

Drumm, A., & Moore, A. (2002). An introduction to ecotourism planning. In A. Drumm & A. Moore (Eds.), *Ecotourism development – a manual for conservation planners and managers* (Vol. 1, pp. 11–54). Arlington, VA: The Nature Conservancy.

Epler Wood, M. (2002). *Ecotourism: Principles, practices and policies for sustainability.* UNEP. New York, NY: United Nations.

Ezaki, A., & Bricker, K. S. (2012). The International Ecotourism Society: A brief history. In K. S. Briker, R. Black, & S. Cottrell (Eds.), *Sustainable tourism and the millennium development goals: Effecting positive change* (pp. xxi–xxv). Burlington, MA: Jones and Bartlett Learning.

Farrell, T., & Marion, J. (2002). The protected area visitor impact management (PAVIM) framework: A simplified process for making management decisions. *Journal of Sustainable Tourism, 10*(1), 31–51.

Fennell, D. A. (2008). *Ecotourism* (3rd ed.). London: Routledge.

Frost, P. G. H., & Bond, I. (2008). The CAMPFIRE programme in Zimbabwe: Payments for wildlife services. *Ecological Economics, 65*, 776–787.

Guarte, J. M., & Barrios, E. B. (2006). Estimation under purposive sampling. *Communications in Statistics – Simulation and Computation, 35*(2), 277–284.

Haligah, I. (1998). *The underutilised tourist resources at the Kalakpa resource reserve* (BA (Honours) thesis). Department of Geography and Resource Development, University of Ghana, Legon, Accra.

Honey, M. (1999). *Ecotourism and sustainable development: Who owns Paradise?* Washington, DC: Island Press.

Honey, M. (2008). *Ecotourism and sustainable development: Who owns Paradise?* (2nd ed.). Washington, DC: Island Press.

IUCN. (2010). *Parks and reserves in Ghana; management effectiveness assessment of protected areas.* Gland: Author.

Kruger, O. (2005). The role of ecotourism in conservation: Panacea or Pandora's box? *Biodiversity and Conservation, 14*, 579–600.

Landell-Mills, N., & Porras, I. (2002). *Silver bullet or fools' gold? A global review of markets for forest environmental services and their impact on the poor.* London: IIED.

Lindberg, K., & Enriquez, J. (1994). *An analysis of ecotourism's economic contribution to conservation and development in Belize: A report* (Vol. 2, p. 82). Washington, DC: World Wildlife Fund.

Ormsby, A., & Mannie, K. (2006). Ecotourism benefits and the role of local guides at Masoala National Park, Madagascar. *Journal of Sustainable Tourism, 14*(3), 271–287.

Petrovska, E., Reckoski, R., & Reckoska, G. (2009). Participants in the ecotourism activity and eco-tour planning. *TOURISMOS: An International Multidisciplinary Journal of Tourism, 4*(4), 259–272.

Pradhan, H. (2001). *Sustainable mountain development through ecotourism* (PhD dissertation). Asian Institute of Technology, Bangkok.

Roberts, J. T., & Thanos, N. D. (2003). *Trouble in paradise: Globalisation and environmental crises in Latin America*. New York, NY: Routledge.

Ross, S., & Wall, G. (1999). Ecotourism: Towards congruence between theory and practice. *Tourism Management, 20*, 123–132.

Rubin, H. J., & Rubin, I. S. (2005). *Qualitative interviewing: The art of hearing data* (2nd ed.). Thousand Oaks, CA: Sage.

Sarrasin, B. (2013). Ecotourism, poverty and resources management in Ranomafana, Madagascar. *Tourism Geographies: An International Journal of Tourism Space, Place and Environment, 15*(1), 3–24.

Scheyvens, R. (1999). Ecotourism and the empowerment of local communities. *Tourism Management, 20*, 245–249.

Segbefia, A. Y. (2008). Community approach to tourism development in Ghana. In O. Akyeampong & A. B. Asiedu (Eds.), *Tourism in Ghana: A modern synthesis* (pp. 54–68), Accra: Assemblies of God Literature Centre Limited.

Spenceley, A., & Snyman, S. (2012). High-end ecotourism's role in assisting rural communities in reaching the millennium development goals. In K. S. Bricker, R. Black, & S. Cottrell (Eds.), *Sustainable tourism & the millennium development goals: Effecting positive change* (pp. 89–106). Burlington, MA: Jones & Bartlett Learning.

Stone, M., & Wall, G. (2004). Ecotourism and community development: Case studies from Hainan, China. *Environmental Management, 33*(1), 12–24.

Stronza, A., & Gordillo, J. (2008). Community views of ecotourism. *Annals of Tourism Research, 35*(2), 448–468.

Tamakloe, W. (2000). *State of Ghana's environment – challenges of compliance and enforcement* (pp. 1–3). Accra: Environmental Protection Agency.

TIES. (2013). *Fact sheet: Global ecotourism*. The International Ecotourism Society, Size of Global Ecotourism.

UN. (2003). *Poverty alleviation through sustainable tourism development*. Bangkok: United Nations Economic and Social Commission for Asia and the Pacific.

UNEP. (2001). Industry and environment. *Ecotourism and Sustainability, 24*, 3–4.

UNWTO. (2002). *The world ecotourism summit* (final report). Madrid: Author.

Weaver, D. B. (2001). *The encyclopedia of ecotourism*. Wallingford: CABI.

World Wildlife Federation. (2001). *Guidelines for community-based ecotourism development*. Retrieved August 12, 2011, from: http://assets.panda.org/downloads/guidelinesen.pdf

Yegidis, B. L., & Weinbach, R. W. (2009). *Research methods for social workers*. New York, NY: Pearson Education.

Yin, R. K. (2002). *Case study research, design and methods* (3rd ed.). Newbury Park, CA: Sage.

Factors that influence support for community-based ecotourism in the rural communities adjacent to the Kgalagadi Transfrontier Park, Botswana

Naomi Moswete[a] and Brijesh Thapa[b,c]

[a]Department of Environmental Sciences, University of Botswana, Gaborone, Botswana;
[b]Department of Tourism, Recreation & Sport Management, University of Florida, Gainesville, FL, USA; [c]Department of Tourism Management, Tshwane University of Technology, Pretoria, South Africa

Community-based tourism (CBE) has become an important livelihood option for rural communities in Botswana. The growth of CBE has been facilitated via community-based natural resources management initiatives that have yielded positive and tangible benefits to some regions more than others. The south-western region of the country lacks the level of tourism development of other areas, but has the opportunity to capitalise via CBE based on Kgalagadi Transfrontier Park area. Given the paucity of information and research on CBEs in the region, there is a dire need for additional baseline data. This study empirically explored knowledge, concern, perceptions of and support for CBE among residents living adjacent to the Transfrontier Park. Data were collected via a semi-structured questionnaire among 746 households in 9 villages. Results highlight the diverse array of factors that were likely to influence residents' perception and support of CBE development in the area. In addition to descriptive analysis, two models were tested via hierarchical regression to examine the factors that influence residents' support for CBE development. Overall, four independent variables were important predictors of residents' CBE support with environmental being the most important factor followed by economic, socio-cultural, and knowledge of ecotourism. This study contributes to the emerging literature in the region, as well as assists policy-makers, planners, and other stakeholders with respect to what should be considered when assessing the communities for CBE development.

Introduction

Ecotourism has become an important tool for numerous developing countries to aid in economic development, environmental protection, and preservation of cultural environments (Honey, 1999; Nyaupane & Thapa, 2004; Reid, 1999; Snyman, 2012; Stronza, 2007). This form of tourism is considered a better development and management strategy with the potential to alleviate the negative effects of mass tourism (Fennell, 2003; Parker & Khare, 2005; Reid, 1999; Scheyvens, 1999). In addition, the key values of sustainability, cultural sensitivity, education, and responsibility have led to the recognition of ecotourism as a prominent resource to resolve socio-economic concerns of destination communities (Weaver, 2002; Wood, 2002).

In the past few decades, ecotourism has also been recognised as one of the fastest growing tourism market segments in various countries within sub-Saharan Africa (Sidinga, 1999; United Nations World Tourism Organization, 2011). The promotion of eco-tourism has been based on it being small-scale, low-impact, and community-oriented with benefits accrued at the local community (Fennell, 2003; Government of Botswana [GOB], 2007; Hancock & Potts, 2002; Honey, 1999; Saarinen, Becker, Manwa, & Wilson, 2009; Scheyvens, 1999). The growth of ecotourism, especially community-based tourism (CBE), has been advocated and implemented in the sub-Saharan African region (e.g. Bots-wana, Namibia; South Africa, Kenya, Tanzania, Uganda, and Zambia) to actively involve communities residing in the periphery of protected areas, and to enhance citizen income power (Botswana Tourism Organisation, 2008; Jones, 2005; Lepp, 2004; Murphree, 2001; Nelson, 2004; Saarinen, 2011; Spenceley, 2008; Suich, 2010).

It has been identified that CBE activities that occur in and around protected areas have generated substantial revenues to the national economy and to local communities (Mugisha, 2002; Ormsby & Mannie, 2006; Snyman, 2013). For example, most employment opportu-nities in the northern parks and reserves in Botswana are attributable to tourism (Botswana Review, 2013). CBE may also help rural residents break free of agricultural dependence by building awareness of alternative and complementary economic activities, such as commu-nity-owned game farming or sustainable collection of forest resources (Ashley, 2000; Mbaiwa, 2008). According to Lindberg (2001), local communities who participate in CBE and receive tangible benefits tend to become cautious in their use of natural resources and, therefore, more likely to support tourism and conservation. This has been evident in the Sankuyu (Mbaiwa, 2008; Snyman, 2014), Khawa (Moswete, 2009), Okavango Community Trust (Snyman, 2014), and Basarwa communities in Botswana (Mbaiwa, 2008).

In Uganda, Lepp (2004) identified the role of tourism in the provision of basic needs such as improved housing, education, and jobs as well as cohesiveness and pride in a buffer community of Kibale National Park. In Namibia, rural communities have established conservancies, which have offered them conditional user rights over wildlife (Ashley, 2000). The communities have become involved in ecotourism development by forming small-scale enterprises (e.g. campsite, community craft-market). They have been involved in CBE businesses via engagement in joint venture[1] agreements with tourism investors (e.g. safari lodges and hunters) who in turn assist them to open and operate such businesses (Ashley, 2000). In Namibia, CBE is recognised by several stakeholders, including the gov-ernment, as a conservation and rural tourism success story (Ashley, 2000; Snyman, 2012, 2013).

In addition, well-managed projects and enterprises can restore degraded rangelands (Lepp, 2008; Mbaiwa & Sakuze, 2009), revive cultures (Moswete, Thapa, & Lacey, 2009), protect and preserve endangered species of fauna and flora (Mugisha, 2002), reduce resource conflicts (Mbaiwa, 2008), and improve the living standards of rural commu-nities (Ashley, 2000; Avila Foucat, 2002). However, in order for communities to fully benefit from CBE-related activities within their localities, there is a need to build capacity in order to understand the concept of, and principles of ecotourism, tourism business, and entrepreneur-ship. Overall, CBE is described and practised as sustainable tourism (Fennell, 2003), and is premised on the following principles (Honey, 1999; Nelson, 2004; Snyman, 2012, 2013):

- More benefits accrue to host communities;
- More consultative and democratic planning;

- Greater local community participation and involvement;
- Allow only tourism types that have low environmental impacts;
- Commitment to environmental protection and conservation of natural resources;
- Raise awareness to countries' political and, social and cultural climate;
- Empowers the local community as it promotes the use of indigenous knowledge, material and labour, and provides the opportunity for the local population to generate economic benefits from tourism.

CBE initiatives have demonstrated the propensity for local economic development along with environmental conservation and cultural preservation in various destinations within the sub-Saharan African region. Such prospects have resulted in the ecotourism industry being identified as an alternative option for economic growth in remote parts, especially in Botswana (Arntzen et al., 2003; Mbaiwa, 2008; Moswete, 2009). Hence, ventures and enterprises, which are communally owned and managed, have been encouraged and promoted as CBE by the national government (GOB, 2007). The growth of CBE in the sub-Saharan African region, especially in Botswana, has been facilitated via community-based natural resources management (CBNRM) initiatives.

CBNRM and tourism in Botswana

The CBNRM framework was formulated in the early 1990s with the aim of alleviating poverty and advancing natural resource conservation by strengthening rural economies and empowering communities to manage their own resources (e.g. fauna, flora) for long-term environmental, social, and economic benefits (GOB, 2007). Since then, the formation and use of Community-Based Organization (CBO) or Trusts, as they are popularly known in Botswana, has become an instrumental strategy for rural people. The implementation of CBNRM acts as a forum for rural people to negotiate their interests, problems, goals, and aspirations in a democratic and participatory manner (Arntzen et al., 2003). The Botswana CBNRM initiative is connected to CBE/ecotourism. Under the CBNRM programme, rural or local communities are encouraged to form CBE enterprises or projects in which they can collectively collaborate to establish CBE-related businesses (GOB, 2007).

CBE is important for Botswana (citizens) mainly in the remote areas of the country. The ecotourism industry has become vital for the country, specifically for rural development and conservation of natural and cultural resources. The government has so far formulated policies, strategies, and programmes to expand the sector. Current pieces of legislation include the National Ecotourism Strategy (Botswana Tourism Development Program, 2003) in which more rural communities are actively involved in tourism-related enterprises and projects to the benefit of people who live with the resources (e.g. wildlife). The CBNRM policy was initiated in 2007 and one of its aims was to 'enhance economic and social development in rural areas by providing qualified communities opportunities to earn benefits from natural "and cultural" resource conservation' (GOB, 2007, p. 5). The government has also established the Citizen Entrepreneurial Development Agency through which citizens can access financial support to venture into businesses that include tourism (e.g. game farms; guinea-fowl, and rabbit parks) (GOB, 2007; Hancock & Potts, 2002). Overall, CBE has been able to provide benefits to various communities and individuals (Arntzen et al., 2003; Mbaiwa, 2013; Moswete et al., 2009; Sebele, 2010). Two brief case studies are presented below to illustrate success stories of CBE projects in Botswana.

The Goo-Moremi Mannonnye Community Trust is an example of a success story of CBE in the central region (Elijah, 2014; White, 2000). Goo-Moremi village is situated in the Tswapong hills in an area demarcated as a conservation zone known as Goo-Moremi Mannonnye Conservation area (White, 2000). The Gorge is designated as a National Monument due to its unique features as an ancient, natural gorge that is home to endangered cape vultures and intimately connected to the heritage and history of the people of Goo-Moremi (Elijah, 2014; Geoflux, 2009). The community established a CBO (known as a Trust) and engaged in a joint venture partnership with a private operator. The community initiated the project with the assistance of the Kalahari Conservation society (a local non-governmental organisation) and the Botswana Tourism Organisation. The accrued benefits included preservation of culture, knowledge of the importance of conservation, employment, skills, and knowledge of guiding. Some of the job opportunities gained by the CBO/Trust included tour guides, housekeeping, management positions, and security guards (Elijah, 2014).

Another example is the Sankuyo community located in the Ngamiland region of northern Botswana. The community is largely dependent on farming (arable and small stock agriculture) and also engages in the collection of veldt resources and forest foods for subsistence. More than two decades ago, the community established a CBO called Sankuyo Tshwaragano Management Trust. Since then, they have operated a joint venture partnership in hunting and photographic safaris with a private operator in two Controlled Hunting Areas (NG33 and NG34). The joint venture partnership benefits included increased employment opportunities, income, game meat, sanitary facilities, social capital, transportation, reduced rural–urban migration, improved village image, and above all, a reduction in illegal hunting of wild animals (Arntzen et al., 2003; Mbaiwa, 2013).

Rural communities in tourism-biodiversity rich spots of Botswana, such as the Ngamiland district, Okavango Delta, and the eastern regions including Bobirwa sub-district, tend to be highly knowledgeable about CBE and the general business of tourism (Arntzen et al., 2003; Mbaiwa, 2013). There are ample CBE enterprises and projects that have benefited communities in these remote parts of the country (Arntzen et al., 2003; Mbaiwa, 2013; Moswete et al., 2009; Sebele, 2010). It is in these regions that residents have high repute and understanding of CBE and the business of tourism. However, the south-western region of the country is in the early stages of tourism. Only a small proportion of the communities have knowledge of ecotourism, while a few have ventured in the accommodation sector (Moswete, 2009). The few villages such as Khawa (KD 15), Zutshwa (KD 2), Ngwatle, Ukhwi, and Ncaang (KD 1) have established CBO/Trusts that offer activities that include safari-related tourism, arts and craft, campsites, and photographic tourism, but only as small-scale operations.

Overall, CBE initiatives in Botswana have yielded positive, tangible benefits in some regions more than others. The opportunity for further development of CBE enterprises in the south-western region (e.g. Kgalagadi Transfrontier Park (KTP)[2] area) is evident, but will need additional engagement from the national government as well as local communities. Hence, there is a need to further examine the situational context and the potential for local support and development for CBE programmes. Moreover, there is paucity of information and empirical research about CBE in the Kgalagadi region, especially within local communities living adjacent to the KTP. The need for additional information about CBE, knowledge or awareness of ecotourism among residents, and associated support for development in the area have been emphasised (Chanda, Totolo, Moleele, Setshogo, & Mosweu, 2003; Moswete et al., 2009; Moswete, Thapa, & Child, 2012). Therefore, the purpose of this study was to empirically explore residents' ecotourism knowledge, community concern, and perceptions of and support for CBE. More specifically, also to identify demographic indicators and associated factors that influence support for CBE in the rural communities adjacent to KTP.

Methods

Study site

The Kgalagadi region forms part of the first formally declared Transfrontier Park[3] in southern Africa – the KTP (South African Park Board & Department of Wildlife & National Parks [SANP & DWNP], 1999). The KTP is a unique feature to the Republic of Botswana and the Republic of South Africa measuring about 38,000 km^2 of the Kalahari ecosystem (SANP & DWNP, 1999). The park is made of two adjoined National Parks. On the Botswana side, the park was called Gemsbok National Park (GNP) (28,400 km^2), while the South African frontier was referred to as the Kalahari Gemsbok National Park (KGNP) (9591 km^2). The KTP became a Transfrontier Park when the two parks were merged into a single, co-managed, and protected area. There are no international boundaries – hence, there is free movement of people and animals inside the park area. Also, there are no communities that live inside the boundaries of the KTP (Peace Parks Foundation, 2009; SANP & DWNP, 1999).

The Kgalagadi District is located in south-western Botswana, and is over 600 km from the capital, Gaborone (Figure 1). The district is divided into two sub-districts, the north and south, both situated within the Kalahari Desert region. Kgalagadi north covers 44,004 km^2, while the southern block comprises 66,066 km^2 in land area (Kgalagadi District Development Plan KDDP 6, 2003–2009). Of the 193 villages and settlements, Tsabong, is the most highly populated village in Kgalagadi with more than 6000 inhabitants, thus it acts as the centre and has been designated as the main administration headquarters (GOB, 2002). Collectively, the district population occupies a network of 193 settlements within the Kgalagadi Communal Areas, and the average village/settlement size is 198 inhabitants. Settlements are often small with fewer than 500 people, comprising a few household clusters usually inhabited by people with a nomadic background. Villages are more formal, and are officially recognised establishments with at least 500 persons. They have basic facilities and services, such as water, health clinics, postal services, and schools. The level of available services is dependent on the village classification (Ministry of Finance & Development Planning, 2002). The main economy has primarily been based on raising small-scale livestock and nominal arable farming. Other traditional livelihood activities include subsistence hunting and gathering (Chanda et al., 2003), while safari-based tourism provides opportunities to a few community-based projects and individuals (Moswete et al., 2009).

The Kgalagadi District, incorporating KTP offers a wide range of ecotourism resources and products. Eco-resources include nature, desert landscape, unique sand dunes (ridges), salt pans, culture, and history. With respect to cultural heritage resources, artefacts dating to the early, middle, and late Stone Ages have been uncovered in the KTP and the surrounding villages (GOB, 2001). Primarily, the district is endowed with rich nature and cultural-based heritage resources including history, tribal stories, and lifestyle, as well as the rich intangible heritage of the different ethnic groups including the San/Basarwa (Ministry of Local Government [MLG], 2005). Handicrafts made from ostrich eggshells (head bands, bracelets, necklaces, belts and floor mats) are produced mainly by the San. Because of desert conditions with incidents of recurring droughts, inadequate rainfall, and infertile soils for arable and pastoral agriculture, poverty levels are relatively high. Unemployment levels within Kgalagadi communities are high due to low levels of commerce. Thus, livestock farming (e.g. goats, sheep, donkey, poultry, and cattle) and park-based tourism provide employment

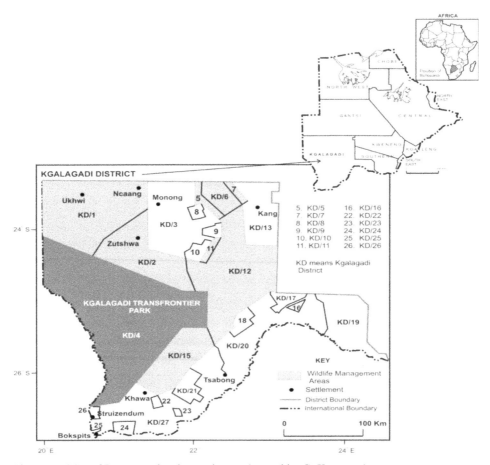

Figure 1.   Map of Botswana showing study area (created by G. Koorutwe).

opportunities for residents (Moswete et al., 2009). Hence, ecotourism has been identified as a sector through which the Kgalagadi region's economy could diversify, and residents are encouraged to invest in tourism initiatives with particular emphasis on communally owned ecotourism enterprises or projects (van der Jagt & Rozemeijer, 2002).

Sample

The study was conducted in nine rural communities located close to the boundaries of the KTP. A stratified sampling method based on the geographic location or proximity of villages to the park was used. In all, nine communities were selected, with five in the north and four in the south. For sampling purposes, a list of villages and associated population sizes contained in the 2001 population census report was obtained from the Central Statistics Office (CSO, 2001). A systematic sampling of residents was utilised to select households from the villages of Bokspits, Khawa, Tsabong, Struizendum, in south Kgalagadi, and Kang, Ncaang, Ukhwi, Tshane, and Zutshwa in north Kgalagadi. Like many rural villages in Botswana, the study site does not have streets and avenues that can be used to classify households or residential blocks. Instead, households tend to be demarcated or separated by paths, tracks, roads, rock outcrops, hills or valleys. Hence, every other home or plot that

154

intersects paths and roads was selected and visited for an interview. Collectively, the sampled village/settlements had a total population of 13,619 inhabitants and 3331 households. The total populace for the entire Kgalagadi District was approximately 43,000, with more people living in the Kgalagadi north (25,938) than in the south (16,111) (CSO, 2001). The most recent population census reports an increase in the total number of people living in the Kgalagadi region to approximately 50,000 (CSO, 2011).

Data collection

A semi-structured questionnaire interview ($n = 746$ households) with open- and closed-ended questions was conducted among residents in nine villages. The villages covered were Ncaang ($n = 37$), Ukhwi ($n = 59$), Kang ($n = 122$), Zutshwa ($n = 55$), and Tshane ($n = 89$) in the Kgalagadi north region, and Bokspits (53), Khawa (75), Tsabong (212), and Struizendam (44) in the south (Table 1). In this study, a household is a group of one or more persons living together in the same home or dwelling in which they cook and eat from the same pot and plan and do projects together. As such, the head of the household was contacted and requested to participate. Culturally, the head of the household would be a male individual (father). In the absence of the head, the female adult (mother) or any adult living permanently (or having lived for at least one year) in the household, and aged 18 years or older, was interviewed.

Operationalisation of variables

The socio-demographic characteristics of the respondents were age, level of education, length of residence, employment status, household income, employment and distance to the park.[4] Information about *knowledge of ecotourism* (Avila Foucat, 2002; Brandon, 2007; Dwyer, Gursoy, Sharma, & Cater, 2007; Lai & Nepal, 2006; Kuvan & Akan, 2005) was operationalised with six items with True, False or Do not Know categories (Table 2). *Perception about CBE* (Lai & Nepal, 2006); was measured with 14 items on a 5-point Likert-type scale of 1 = strongly disagree to 5 = strongly agree (Table 3). *Community concern* (Gursoy, Jurowski, & Uysal, 2002; Jurowski & Gursoy, 2004) was measured

Table 1. Study sample for residents per village/settlements, household and population.

Village/ communities	Total village population (n) (2001)	Total households (n)*	30% of households	Household sampled
North Kgalagadi				
Ncaang	175	43	13	37
Ukhwi	453	114	34	59
Zutshwa	469	118	35	55
Tshane	858	209	63	89
Kang	3744	913	274	122 (82)**
South Kgalagadi				
Khawa	517	128	39	75
Struizendam	313	76	23	44
Bokspits	499	122	37	53
Tsabong	6591	1608	482	212 (145)**
Total (9)	13,619	3331	1000	746

*Household estimate = total population/4.1.
**Number in parentheses is 30% of the original 30%.

Table 2. Ecotourism knowledge (percentages) among residents adjacent to the KTP.

Statements	True	False	Not true
Ecotourism encourages conservation of natural resources	90.9	1.2	7.9
Ecotourism promotes preservation of cultural traditions	83.8	4.0	12.2
Ecotourism encourages local participation in planning & decision-making	65.4	6.4	27.7
Ecotourism ensures economic benefits for local communities	69.3	7.2	23.1
Ecotourism encourages sustainable use of wildlife in local communities	90.9	1.7	7.1
Ecotourism promotes sustainable harvesting of veldt resources	82.2	5.8	11.7

Note: Sample size ~ 746.

Table 3. Residents' perception (percentages) about community-based ecotourism.

Statements	Strongly disagree	Disagree	Neutral	Agree	Strongly agree
CBE increases income and standard of living in the community	1.2	6.2	10.2	62.3	19.8
CBE increases opportunities for the community	1.3	10.2	7.5	61.5	19.0
CBE promotes equal sharing of benefits form community projects	2.3	10.7	20.9	52.1	13.7
CBE provides educational experiences for local communities	1.2	4.3	11.0	57.9	25.2
CBE creates problems to local people in my village*	12.6	57.8	13.0	13.8	2.8
CBE enhances the quality of life of local communities	1.9	8.2	12.6	63.9	12.9
CBE promotes meeting new people & cultural exchange	1.1	2.8	5.6	63.9	26.0
CBE improves understanding & image of my community	2.3	5.8	8.8	64.1	16.9
CBE enhances local arts and crafts in communities	1.9	3.9	7.2	65.8	23.6
CBE discourages preservation of cultural resources*	16.6	50.1	8.2	19.8	4.8
CBE provides casual earning opportunities by selling grass, crafts	2.7	9.4	8.3	61.7	17.7
CBE protects and supports wildlife resources	0.5	0.9	3.8	68.5	26.0
CBE supports conservation of forests or veldt resources	0.4	1.1	5.6	68.9	23.6
CBE increases support for natural resource conservation	0.5	1.6	5.6	68.4	23.2

Note: Sample size ~ 746
*Items reverse coded prior to analysis.

with 5 items on a 5-point Likert scale whereby, 1 = not at all concerned to 5 = extremely concerned (Table 4). *Support for CBE development* (Lai & Nepal, 2006; Nelson, 2004; Nyaupane & Thapa, 2004; Sikaraya, Teye, & Sonmez, 2002) was measured by 6 items on a 5-point Likert scale of 1 = strongly oppose to 5 = strongly support (Table 5). All the operationalised variables along with the respective frequency distributions are reported in the corresponding tables.[5]

Table 4. Residents' perception (percentages) of community concern about tourism.

Statements	Not at all concerned	Somewhat concerned	Moderate concern	Very concerned	Extremely concerned
Destroy our environment	15.8	10.1	14.2	41.0	18.9
Change our cultural traditions	13.3	9.1	11.9	39.0	26.7
Increase social ills (e.g. crime)	4.8	4.6	7.7	39.1	43.4
Increase incidents of HIV/ AIDS infections	3.9	4.2	5.1	30.3	56.2
Loss of grazing land for our livestock if more hotels & infrastructure are built	12.6	7.8	14.2	44.8	20.6

Note: Sample size ~ 746.

Table 5. Residents' support (percentages) for community-based ecotourism in Kgalagadi.

Statements I support	Strongly oppose	Oppose	Neutral	Support	Strongly support
Promotes local involvement in tourism activities	1.1	1.6	7.1	72.5	17.4
Promotes preservation of local culture and traditions	1.3	3.8	10.5	59.0	24.8
Promotes environmental education for local people	0.8	2.0	8.3	64.2	24.0
Encourages local participation in tourism planning & development	0.9	3.8	11.7	62.7	20.2
Promotes collective income for the community	1.9	4.8	14.5	60.9	17.4
Encourages conservation of natural resources	0.8	1.2	3.9	65.0	28.6

Note: Sample size ~ 746.

Data analysis

First, the suitability of the data was assessed prior to a factor analysis using Bartlett's test of sphericity and the Kaiser–Meyer–Oaklin (KMO) measure of sampling adequacy. The data revealed the test of sphericity as highly significant (approximate $\chi^2 = 6105.709$, df = 253, $p < .001$), and KMO at a 0.891, that exceeded the recommended cut-off of 0.60. Both measures indicated that the data were appropriate for factor analysis (Tabachnick & Fidell, 2001). Factor analysis with a principal component approach and variance rotation was conducted for the 23 items. Five factors were generated and accounted for 58.05% of the total variance that explained 15.92%, 12.19%, 10.83%, 10.24%, and 8.87% of the variance, respectively. Data with a factor loading of 0.40 and higher were retained and ranged from 0.528 to 0.798. The respective items within each index along with the quantity of items and the corresponding Cronbach's alpha values (range from 0.68 to 0.86) are reported in Table 6.

In addition, a correlation analysis was conducted to guard against multicollinearity (Callaghan & Chen, 2008). The bivariate correlations, means, standard deviations, reliabilities and the number of items per the multi-item-constructs are presented in

157

Table 6.   Factor loadings and reliabilities.

	No of items	Loading	% Of variance explained	Cronbach alpha
CBE support (Y_1)	6		15.92	.86
Encourages local participation in tourism planning and development		.764		
Encourages conservation of natural resources		.745		
Promotes environmental education for local community		.738		
Promotes local involvement in tourism activities		.733		
Promotes preservation of local culture and traditions		.728		
Promotes collective income for local communities		.690		
Concern (X_2)	5		12.19	.79
Destroy the environment		.779		
Increase social ills (e.g. crime)		.770		
Change our cultural traditions		.735		
Increase incidents of HIV/AIDS infections		.733		
Loss of grazing land for our livestock if more hotels and infrastructure is built		.671		
Economic (X_5)	5		10.83	.74
Increase income and standard of living in the community		.758		
Increases job opportunities for the community		.710		
Promotes equal sharing of benefits from community projects		.609		
Promotes educational experiences for the local community		.532		
Enhances the quality of life of local communities		528		
Environmental (X_3)	3		10.24	.82
Supports conservation of forest or veldt resources		.798		
Increases support or natural resources for conservation		.781		
Protects and supports wildlife resources		.769		
Socio-cultural (X_4)	4		8.87	.68
Improves understanding and image of my community		.729		
Enhances local arts and crafts in local communities		.688		
Promotes meeting new people and cultural exchange		.554		
Provides casual earning opportunities by selling grass, crafts, firewood		.546		

Table 7. Also, the highest correlation resulted between two covariates (i.e. *age* and *years at residence*), and registered at 0.689, which was below 0.70. As a rule, Meyers, Gamst, and Guarino (2006, p. 181) 'recommend that two variables correlated in the mid 0.70s or higher should not be used together in a regression'. Furthermore, the two constructs (i.e. *age* and

Table 7. Correlation matrix.

Variables	Z_1	Z_2	Z_3	X_1	X_2	X_3	X_4	X_5	Y_1
Covariates									
Age (Z_1)	1.000								
Education (Z_2)	-.594**	1.000							
Years of residence (Z_3)	.689**	-.489**	1.000						
Independent									
Knowledge (X_1)	.059	-.069	.036	1.000					
Concern (X_2)	.101**	-.160**	.169**	.096**	1.000				
Environmental (X_3)	-.021	-.049	-.041	.234**	.059	1.000			
Socio-cultural (X_4)	-.016	-.049.	.009	.180**	.072	.508**	1.000		
Economic (X_5)	.006	-.068	-.039	.265**	.086*	.502**	.575**	1.000	
Dependent									
CBE support (Y_1)	.068	-.129**	.106**	.301**	.122**	.505**	.469**	.479**	1.000
Number of Items	—	—	—	5	5	3	4	5	6
Mean	37.71	.601	28.512	4.824	3.781	4.155	3.967	3.852	4.034
Standard deviation	14.854	.490	19.837	1.399.	.886	.579	.584	.599	.560
Reliability	—	—	—	—	.79	.82	.68	.74	.86

*Correlations significant at the .05 level (two-tailed).
**Correlations significant at the .01 level (two-tailed).

years at residence) were conceptually different and were used in the subsequent analysis. The bivariate correlations among the five independent variables and the dependent measure ranged from 0.059 to 0.575.

Furthermore, in SPSS 'collinearity diagnosis', the tolerance value obtained for each of the variables employed was 0.947 or less. However, 0.947 was the highest, which was not less than 0.10. The commonly used cut-off mark to determine the presence of multicollinearity is the Tolerance (TOL) value of less than 0.10 or variance inflation factor (VIF) value of above 10 (Pallant, 2013). Therefore, in this analysis, VIF was 2.292 (highest), which was below the cut-off of 10. Pallant (2013, p. 164) recommends 'cut-off points for determining the presence of multicollinearity (Tolerance value of less 0.10, or a VIF value of above 10)'. Collectively, multicollinearity assumption was not violated for the data analysis (Allison, 1999; Hair, Anderson, Tathan, & Black, 1998; Osborne & Waters, 2002; Pallant, 2013).

Results

Demographics

Based on the total sample, there were more females (55%) than males (45%). The difference in gender could be cultural, since during the time of the survey, male household heads were noticeably absent. Possibly, they were at work in farms, fields or cattle-posts, while females stayed home to tend to household chores and children. The youngest respondent was 18 and the oldest was 92 years of age, with 41% in the age bracket of 18−30 and 24% in the 31−40 age brackets. The 41−50 age groups were the third largest and constituted 16% of the total sample. Residents who were 61 years and older were representative of 10% of the total sample. Literacy levels varied by village and there were vast differences across communities. Sixteen percent had no formal schooling, 21% had attained primary education, 32% had junior certificate (US Grade 8) and 18% had secondary education equivalent to the US high school education. Only 6% of the respondents had some form of university education. Approximately 67% of the respondents were native residents, born and raised in Kgalagadi as children. Seventeen per cent had lived in the Kgalagadi for 1−5 years, while 10% had lived in area for at least 10 years. Length of residency in the study area averaged 28.5 years. Finally, there were more than eight ethnic groups of the respondents with Bakgalagadi (28%), Batlharo (21%), Bangologa (14%), Coloreds (13%), San/Basarwa (7%), and others.

Household income and employment

Residents were asked to indicate their total household income in Pula[6] per month. Overall, the total monthly household income displayed two extreme cases: very low total income for some residents (e.g. 26% earned under P500 (US $71), and very high for other members of the community (e.g. 30% earned more than P3000 (US $429). The median monthly household income ranged between P1001 and P1500 (US $143−$214). The main source of household income resulted from employment. A total of 31% indicated involvement in formal employment, 24% were self-employed, and 19% had part-time employment while about 25% said were unemployed. In addition, 80% of the respondents stated that at least 1−2 persons in the household or family were employed.

Interestingly, in rural Botswana, especially in the remote villages of the Kalahari, most jobs are created through welfare programmes known as Ipelegeng (formally known as drought relief projects). Such jobs are provided by the District Councils through the MLG (Chanda et al., 2003). Some resident communities were involved in livestock farming (sheep, goats, donkey, horse, and cattle); small businesses (e.g. carving, tannery, and beadwork) and tourism (e.g. campsites, arts/crafts, tour guides, and lodges/guesthouse/motels). Others subsisted on remittances from family members who were working outside the villages. In addition, 14.5% indicated involvement in CBNRM tourism via the local CBO/Trust.[7] Individual gains were mentioned to include employment opportunities (safari-related tourism), game meat and business opportunities (e.g. making and selling of crafts).

Regression analysis

The data were analysed using SPSS hierarchical regression with *knowledge of ecotourism, community concern, environmental, socio-cultural* and *economic perceptions about CBE* as the independent variables; *age, education* and *years at residence* as covariates; and *CBE support* as the dependent variable. The three covariates (*age, education*, and *years at residence*) were included in the analysis because past research has shown that CBE support was related to age (Andereck & Vogt, 2000; Huh & Vogt, 2008; Walpole & Goodwin, 2001); and age was also found to have an influence on the support of protected areas or parks/reserves (De Boer & Baquete, 1998). Also, education was identified to have had effects with support for tourism development (Sikaraya et al., 2002) and years at residency (Gursoy et al., 2002; McGehee & Andereck, 2004; Mehta & Heinen, 2001). The results of the regression analyses are reported in Table 8.

For the first analysis, the hierarchical regression with *age, education* and *years at residence* was employed to assess residents' *CBE support* within their local communities.

Table 8. Hierarchical regression analysis with CBE support as dependent variable.

	Model I			Model II		
	B	β	T-value	B	β	T-value
Covariates						
Age (Z_1)	−.003	−.071	−1.301	−.002	−.050	−1.133
Education (Z_2)	−.144	−.126	2.760**	−.055	−.048	−1.301
Years at residence (Z_3)	.003	.093	1.837	.003	.122	2.977**
Independent variables						
Knowledge (X_1)				.057	.142	4.684***
Concern (X_2)				.023	.037	1.237
Environmental (X_3)				.034	.282	7.936***
Socio-cultural (X_4)				.173	.181	4.832***
Economic (X_5)				.182	.194	5.134***
R^2		.021			.383	
Adj. R^2		.017			.377	
F-value		5.350***			57.055***	
df		(3739)			(8734)	
ΔR^2					.364	
ΔF					86.227***	
VIF					<2.292	

*$p < .05$.
**$p < .01$.
***$p < .001$.

Model I shows the effect of the three covariates on residents' support of CBE, and the relationship was significant ($F = 5.350, p < .001$). While these three variables explained 2.1% of the variance in *CBE support*, only *education* was significant with a negative relationship ($\beta = -0.126, p < .01$). This implies that as *education* increases, residents' *CBE support* in and around the KTP decreases. *Age* and *years at residency* were not significant factors in terms of determining support among residents. So, the question of interest is, if the three covariates were controlled, then would the five independent variables still be able to predict a significant amount of variance in *CBE support* on the study population?

Model II shows the effect of all the variables (i.e. three covariates and five independent variables) on *CBE support*. It also shows that when the three covariates (*age, education,* and *residency*) were controlled for, the independent variables (*knowledge of ecotourism, community concerns, environmental, socio-cultural, and economic*) were able to predict a significant amount of variance in *CBE support*. This model explained 38.3% of the variance in *CBE support* with the five independent variables accounting for 36.2% of additional variance when the covariates were controlled for. Model II was highly significant ($F = 57.055, p < .001$). The change in F due to the addition of the five independent variables was also highly significant ($F = 86.277, p < .001$). Of the three covariates, only *years at residence* had a significant effect on *CBE support* ($\beta = 0.122, p < .01$). This relationship indicates that as *years at residence* in the community increases, residents' *CBE support* in and around the KTP also increases.

Four of the five independent variables (*knowledge of ecotourism, environmental, and socio-cultural,* and *economic*) had positive significant effects on *CBE support*. The results identified that as *knowledge of ecotourism* increases, residents' *CBE support* in and around the KTP increases too ($\beta = 0.142, p < .001$). Similarly, as the level of *environmental* perceptions increases, resident' *CBE support* in and around the KTP increases ($\beta = 0.282, p < .001$). Also, as the level of *socio-cultural* perceptions increases, residents' *CBE support* in and around the KTP increases ($\beta = 0.181, p < .001$). A similar positive relationship was evident for *economic* and *CBE support* ($\beta = 0.194, p < .001$). Overall, four independent variables were important predictors of residents' *CBE support* with *environmental* being the most important factor followed by *economic, socio-cultural* and *knowledge of ecotourism*.

Discussion

This study empirically explored perceptions of and factors that influence support for CBE among residents from nine villages living adjacent to the KTP. Two models were analysed. While the first overall model that examined the effects of the three covariates (education, age, and years at residency) on CBE support was statistically significant, only education displayed a significant negative relationship. This finding was interesting and might be due to residents with a high level of knowledge of the area and those with formal training understanding the issues that pertain to management of the KTP better. Such residents might more readily acknowledge any inequalities or imbalances in benefits sharing or a lack of development of ecotourism (Moswete et al., 2012).

For the second overall model, four independent variables (knowledge of ecotourism, environmental, socio-cultural, and economic) were able to statistically predict significant positive relationships for CBE support when the three demographic covariates (age, education, and residency) were controlled for. Also, only one covariate, years at residence, had a significant effect on CBE support. This finding is logical as length of residence has a tendency to create a stronger community attachment, which in turn positively impacts support (Nicholas, Thapa, & Ko, 2009). Similarly, other studies (Gursoy et al., 2002; McCool & Martin, 1994; McGehee & Andereck, 2004; Kibicho, 2004; Mehta & Heinen, 2001) have identified that the number of years of residence has an influence on residents' support for tourism development. Also, local residents who had lived in the community much longer expressed their desire to experience more tourism growth and were very supportive of further developments (Andereck, Valentine, Knopf, & Vogt, 2005; McGehee & Andereck, 2004). Indeed, respondents who had lived longer in the nine villages adjacent to the boundary of the KTP of Botswana and South Africa demonstrated a strong support for CBE development in their area. Interestingly, the relationship between age and support for CBE development with regard to the KTP communities was not a significant factor. This finding was surprising as based on previous research; increase in age does have a significant relationship with respect to support (De Boer & Baquete, 1998).

The positive relationship between knowledge of ecotourism and CBE support makes sense as with increased knowledge; residents would be more supportive of CBE initiatives (Lepp, 2008; Moswete et al., 2012; Snyman, 2012, 2013). This finding was similar to previous studies in which high awareness and knowledge about tourism was positively associated with support for tourism development within local communities. According to Sikaraya et al. (2002), local people who accrued socio-economic benefits from tourism had a high level of knowledge of tourism 'as a business' and thereby strongly supported its development in their communities.

Similarly, residents with positive perceptions of environmental resources (e.g. fauna, flora,) in and around the KTP area were more likely to show support for the environment. Furthermore, positive perceptions and support of CBE could be due to the fact that the government has been engaged in capacity building and formal training to enable rural communities to venture into CBNRM-ecotourism. The government through the Ministry of Environment, Wildlife and Tourism has held training workshops in remote villages, especially those residing closer to protected areas (National Parks and Reserves). The government has also engaged in educating residents about the importance of conservation and safeguarding of natural resources that include – wild animals, birds and vegetation, including rare and endangered species. Also, communities appear to have started to appreciate conservation programmes and several have established CBNRM–CBOs for tourism (Mbaiwa, 2008; Moswete et al., 2009, 2012; Mulale, 2005).

Residents' CBE support also increases with an increase in economic perceptions. This positive relationship is reasonable, as when residents accrue benefits from tourism in their area, they tend to perceive ecotourism and CBE development favourably (Moswete et al., 2009, 2012). This finding was supported by previous research, in which local residents in communities where tourism growth was still at an early stage tended to view potential benefits of tourism favourably and ultimately indicated support for its development (Ko & Stewart, 2002; Sikaraya et al., 2002; Wilson, Fesenmaier, Fesenmaier, & Van Es, 2001). In this study, only a handful of members from the nine villages had jobs (mainly part time) at the Park and/or with Safari campsites that brought visitors to the park. Others worked with safari operators during hunting expeditions. However, it can be argued that a high level of knowledge of ecotourism did not necessarily equate to recognition of accrued benefits, as many members did not receive significant benefits and royalties from KTP-based tourism. Their perspectives could be different in this case because they are living in the periphery of the park with which they have an historical identity and a cultural and spiritual attachment and/or pride associated with its proximity. Thus, even if individuals were not recipients of significant benefits from CBE and or ecotourism enterprises from villages near the park, they still noted positive attitudes and perceptions towards ecotourism development. This could also be because their knowledge of ecotourism was high, which indicated that even if they obtained nominal benefits they were aware that ecotourism can generate benefits. Therefore, when policy-makers, CBO, and KTP authorities work towards improving ecotourism within the Kgalagadi region, efforts have to be made to increase economic benefits (Moswete, 2009; Moswete et al., 2012). Basically, unless communities are given an opportunity to participate in the development of interventions designed to improve their livelihoods, they will continue to lack the benefits (Child, 2009; Manwa, 2003; Moswete, 2009; Moswete et al., 2009; Sebele, 2010; Snyman, 2014).

There was a strong and significant relationship between socio-cultural perceptions and support for CBE development. With both factors in perspective, it is noteworthy that in all nine villages, a CBNRM-tourism-related CBO/Trust had been formed. For example, Nqwaa Khobee Xeya Development Trust consists of three communities – Ncaang, Ngwatle, and Ukhwi in Kgalagadi north, and Khawa Kopanelo Development Trust consists of one village in Kgalagadi south (Arntzen et al., 2003; Chanda et al., 2003; Mbaiwa, 2013; Moswete et al., 2009). Some residents of the greater Kgalagadi were already accruing benefits in terms of income via handicrafts sales, employment in safari-related enterprises, infrastructure (e.g. communally owned guest houses), and craft outlets where individual families assemble to make and display their arts, leading to improved relationships between individuals and families (Moswete et al., 2009). However, such activities and benefits were not spread equally within the study area, and it is important for the respective communities to view CBE development positively, as well as venture into the ecotourism industry that is linked to the KTP.

Remarkably, community concern did not have a significant relationship with CBE support. However, most respondents expressed varying concerns about potential growth of tourism in the community. Residents generally expressed concern with respect to environmental impacts (e.g. potential to damage the local environment, loss of grazing land for livestock) and socio-cultural impacts (e.g. changes in the local cultural traditions, increase in crime and the incidence of HIV/AIDS infections). Previous studies have documented that local residents who were concerned about impacts due to the negative effects of tourism in their communities still expressed strong support for park-based tourism development (Dwyer et al., 2007; Stem, Lassoie, Lee, Deshler, & Schelhas, 2003). Other studies concluded that despite the community concerns, residents were supportive because they perceived tourism as an economic tool (Andereck et al., 2005; Burns & Howard, 2003; Gursoy & Rutherford, 2004; McGehee & Andereck, 2004).

Overall, the results of this study highlight the diverse array of factors that were likely to influence local residents' perceptions and support of CBE development in the area. Largely, residents noted a significant number of positive perceptions about potential benefits from CBE development or from the KTP that did not reflect actual, derived benefits. This could be because ecotourism development in the area is fairly new. Consequently, residents may not have had time to accrue the potential financial benefits.

Noteworthy is the fact that only about 40% of the variance in the dependent variable (i.e. community-based ecotourism) was explained by the set of independent variables. While 40% is respectable (Pallant, 2013, p. 167), it leaves about 60% of the variance unexplained. One explanation may be the fact that ecotourism development is relatively new in the area. Thus, the nearly 40% of variance explained was reasonably substantial when one considers community-based ecotourism 'as a variable that may be complexly determined' (Meyers et al., 2006, p. 167). That said, there may be other variables which influence community-based ecotourism that were not captured in this study. Additional explanatory variables such as level of involvement with the Park, whether the individual has benefited from tourism in the past, and residential distance from the Park are worth considering in future analysis.

Conclusion

A systematic analysis of residents' attitudes and perspectives about tourism can help government planners, local authority decision-makers, protected area authorities, and tourism developers, and promoters to identify stakeholder concerns and issues in order for appropriate policies and actions to be formulated and implemented (Byrd, 2007; De Lopez, 2001; Weladji, Moe, & Vedeld, 2003). Also, strategic planning of Transfrontier protected areas is a complex task due to the interdependence of multiple stakeholders that ought to be involved in management and conservation of shared resources (Kelson & Lilieholm, 1999; Schoon, 2008). Ecotourism development and successes in and around parks and protected areas rely heavily on local communities' support and willingness to participate in park-based tourism and conservation projects (Lai & Nepal, 2006; Ormsby & Mannie, 2006; Sikaraya et al., 2002; Stem et al., 2003). Therefore, it is paramount that residents' perspectives be understood so that they can play a lead role in the issues that pertain to ecotourism development and planning in their area (Lepp, 2004, 2008; Parker & Khare, 2005; Stem et al., 2003). It is also important that factors that affect or influence residents' support for conservation of protected areas within their local communities are identified to benefit policy reviews and implementation (Allendorf, 2007; Bruyere, Beh, & Lelengula, 2009; Kelson & Lilieholm, 1999; Moswete, 2009; Ormsby & Mannie, 2006).

Since CBE has become an important livelihood option for rural communities in Botswana, the KTP plays a vital role in the conservation of resources and the development of ecotourism. It is notable that there are relatively few studies that empirically examined relationships by incorporating these constructs to evaluate support for CBE in a desert setting of a developing country in Africa. From an academic point of view, this study contributes to the emerging literature in the Kgalagadi region where tourism development is limited. From the perspective of decision-makers, planners, and ecotourism developers, this study provides insights in to what should be considered when assessing the Kgalagadi communities for ecotourism development. These empirical results extend our understanding of residents' perceptions and support for CBE development in and around KTP. Based on the findings of this study, the factors that influence support for CBE development can be further examined and applied in other diverse geographical locations.

Acknowledgements

The authors would like to thank Professor William Darley for valuable assistance with respect to the data analysis. Also, much appreciation is extended to the respondents from various communities who spent the time to respond to the survey as well as discuss myriad issues about the KTP with the primary author. The authors would like to thank the reviewers for their encouraging responses and observations that helped us to improve this manuscript.

Disclosure statement

No potential conflict of interest was reported by the authors.

Notes

1. A joint venture requires a community and a private company to work together, sharing the risks and responsibility of a joint enterprise. It generally offers a community more decision-making power and training (van der Jagt & Rozemeijer, 2002, p. 39).

2. The KTP is the first transboundary protected area to be created in southern Africa with dual own-ership between Botswana and South Africa.
3. Relatively large area that straddles frontiers (boundaries) between two or more countries and covers a large-scale natural system encompassing one or more protected areas (World Bank, 1996, p. 10).
4. For the regression analysis, only age, education, and years at residence were used.
5. Due to space restrictions, the frequencies are only illustrated in the tables and not described in a text format.
6. Pula is Botswana currency (BWP): Botswana Pula (US $1.00–BWP 7.00).
7. There are several CBNRM-related CBO/Trust in the local area.

References

Allendorf, T. D. (2007). Residents' attitudes toward three protected areas in southwestern Nepal. *Biodiversity Conservation, 16*(7), 2087–2102.

Allison, P. D. (1999). *Multiple regressions: A primer.* Thousand Oaks, CA: Pine Forge Press.

Andereck, K. L., Valentine, K. M., Knopf, R. C., & Vogt, C. A. (2005). Residents' perceptions of community tourism impacts. *Annals of Tourism Research, 32*(4), 1056–1076.

Andereck, K., & Vogt, C. (2000). The relationship between residents' attitudes towards tourism and tourism development options. *Journal of Travel Research, 39*(1), 27–36.

Arntzen, J. W., Molokomme, D. L., Terry, E. M., Moleele, N., Tshosa, O., & Mazambani, D. (2003). *Main findings of the review of community-based natural resources management in Botswana.* Occasional Paper No. 14. Gaborone: IUCN/SNV CBNRM Support Programme.

Ashley, C. (2000). *The impacts of tourism on rural livelihoods: Namibia's experience.* ODI Working Paper 128. London: Chameleon Press.

Avila Foucat, V. S. (2002). Community-based ecotourism management moving towards sustainability in Ventanilla, Oaxaca, Mexico. *Ocean and Coastal Management, 45*(8), 511–529.

Botswana Review. (2013). *Botswana review: Commerce and industry* (33rd ed.). Gaborone: Botswana Export Development and Investment Authority.

Botswana Tourism Development Program. (2003). *Botswana national ecotourism strategy.* Gaborone: Ministry of Commerce and Industry, Department of Tourism.

Botswana Tourism Organisation. (2008). *Botswana eco-tourism best practice manual.* Gaborone: Discover Ltd and Ecoplanet Ltd.

Brandon, A. (2007). The dual nature of parks: Attitudes of neighboring communities towards Kruger National Park, South Africa. *Environmental Conservation, 34*(3), 236–245.

Bruyere, B. L., Beh, A. W., & Lelengula, W. (2009). Differences in perceptions of communication, tourism benefits, and management issues in a protected area of rural Kenya. *Environmental Management, 43*(1), 49–59.

Burns, G. L., & Howard, T. (2003). When wildlife tourism goes wrong: A case study of stakeholder and management issues regarding Dingoes on Fraser Island, Australia. *Tourism Management, 24*(6), 699–712.

Byrd, E. (2007). Stakeholders in sustainable tourism development and their roles: Applying stake-holder theory to sustainable tourism development. *Tourism Review, 62*(2), 6–13.

Callaghan, K., & Chen, J. (2008). Revisiting the collinear data problem. An assessment of estimator 'ill-conditioning' in linear regression. *Practical Assessment, Research and Evaluation, 13*(5), 1–6.

Central Statistics Office. (2001). *Botswana population and housing census.* Gaborone: Ministry of Local Government and Housing.

Central Statistics Office. (2011). *Botswana population and housing census.* Gaborone: Ministry of Local Government and Housing.

Chanda, R., Totolo, O., Moleele, N., Setshogo, M., & Mosweu, S. (2003). Prospects for subsistence livelihood and environmental sustainability along the Kalahari rangelands transect: The case of Matsheng in Botswana's Kalahari. *Journal of Arid Environments, 54*(2), 425–445.

Child, G. (2009). The growth of park conservation in Botswana. In H. Suich, B. Child, & A. Spenceley (Eds.), *Evolution and innovation in wildlife conservation: Parks and game ranches to Transfrontier conservation areas* (pp. 187–200). London: Earthscan.

De Boer, W. F., & Baquete, D. S. (1998). Natural resource use, crop damage and attitudes of rural people in the vicinity of the Maputo Elephant Reserve, Mozambique. *Environmental Conservation, 25*(3), 208–218.

De Lopez, T. T. (2001). Stakeholder management for conservation projects: A case study of Realm National Park, Cambodia. *Environmental Management, 28*(1), 47–60.

Dwyer, P., Gursoy, D., Sharma, B., & Cater, J. (2007). Structural modeling of resident perceptions of tourism and associated development on the sunshine coast, Australia. *Tourism Management, 28*(2), 409–422.

Elijah, B. (2014). *Assessment of benefits and challenges of community-based tourism: A case study of the Moremi-Mannonnye Conservation Trust* (Unpublished undergraduate thesis). University of Botswana, Gaborone.

Fennell, D. (2003). *Ecotourism: An introduction* (2nd ed.). New York: Routledge.

Geoflux. (2009). *Environmental impact assessment for goo-moremi mannonnye conservation area.* Scoping Report. Gaborone, Botswana, Gaborone Geoflux.

Government of Botswana. (2001). *Botswana national atlas.* Gaborone: Government Printers, Department of Surveys and Mapping.

Government of Botswana. (2002). *Game ranching policy for Botswana No. 5 of 2002.* Gaborone: Ministry of Trade, Industry, Wildlife and Tourism, Government Printers.

Government of Botswana. (2007). *Community based natural resources management policy.* Government Paper No. 2, Ministry of Environment, Wildlife and Tourism. Gaborone, Government Printers.

Gursoy, D., Jurowski, C., & Uysal, M. (2002). Resident attitudes: A structural modeling approach. *Annals of Tourism Research, 29*(1), 79–105.

Gursoy, D., & Rutherford, D. G. (2004). Host attitudes toward tourism: An improved structural model. *Annals of Tourism Research, 31*(3), 495–516.

Hair, J. F., Anderson, R. E., Tathan, R. L., & Black, W. C. (1998). *Multivariate data analysis* (5th ed.). Upper Saddle River, NJ: Prentice Hall.

Hancock, P., & Potts, F. (2002). *A guide to starting a tourism enterprise in Botswana.* Community-based natural resource management (CBNRM) Support Programme. Occasional Paper No. 9. Botswana SNV. Gaborone, Botswana.

Honey, M. (1999). *Ecotourism and sustainable development: Who owns paradise?* Washington, DC: Island Press.

Huh, C., & Vogt, C. A. (2008). Changes in residents' attitudes toward tourism over time: A cohort analytical approach. *Journal of Travel Research, 46*(4), 446–455.

van der Jagt, C., & Rozemeijer, N. (2002). *Practical guide for facilitating CBNRM in Botswana.* Community Based National Resource Management Support Programme. Occasional Paper No. 8. SNV, IUCN, Botswana.

Jones, J. L. (2005). Transboundary conservation: Development implications for communities in Kwa Zulu-Natal, South Africa. *International Journal of Sustainable Development and World Ecology, 12*(3), 266–278.

Jurowski, C., & Gursoy, D. (2004). Distance effects on residents' attitudes toward tourism. *Annals of Tourism Research, 31*(2), 296–312.

Kelson, A. E., & Lilieholm, R. J. (1999). Transboundary issues in wilderness management. *Environmental Management, 23*(3), 297–305.

Kibicho, W. (2004). Community tourism: A lesson from Kenya's coastal region. *Journal of Vacation Marketing, 10*(1), 33–42.

Ko, W., & Stewart, P. (2002). A structural equation model of residents' attitudes for tourism development. *Tourism Management, 23*(5), 521–530.

Kuvan, Y., & Akan, P. (2005). Residents' attitudes toward general and forest-related impacts of tourism: The case of Belek, Antalya. *Tourism Management, 26*(5), 691–706.

Lai, P., & Nepal, S. K. (2006). Local perspectives of ecotourism development in Tawushan nature reserve, Taiwan. *Tourism Management, 27*(6), 1117–1129.

Lepp, A. (2004). *Tourism in a rural Ugadan village: Impacts, local meaning and implications for development* (Unpublished PhD dissertation). University of Florida, USA.

Lepp, A. (2008). Attitudes toward initial tourism development in a community with no prior tourism experience: The case of Bigodi, Uganda. *Journal of Sustainable Tourism, 16*(1), 5–22.

Lindberg, K. (2001). Economic impacts. In D. B. Weaver (Ed.), *The encyclopedia of ecotourism* (pp. 363–376). Cambridge: CABI.

Manwa, H. (2003). Wildlife-based tourism, ecology and sustainability: A tug of war among competing interest in Zimbabwe. *Journal of Tourism Studies, 14*(2), 45–55.

Mbaiwa, J. E. (2008). *Tourism development, rural livelihoods, and conservation in the Okavango Delta, Botswana* (Unpublished PhD dissertation). Texas A&M University, USA.

Mbaiwa, J. E. (2013). *Community-based natural resource management (CBNRM) in Botswana: CBNRM status report of 2011–2012.* Prepared for Botswana CBNRM National Forum Secretariat – Kalahari Conservation Society. Gaborone, Botswana.

Mbaiwa, J. E., & Sakuze, L. K. (2009). Cultural tourism and livelihood diversification: The case of Gcwihaba Caves and XaiXai Village in the Okavango Delta, Botswana. *Journal of Tourism and Cultural Change, 7*(1), 61–75.

McCool, S. F., & Martin, S. R. (1994). Community attachment and attitudes toward tourism development. *Journal of Travel Research, 32*(3), 29–34.

McGehee, N. G., & Andereck, K. L. (2004). Factors predicting rural residents' support of tourism. *Journal of Travel Research, 43*(2), 131–140.

Mehta, J. N., & Heinen, J. T. (2001). Does community-based conservation shape favorable attitudes among locals? An empirical study from Nepal. *Environmental Management, 28*(2), 165–177.

Meyers, L. S., Gamst, G., & Guarino, A. J. (2006). *Applied multivariate research: Design and interpretation.* Thousand Oaks, CA: Sage.

Ministry of Finance & Development Planning. (2002). *Revised national policy for rural development.* Government Paper No. 3. Gaborone, Botswana.

Ministry of Local Government. (2005). *Kgalagadi communal areas land management plan for the period 2005–2008.* Final draft. Department of Lands. Gaborone, Botswana.

Moswete, N. (2009). *Stakeholder perspectives on the potential for community-based ecotourism development and support for the Kgalagadi Transfrontier Park in Botswana* (Unpublished PhD dissertation). University of Florida, USA.

Moswete, N., Thapa, B., & Child, B. (2012). Attitudes and opinions of local and national public sector stakeholders towards Kgalagadi Transfrontier Park, Botswana. *International Journal of Sustainable Development and World Ecology, 19*(1), 67–80.

Moswete, N., Thapa, B., & Lacey, G. (2009). Village-based tourism and community participation: A case study of the Matsheng villages in southwest Botswana. In J. Saarinen, F. Becker, H. Manwa, & D. Wilson (Eds.), *Sustainable tourism in Southern Africa: Local communities and natural resources in transition* (pp. 189–209). Clevedon: Channelview.

Mugisha, A. R. (2002). *Evaluation of community-based conservation approaches: Management of protected areas in Uganda* (Unpublished PhD dissertation). University of Florida, USA.

Mulale, K. (2005). *The structural organization of CBNRM in Botswana* (Unpublished PhD dissertation). Iowa State University, USA.

Murphree, M. (2001). A case study of ecotourism development in Mahenye, Zimbabwe. In D. Hulme & M. Murphree (Eds.), *African wildlife and livelihoods: The promise and performance of community conservation* (pp. 177–194). Oxford: James Currey Press.

Nelson, F. (2004). *The evolution and impacts of community-based ecotourism in northern Tanzania.* International Institute for Environment and Development, Paper No. 131, 1–35. London, UK.

Nicholas, L. N., Thapa, B., & Ko, Y. J. (2009). Residents' perspectives of a World Heritage Site: The pitons management area, St. Lucia. *Annals of Tourism Research, 36*(3), 390–412.

Nyaupane, G. P., & Thapa, B. (2004). Evaluation of ecotourism: A comparative assessment in the Annapurna conservation area project, Nepal. *Journal of Ecotourism, 3*(1), 20–45.

Ormsby, A., & Mannie, K. (2006). Ecotourism benefits and the role of local guides at masoala national park, Madagascar. *Journal of Sustainable Tourism, 14*(3), 271–287.

Osborne, J. W., & Waters, E. (2002). Assumptions of multiple regression that researchers should always test. *Practical Assessment and Evaluation, 8*(2), 1–5.

Pallant, J. (2013). *SPSS survival manual.* Berkshire: Open University Press.

Parker, S., & Khare, A. (2005). Understanding success factors for ensuring sustainability in ecotourism development in Southern Africa. *Journal of Ecotourism, 4*(1), 32–46.

Peace Parks Foundation. (2009). *What progress has been made?* Retrieved March 14, 2009, from http://www.peaceparks.org

Reid, D. G. (Ed.). (1999). *Ecotourism development in eastern and southern Africa.* Harare: University of Guelph, Weaver Press.

Saarinen, J. (2011). Tourism development and local communities: The direct benefits of tourism to Ovahimba communities in the Kaokoland, northwest Namibia. *Tourism Review International*, *15*(1–2), 149–157.

Saarinen, J., Becker, F., Manwa, H., & Wilson, D. (Eds.). (2009). *Sustainable tourism in Southern Africa: Local communities and natural resources in transition*. Clevedon: Channelview.

Scheyvens, R. (1999). Ecotourism and the empowerment of local communities. *Tourism Management, 20*(2), 245–249.

Schoon, M. (2008). *Building robustness to disturbances: Governance in southern African peace parks* (Unpublished PhD dissertation). Indiana University, USA.

Sebele, L. S. (2010). Community-based tourism ventures, benefits and challenges: Khama rhino sanctuary trust, central district, Botswana. *Tourism Management, 31*(1), 136–146.

Sidinga, I. (1999). Tourism in sub-Saharan Africa. In D. G. Reid (Ed.), *Ecotourism development in eastern and southern Africa* (pp. 1–28). Harare: University of Guelph, Weaver Press.

Sikaraya, E., Teye, V., & Sonmez, S. (2002). Understanding residents' support for tourism development in the central region of Ghana. *Journal of Travel Research, 41*(1), 57–67.

Snyman, S. (2012). Ecotourism joint ventures between the private sector and communities: An updated analysis of the Torra Conservancy and Damaraland Camp partnership, Namibia. *Tourism Management Perspectives, 4*, 127–135.

Snyman, S. (2013). Household spending patterns and flow ecotourism income into communities around Liwonde National Park, Malawi. *Development Southern Africa, 30*(4–5), 640–658.

Snyman, S. (2014). Partnership between a private sector ecotourism operator and a local community in the Okavango Delta, Botswana: The case of the Okavango Community Trust and Wilderness Safaris. *Journal of Ecotourism, 13*(2–3), 110–127.

South African Park Board & Department of Wildlife & National Parks. (1999, April 12). *South Africa and Botswana sign historic agreement to formalize establishment of Kgalagadi Transfrontier Park*. Botswana. Joint Press Release.

Spenceley, A. (2008). Local impacts of community-based tourism in Southern Africa. In A. Spenceley (Ed.), *Responsible tourism: Critical issues for conservation and development* (pp. 287–301). London: Earthscan.

Stem, C. J., Lassoie, J. P., Lee, D. R., Deshler, D. D., & Schelhas, J. W. (2003). Community participation in ecotourism benefits: The link to conservation practices and perspectives. *Society and Natural Resources, 16*(5), 387–413.

Stronza, A. (2007). The economic promise of ecotourism for conservation. *Journal of Ecotourism, 6*(3), 210–230.

Suich, H. (2010). The livelihood impacts of the Namibian community-based natural resource management programme: A meta-synthesis. *Environmental Conservation, 37*(1), 45–53.

Tabachnick, B. G., & Fidell, L. S. (2001). *Using multivariate statistics*. Boston: Allyn and Bacon.

United Nations World Tourism Organization. (2011). *Tourism highlights: 2011 edition*. Madrid: UNWTO.

Walpole, M. J., & Goodwin, H. J. (2001). Local attitudes towards conservation and tourism around Komodo National Park, Indonesia. *Environmental Conservation, 28*(2), 160–166.

Weaver, D. (2002). Hard-core ecotourists in Lamington National Park, Australia. *Journal of Ecotourism, 1*(1), 19–35.

Weladji, R. B., Moe, S. R., & Vedeld, P. (2003). Stakeholder attitudes towards wildlife policy and Bénoué wildlife conservation area, north Cameroon. *Environmental Conservation, 30*(4), 334–343.

White, R. (2000). *Development and management plan for the Moremi Gorge*. Draft Final Report, Gaborone, Botswana.

Wilson, S., Fesenmaier, D. R., Fesenmaier, J., & Van Es, J. C. (2001). Factors for success in rural tourism development. *Journal of Travel Research, 40*(2), 132–138.

Wood, M. E. (2002). *Ecotourism: Principles, practices and policies for sustainability*. Paris: United Nations Environment Programme.

World Bank. (1996). *Transfrontier conservation areas pilot and institutional strengthening project*. Washington, DC: World Bank, Global Environment Coordination Division.

A review of ecotourism in Tanzania: magnitude, challenges, and prospects for sustainability

John T. Mgonja[a,b], Agnes Sirima[a,b] and Peter J. Mkumbo[a]

[a]Department of Parks, Recreation and Tourism Management, Clemson University, Clemson, SC, USA; [b]Department of Wildlife Management, Faculty of Forestry and Nature Conservation, Sokoine University of Agriculture, Morogoro, Tanzania

In the recent past, the concept of ecotourism has been promoted in Tanzania as an alternative, low-impact form of tourism that supports conservation of natural resources, preserves local culture, and provides economic benefits to the communities. Existing evidence shows that Tanzania has not utilised most of its ecotourism potential. The actual amount of ecotourism activity in the country is highly localised and relatively minimal due to the following factors: accessibility problems in some protected areas, inadequate infrastructure, and insufficient marketing and promotion. There is a need for regulatory authorities to articulate clear policies, regulations, and guidelines that delineate strategies on how to implement ecotourism activities in most parts of Tanzania. Such strategies should describe how to increase accessibility of ecotourism benefits to local communities, increase local community participation, and elucidate better mechanisms of sharing revenues generated from ecotourism. Given the abundance and diversity of natural and cultural resources in Tanzania, there is still room for growth, particularly in the southern, eastern, and western tourism circuits.

Introduction

In recent years, Tanzania has experienced a remarkable growth in nature-based tourism following major transformations in its tourism policies in the 1980s (Wade, Mwasaga, & Eagles, 2001). In the last five years, tourism has increased to become the nation's second leading foreign exchange earner after agriculture (Anderson, 2010). It is estimated that the number of international tourists' arrivals in the country rose from 150,000 in 1990 to 1,095,884 in 2013, amounting to an increase of approximately 630.6% (MNRT, 2014). Currently, the tourism industry supports approximately 250,000 jobs (direct and indirect), generates about 25% of Tanzania's foreign exchange earnings, and contributes to almost 17.8% of the national GDP (Carlson, 2009; MNRT, 2012). According to the Tourism Master Plan, Tanzania seeks to offer a low-density, high-quality, and high-priced tourism experience, which is consistent with the principles of ecotourism (URT, 2002a). It is estimated that over 50% of tourism activities in the country are nature based, focusing mostly on protected areas wildlife resources (Anderson, 2010).

In the recent past, the concept of ecotourism has been promoted in Tanzania as an alternative, low-impact form of tourism as opposed to conventional mass tourism. Ecotourism is viewed by the government of Tanzania as both; a conservation and development tool because it provides conservation benefits to its natural resources as well as social, cultural, and economic benefits to local communities (URT, 1999). Ecotourism is also applauded by many scholars due to its potential to provide more employment and business opportunities to more remote indigenous people than mass tourism (Jusko, 1994). Socially, ecotourism is praised because it stimulates hosts and guests education and helps local communities to revive their ancient festivals and restore their cultural landmarks (Wright, 1993).

Although ecotourism is subject to multiple definitions, it is typically contrasted to traditional mass tourism. Ecotourism is referred as a responsible travel to natural areas that conserves the natural resources and sustains the well-being of local people (Charnley, 2005; Wood, 2002). The literature shows that early definitions of the concept of ecotourism focused more on protection of resources and observers' experience (Ceballos-Lascurain, 1983; International Resource Group, 1992; Smardon, 1994; Tickell, 1994). Commenting on Ceballos-Lascurain's (1983) definition, Fennell (2001) makes the case that this definition is effective in capturing the essence of what ecotourism is, because it focuses on the importance of natural areas, cognitive and affective domains, and behaviour.

In this article, we define ecotourism as 'responsible travel to natural areas that conserves the environment, sustains the well-being of the local people, and involves interpretation and education' (TIES, 2015). In this definition, education is meant to be inclusive of both hosts and guests (TIES, 2015). The strength of TIES definition is that it combines both resource protection and economic development or welfare of the local communities. Similarly, it captures three fundamental principles of sustainability, namely the environment, economy, and community well-being. Ecotourism has also been defined based on resource protection (natural and cultural), economic development, and education (Australian Commonwealth Department of Tourism, 1994; Buckley, 1994; Honey, 1999; 2008). These definitions are also useful since they embrace three important criteria; (1) an emphasis on the protection of both natural and cultural resources, (2) learning opportunities (education), and (3) adherence to the principles of ecological, sociocultural, and economic sustainability. A review of 85 ecotourism definitions showed that there is a definitional change through time and that conceptual variables most common on contemporary definitions are slightly different from those of earlier definitions (Fennell, 2001). Most contemporary definitions show that there is a growing sensitivity to sustainability and benefit to the local communities (Fennell, 2001). This suggests that the concept of ecotourism, just like any other new concept has been evolving over time.

Despite a wide range of publications on ecotourism development worldwide, little has been published regarding ecotourism growth in Tanzania. Therefore, this paper discusses the status of ecotourism in Tanzania, offers some useful insights into ecotourism developments in the country, and discusses major challenges and opportunities of ecotourism practices in the country. The specific objectives of this paper are to: delineate various ecotourism attractions and activities, examine the magnitude and opportunities of ecotourism, and examine the challenges of ecotourism practices in Tanzania.

The paper starts by discussing the shortcomings of mass tourism and emergence of ecotourism in developing countries. Then, it discusses some ecotourism attractions and activities occurring in protected areas as well as other areas in Tanzania. This is followed by a section that examines the magnitude and opportunities of ecotourism, and then a section that examines the challenges of ecotourism practices in Tanzania. The paper concludes with discussion of the limitations of ecotourism practices and future plans for the industry.

This paper is based on the secondary data. Such documents as National tourism policy, tourism act, tourism master plan, and other published articles regarding ecotourism activities in Tanzania and elsewhere were therefore consulted in our review.

Shortcomings of mass tourism and emergence of ecotourism in developing countries

Improvements in air transportation post the Second World War made it easier for people to visit geographically distant destinations in a shorter time than before. This led to the evolution and growth of mass tourism in the 1960s and 1970s in many destinations, such as those in the Mediterranean region, and some developing countries, such as Small Island Developing States (SIDS). Consequently, many developing countries witnessed an increase in the overuse and degradation of natural resources. This is partly due to the fact that many developing countries regarded tourism as a panacea for solving most of their economic problems at a macro-level as well as a valuable tool for alleviating poverty at a micro-level (Long & Nuckolls, 1994; Mann, 2005). The use of tourism as a means of poverty alleviation in developing countries has been supported by many agencies and organisations, including development agencies and donors (e.g. German Organisation for Technical Cooperation agency – GTZ), tourism industry organisations (e.g. Pacific and Asia Travel Association – PATA), NGOs (e.g. International Union for Conservation of Nature – IUCN), multilateral organisations (e.g. the Asian Development Bank), United Nations Development Programme and Environment Programme (Scheyvens, 2007). The need to solve economic problems facing many developing countries coupled with the emergence of globalisation led many governments to jump on the tourism bandwagon without proper planning, leading to many destructive forms of mass tourism.

In the beginning, mass tourism was extolled as a harmless industry that would help developing nations to raise foreign exchange quickly and reduce unemployment rates, as it involved many sectors in the host destination, such as transportation, accommodation, tour operations, tour guiding, and hospitality. However, in many developing countries the benefits of mass tourism were never attained as anticipated (Mowforth & Munt, 2008; O'Neill, 2002; Tosun & Timothy, 2001).

Honey (1999) shows that mass tourism has often resulted in overdevelopment, uneven development, environmental degradation, and invasion by culturally insensitive and economically disruptive foreigners. O'Neill (2002) argues that in some cases, local citizens were left worse off because of the opportunity costs of developing a tourism industry as well as an overdependence on an unpredictable tourism industry. It is further argued by O'Neill that mass tourism is manipulative in nature because some governments, particularly in developing countries, provide subsidies in the form of tax breaks and other investment incentives that tend to favour investors over the locals (O'Neill, 2002). Similarly, Telfer (2003, p. 100) stresses that 'Overseas companies and investors which come into a country under pro-globalisation policies can push out small, local investors or businesses who find they cannot compete'.

Additional shortcomings of mass tourism are related to revenue leakages. According to the World Bank estimates, up to fifty-five percent of revenues generated from tourism in developing countries leak back to developed nations (Lindberg & Lindberg, 1991). A similar argument was raised by Scheyvens (2007) pointing out that the economic benefits of tourism are normally minimal because foreign companies, which dominate many developing countries, repatriate their profits. The United Nations Conference on Trade and Development (UNCTAD) estimates that an average of 40–50% of foreign exchange earnings return to the home countries of the investors (Plüss & Backes, 2002). The Tourism Confederation of Tanzania (2009) showed that all-inclusive tour packages can result in leakage of about 60% of revenues. Studies conducted by a number of scholars indicate that such leakages are often substantial, especially in smaller countries with the tourism industry dominated by foreign investors (Akama, 1997; Britton, 1987; English, 1986; Khan, Chou, & Wong, 1990; Richards, 1983; Steward & Spinrad, 1982). Because of leakages, developing countries tend to capture little of the scarcity rent offered by their resources and quickly lose much of what they do capture (Lindberg & Lindberg, 1991). Other shortcomings frequently associated with mass tourism in developing countries include: high rates of foreign ownership, contributing to a loss of control over local resources; widely fluctuating earnings due to seasonality of tourism in some places; environmental destruction; increasing crime rates; overcrowding; overloaded infrastructures; and the perceived loss of cultural identity (Brohman, 1996). Most articulated criticisms of mass tourism concur with Jafari's idea of 'cautionary platform', which asserts that tourism has a wide range of negative impacts, including cultural commodification, social disruption, and environmental degradation (Jafari, 2001).

Due to many problems associated with conventional mass tourism, many scholars and practitioners promote ecotourism as a means of achieving sustainability in tourism development (Liu, 2003). Several scholars argue that ecotourism, along with allied concepts such as sustainable tourism and alternative tourism, evolved out of dissatisfaction with traditional mass tourism which was seen as environmentally, economically, and socially damaging and harmful to local cultures (Brohman, 1996; Fennell, 2007; Honey & Stewart, 2002; Jafari, 2001; O'Neill, 2002; Zhong & Xiao, 1999). Ecotourism is thus viewed as a potential tool for protection of natural resources as well as a tool for attaining sustainable tourism and hence sustainable development in many developing countries where tourism is prominent. Some scholars argue that even the term 'ecotourism' means quite simply 'ecologically sound tourism' (Shores, 1992). It is argued that perhaps the most prominent direct benefit of ecotourism is its allocentric propensity, which tends to distribute net benefits to local people thereby creating incentives to protect those natural areas that draw tourists (Shores, 1992). It is contended that ecotourists travel to more peripheral areas and so have a higher tendency to consume local goods, thereby enhancing multiplier effects as well as increasing local participation in tourism development (Weaver, 1999).

Ecotourism is considered to be one of the fastest growing segments of tourism (Fennell, 1999; Wally, 2001) and it originates from the ethics of conservation and sustainable development (Wood, 2002). Ecotourism serves as a niche market for environmentally concerned travellers (Wood & Crouch, 2001). Studies indicate that tourism activities in developing countries account for a much higher proportion of ecotourism activity (Daniel, Carey, & Jones, 1993; Eagles & Cascagnette, 1995; Holing, 1991), because most of these countries have more natural, relatively undisturbed, and unspoiled areas compared to developed countries (Cater & Lowman, 1994). Proponents of ecotourism assert that ecotourism is different from other forms of tourism, such as nature tourism. These scholars maintain that 'while nature tourism is defined on the basis of what travellers do, ecotourism focusses on the impact of their travel on both the environment and the people in the host country' (Medina, 2005, p. 283). Similar to Medina, Ziffer distinguishes between the concepts of ecotourism and nature tourism by claiming that 'ecotourism is a more comprehensive concept based on a planned approach by the destination authorities, whereas nature tourism is more consumer-based and not ecologically sound' (Ziffer, 1989, p. 6).

Ecotourism attractions and activities in Tanzania

Tanzania is one of sub-Saharan Africa's most popular and rapidly growing nature-based tourism destinations (CNN travel poll, 2013; UNWTO, 2014). A similar view was echoed by Honey (2008) who argued that Tanzania is the richest country in the world in term of its wildlife, having more elephants, lions, zebras, antelopes, and other large mammals than any other country in Africa. Tanzania is extoled for possessing a rich store-house of biological diversity, which constitutes some of the world's greatest natural wonders. Tanzania is one of the top 25 global hotspots (Myers, 1990; Myers, Mittermeier, Mittermeier, Da Fonseca, & Kent, 2000). These hotspots are characterised by a high level of species endemism and account for a disproportionate share of global biodiversity. Over 25% of Tanzanian land is managed under different levels of protection (URT, 2013), among them include:16 national parks, 34 game reserves, 38 game controlled areas, 1 conservation area, 3 marine parks, and 15 marine reserves (Mwaipopo, 2008; URT, 2007). Additionally, Tanzania is applauded as the only country in the World, which has allocated more than 25% of its total area for conservation of natural resources under different forms of protected areas (URT, 2013). Tanzania has also been widely known for its unparalleled wildlife and abundant natural resources, which are considered among the finest in the world (World Economic Forum, 2011).

As in most ecotourism destinations, such as Kenya or Costa Rica, ecotourism activities in Tanzania are strongly linked to protected areas and, in some cases, their surrounding neighbourhoods. Existing evidence shows that currently, most ecotourism activities in Tanzania take place within a relatively small designated part of protected areas; and in most cases ecotourism activities take place only in a few, more accessible parks. The majority of accessible parks are located in the northern part of the country, commonly known as northern tourist circuit. The circuit consists of famous protected areas, such as Serengeti, Lake Manyara, Tarangire, Arusha, Kilimanjaro, and Mkomazi national parks, and Ngorongoro conservation area authority. Combined, these protected areas account for over 90% of the total parks' visitations countrywide. Walking safaris, campsites, and community-based tourism are typical examples of the various forms of ecotourism in Tanzania.

Walking safaris allow visitors to explore nature up-close and offer direct contact with local residents. The literature shows that ecotourism in the form of walking safaris are rapidly increasing in the Ngorongoro conservation area (Charnley, 2005). Walking safaris in Ngorongoro involve Maasai (local guide) taking visitors on foot through different physical landscapes, such as forests, craters, mountains, and plains over routes that can take a day to several weeks depending on visitors' curiosity and local guide availability (NCAA, 2002). Sometimes walking safaris involve visitors spending a day or a number of days in a bush camp, in a Maasai cultural house (known as *boma*), or a combination of both. In some instances; Maasai donkeys are used as a means of transport to carry loads, such as food, water, and bags (Shivji & Kapinga, 1998; Wilson, 2011). It is also maintained that walking safaris enable visitors to get up-close, and tread into the personal space of the wild animals, this includes feeling the air they breathe, where they eat, sleep, play, and breed, and thus creating a unique experience (Kaur & Singh, 2008). Walking safaris are regarded as prime examples of ecotourism because they are compatible with local peoples' (Maasai) way of life. Additionally, walking safaris provide local people with opportunities to participate directly in tourism activities by offering them job opportunities that are built on their existing skills and do not necessarily interfere with their traditional life pattern (Charnley, 2005). Some scholars contend that for the Maasai guiding tourists on walking safaris is similar to herding livestock as they can apply the same skill set—the ability to walk long distances for long periods of time, the ability to detect and avoid predators, the ability to find drinking water, a good sense of direction, and familiarity with the local landscape. (DeLuca, 2002, p. 216)

Table 1 presents ecotourism attractions and activities in national parks/protected areas in the country. Other areas where many ecotourism activities take place in the country include: all 47 Cultural Tourism Programmes (CTP) in the country, cultural and natural world heritage sites in Tanzania (such as Kilimanjaro national park, Serengeti national park, Selous game reserve, Ngorongoro conservation area authority, Kondoa rock-art sites, Kilwa ruins, and the ruins of Songo Mnara), cultural and natural national heritage sites (e.g. mount Meru, mount Uluguru, etc.), nature reserves (e.g. Amani nature reserve, Uluguru nature reserve, Nilo nature reserve, Magamba nature reserve, Chome nature reserve, Kilombero nature reserve, Mkingu nature reserve), marine parks (e.g. Mafia island marine park, Mnazi bay, Ruvuma estuary marine park, Tanga coelocanthy marine park), marine reserves, such as Maziwe island marine reserve, Kwale island marine reserve, Mbarakuni island marine reserve, Mwewe island marine reserve, Kirui island marine reserve, Ulenge island marine reserve, Nyororo island marine reserve, Shungi mbili island marine reserve, and Dar es Salaam marine reserves system (DMRs) comprises seven islands of Bongoyo, Pangavini, Fungu Yasin, Mbudya Sinda, Makatobe, and Kendwa (TTB, 2013; UNESCO, 2014; URT, 2007; URT, 2015).

The magnitude and opportunities for ecotourism in Tanzania

Since 2000, the Tanzanian government has focused on the development of ecotourism in the country (URT, 1999). Although it is difficult to quantify the number of tourists who are purely ecotourists, it can be argued that most tourists who choose to visit Tanzania do so due to the high-quality nature-based/ecotourism attractions (Table 1). Anderson (2010) estimates that at least 50% of tourists visiting Tanzania follow nature-based tourism. The classification of Tanzania as one of the sub-Saharan Africa's most popular and rapidly growing nature-based tourism destinations by CNN travel poll (2013) and UNWTO (2014), the richest country in the world in terms of its wildlife by Honey (2008) and one of the top 25 global 'hotspots' by Myers et al. (2000) and Myers (1990) justifies further why there is an influx of tourists, particularly nature-based tourists travelling to Tanzania. Most protected areas in Tanzania (Table 1) support some forms of ecotourism or have a high potential of becoming ecotourism destinations.

Park regulations given by Tanzania National Parks (TANAPA) to tourists have to a large extent made it possible to maintain the quality of these natural and cultural attractions. Such regulations state that when in the park, visitors should not disturb or feed animals, make noise or any sort of disturbance which offend other visitors, pick or destroy flowers and plants, litter, burn cigarettes or matches, carry pets, be involved in hunting or collection of plant and animal samples, go for a walking safari without park official armed guides/rangers, or practice off-road driving at any time. The regulations also stipulate that visitors should always stay on the authorised trails during walking safaris. Similarly, visitors should conduct all tourism activities between 6am and 7pm. For the rest of the time, visitors are expected to stay in their chosen accommodation location (i.e. lodges, camps and/or campsites). The main objective of these regulations is to sustain the resources while providing visitors with a positive and unforgettable experience.

Table 1.   Ecotourism attractions and activities in national parks/protected areas in Tanzania.

National park/ Protected area	Visitors in 2013	Tourism activities	Comments
Serengeti	452,485	Hot air balloon safaris, walking safaris, picnicking, game drives, Maasai rock paintings and musical rocks.	Mass tourism and ecotourism
Ngorongoro	350,970	Walking safaris, picnicking, game drives, site seeing (e.g. Ngorongoro Crater, Olduvai Gorge, Ol Doinyo Lengai volcano and Lake Natron's flamingos.	Mass tourism and ecotourism
Lake Manyara	187,773	Game drives, canoeing, cultural tours, picnicking, mountain bike tours, abseiling, and forest walks.	Mostly ecotourism
Tarangire	165,949	Walking safaris, day trips to Maasai and Barabaig villages, ancient rock paintings in the vicinity of Kolo on the Dodoma road.	Mostly ecotourism
Arusha	71,930	Forest walks, bird watching, numerous picnic sites, Mt. Meru climbing.	Mostly ecotourism
Mt. Kilimanjaro	53,254	Mt. Kilimanjaro climbing, hiking Shira plateau, nature trails on the lower reaches, Trout fishing, visit the Chala crater lake on the mountain's southeastern slopes and bird watching	Mostly ecotourism
Mikumi	45,888	Game drives and guided walks.	Mostly ecotourism
Ruaha	21,766	Bird watching, game drives, site seeing including cultural and historical sites.	Mostly ecotourism
Saadani	14,709	Boat safari, watching green turtle breeding site, snorkelling in the caves with colourful fish and green turtles, lunch and sun bathing, walking safari on natural trails of Saadani, game drives, relax on the cleanest beach	Mostly ecotourism
Udzungwa	7131	Hiking to the waterfalls, camping safaris. Site seeing, bird watching	Mostly ecotourism
Saanane	5150	Game viewing, bird watching, rock hiking, boat cruise, walking, picnics, bush lunch, meditation photographing/filming, and sport fishing. Ideal place for wedding, engagement, team building, family day, and birthdays	Mostly ecotourism
Mahale	1094	Chimp tracking, hiking to the sacred peek, camping safaris, snorkelling, sports fishing, water sports activities	Mostly ecotourism
Katavi	4275	Walking, driving, and camping safaris, visiting the tamarind tree inhabited by the spirit of the legendary hunter Katabi (for whom the park is named) – offerings are still left here by locals seeking the spirit's blessing.	Mostly ecotourism
Gombe	1771	Chimpanzee trekking, hiking, bird watching, swimming, and snorkelling; Site seeing including dhow building	Mostly ecotourism
Mkomazi	1806	Game drives, camping, site seeing, bird watching, walking safari, and hiking (uphill). Learn more about conservation and rhinoceros at Mkomazi rhino sanctuary.	Mostly ecotourism

(Continued)

Table 1. Continued.

National park/ Protected area	Visitors in 2013	Tourism activities	Comments
Rubondo	908	Game drives, bird watching, walking safaris.	Mostly ecotourism
Kitulo	433	Hiking, open walking across grasslands to watch birds and wildflowers, Matema beach on Lake Nyasa.	Mostly ecotourism

Source: TANAPA (2012).

A close look at these regulations indicates clearly that they are consistent with the principles of ecotourism, which requires that those who implement, participate in, and market ecotourism activities should adopt the ecotourism principles (TIES, 2015). More specifically, the ecotourism principles require practitioners to; (1) minimise physical, social, behavioural, and psychological impacts, (2) build environmental and cultural awareness and respect, (3) provide positive experiences for both visitors and hosts, (4) provide direct financial benefits for conservation, (5) generate financial benefits for both local people and private industry, (6) deliver memorable interpretative experiences to visitors that help raise sensitivity to host countries' political, environmental, and social climates, (7) design, construct and operate low-impact facilities, (8) recognise the rights and spiritual beliefs of the indigenous people in their community and work in partnership with them to create empowerment (TIES, 2015).

Tanzania has a good opportunity to further develop its ecotourism industry due to its unspoilt natural and cultural resources, particularly in the southern, eastern, and western parts of the country where many people still live in abject poverty. The southern and western parts of the country have many undeveloped and underutilised natural and cultural resources which can serve as magnificent ecotourism attractions. Ecotourism activities in and around these areas may provide opportunities for visitors to experience powerful manifestations of nature and culture as well as learn about the importance of biodiversity conservation and local cultures (Drumm, Moore, Soles, Patterson, & Terborgh, 2004). If ecotourism is promoted in these areas, local communities living in or adjacent to these areas may benefit in a number of ways, including diversifying their economies, getting jobs, and hence improving their living standards. Similarly, ecotourism can generate income for conservation programmes and therefore enhance conservation of endangered ecosystems and species in these areas. This is particularly important because protected areas in Tanzania are state owned and therefore, funds for managing these resources are normally scarce.

Some challenges of ecotourism practices in Tanzania

Existing evidence shows that Tanzania has not utilised most of its ecotourism potential. Currently, ecotourism activities are relatively minimal due to such factors as: accessibility problems to some protected areas (particularly in the southern and western parts of the country), inadequate infrastructure, insufficient marketing and promotional campaigns, lack of access to capital, and lack of ecotourism certification programmes throughout the country.

Local people to a large extent have extensive knowledge of their areas including cultural and spiritual aspects which are pertinent in ecotourism; however, they tend to lack the formal education and training necessary to operate ecotourism businesses. Likewise, local people in rural areas have limited access to capital required to run ecotourism businesses. These challenges limit the chances of local people to participate in ecotourism endeavours and to a large extent contribute to revenue leakages from rural areas to large cities or other countries. Revenue leakages occur because investors from large cities and foreign countries normally have more access to capital than local people.

In addition to funding struggles, the sustainability of the ecotourism attractions in the country has been continuously jeopardised by other factors, such as deforestation, poaching, and human encroachment due to rapid population growth. For instance, a recent National Environmental Management Council of Tanzania (NEMC) report demonstrated that the rate of deforestation per year in Tanzania is about 1.1% which is double the global deforestation rate which stands at 0.5% per year (NEMC, 2013). Although there are several government regulations and guidelines such as The Forest Act of 2002 as indicated in the URT (2002b) that governs the utilisation of such forests, there has been a lack of urgency in addressing deforestation issues in the country. Healthy forests offer a wide range of ecotourism activities, such as nature trails, picnic and camping sites, boardwalks, and canopy walks.

Similarly, over the past few years, wildlife trafficking in Tanzania has become more organised, more widespread, and more dangerous than ever. Thus, elephant and rhino poaching have become both an economic and national security issue. The rapid loss of elephants would bring a significant negative effect to the nation. Elephants are a key species in the Savannah ecosystem and would have a cascading effect on the region if they were to go extinct. If the government wishes ecotourism to flourish, then concrete action needs to be taken to enhance conservation and protection of these natural heritages and ecosystems. One way of doing this is to empower local communities living near protected areas to invest in ecotourism. Such investments in ecotourism can provide the local communities with motivation to conserve forests as well as wildlife. When local people get income and employment from ecotourism, they are more likely to protect the natural resources through sustainable exploitation. Ecotourism can play a significant role in the revival of stagnant economies in many rural areas in Tanzania. However, ecotourism activities must be executed in a manner that will not only protect the natural resources but also consider the needs and values of each indigenous community. Careful planning and implementation is required to reduce associated negative impacts. It has been suggested by other scholars that ecotourism activities if not well planned may constitute the early stages of such cycles of tourism development, thereby running the risk of serving to open up new destinations for activities associated with mass tourism (France, 1997).

Conclusions and recommendations

Since the formal introduction of the term 'ecotourism' almost three decades ago, controversy over appropriate use of the term and inconsistency in its application has somewhat hindered the development of the concept and its practical realisation at specific sites. The lack of clear operating ecotourism principles and guidelines in Tanzania has more or less created confusion among practitioners on how to operate their businesses in a manner consistent with ecotourism principles. Although these guidelines exist elsewhere, the government of Tanzania has been slow in adopting and implementing these guidelines.

Tanzania is relatively a huge country and largely a nature-based tourism destination. Due to this, it is not practically feasible to regard it as an ecotourism or as a mass tourism destination as a whole. More specifically, tourism activities in Tanzania need to be seen along a continuum with conventional mass tourism on one side and ecotourism on the other. For example, it is logical and practically correct to place Ngorongoro conservation area authority and Serengeti national park on one side of the spectrum (mass tourism) and the rest of the national parks on the other side of the spectrum (ecotourism), as indicated in Table 1. Even in Serengeti national park and Ngorongoro conservation area authority where mass tourism is cited, there are still some aspects of ecotourism activities taking place, such as walking safaris. It can be generally concluded that in Tanzania, there are more ecotourism practices than mass tourism, as indicated in Table 1. However, these practices need more appropriate ecotourism guidelines from the regulatory authority so as to fully operate according to ecotourism principles.

Similar to other ecotourism destinations in the world, the impacts of ecotourism activities in Tanzania are highly confined. In some parks, particularly in the Northern tourist circuit, carrying capacity problems have been observed. These problems to a large extent are associated with high visitor numbers, resource destruction, and poor visitor management techniques.

Tourism activities within certain protected areas such as Mikumi, Lake Manyara, Tarangire, Ngorongoro, Kilimanjaro, Arusha, and Serengeti have also stimulated the establishment of tourism related services in areas adjacent to park entry points, creating locally significant amounts of economic activities to surrounding communities. Some of the tourism services in these areas include: accommodation facilities, food services, porter service, village tours, hand crafts and souvenirs, and cultural dance performances. These services are currently not operating according to ecotourism principles per se. People offering these services therefore, need to be provided with training and guidelines to transform their services into fully functioning ecotourism endeavours.

To achieve full potential of ecotourism in Tanzania, practitioners and regulatory authorities need to take the following issues into account. First, tourism regulatory authorities need to make sure that ecotourism benefits are readily accessible to local people whose livelihood depends on the natural resources where ecotourism activities takes place. Second, community participation in ecotourism activities needs to be improved (Michael, Mgonja, & Backman, 2013). One way of increasing local people participation is through provision of education and training that is consistent with communities' lifestyles (Michael, Sirima, & Marwa, 2013). A good example of this would be community capacity building on ecotourism-related techniques that promote local culture and protect natural resources. Tour-guiding skills could be a starting point. From our synthesis it is clear that there has been no systematic review of ecotour guide training in Tanzania. Ecotour guides are regarded as important cultural brokers or mediators who are sensitive to the economic, environmental, and cultural environment (Gurung, Simmons, & Devlin, 1996). Third, tourism regulatory authorities need to find better mechanisms of reducing revenue leakages. One way of achieving this could be through supporting community lodges that operate according to ecotourism principles (Sirima & Ladislaus, 2012). An alternative and perhaps more effective way may be through regulations, laws, and policies. An example of this would be the use of ecotourism certification systems. Through certification schemes, it would be possible for regulatory authorities to control businesses that did not fulfil the core criteria of ecotourism but were marketed as such, thereby discrediting and discouraging other businesses that follow the core criteria of ecotourism. Fourth, the regulatory authorities should adopt or develop ecotourism guidelines and make sure that all practitioners follow these guidelines. The key to the successful ecotourism destination is well-defined policies and regulations that show individuals how to implement ecotourism activities.

Records show that tourism is indeed highly significant for the development of the country. Likewise, there is tremendous opportunity for major growth in the Tanzanian eco-tourism industry, based on the projected increase in global travel and increasing demand for authentic nature experiences. Given the abundance and diversity of natural and cultural resources in Tanzania, there is still room for growth particularly in the southern, western, and eastern tourism circuits.

In terms of diversification, Tanzania has already taken a major step in diversifying its products by developing cultural tourism enterprises. Currently there are over 50 cultural tourism enterprises in the country. However, poor benefit sharing mechanisms, lack of guidelines, and tour-guiding techniques constitute a major drawback in the development of such initiatives. Thus, to achieve the intended ecotourism objectives in the country, the regulatory authorities need to pay more attention on issues related to capacity building and development of ecotourism guidelines to guide current and future practices. Likewise, the government of Tanzania should promote ecotourism among the indigenous people instead of depending mainly on international visitors and investors.

Disclosure statement

No potential conflict of interest was reported by the authors.

References

Akama, J. S. (1997). Tourism development in Kenya: Problems and policy alternatives. *Progress in Tourism and Hospitality Research, 3*(2), 95–105.

Anderson, W. (2010). Determinants of all-inclusive travel expenditure. *Tourism Review, 65*(3), 4–15.

Australian Commonwealth Department of Tourism. (1994). *National ecotourism strategy.* Canberra: Australian Government Publishing Service.

Britton, S., & Clarke, W. (1987). *Ambiguous alternative: Tourism in small developing countries.* Suva: The University of the South Pacific.

Brohman, J. (1996). New directions in tourism for third world development. *Annals of Tourism Research, 23*(1), 48–70.

Buckley, R. (1994). A framework for ecotourism. *Annals of Tourism Research, 21*(3), 661–665.

Carlson, L. (2009). *Tanzania tourism and travel news.* Retrieved October 30, 2014, from http://www.tanzaniainvest.com

Cater, E., & Lowman, G. (1994). *Ecotourism: A Sustainable Option?* Chichester: John Wiley & Sons.

Ceballos-Lascurain, H. (1983). Tourism, ecotourism and protected areas. In J. A. Kusler (Ed.), *Ecotourism and resource conservation* (Vol. 1, pp. 24–34). Ecotourism Conservation Project. Merida, Mexico: Berne, N.Y.

Charnley, S. (2005). From nature tourism to ecotourism? The case of the ngorongoro conservation area, Tanzania. *Human Organization, 64*(1), 75–88.

CNN travel poll. (2013). *Tanzania voted best safari country in Africa: A new poll crowns the East African country the king of safaris.* Retrieved October 10, 2014, from http://travel.cnn.com/tanzania-voted-best-country-watch-african-animals-run-wild-182326

Daniel, J., Carey, A., & Jones, L. (1993). *The buzzworm magazine guide to ecotravel.* Boulder, CO: Buzzworm Books.

DeLuca, L. M. (2002). *Tourism, conservation, and development among the Maasai of Ngorongoro district, Tanzania: Implications for political ecology and sustainable livelihoods.* Ph.D. dissertation, Department of Anthropology, University of Colorado.

Drumm, A., Moore, A., Soles, A., Patterson, C., & Terborgh, J. E. (2004). *Ecotourism development: A manual for conservation planners and managers* (Vol. 2, pp. 1–107). Arlington, VA: The Nature Conservancy.

Eagles, P. F., & Cascagnette, J. W. (1995). Canadian ecotourists: Who are they? *Tourism Recreation Research, 20*, 22–28.

English, E. (1986). *The great escape? An examination of North–South tourism*. Ottawa: The North-South Institute.

Fennell, D. A. (1999). *Ecotourism: An introduction*. New York, NY: Routledge.

Fennell, D. A. (2001). A content analysis of ecotourism definitions. *Current Issues in Tourism*, *4*(5), 403–421.

Fennell, D. A. (2007). *Ecotourism*. London: Routledge.

France, L. (1997). Introduction. In L. France (Ed.), *The Earthscan reader in sustainable tourism* (pp. 1–22). London: Earthscan.

Gurung, G., Simmons, D., & Devlin, P. (1996). The evolving role of the tourist guides: The Nepali experience. In R. Butler & T. Hinch (Eds.), *Tourism and indigenous peoples* (pp. 108–127). London: International Thomson Business Press.

Holing, D. (1991). *A guide to earth trips: Nature travel on a fragile planet*. Los Angeles, CA: Living Planet Press.

Honey, M. (1999). *Ecotourism and sustainable development: Who owns the paradise?* Washington, DC: Island.

Honey, M. (2008). *Ecotourism and sustainable development* (2nd ed.). Washington, DC: Island Press.

Honey, M., & Stewart, E. (2002). The evolution of 'green' standards for tourism. In M. Honey (Ed.), *Ecotourism and certification* (pp. 33–71). Washington, DC: Island.

International Resources Group. (1992). *Ecotourism: A viable alternative for sustainable management of natural resources in Africa* (Agency For Int'l Dev. Bureau For Aft., 1992). Washington, DC: Author.

Jafari, J. (2001). The scientification of tourism. In V. L. Smith & M. Brent (Eds.), *Hosts and guests revisited: Tourism issues of the 21st Century* (pp. 28–41). New York, NY: Cognizant Communication.

Jusko, J. (1994). CHIC addresses threats to tourism. *Hotel and Motel Management*, *209*(13), 6–29.

Kaur, T., & Singh, J. (2008). Up close and personal with Mahale chimpanzees – a path forward. *American Journal of Primatology*, *70*(8), 729–733.

Khan, H., Chou, F., & Wong, E. (1990). Tourism multiplier effects on Singapore. *Annals of Tourism Research*, *17*, 408–418.

Lindberg, K., & Lindberg, K. (1991). *Policies for maximizing nature tourism's ecological and economic benefits* (pp. 20–21). Washington, DC: World Resources Institute.

Liu, Z. (2003). Sustainable tourism development: A critique. *Journal of Sustainable Tourism*, *11*(6), 459–475.

Long, P. T., & Nuckolls, J. S. (1994). Organizing resources for rural tourism development: The importance of leadership, planning and technical assistance. *Tourism Recreation Research*, *19*(2), 19–34.

Mann, S. (2005). *Tourism and the World Bank*. Paper presented at the Development Studies Association Conference, Milton Keynes.

Medina, L. K. (2005). Ecotourism and certification: Confronting the principles and pragmatics of socially responsible tourism. *Journal of Sustainable Tourism*, *13*(3), 281–295.

Michael, M., Mgonja, J. T., & Backman, K. F. (2013). Desires of community participation in tourism development decision making process. A case study of barabarani, Mto Wa Mbu, Tanzania. *American Journal of Tourism Research*, *2*(1), 84–94.

Michael, M., Sirima, A., & Marwa, E. (2013). The role of local communities in tourism development: A grassroots perspective from Tanzania. *Journal of Human Ecology*, *41*(1), 53–66.

MNRT. (2012). *The international visitors' exit survey report*. Dar es Salaam: Ministry of Natural Resources and Tourism.

MNRT. (2014). *The international visitors' exit survey report*. Dar es Salaam: Ministry of Natural Resources and Tourism.

Mowforth, M., & Munt, I. (2008). *Tourism and sustainability: Development, globalization and new tourism in the third world*. New York: Routledge.

Mwaipopo, R. N. (2008). *The social dimensions of marine protected areas: A case study of the Mafia Island Marine Park in Tanzania*. Dar es Salaam, Tanzania: International Collective in Support of Fishworkers.

Myers, N. (1990). The biodiversity challenge: Expanded hot-spots analysis. *Environmentalist*, *10*(4), 243–256.

Myers, N., Mittermeier, R. A., Mittermeier, C. G., Da Fonseca, G. A., & Kent, J. (2000). Biodiversity hotspots for conservation priorities. *Nature*, *403*(6772), 853–858.

NCAA. (2002). *Walking safaris in the Ngorongoro conservation area*. Arusha: Pamphlet produced by NCAA, Norwegian Agency for Development Cooperation, and National Outdoor Leadership School.

NEMC. (2013). *Global warming and climate change forum*. National Environmental Management Council, Retrieved September 13, 2015, from http://www.ippmedia.com/frontend/?l=62180

O'Neill, A. C. (2002). What globalization means for ecotourism: Managing globalization's impacts on ecotourism in developing countries. *Indiana Journal of Global Legal Studies*, *9*(2), 501–528.

Plüss, C., & Backes, M. (2002). *Red card for tourism? 10 principles and challenges for a sustainable tourism development in the 21st century*. Freiburg, Germany: Schwarz auf Weiss.

Richards, V. A. (1983). Decolonization in Antigua: Its impact on agriculture and tourism. In P. Henry & C. Stone (Eds.), *The newer Caribbean: Decolonization, democracy and development* (pp. 15–35). Philadelphia, PA: Institute for the Study of Human Issues.

Scheyvens, R. (2007). Exploring the tourism-poverty nexus. *Current Issues in Tourism*, *10*(2–3), 231–254.

Shivji, I. G., & Kapinga, W. B. L. (1998). *Maasai Rights in Ngorongoro, Tanzania* (Vol. 38). Papua New Guinea: IIED.

Shores, J. N. (1992, February). *The challenge of ecotourism: A call for higher standards* (pp. 10–21). Paper presented at the 4th world congress on national parks and protected areas, Caracas, Venezuela.

Sirima, A., & Ladislaus, M. (2012). Unlocking the opportunities for displaced communities: Can tourism offset the conservation costs? *Asia-Pacific Journal of Innovation in Hospitality and Tourism*, *1*(1), 65–84.

Smardon, C. R. (1994). Ecotourims: Blessing or bane to sustainable development. *LALUP (Newsl. Landscape/Land Use Plan*. Committee Am. Society Landscape Architects).

Steward, S., & Spinrad, B. (1982). *Tourism in the Caribbean: The economic impact*. Toronto, ON: Renouf.

TANAPA. (2012). *Tanzania national parks*, Retrieved July 31, 2015, from http://www.tanzaniaparks.com/

Telfer, D. J. (2003). Development issues in destination communities. In S. Singh, D. J. Timothy, & R. K. Dowling (Eds.), *Tourism in destination communities* (pp. 155–180). New York, NY: CABI.

Tickell, C. (1994). Foreword. In E. Cater & G. Lowman (Eds.), *Ecotourism: A sustainable option?* (pp. ix–x). Brisbane: John Wiley and Sons.

TIES. (2015). *The international ecotourism society. Principles of ecotourism*. Retrieved August 9, 2015, from https://www.ecotourism.org/what-is-ecotourism

Tosun, C., & Timothy, D. J. (2001). Shortcomings in planning approaches to tourism development in developing countries: The case of Turkey. *International Journal of Contemporary Hospitality Management*, *13*(7), 352–359.

Tourism Confederation of Tanzania. (2009). *Tanzania tourism value chain study*. Final Report. Dar es Salaam, Tanzania.

TTB. (2013). *Tanzania cultural tourism program*. Tanzania Tourist Board. Retrieved December 13, 2015 from http:// tanzaniaculturaltourism.go.tz/docs/new_cultural.pdf

UNESCO. (2014). *UNESCO world heritage center, United Republic of Tanzania*. Retrieved October 10, 2015, from http://whc.unesco.org/en/statesparties/tz

UNWTO. (2014). *Tourism highlights, United Nations World Tourism Organization*. Retrieved October 20, 2015, from http://dtxtq4w60xqpw.cloudfront.net/sites/all/files/pdf/unwto_highlights14_en_hr_0.pdf

URT. (1999). *National tourism policy*, United Republic of Tanzania, Ministry of Natural Resources and Tourism, Dar es salaam, Tanzania.

URT. (2002a). *Tourism master plan, strategy and action*. United Republic of Tanzania, Ministry of Natural Resources and Tourism, Dar es Salaam, Tanzania.

URT. (2002b). *The forest act of Tanzania*. Retrieved September 12, 2015 from http://theredddesk.org/sites/default/files/forest_act_tanzania.pdf

URT. (2007). *Marine parks and reserve units*. United Republic of Tanzania, Ministry of Livestock and Fisheries Development. Retrieved October 15, 2015, from http://www.marineparks.go.tz/parks-reserves/

URT. (2013). *The 2013 Tourism Statistical Bulletin*. United Republic of Tanzania, Ministry of Natural Resources and Tourism, Tourism Division, Dar es Salaam, Tanzania.

URT. (2015). *World heritage sites in Tanzania*. Retrieved July 31, 2015 from http://whc.unesco.org/en/statesparties/tz

Wade, D. J., Mwasaga, B. C., & Eagles, P. F. (2001). A history and market analysis of tourism in Tanzania. *Tourism Management, 22*(1), 93–101.

Wally, M. (2001). *Ecotourism and sustainable wildlife management*: *Experiences in the Gambia*. Retrieved October 20, 2015, from http://www.fao.org/fileadmin/templates/lead/pdf/02_article_en.pdf

Weaver, D. B. (1999). Magnitude of ecotourism in Costa Rica and Kenya. *Annals of Tourism Research, 26*(4), 792–816.

Wilson, R. T. (2011). The one-humped camel and the environment in Northern Tanzania. *Journal of Camel Practice and Research, 18*(1), 25–29.

Wood, M. E. (2002). *Ecotourism: Principles, practices and policies for sustainability.* Paris: United Nations Environment Program.

Wood, S., & Crouch, G. (2001). Ecotourism. *Business and Economic Review, 47*(2), 19–21.

World Economic Forum. (2011). *The travel & tourism competitiveness report, beyond the downturn.* Retrieved October 25, 2015, from http://www.weforum.org/ttcr

Wright, P. (1993). Ecotourism: Ethics or eco-self? *Journal of Travel Research, 31*(3), 3–9.

Zhong, L., & Xiao, D. (1999). Ecotourism and its planning and management, a review. *Acta Ecologica Sinica, 20*(5), 841–848.

Ziffer, K. A. (1989). *Ecotourism: The uneasy alliance.* Washington, DC: Conservation International and Ernst & Young.

Climate change risks on protected areas ecotourism: shocks and stressors perspectives in Ngorongoro Conservation Area, Tanzania

N. P. Mkiramweni[a], T. DeLacy[b], M. Jiang[b] and F. E. Chiwanga[a]

[a]Faculty of Forestry and Nature Conservation, Department of Wildlife Management, Sokoine University of Agriculture, Morogoro, Tanzania; [b]College of Business, Tourism and Events Research Group, Victoria University, Melbourne, Australia

ABSTRACT
Protected areas are increasingly becoming important sites for ecotourism worldwide. Due to the high dependence on climate and natural ecosystems, protected areas ecotourism is, however, considered to be at risk of climate change. This study was conducted between January 2012 and April 2014 in the Ngorongoro Conservation Area with the aim of identifying climate related shocks and stressors and implied effects on ecotourism. Along with this aim, the study assessed ecotourism stakeholders' awareness and perceptions on climate change in the area. It was found through focus group discussion and semi-structured interview that recurrent droughts, political unrests in a neighbouring country, global terrorism and disease outbreaks have been the key shocks. It was found further that water shortages, vegetation change, biodiversity loss and recurrent livestock and human diseases are the key stressors. Understanding these provides grounds for conducting an in-depth vulnerability assessment and developing adaptation strategies for ecotourism.

Background: climate change and protected areas ecotourism

Climate change is increasingly recognised as one of the serious risks for ecotourism in protected areas (PAs) (Hannah, 2008). The Intergovernmental Panel on Climate Change (IPCC, 2007) defines climate change as 'a change in the state of the climate that can be identified by changes in the mean and/or variability of its properties, and that persists for an extended period, typically decades or longer as a result of natural variability or human activity' (p. 30). Because of climate change, there will be changes in the mean and variance of rainfall and temperature that may lead to extreme weather events (IPCC, 2007). These events will, in turn, affect ecosystems, water availability, agriculture production and food prices (IPCC, 2014). The IPCC (2007) emphasises that sectors that depend on climatic sensitive resources are at risk of such effects. Protected areas ecotourism (PAE) is arguably at risk of climate change because it relies on key resources such as wildlife, landscapes and infrastructures that are sensitive to climate change (Becken & Job, 2014; Hambira, Saarinen, Manwa, & Atlhopheng, 2013; Nyaupane & Chhetri, 2009; Scott, Jones, & Konopek, 2007; Steyn & Spencer, 2012). Reducing risk is, therefore, a necessary condition not only to reduce vulnerability but also to ensure long-term sustainability of ecotourism.

Risk and vulnerability are concepts that have been frequently used in climate change studies. On the one hand, risk is the potential of climate change to harm a system – or any of its components (Leiserowitz, 2006). On the other hand, vulnerability denotes a condition whereby a system or any of its components is susceptible to or unable to cope with adverse effects of climate change (Füssel, 2007; IPCC, 2007). Many researchers (such as Calgaro, Lloyd, & Dominey-Howes, 2014; Hinkel, 2011; Jopp, DeLacy, & Mair, 2010) advise that risk and vulnerability can be reduced through adaptation, but this should be preceded by risk and vulnerability assessments (VAs). These assessments are practical actions for collecting information on risk factors and the extent and nature of vulnerability (IPCC, 2014). Usually, risk assessment (RA) and VA can take place at the local/destinations, at national, regional or international levels with the goal of creating grounds for developing adaptation actions.

At the local level, vulnerability is triggered or exacerbated by many risk factors which are not necessarily restricted to climate change (Birkmann, 2007). These include: catastrophes associated with natural hazards or extreme weather; awareness, perceptions or knowledge about climate change of those involved in developing adaptation actions; and markets or policy failures (Heltberg, Siegel, & Jorgensen, 2009; Klint et al., 2012). In climate change studies, risk factors associated with physical catastrophes are referred to as shocks and stressors (Calgaro et al., 2014; Klint et al., 2012). Shocks are incidents that occur suddenly and last for a very short period of time (Klint et al., 2012). They include tsunamis, earthquakes, storms, volcanic eruptions, landslides, avalanches and wildfires, to mention a few (Calgaro et al., 2014; Klint et al., 2012; Sharpley & Telfer, 2008). Regardless of whether they are climatic or not, shocks may severely disrupt ecotourism especially when their occurrence coincides with high seasons of tourists and income flow (Calgaro et al., 2014). Conversely, those incidents occurring at a slow pace with their effects being observed for a long-term (that is, after a tipping point has been reached) are referred to as stressors (Calgaro et al., 2014). These include land degradation, biodiversity loss and water shortages, just to mention a few. Both shocks and stressors can destabilise and reduce the viability of ecotourism business (Calgaro et al., 2014).

With regard to assessment, Romieu, Welle, Schneiderbauer, Pelling, and Vinchon (2010), suggest that assessing vulnerability (and risk factors) need to begin with the identification of shocks and stressor factors – the focus of this study. Understanding these provides park and tourism managers grounds for assessing vulnerability as well as developing appropriate adaptation strategies for ecotourism (Hahn, Riederer, & Foster, 2009; Hinkel, 2011). Besides, other researchers (Adger et al., 2009; Chaudhary & Bawa, 2011; Leiserowitz, 2006) suggest that RA and VA need to include the assessment of stakeholders' awareness, perceptions on and knowledge of climate change. The assessment of stakeholders' awareness, perceptions on and knowledge of climate change is very crucial aspects of RA and VA because these can enhance or limit the whole process of adaptation (Klint et al., 2012). Davidson, Williamson, and Parkins (2003) state that 'if stakeholders do not draw a causal connection between climate change and local consequences, then they may not perceive climate change as a risk issue and consequently fail to assess and act on potential adaptation responses' (p. 2257).

Climate change and PAE in Tanzania

The government of Tanzania reports that climate change is already affecting some of its PAs (United Republic of Tanzania [URT], 2008). For instance, floods and severe droughts have been common in many Tanzania's PAs. Beside these catastrophes, the report explains further that there is an alarming encroachment of PAs by local communities. The government is convinced that these catastrophes will affect ecotourism unless effective adaptation measures have been taken.

Ngorongoro Conservation Area (NCA) is one of the very important PAs for ecotourism in Tanzania. It operates under the multiple land use system where wildlife, people and livestock co-exist harmoniously – making their interactions a highly complex system. The ecotourism product of NCA is based on natural and cultural resources such as wildlife, archaeological sites, beautiful landscapes and lifestyles/cultures of the local community (Galvin, Thornton, Boone, & Sunderland, 2004). According to IPCC (2007), these resources are sensitive to the impacts of climate change. Furthermore, Smit and Wandel (2006) assert that vulnerability to climate change may be high in areas where there are complex human–environment interactions.

Despite climate change being one of the Tanzania's political agenda, information on climate change-related shocks and stressors, particularly in NCA, is scarce. Given that climate change will escalate in future (IPCC, 2007); this scarcity raises a question as to whether Tanzania will effectively address risks and vulnerabilities associated with climate change in NCA. The purpose of this study was to assess shocks and stressors that can exacerbate the vulnerability of ecotourism to climate change in NCA. Along with this, the study assessed awareness and perceptions on climate change among local ecotourism stakeholders. To achieve these, the study was guided by the following research questions: (a) How do ecotourism stakeholders perceive and consider climate change in their actions? (b) What incidents have affected tourism business in NCA for the past 25 years? (c) What incidents have affected livelihoods of the local community in NCA for the past 25 years? (d)What incidents have affected the conservation of natural resources in NCA for the past 25 years?

Methodology

This qualitative study was based on a case study research strategy. The application of this strategy enhanced our understanding of the dynamics present in NCA. Case study research strategy is particularly appropriate in a new topic study – such as climate change (Eisenhardt, 1989; Eriksen, O'Brien, & Rosentrater, 2008). The choice of NCA (Figure 1) as a study area was based on the observation made by Smit and Wandel (2006) that vulnerability to climate change may be high where there is a strong human–environment interaction. Moreover, NCA shares ecosystem with the surrounding PAs such as Serengeti, Loliondo, Maswa and Grumet in Tanzania. These PAs together with the Masai-Mara in Kenya form the Serengeti-Mara ecosystem (Sinclair & Norton-Griffiths, 1995) (see Figure 2). We believe that the use of NCA as a case study would enable a replication of findings in the surrounding PAs. However, to facilitate an understanding of vulnerability in such a complex case study it was important to begin this study with description of the nature of interactions between elements that make up the NCA ecotourism system (see Figure 3).

Ecotourism system of NCA and interacting elements

This study showed that NCA ecotourism is a coupled human–environmental system composed of the key stakeholders: the local community (that is, the Maasai); resource conservators; tourism businesses; and tourists. The environmental resources such as wildlife, landscapes, soils and water are central to ecotourism and the interactions among these players. The nature of interactions is mapped by arrows as shown in Figure 3. As Figure 3 shows, the local community exists in the use of environmental services such as water, medicines or herbs, pasture, housing materials, recreation and food; and tourism businesses depend on environmental services such as water, flora and fauna to attract tourists. Furthermore, tourism businesses draw income from tourists who enjoy the appealing of natural resources and services such as accommodation, food and beverages, guiding and transportation.

Moreover, the local community depend on tourists for direct income and exchange of cultural experiences. Similarly, the community depend on tourism businesses for casual employment, deployment of tourists into their centres (known locally as cultural *bomas*) and transport services. The community further depend on park managers (PMs) for the provision of services such as education, health, transport, food especially during crisis and security. In turn, PMs depend on tourism businesses for income levies; also on tourists

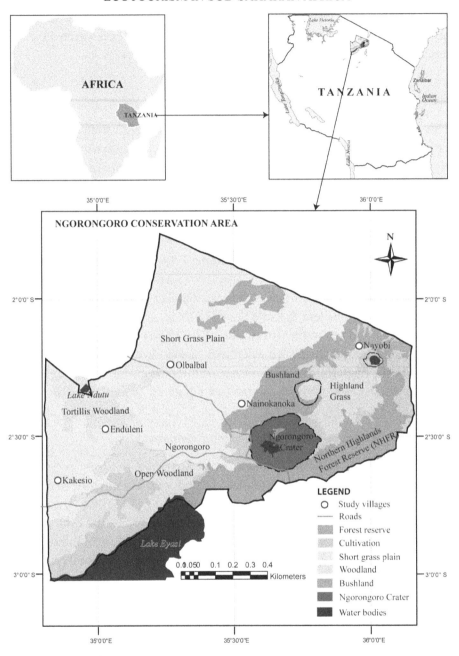

Figure 1. (Colour online) Map showing the study area.

for direct income (such as entry fees). The income generated from ecotourism is used to pay for conservation services and to provide social services to support the existence and survival of the local community. PMs recognise the contribution of the local community to the conservation of natural resources. This is because the lifestyles and cultures of the local community contain values which enable them to live harmoniously with wild ecosystem.

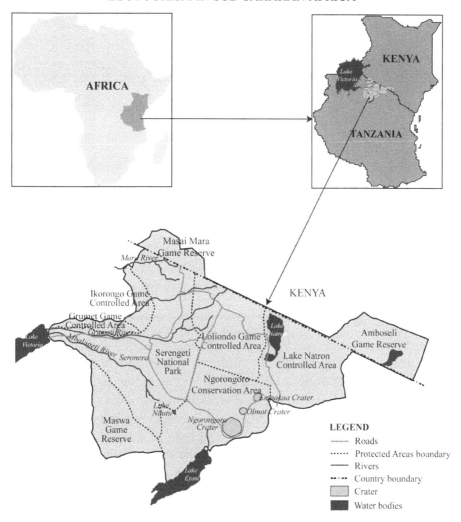

Figure 2. (Colour online) Map showing the Serengeti-Mara ecosystem.

The identification of these interacting components assisted in the sampling of research participants as well as in understanding how the impact of climate change on one of these elements can induce effects on other element(s) and the system at large.

Sample size and data collection

This study involved 58 participants. Of them, 45 were sampled from the local community. Others included: five lodge managers (LMs), five tour guides (TGs) and three PMs. Convenience and snow ball sampling techniques were used to recruit these participants. While the former uses the most convenient and accessible people to participate in the research (Reynolds & Braithwaite, 2001), the latter is used for recruiting participants 'with very specific characteristics, rare

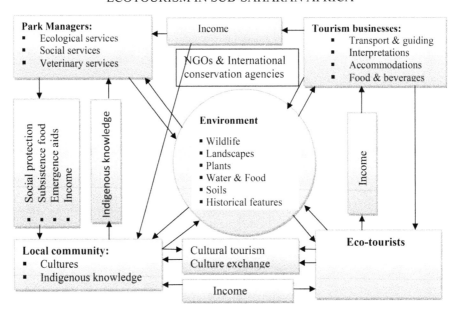

Figure 3. Ecotourism system of the NCA.

experiences or who may be difficult to identify with other recruitment methods'
(Hennink, Hutter, & Bailey, 2011, p. 100). Focus group discussions (FGDs)
were used to collect data from the local community whereby 3 groups composed
of 9–10 people were formed. Additionally, in-depth interviews were used to
collect data from tourism mangers, TGs and PMs. A semi-structured questionnaire was used to guide both the interviews and FGDs. Direct observation was
also used.

Data analysis

The data were analysed with the aid of NVivo (version 9), a sophisticated computer programme that facilitates filling and quickly displaying out the data whenever
needed (Bazeley & Jackson, 2013; Marshall, 2011). The analysis involved coding of
the key themes: perceptions, shocks and stressors. By using the coding tree, the key
themes were coded as parent nodes followed by the responses under each theme
which were coded as sub-themes. The analysis was then run to identify issues
emerged from each theme, as were said by the participants.

Results and discussion

Perceptions towards climate change

Table 1 indicates awareness and different perceptions among PMs, LMs, TGs
and local community members in relation to climate change. These were captured during both interviews and FGDs.

Park managers

The data showed widespread perceptions among PMs that climate is changing and its effect is observable across NCA. This was shown by all three managers who participated in interviews. Some responses from PMs are shown in Table 1. PMs referred to the recurrent droughts, vegetation change and infrastructure damage as the major consequences of climate change in the study area. However, with respect to the effect of climate change on ecotourism, there was a divergence of opinions among the managers. While two of them believed that climate change is yet to affect ecotourism, the rest highlighted that climate change is already affecting ecotourism in NCA. Becken and Hay (2007) observed that some PMs tend to consider climate change in national parks as stable. This is based on the fact that there is significant protection accorded to these areas by national and international conservation communities. Due to this, some managers think that climate change will not affect PAE. All managers, however, considered their level of knowledge about climate change as low, thinking that their answers might not be correct. They suggested for attending training or exposed to practical interventions related to climate change.

Lodge managers

With respect to LMs, findings showed that all were aware of climate change (Table 1). However, in terms of its effect on ecotourism, all the managers acknowledged that by then they had not experienced serious effects of climate change. Among them, two managers considered climate change as a future threat to ecotourism. Others think climate change is an exaggeration and the future of ecotourism is probably safe. In addition, all LMs consistently referred to issues such as economic downturns, terrorism, disease outbreaks and political instability as the major issues that have affected or can affect ecotourism. However all interviewed LMs were not able to link such issues with climate change.

Tour guides

As with TGs, the results showed a consistence of perceptions among them in terms of climate change. All the interviewed TGs were aware of climate change. However, there was a divergence of views among them in terms of the current and future climate change effects on ecotourism. Referring to damage on road infrastructure, two TGs acknowledged that ecotourism is at risk of climate change. Others saw it as something that would not affect ecotourism. One TG said:

> It won't happen that wildlife will perish [as] they migrate during severe droughts and return when the condition is favourable. Some [wildlife] will remain and continue to attract visitors even if droughts intensify in the future ...

Table 1. Awareness and perceptions towards climate change.

Research question		Have you considered climate change as a threat to ecotourism in the NCA? If yes, why?
Some key answers	PMs	
	PM1	No	'Leave aside the reason that I am not [an] expert in climate change, I think this [climate change] is not a big issue for eco-tourism currently'
	PM2	Yes	'Considerable changes in vegetation might be due to climate change … we have seen also roads have been damaged severely in recent years'
	PM3	Yes	'May be in the future ecotourism will be affected if the situation continues like this, but as it is now there has been no effect', I can see a lots of droughts nowadays and almost two years now heavy rainfall is damaging the roads
	HMs	
	HM1	Yes	'Climate change is occurring. Last year heavy rainfall have damaged the road at Mtowambu; we had never experienced this before. For almost a week or so we didn't receive tourists'.
	HM2	No	' … I don't think if climate change is occurring … think of exaggerations by experts … variations [in climate] we can see are just normal'.
	HM3	No	' …I don't think if climate change will wipe out all wildlife …visitors are interested in wildlife and will continue visiting NCA'.
	HM4	No	'Tourism has existed here for many decades. Do you think it will just be affected by what you call climate change?'
	TGs	
	TG1	Yes	'We are seeing a lot of changes in environment which may affect wildlife and tourism in the future, you know tourists are interested to see some species of animals but if any of those species perishes, a group of them [tourists] may go to other parks indefinitely'.
	TG2	No	'Even if heavy rainfall may destroy the roads elsewhere, still tourism will persist because the rainfall comes during off-[tourism] season'
	TG3	No	'The impact of climate change is observable in livestock but not in tourism'.
	TG4	Yes	'Climate change might not affect us directly but since NCA is connected to other parts through roads, we may face the problems especially if heavy rainfall breaks roads as it was the case in Mtowambu last year'.
	TG5	No	'It won't happen that wildlife will perish … they migrate during severe droughts and return when the condition is favourable, some will remain even if drought [severity] increases, only the itinerary may change'.
	Local community	
	FGD1	Yes	'If the severe droughts escalate in future, there will be likelihood that the indigenous people will eat all edible wildlife … and there will be little tourism.
	FGD2	Yes	'If drought continues to affect our livestock, we will be forced to leave NCA. Those animals which do not migrate will be at risk of droughts as it is the case of livestock, so ecotourism will be at a slight risk.
	FGD3	Yes	'It is affecting livelihoods of local people and hungry people cannot participate in tourism'.

Beside these perceptions, all the TGs considered their knowledge on climate change as low, lamenting that their responses may not be correct. They had opinions that if they were trained on climate change, their knowledge would improve and provide correct answers wherever asked about climate change.

The local community

All participants from the local community were aware of climate change, but considered their knowledge about it as low. Most of them perceived that climate change would not affect ecotourism directly, but rather the effect would occur only if wildlife perished. During FGDs, some participants considered those animals which do not migrate as being at risk of droughts and so is ecotourism.

Shocks and stressors

Table 2 shows a summary of shocks and stressors which were said by the research participants.

Shocks

This study identified that recurrent droughts, disease outbreaks, political unrests and global terrorism emerged as key shocks (Table 2). Recurrent severe droughts were highlighted during FGDs as one of the most risky shocks to livelihoods. It is predicted by climate change scientists that the frequency, duration and severity of droughts will increase, as a result of climate change, and this increase will affect various sectors of the economy including overlapping sectors such as agriculture and tourism (IPCC, 2007; Ding, Hayes, & Widhalm, 2011; Mishra & Singh, 2010). The FGDs participants showed that since the1990s severe droughts have caused massive deaths of livestock leading to hunger and starvation among the local community members. This consequently makes some local community members engage themselves in poaching of some wildlife and plant species which are potential for ecotourism. Likewise, the interviewees said that severe droughts accelerate disease complications and malnutrition which in 2012 was associated with some deaths of children. In respect of the effect of droughts on wildlife, the PMs did not mention any wildlife death caused by droughts, but acknowledged that there might be some indirect effects. They also warned that if this happens ecotourism will be at a high risk of losing its key resources.

It was learnt further that disease outbreaks such as the Rift Valley fever (RVF) and swine flu (SF) which occurred in 2007/2008 and 2009 respectively affected negatively the flow of tourists to NCA. The participants reported that RVF and SF were the most severe disease outbreaks that reduced the number of visitors to not only NCA but also to the whole country. For example, the

Table 2. Summary of shocks and stressors emerged from the research.

Key shocks and stressors	Some answers from participants
Shocks	
Political unrest and global terrorism	'Bombing in Mombasa and Dar es Salaam coincided with the high tourism season and this affected us' '... Post-election violence of 2007 in Kenya reduced the number of tourists coming through Kenya but not those coming through South Africa and Zanzibar'.
Disease outbreaks	'Swine flu that affected Kenya and Northern Tanzania affected tourism ... decreased the number of tourists'. 'Media coverage escalated the problem ...'.
Recurrent droughts	'Our livestock is continuously dying because of droughts'. 'Even animals and plants in the crater will likely die because of droughts ... there will be no tourism ...' 'Malnutrition is killing our children as there is no food'.
Stressors	
Water shortage	'Increased tourism development in the area has increased water usage leading to water shortage ... if this trend grows unchecked, it will threaten wildlife and the local community'. 'Low rainfall and recurrent droughts have led to water shortages in many parts of the NCA and this will affect tourism' ... 'we have no access to clean water ... as you can see our kids are very dirty, do you think we like this situation? ... even tourists will not like to find us in this situation'.
Environmental degradation	'In certain circumstances tour guides off-road, especially when they want to show their tourists a rare animal ...' 'Forest destruction used to be a serious issue especially in the eastern part of the 'Northern Highland Forest'. 'Forest destruction threatens the water catchment'.
Biodiversity and habitat loss	'Some animal species are at risk of extinction. We have experienced a declining trend of wildebeests, hyenas and lions. There are many factors causing the decline of these animals including inbreeding, inadequate prey and maybe the climate change'.
Change in vegetation structure	There is notable change in vegetation – probably due to the climate change. Lerai forest is the habitat at risk of loss due to disappearance of acacia trees'. 'If the withdrawal of water in Lerai ponds continues unchecked, habitat for hippopotamus may disappear ... yeah! Signs of climate change are clear. We can see how vegetation has changed' ... 'We have noted the invasion of a new weed called *Datura stramonia*'. 'Invasive long grass species in short grassland is obvious'.
Recurring human, livestock and wildlife diseases.	'Diseases such as *distemper* and *pathogenic bacterium* are affecting lions and wildebeests' ... 'Tourism is not currently affected by diseases, but in the future, if the diseases persist without control measures, we will end up having no wildlife and tourism at all – you know tourists are drawn by wildlife'. 'The most common diseases [affecting human] are malaria and HIV/AIDS' ... 'we cannot participate effectively in cultural tourism if we are sick'.

number of international tourists travelling to NCA declined from 641,951 in 2008 to 576,643 tourists (10%) in 2009 mainly due to SF (URT, 2010). Even though most of these incidents occurred outside the boundaries of Tanzania, according to the interview, ecotourism in NCA was affected because some international visitors to Kenya tend to extend their journeys to Tanzania. In East Africa, RVF outbreaks are associated with extreme precipitation and floods (Baylis & Risley, 2013; Martin et al., 2008). Scientists have consistently shown that there is a close relationship between the occurrences of RVF and SF and local climate variability. This is because some of these viruses are transmitted by vectors: mosquitoes, ticks and fleas which are sensitive to local climate change and variability (Mandell & Flick, 2010; Martin et al., 2008).

Likewise, the incidents such as political unrests and global terrorism were found prominent through the interview, particularly with LMs. Political unrests involving civil disobedience and kidnapping of international tourists reported in 1997, 1998 and 2007/2008 in Kenya plus global terrorist acts which took the form of bombings in the Embassies of the USA in Tanzania and Kenya were mostly mentioned during the interview. Similarly, the September 11th incident that involved bombing of the World Trade Centre in the USA emerged as an incident that affected ecotourism. According to the participants, these incidents caused a significant reduction of international tourists, especially those coming from USA.

Although these incidents are non-climatic some researchers have linked them to climate change and variability (Buhaug, Gleditsch, & Theisen, 2010; Hendrix & Glaser, 2007; Raleigh, 2010). This is because the impact associated with temperature, precipitation and drought anomalies cause resource scarcity in most parts of the world. In turn, resource scarcity leads to poverty which can, thereafter, exacerbate crime rates (Raleigh, 2010). It is important, however, to note that climate change is not the only issue that trigger crimes. Crime incidents can be caused also by poor re-distribution of resources among community members.

Stressors

This study found that water shortage, vegetation change, biodiversity loss and diseases were frequently mentioned as key stressors (Table 2). Water shortage was mentioned by all local community participants as a serious problem for livestock and people's livelihoods. It was found that water supply for livestock and domestic uses had decreased tremendously since 2000s. Participants associated this decrease with reduced rainfalls, increased frequencies and intensities of droughts and ill-defined water right policies. One interviewee was quoted:

> ... Nowadays the seasonal ponds that we depend on dry up very quickly during severe droughts and there has been no plan to drill ponds or share water with lodges.

Although there was a project to increase water supply to the local community, all the PMs said that droughts had affected its implementations. One of PMs said:

> Droughts had caused many drilled water holes to dry and hindered our efforts to supply water to the local community.

However, the issue of water shortage was not raised by LMs and TGs implying that water was not a big problem for them. Although there was no reported serious effect of water shortage on ecotourism, TGs, LMs and PMs were sceptical that in the future climate change coupled with increased human activities in NCA may exacerbate the problem. Some of them had opinions that this will consequently affect ecotourism.

Vegetation change is another stressor that was mentioned by some of the participants, mainly the PMs. The interviewed PMs associated this change with increased invasive plant species such as Mexican poppy (*Argemone mexicana*), Thorn apple (*Datura stramonia*), Prickly pear cactus (*Opuntas ficus-indica*), Custard oil, *Bidens schimperi* and *Gutenbergis cordfolia*. The PMs considered Mexican poppy (*A. mexicana*) as the most dangerous invasive species due to its 'double effect' on herbivores. According to these experts, double effect means that the invasive species can limits the rangelands by inhibiting the growth of some native grass species important for herbivores and, if swallowed, it can kill the herbivores. Although these experts were not able to link climate change with invasions, many studies have consistently associated invasive species with climate change (Hellmann, Byers, Bierwagen, & Dukes, 2008; Steffen et al., 2009). Hellmann et al. (2008) assert that invasive species respond to climate change and their responses – in PAs – may pose ecological, environmental and economic consequences for ecotourism. Climate change may create suitable conditions for invasive species to compete for space, nutrients and water with previously thriving native species (Steffen et al., 2009). The invasive species may consequently occupy the area if the native species is under stress from climate change or other factors. Estes, Atwood, and Estes (2006) report that in NCA drought causes depletion of the grassland which in turn becomes a favourable site for invasive species. Invasive species such as *B. schimperi*, *G. (Earlangea) cordifolia* and *Eleusine jaegeri* are very prominent in NCA. Although currently the effect of vegetation change seems minor when acting alone, its cumulative consequences can cause dramatic negative impacts for NCA ecosystem and ecotourism. For instance, the short grass in the Ngorongoro Crater enables the calves of wildebeests (*Connochaetes taurinus*), zebra (*Equus burchelli*), Grant's and Thomson's gazelles (*Gazella grant* and *Gazella thomsonii*, respectively) to view from far predators and can camouflage quickly. Likewise, the presence of the short grass in this area provides spectacular scenery that also facilitates viewing of wildlife species during safari drives.

Climate change was also associated with the decline of some wildlife species. It was revealed that since 1960s populations of some wildlife such as elephants, black rhinos, lions, and elands have dramatically declined. Although there has been no scientific research conducted previously to establish whether this decline is really caused by climate change, the PMs acknowledged that climate change could have exacerbated factors such as poaching, diseases, droughts and vegetation change. Although poaching is a non-climatic stressor, this study established that there is a close relationship between climate change and poaching occurring in NCA. This research found that because of the droughts which have resulted into low livestock production, some local community members are forced to engage in poaching as a coping strategy. One of the interviewees revealed secretly that elands are the most preferred edible wildlife. Figure 4 illustrates that the population of elands in NCA was higher from 1960s to mid-1980s, but later on the population declined. As Figure 4 shows, such a decline occurred in both wet and dry seasons, but the decline was rampant during dry seasons where the drought was so intense. Besides, it is a taboo for the Maasai to feed on wildlife. However, poor livestock productivity due to droughts and lack of alternative livelihood might have forced them to.

With regard to the black rhino population, Fyumagwa and Nyahongo (2010) report that, in 1974s there were about 700 black rhinos in NCA, but the number decreased in the 1980s to only 67 rhinos. In 1990s the population dropped further to 10 rhinos. This study noted further that between 2001 and 2005 there was only one rhino in NCA during both dry and wet seasons. Poaching for horns was highlighted by participants as the main factor for the decline of black rhinos. Fyumagwa and Nyahongo (2010) report that in 1980s, illegal immigrants from Somalia engaged in poaching rhinos and elephants using heavy firearms. Over many decades Somalia communities have faced serious poverty due to droughts. As such, poaching rhinos might be one of the adaptive strategies for some people from Somalia. According to the intervie-wees, other climatic related issues such vegetation changes, diseases and

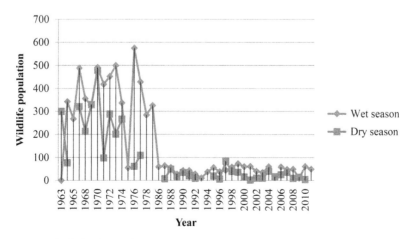

Figure 4. Trend of eland population in NCA, 1963–2011.

197

inbreeding might have directly contributed to the decline of rhinos; the latter two taking the lead.

Similarly, it was highlighted that loss of biodiversity in NCA is not confined only to wild animals but also to some plant species. Nevertheless, neither this nor previous research have established the list of plant species that are in danger of extinction. However, PMs highlighted a serious decrease in some vegetation in the area in recent years. For example, Yellow fever trees (*Acacia xanthophloea*) which form the Lerai forest in the Crater were disappearing. If this disappearance is allowed to persist there will be negative consequences for ecotourism as the forest provides a micro-habitat for elephants, black rhinos (especially during the night), baboons, velvet monkeys, waterbucks, bushbucks and leopards.

Moreover, recurring livestock and human diseases were mentioned as another stressor. It was highlighted that, besides droughts, diseases cause deaths of livestock and reduced income. The PMs explained that some of the livestock diseases have been in existence since 1960s and others were diagnosed in the late 1990s. The IPCC (2007) warned that climate change would result in occurrence of diseases in areas with no previous history of occurrences. Given this warning, the newly diagnosed diseases in recent years may be associated with climate change. For example, one park manager informed that vector-borne diseases from ticks can cause more than 34% of calves' deaths within their first year of life during critical period of droughts. Both the local community and PMs informed further that diseases occurred in 2007/2008 when drought was intense were behind the loss of about 90% of newly born livestock in NCA. Examples of livestock diseases that existed before 1990s include foot and mouth disease, contagious bovine pluero-pneumonia, east coast fever, anaplasmosis, babesiosis, anthrax, mastitis, otitis, malignant catarrhal fever, tuberculosis, helminthosis and eye infection (URT, 2010). Others are fleas, foot-rot, diarrhoea, RVF, heart-water, pneumonic pasteurellosis and mange. The newly diagnosed diseases include bovine cerebral thailerosis, contagious caprine pluero-pnuemonia and *peste des petit* ruminants, which affects young ruminants. Similarly, malaria and HIV/AIDS were mentioned as critical to man. According to the FGDs discussants, these diseases are mainly acquired by the local community members who migrate to towns and cities to escape poverty caused by loss of livestock.

Although this study did not establish any direct link between livestock and human diseases and climate change, climate change might have exacerbated them. This will consequently affect ecotourism. Interviews and FGDs provided two major possibilities where ecotourism can be affected by climate change: exacerbation of illegal activities including poaching and robbery which may ultimately tarnish the image of NCA to visitors.

Conclusions and recommendations

This study assessed climate change-related shocks and stressors experienced by NCA over the last 25 years. The purpose was to establish whether or not these risk factors had implications for ecotourism. Additionally, the study assessed the awareness and perceptions about climate change among local ecotourism stakeholders.

The assessment of shocks and stressors revealed the ways in which ecotourism in NCA can be put at risk of climate change. The study showed that severe droughts and livestock diseases disrupted the local community's livelihoods leading to negative consequences for the people's use of natural resources. The taboos and cultural values such as those prohibiting the local community from consuming wildlife and those that for decades have enabled the community to conserve natural resources are now degrading as a result of climate change. The emerging picture from this study reveals that climate change is one of many factors now which has started, in synergistic ways, to degrade the basis for harmonious existence of human with nature. Additionally, the shocks related to civil disobedience in neighbouring nation and global terrorism incidents which, in some ways, affected tourism businesses in NCA provides another way in which climate change can affect ecotourism.

Likewise, the identified stressors such as biodiversity loss and change in vegetation-cover provide a further reminder that ecotourism resources are undergoing degradation probably due to climate change. Given that climate change will proceed into the future, this puts ecotourism at risk of losing its appeal to visitors unless adaptation measures are taken. This study noted that although the identified stressors are yet to affect ecotourism, there is a need to design appropriate adaptation measures to reduce risk of PAE to climate change.

Risk and VAs are practical and policy actions aimed at providing information necessary for developing adaptation strategies (Füssel, 2007). By identifying the shocks and stressors, this study has laid a foundation for undertaking VA. The identified shocks and stressors can be used as entry points for an in-depth assessment of risk and vulnerability factors owing to designing appropriate adaptation strategies for the NCA and surrounding ecosystem.

More often, the awareness, perceptions and knowledge of climate change among stakeholders can influence the designing and implementation of adaptation strategies (Adger et al., 2009). This study found a divergence of perceptions among local ecotourism stakeholders about climate change. Many stakeholders were aware of climate change, but some of them perceived that ecotourism is not at risk. Others saw it as a future threat. Likewise, there were stakeholders who considered climate change as an exaggeration by scientists. With respect to knowledge, all stakeholders who participated in this assessment considered their knowledge of climate change as low. In this article, we consider that those acknowledging ecotourism as being at risk, whether today or in the future, stand a better chance to develop effective adaptation strategies than those with the opposite feelings. However, a lack of common understanding and inadequate knowledge among them can limit the development of such strategies altogether. Thus, addressing the divergence of opinions and knowledge gaps among stakeholders in order to attain a common understanding of climate change will increase the effectiveness of all stakeholders in designing and implementing adaptation strategies. This suggests for further investigation on stakeholders' knowledge gaps about climate change.

Disclosure statement

No potential conflict of interest was reported by the authors.

References

Adger, W. N., Dessai, S., Goulden, M., Hulme, M., Lorenzoni, I., Nelson, D. R., ... Wreford, A. (2009). Are there social limits to adaptation to climate change? *Climate Change*, *93*(3), 335–354.

Baylis, M. & Risley, C. (2013). *Infectious diseases, climate change effects on infectious diseases*. New York, NY: Springer.

Bazeley, P., & Jackson, K. (2013). *Qualitative data analysis with NVivo*. London: Sage Publications.

Becken, S., & Hay, J. (2007). *Tourism and climate change: Risks and opportunities*. Clevdon: Channel View Publications.

Becken, S., & Job, H. (2014). Protected areas in an era of global–local change. *Journal of Sustainable Tourism*, *22*(4), 507–527. doi:10.1080/09669582.2013.877913

Birkmann, J. (2007). Risk and vulnerability indicators at different scales: Applicability, usefulness and policy implications. *Environmental Hazards*, *7*(1), 20–31. doi:10.1016/j.envhaz.2007.04.002

Buhaug, H., Gleditsch, N. P., & Theisen, O. M. (2010). Implications of climate change for armed conflict. In R. Mearns & A. Norton (Eds.), *Social dimensions of climate change: Equity and vulnerability in a warming world* (pp. 75–101). Washington, DC: World Bank.

Calgaro, E., Lloyd, K., & Dominey-Howes, D. (2014). From vulnerability to transformation: A framework for assessing the vulnerability and resilience of tourism destinations. *Journal of Sustainable Tourism*, *22*(3), 341–360. doi:10.1080/09669582.2013.826229

Chaudhary, P., & Bawa, K. S. (2011). Local perceptions of climate change validated by scientific evidence in the Himalayas. *Biology Letters*. doi:rsbl20110269

Davidson, D. J., Williamson, T., & Parkins, J. R. (2003). Understanding climate change risk and vulnerability in northern forest-based communities. *Canadian Journal of Forest Research*, *33*(11), 2252–2261. doi:10.1139/x03-138

Ding, Y., Hayes, M. J., & Widhalm, M. (2011). Measuring economic impacts of drought: A review and discussion. *Disaster Prevention and Management*, *20*(4), 434–446. doi:10.1108/09653561111161752

Eisenhardt, K. M. (1989). Building theories from case study research. *Academy of Management Review, 14*(4), 532–550.

Eriksen, S., O'Brien, K., & Rosentrater, L. (2008). *Climate change in Eastern and Southern Africa: Impacts, vulnerability and adaptation.* Oslo: University of Oslo.

Estes, R. D., Atwood, J., & Estes, A. (2006). Downward trends in Ngorongoro Crater ungulate populations 1986–2005: Conservation concerns and the need for ecological research. *Biological Conservation, 131*(1), 106–120. doi:10.1016/j.biocon.2006.02.009

Füssel, H. M. (2007). Vulnerability: A generally applicable conceptual framework for climate change research. *Global Environmental Change, 17*(2), 155–167. doi:10.1016/j.gloenvcha.2006.05.002

Fyumagwa, R. D., & Nyahongo, J. (2010). Black rhino conservation in Tanzania: Translocation efforts and further challenges. *Pachyderm, 47,* 59–65.

Galvin, K. A., Thornton, P. K., Boone, R. B., & Sunderland, J. (2004). Climate variability and impacts on East African livestock herders: The Maasai of Ngorongoro Conservation Area, Tanzania. *African Journal of Range & Forage Science, 21*(3), 183–189. doi:10.2989/10220110409485850

Hahn, M. B., Riederer, A. M., & Foster, S. O. (2009). The livelihood vulnerability index: A pragmatic approach to assessing risks from climate variability and change – A case study in Mozambique. *Global Environmental Change, 19*(1), 74–88. doi:10.1016/j.gloenvcha.2008.11.002

Hambira, W. L., Saarinen, J., Manwa, H., & Atlhopheng, J. R. (2013). Climate change adaptation practices in nature-based tourism in Maun in the Okavango Delta area, Botswana: How prepared are the tourism businesses? *Tourism Review International, 17*(1), 19–29.

Hannah, L. (2008). Protected areas and climate change. *Annals of the New York Academy of Sciences, 1134*(1), 201–212. doi:10.1196/annals.1439.009

Hellmann, J. J., Byers, J. E., Bierwagen, B. G., & Dukes, J. S. (2008). Five potential consequences of climate change for invasive species. *Conservation Biology, 22*(3), 534–543. doi:10.1111/j.1523-1739.2008.00951.x

Hendrix, C. S., & Glaser, S. M. (2007). Trends and triggers: Climate, climate change and civil conflict in Sub-Saharan Africa. *Political Geography, 26*(6), 695–715. doi:10.1016/j.polgeo.2007.06.006

Hennink, M., Hutter, I., & Bailey, A. (2011). *Qualitative research methods.* London: Sage.

Heltberg, R., Siegel, P. B., & Jorgensen, S. L. (2009). Addressing human vulnerability to climate change: Toward a 'no-regrets' approach. *Global Environmental Change, 19*(1), 89–99. doi:10.1016/j.gloenvcha.2008.11.003

Hinkel, J. (2011). Indicators of vulnerability and adaptive capacity: Towards a clarification of the science–policy interface. *Global Environmental Change, 21*(1), 198–208. doi:10.1016/j.gloenvcha.2010.08.002

IPCC. (2007). Climate change impacts, adaptation and vulnerability: Contribution of working group II to the fourth assessment report of the Intergovernemntal Panel on Climate Change Geneva, Switzerland.

IPCC. (2014). Adaptation needs and options. In: *Climate Change 2014: Impacts, adaptation and vulnerability* (pp. 833–868). New York: Author.

Jopp, R., DeLacy, T., & Mair, J. (2010). Developing a framework for regional destination adaptation to climate change. *Current Issues in Tourism, 13*(6), 591–605. doi:10.1080/13683501003653379

Klint, L. M., Jiang, M., Law, A., Delacy, T., Filep, S., Calgaro, E., … Harrison, D. (2012). Dive tourism in Luganville, Vanuatu: Shocks, stressors, and vulnerability to climate change. *Tourism in Marine Environments, 8*(1–2), 1–2.

Leiserowitz, A. (2006). Climate change risk perception and policy preferences: The role of affect, imagery and values. *Climatic change*, *77*(1–2), 45–72. doi:10.1007/s10584-006-9059-9

Mandell, R. B., & Flick, R. (2010). Rift Valley fever virus: An unrecognised emerging threat? *Human vaccines*, *6*(7), 597–601.

Marshall, H. (2011). *A hand out on introduction to NVivo 9* (Unpublished manuscript). RMIT University, Centre for Applied Social Research, Melbourne.

Martin, V., Chevalier, V., Ceccato, P. N., Anyamba, A., De Simone, L., Lubroth, J., & Domenech, J. (2008). The impact of climate change on the epidemiology and control of Rift Valley fever. *Revue Scientifique et Technique, Office International des Epizooties, 27* (2), 413–426.

Mishra, A. K., & Singh, V. P. (2010). A review of drought concepts. *Journal of Hydrology, 391* (1), 202–216. doi:10.1016/j.jhydrol.2010.07.012

Nyaupane, G. P., & Chhetri, N. (2009). Vulnerability to climate change of nature-based tourism in the Nepalese Himalayas. *Tourism Geographies, 11*(1), 95–119. doi:10.1080/14616680802643359

Raleigh, C. (2010). Political marginalization, climate change, and conflict in African Sahel states. *International Studies Review, 12*(1), 69–86. doi:10.1111/j.1468-2486.2009.00913.x

Reynolds, P. C., & Braithwaite, D. (2001). Towards a conceptual framework for wildlife tourism. *Tourism Management, 22*(1), 31–42.

Romieu, E., Welle, T., Schneiderbauer, S., Pelling, M., & Vinchon, C. (2010). Vulnerability assessment within climate change and natural hazard contexts: Revealing gaps and synergies through coastal applications. *Sustainability Science, 5*(2), 159–170. doi:10.1007/s11625-010-0112-2

Scott, D., Jones, B., & Konopek, J. (2007). Implications of climate and environmental change for nature-based tourism in the Canadian Rocky Mountains: A case study of Waterton Lakes National Park. *Tourism Management, 28*(2), 570–579.

Sharpley, R., & Telfer, J. D. (2008). *Tourism and development in the developing world.* New York, NY: Routledge.

Sinclair, A. R. E., & Norton-Griffiths, M. (1995). *Serengeti: Dynamics of an ecosystem.* Chicago: University of Chicago Press.

Smit, B., & Wandel, J. (2006). Adaptation, adaptive capacity and vulnerability. *Global Environmental Change, 16*(3), 282–292. doi:10.1016/j.gloenvcha.2006.03.008

Steffen, W., Burbidge, A. A., Hughes, L., Kitching, R., Lindenmayer, D., Musgrave, W., … Werner, P. A. (2009). *Australia's biodiversity and climate change.* Melbourne: Csiro Publishing.

Steyn, J. N., & Spencer, J. P. (2012). Climate change and tourism: Implications for South Africa. *African Journal for Physical, Health Education, Recreation and Dance, 18*(1), 1–19.

United Republic of Tanzania. (2008). *State of the environment report.* Dar es Salaam: Vice President's office, Division of Environment.

United Republic of Tanzania. (2010). *Ngorongoro Conservation Area general management plan.* Tanzania: NCA.

The influence of homestay facilities on tourist satisfaction in the Lake Victoria Kenya Tourism Circuit

Eliza Buyeke Ogucha[a], Geoffrey K. Riungu[b], Frimar K. Kiama[a] and Eunice Mukolwe[a]

[a]Department of Tourism and Hospitaliy Management, KISII University, Kisii, Kenya;
[b]Department of Parks, Recreation And Tourism Management, Clemson University, Clemson, SC, USA

Kenya is one of the leading tourist destinations in Africa, which creates the need to foster closer linkages between the tourists and the local community members. As such, many homestay facilities have come up in the recent past to cater for the accommodation needs of the tourists. Yet information on the tourists' satisfaction levels regarding the homestay facilities in Kenya currently remains largely unknown. The study therefore determined the influence of facilities and services offered by homestays on tourist satisfaction within the Lake Victoria area of the western tourist circuit. The study was conducted through survey design comprising a randomly selected sample of 20 homestay facilities (with a total of 42 respondents) that were identified through the Kenya Community-Based Tourism Network database (KECOBAT). The findings indicated that 71% were not satisfied with the homestays. This was largely attributed to deficient tangible factors of service quality of which the study also revealed were a better predictor of tourist satisfaction in homestays than intangible factors. Therefore it may be prudent for the homestay owners to ensure that they have adequate facilities (not necessarily high quality but should be functional) to ensure repeat business especially through recommendations.

1. Introduction

In Kenya, tourism accounts for 11% of the Gross Domestic Product (Kenya National Bureau of Statistics [KNBS], 2014) and drives the achievement of the Vision 2030-Kenya's development blueprint. Kenya registered Ksh 93.97 billion from tourism in the year 2013 down from Ksh 96.02 billion in the previous year. This represented a 2.2% declined tourism performance. Tourism arrivals were also on a decline from 1.71million visitors in 2012 to 1.52 million in 2013 (KNBS, 2014). This was attributed to increased competition from other destinations as well as incidences of terror attacks. Despite the fluctuations experienced in the tourism industry, it is still regarded as a significant sector in Kenya's economy and its multiplier effect has the capacity to promote regional development, create new commercial and industrial enterprises, stimulate demand for locally produced goods and services, and provide a market for agricultural products.

Product diversification is seen as a salient possibility in tourism growth and regional development, and homestay provides such an opportunity especially for the accommodation industry. Kenya Community-Based Tourism Network (KECOBAT, 2015) recognise a homestay to be a home owner-occupied private residence where the primary aim is residence and the secondary purpose is providing accommodation to a few paying guests. It is neither a hotel nor a motel. It is a non-commercialised, private residence with paying guests who enjoy staying in the comfort and security of a family home. It is normally considered to be a safe and affordable housing for visitors looking to experience and learn the host's lifestyle.

Wall and Long (1996) state that locally owned and operated homestays constitute suitable tourist accommodation and a unique chance for the local community to participate in tourism activities. People's inclination to seek out novelty, including that of traditional cultures, heritage and other aspects of the local culture, staying at the facilities built by the local community members may become a new paradigm of tourism in Kenya. Homestay as an accommodation option provides an opportunity through which an individual or group may be exposed to the authentic culture, language and social structures of another country (Agyeiwaah, Akyeampong, & Amenumey, 2013; Wang, 2007; Welsh, 2001).

The money-making activities of tourism has the potential to bring tourist taxes for the government provided that policies and guidelines are established in ensuring the sustainable development (Yassin, Shaffril, Hassan, Othman, & Samah, 2010). Economic considerations are a primary motivation for increasing local involvement in tourism as pointed out by Hinch and Butler (1996) who concluded that more local houses become homestays as tourists numbers increase as a result of affordable homestay prices. Evidently this is because some tourists are motivated to choose homestay because of the cheap price (Hsu & Lin, 2011).

Tourists who stay at locally owned homestay facilities are a major growth area, that has been used to boost local culture, and that they can aid the seasonal and geographic spread of tourism (Richards, 2011). Tourist visiting the hinterland of Kenya has shown tremendous interest in travelling to cultural/heritage destinations (Akama & Sterry, 2002), and are now showing increased propensity to stay at the local homestay facilities.

Tourists will generally be satisfied with the quality of services offered to them if the services are provided in satisfactory manner (Sureshchander, Rajendran, & Anantharaman, 2002), which may encourage their longer stays and return visits. However, in Kenya, there is no adequate oversight to monitor the operations of the homestays and therefore, the quality of services offered in these homestay facilities is currently not well known. As a result of limited research on homestays in Kenya (Kimaiga, Kihima, & Pepela, 2015), the study therefore attempted to establish whether tangible and intangible factors of service quality significantly affected tourism satisfaction.

1.1. *The scope of the study*

The study only focused on KECOBAT-registered homestays. The sample was derived from the stated database and used in the analysis. Furthermore, the study did not distinguish between international or domestic tourists in identifying respondents. It also defined a tourist as a person who travels to a location other than his own home for business, leisure, education, pleasure and staying in homestays, guest houses, farm houses and stays for more than 24 hours. Finally, tourist satisfaction was defined as a person's feeling of pleasure or disappointment results from comparing a product perceived performance in relation to his or her expectation (Kotler & Armstrong, 1996).

In this study tourist satisfaction was measured in terms of tourist likelihood to recommend the homestay.

2.   Theoretical framework

The study focused on identifying the homestay destination attributes which influence tourists' satisfaction. Therefore, this research is based on the consumer behaviour model, whereby, consumer satisfaction is viewed as a function of both expectations related to certain attributes and judgments of performance regarding these attributes (Clemons & Woodruff, 1992). Expectancy-disconfirmation theory has become one of the most commonly adopted approaches used to examine the satisfaction. It has been applied in diverse contexts, like, examining organizational behavior, citizen satisfaction as well as visitor experiences (Oliver, Balakrishnan, & Barry 1994; Van Ryzin 2013). As described by Oliver (1980), expectancy–disconfirmation theory consists of two sub-processes having independent effects on customer satisfaction: the formation of expectations and the disconfirmation of those expectations through performance comparisons. Expectancy–disconfirmation theory holds that consumers first form expectations of products' or services' (the tangible and intangible aspects in this study) performance prior to purchase or use. Subsequently, purchase and use contribute to consumer beliefs about the actual or perceived performance of the product or service. The consumer then compares the perceived performance to prior expectations, with the outcome being consumer satisfaction (Clemons & Woodruff, 1992).

Moreover, a consumer's expectations are: (a) confirmed when the product or service performance matches prior expectations, (b) negatively disconfirmed when product or service performance fails to match expectations and (c) positively disconfirmed when perceived the product or service performance exceeds expectations. Dissatisfaction comes about when a consumer's expectations are negatively disconfirmed; that is the product performance is less than expected (Patterson, 1993). The study measures the overall satisfaction of tourists' experiences in homestays whereby the hosts are generally expected to exhibit cultural/heritage of the destinations. The satisfaction was characterised with the tourist's assessment of both the tangible and intangible factors at the homestay. It is necessary to measure tourist satisfaction at homestays because (dis)satisfaction of either of the factors can lead to (dis)satisfaction with the overall destination.

2.1.   *Tangible and intangible factors*

The tangible factors of service quality include the interior layout and design of the homestay. Ransley and Ingram (2001) argued that good design can lead to greater profitability and that many of the messages homestays wish to convey to their guests can be effectively communicated through the design of the homestay. Another aspect of the tangible factors in homestay facilities is the ambient conditions that can include colour, lighting, equipment and overall cleanliness of the places inside the homestays.

Yoshida and James (2011) noted that physical environment had been overlooked and regarded as being unimportant towards quality perceptions. However, this was primarily limited to service encounters characterised by relatively short durations, for example, encounters with travel agencies. Thus with the duration of service encounters in homestays being long, tangible factors are likely to play a significant role in customer satisfaction. Studies (Wakefield & Blodgett, 1999; Yoshida & James, 2011) demonstrate that the tangible physical environment plays an important role in generating excitement in leisure settings; and this in turn, plays a significant role in determining customers' repatronage intentions and willingness to recommend.

On the other hand, intangible aspects of service quality are those aspects that are not touched. The dimensions of intangibles in service quality are reliability, responsiveness, assurance and empathy. The dimension of reliability is defined as 'delivering the promised performance dependably and accurately' (Schneider & White, 2004, p.32). Furthermore, reliability includes the service provider being able to performing a task correctly at the first attempt and it is one of the most important service components of customers (Parasuraman, Berry, & Zeithaml, 1991).The dimension of responsiveness is defined as 'willingness of the organization to provide prompt service and help customers' while assurance is defined as 'ability of the organization's employees to inspire trust and confidence in the organization through their knowledge and courtesy' (Parasuraman, Zeithaml, & Berry, 1988, p. 23). Moreover, Kandampully, Mok, and Sparks (2001) asserted that guests expect to feel safe in their encounters with employees. In the case of homestays, the tourists may also need to feel safe with other members of the household. Finally, the dimension of empathy is explained as 'the caring, individualized attention the firm provides its customers' (Parasuraman et al., 1988, p.23). These dimensions constitute an important role of service and form a significant part of the multiple-item scale for measuring service quality referred to as 'SERVQUAL' model (Parasurman et al., 1991).

3. Methodology

The study adopted a descriptive survey design to determine the level of tangible and intangible factors of service quality provided and their influence towards tourist satisfaction. The Lake Victoria tourist circuit is as a result of a 2014 restructuring from the former Nyanza and Western Tourism Circuits meant to conform to Kenya's new counties systems. The region comprises 10 counties, namely Kisumu, Migori, Homa Bay, Nyamira, Siaya, Kisii, Kakamega, Busia, Vihiga and Bungoma. According to KECOBAT, the number of registered homestays was around 100 (it was in its initial stages of recruiting members). The expected number of unregistered homestays was estimated to be much higher. However, the scope of the study was limited to registered members only.

The research was carried out on homestays located in three selected counties of the Lake Victoria Kenya Tourism Circuit that included Siaya, Kisumu and Kakamega counties. This is because they accounted for an estimated 65% of the registered members, indicating that homestays were more vibrant in these areas. Additionally, the region is endowed with rich cultural attractions, wonderful landforms, and high-altitude climate suitable for sports, forests and wildlife (Kiprutto, Akama, & Sitati, 2007).

The study used 20 homestays from the 3 counties, and this was deemed representative of the population since it accounted for at least 30% of the total population (Borg & Gall, 2003; Mugenda & Mugenda, 2003). Further, the study identified 44 respondents (however the study used 42 respondents as 2 cases were deemed to be outliers) based on convenience sampling on the total number of homestays considered in the study. In circumstances where there were more than one adult tourist in the same homestay each of them was issued with a questionnaire.

3.1. *Data collection procedure*

A set of structured tourists' questionnaires were used to collect data. Closed-ended questions in the questionnaires were used to help to standardise and quantify responses from the research. The questionnaires were divided into four sections. Section A collected background information, including demographics such as gender and age, and details of the facilities and services provided at each homestay facilities. Section B collected information about the tourists' perception of tangible factors in the homestay. Further, Section C collected information about the tourists' perception of intangible factors in the homestay. Finally, Section D collected information about the tourists' satisfaction which was operationalised on the likelihood of the visitor recommending the homestay to his/her friends and family. Responses to questions in sections B, C and D were based on a five-point *Likert scale*.

One Research assistant was recruited and trained to aid in the collection of data. The questionnaires were administered by drop-off survey whereby the researcher goes to the homestay and hands the survey to respondents. The researcher returns to pick it up.

3.2. *Data analysis and presentation*

After data collection, the questionnaires were evaluated for errors before analysis. Data were then coded and screened using SPSS to check for inconsistencies. Two cases were identified as outliers using Mahalanobis distance and studentised deleted residual method and thus deleted. Descriptive statistics and multiple regression was then performed on the data to test the relationship between tangible and intangible factors of service quality in homestays as predictors of tourist satisfaction.

4. Findings and interpretation

The study was fairly balanced in terms of gender with an estimated 57% of the respondents being male. However, in terms of tourist distribution regarding age, 52.4% of the respondents were around 18–27 years followed by ages 28–37 years with 31%. These two age groups accounted for an estimated 83% of the total sample size.

The study also revealed an estimated 74% of the respondents had visited the homestays for the first time with the rest (26%) having visited the homestay more than once. This can be an indication of a low customer retention rate. Further, 24% out of the 74% first time tourists in the homestay were there for business purposes with the rest being there for leisure purposes and visiting friends and relatives.

Tourist satisfaction was operationalised in terms of the respondent's likelihood to recommend the homestay to family and friends. The results indicated that 29% of the respondents were satisfied (would recommend the homestay), with 71% indicating that they were not satisfied with the homestay. This may give insight on the prevailing tangible factors and intangible factors of service quality in homestays.

In order to test for moderation (interaction) between tangible factors and intangible factors, the predictors were mean centred (Dawson, 2013) and linear regression performed. After testing for moderation, the interaction variable (tangible*intangible) was excluded from the analysis since it had a low tolerance <0.0001 (Tabachnick & Fidell, 2012). This is because the variable was deemed to be highly related to the others in the set hence may present issues of multicollinearity. Therefore the only predictors used in the linear regression analysis were tangible factors and intangible factors.

The results given in Table 1 indicated that the relationship between tangible factors, intangible factors and the likelihood of the tourist to recommend the homestay was significant $F (2, 39) = 42.103 \, p < .05$.

Additionally, tangible factors and intangible factors of service quality explained 66.7% of the variance of a tourist's likelihood to recommend a homestay (adjusted $R^2 = .667$ as illustrated in Table 2).

Table 1. ANOVA[a].

Model		Sum of squares	df	Mean square	F	Sig.
1	Regression	17.705	2	8.852	42.103	.000[b]
	Residual	8.200	39	.210		
	Total	25.905	41			

[a]Dependent variable: likelihood to recommend the homestay to friends and family.
[b]Predictors: (constant), overall perception of intangible factors in the homestay, overall perception of tangible factors in the homestay.

The results also indicated that tangible factors of service quality ($\beta = .667$, $p = .012$) are a better predictor of tourist's likelihood to recommend homestays than intangible factors of service quality ($\beta = .35$, $p = .008$ see Table 3). Overall increasing both tangible and intangible factors of service quality would result in an increase in the tourist likelihood to recommend the homestay.

The regression prediction equation is depicted as follows:

$$Y = .667X_1 + .35X_2 - 2.417 + e,$$

where Y is the tourists likelihood to recommend, X_1 the tangible factors, X_2 the intangible factors and e the error term.

5. Discussion

An estimated 83% of the respondents were aged between 18 and 37 years. This may be because 'Millennials' (refers those born after 1980) are normally more liberal and open to change (PewReseacrhCenter, 2010) hence can try out homestay facilities with an intention to learn new cultures and experiences. Additionally, due to the relative low cost of homestays it may appeal to this group as opposed to more mature groups who may have more expansive budgets to work with.

The overall satisfaction of visitors at homestay facilities in the study was found to be low. Good service quality is normally vital to retain customers. Customers will recognise and value the outstanding service offered to them. Over time, they will exhibit loyalty behaviours, such as continued purchasing and increased referrals (Chi & Gursoy, 2009). Hospitality operators must recognise the needs of their customers for a successful business and employees; need to have the flexibility and training to react immediately to satisfy customer requests.

The low levels of satisfaction with the quality of homestay facilities may account for the tourists' changes in eating habits where the tourists in the study were found to eat mostly outside the homestay facility. It would be inconclusive to adduce that there is low

Table 2. Model summary.

Model	R	R^2	Adjusted R^2	Std. error of the estimate
1	.827[a]	.683	.667	.45854

[a]Predictors: (constant), overall perception of Intangible factors in the homestay, overall perception of tangible factors in the homestay.

Table 3. Coefficients[a].

Model	Unstandardised coefficients		Standardised coefficients		
	B	Std. error	β	T	Sig.
1 (Constant)	−2.417	.762		−3.170	.003
Overall perception of tangible factors in the homestay	.667	.253	.420	2.630	.012
Overall perception of Intangible factors in the homestay	.350	.126	.445	2.787	.008

[a]Dependent variable: likelihood to recommend the homestay to friends and family.

preference for foods in the homestay facilities considering the lack of reasonable data. Many facets of the institutional setting can affect tourists' satisfaction, some of which operate directly on their eating behaviours, while others are more subtle. Therefore, a high degree of involvement of the institutions with food service quality and tourists perception is an important factor for success for the homestay facility catering and meal provision sector (Cranage, Conklin, & Bordi, 2003).

Furthermore, the study indicated a low customer retention rate with only 26% of the respondents having stayed at the homestay more than once. This may be explained by the prevailing low customer satisfaction levels. This is because if tourists are perceived to be satisfied, they will always come back to the premise and enhance the business for the homestay facility (Sureshchander et al., 2002). In retrospect, the recent introduction of the homestay concept in Kenya may provide an explanation as to why there are a high number of first time visitors in homestay facilities and conversely the low number of repeat visitors.

Tangible and intangible factors of service quality explained 66.7% of the variance of a tourist's likelihood to recommend a homestay. This was an indication that there may be other variables that can significantly influence tourists' satisfaction regarding homestays. Some hypothesised variables may include changes in health condition of the visitors while at the homestay, 'culture shock' and probably having a relatively low amount of time at the homestay to get over it, or even the influence of a spouse, partner or child who may have been 'pushed' or coerced into staying in a homestay. Such variables can be examined in subsequent studies on tourist satisfaction at homestays.

The study also indicated that tangible factors of service quality are a better predictor of tourist satisfaction in homestays than intangible factors of service quality. Although intangible factors of service quality influence consumers' likelihood to recommend a homestay, the intangible aspects are by nature subject to employee heterogeneity or inconsistency. Wakefield and Blodgett (1999) suggested that an attractively designed physical environment, on the other hand, can more consistently generate a positive influence on consumers' feelings about the place. They further noted that the physical environment plays a critical role in determining customers' subsequent behavioural intentions in leisure service settings.

6. Conclusion and recommendations

Tourism is one of the vibrant and promising economic segments in the world today. Many countries of the world have integrated their economic advancement with tourism. Tourists who want to stay with the local communities can be said to be motivated by the desire to know the traditions and cultures of the local area. Homestay provides such opportunities. Consequently, the low levels of tourist satisfaction should be of concern to homestay facilities' administrators as well as the regulatory bodies charged with oversight responsibilities because for there to be an influence on service quality, regular inspection is required.

However, the high number of first time visitors to homestay facilities is an indication of the novelty of the idea in the Lake Victoria tourism circuit. Therefore if the homestays are able to take advantage of this by offering functional tangible facilities as well as efficient intangible elements of service quality, then this sector is likely to have prolonged growth. This would ultimately have a more direct effect on the economic and social status of the community and, on a larger scale, the country.

The study recommends that the tangible factors like the aesthetics of the homestays be improved. This is not necessarily an overhaul of these facilities but quick and regular maintenance of facilities like a cracked window, door knobs and regular cleaning of dust motes. Further, homestay facilities may develop or assign specific bathrooms to visitors to avoid sharing.

With respect to food service, whereby the study revealed that visitors occasionally eat out, the study recommends that a description of what is going to be prepared and the nutritional components of the food be provided to the visitors beforehand. Also homestays may invite visitors to the kitchen to participate in food preparation. Finally, give the visitors an opportunity to choose what they want to eat from a select menu beforehand, prior to them visiting the homestay facility.

KECOBAT may also arrange for training programmes for homestays to help improve and maintain the service quality, for example, customer care, training on proficiency in English and other foreign languages. Moreover, it should certify the homestay facilities in a rating system according to their quality control and to encourage competition between homestay providers.

Finally due to the limited scope of the study, possible suggestions for future research would be a study that focused on determining international and domestic motivations over their choice of homestay accommodation. Additionally, the economic impact of homestay facilities in the rural parts of Kenya may also be studied.

Disclosure statement

No potential conflict of interest was reported by the authors.

References

Agyeiwaah, E., Akyeampong, O., & Amenumey, E. K. (2013). International tourists' motivations to choose homestay: Do their socio-demographics have any influence? *Tourism and Hospitality Research, 13*(1), 16–26. doi:10.1177/1467358413517895

Akama, J. S., & Sterry, T. (2002). *Cultural tourism in Africa: Strategies for the new millennium.* Proceedings of the ATLAS Africa International Conference December 2000, Mombasa, Kenya.

Borg, W. R., & Gall, M. D. (2003). *Educational research* (5th ed.). White Plains, NY: Longman.

Chi, C. G., & Gursoy, D. (2009). Employee satisfaction, customer satisfaction, and financial performance: An empirical examination. *International Journal of Hospitality Management, 28,* 245–253. doi:10.1016/j.ijhm.2008.08.003

Clemons, D. S., & Woodruff, R. B. (1992). Broadening the view of consumer (dis)satisfaction: A proposed means-end disconfirmation model of CS/D. In C. T. Allen, T. J. Madden, T. A. Shimp, R. D. Howell, G. M. Zinkhan, D. D. Heisley, … R. L. Jenk, (Eds.), *Marketing Theory and Applications* (pp. 413-421). Chicago: American Marketing Association.

Cranage, D. A., Conklin, M. T., & Bordi, P. L. (2003). Can young adults be influenced to eat healthier snacks: The effects of choice and nutritional information on taste, satisfaction and intent to purchase? *Foodservice Research International, 14*, 125–137.

Dawson, J. F. (2013). Moderation in management research: What, why, when, and how. *Journal of Business and Psychology.* Retrieved from http://link.springer.com/article/10.1007/s10869-013-9308-7/fulltext.html

Hinch, T., & Butler, R. (1996). Indigenous tourism: A common ground for discussion. In R. Butler & T. Hinch (Eds.), *Tourism and indigenous peoples* (pp. 3–21). London: International Thomson Business Press.

Hsu, S. L., & Lin, Y. M. (2011). Factors underlying college students' choice homestay accommodation while travelling. *World Transaction on Engineering and Technology Education, 9*(3), 196–202.

Kandampully, J., Mok, C., & Sparks, B. (2001). *Service quality management in hospitality, tourism, and leisure.* London: Routledge.

Kenya community based tourism network-KECOBAT. (2015). Retrieved from http://www.kecobat.org/programmes/homestays-development.html

Kenya National Bureau of Statistics. (2014). *Kenya facts and figures 2014.* Retrieved from http://www.knbs.or.ke/index.php?option=com_phocadownload&view=category&id=20&Itemid=1107

Kimaiga, R. K., Kihima, B. O., & Pepela, A. W. (2015). The role of homestay operators' knowledge and skills in enhancing their business. *Journal of Tourism Research & Hospitality, 4*(2), 2–11.

Kotler, P., Armstrong, G. (1996). *Principles of marketing.* New Jersey: Prentice-Hall.

Kiprutto, N., Akama, J., & Sitati, N. (2007). *Marketing of the north rift region as a tourist destination in Kenya* (Masters thesis). Department of Tourism and Tour Operations Management, Moi University, Kenya.

Mugenda, O. M., & Mugenda, A. G. (2003). *Research methods: Quantitative and qualitative approaches.* Nairobi: Acts Press.

Oliver, R. L. (1980). A cognitive model of the antecedents and consequences of satisfaction decisions. *Journal of marketing research, 17*(4), 460–469.

Oliver, R. L., Balakrishnan, P. S. & Barry, B. (1994). Outcome satisfaction in negotiation: A test of expectancy disconfirmation. *Organizational Behavior and Human Decision Processes, 60*(2), 252–275.

Parasuraman, A., Berry, L. L., & Zeithaml, V. A. (1991). Refinement and reassessment of the SERVQUAL scale. *Journal of Retailing, 67*(4), 420–450.

Parasuraman, A., Zeithaml, V. A., & Berry, L. L. (1988). Communication and control process in the delivery of service quality. *Journal of Marketing, 52*(2), 35–48.

Patterson, P. G. (1993). Expectations and product performance as determinants of satisfaction for a high-involvement purchase. *Psychology & Marketing, 10*(5), 449–465.

PewResearchCenter. (2010). *Millenials: Confident. Connected. Open to change.* Retrieved from http://www.pewsocialtrends.org/2010/02/24/millennials-confident-connected-open-to-change/

Ransley, J., & Ingram, H. (2001). What is a 'good' hotel design? *Facilities, 19*(1/2), 79–87. MCB University Press.

Richards, G. (2011). Production and consumption of African cultural tourism and homestay facilities. *Annals of Tourism Research, 22*(2), 261–283.

Schneider, B., & White, S. S. (2004). *Service quality: Research perspectives.* Thousand Oaks, CA: Sage.

Sureshchander, G. S., Rajendran, C., & Anantharaman, R. N. (2002). The relationship between service quality and customer satisfaction: A factor specific approach. *Journal of Service Marketing, 16*(4), 363–379.

Tabachnick, R. G., & Fidell, L. S. (2012). *Using multivariate statistics* (6th ed.). Boston: Pearson.

Van Ryzin, G. G. (2013). An experimental test of the expectancy-disconfirmation theory of citizen satisfaction. *Journal of Policy Analysis and Management, 32*(3), 597–614.

Wakefield, K. L., & Blodgett, J. G. (1999). Customer response to intangible and tangible service factors. *Psychology and Marketing, 16*, 51–68. doi:10.1002/(SICI)1520-6793(199901)16:1<51::AID-MAR4>3.0.CO;2-0

Wall, G., & Long, V. (1996). Balinese homestays: An indigenous response to tourism opportunities. In R. Butler & T. Hinch, (Eds.), *Tourism and indigenous peoples* (pp. 27–48). London: International Thomson Business Press.

Wang, Y. (2007). Customized authenticity begins at home. *Annals of Tourism Research, 34*(3), 789–804.

Welsh, A. K. (2001). *Homestay: The perceptions of international students at a tertiary institution in New Zealand* (Unpublished master's thesis). University of Auckland, Auckland.

Yassin, S. M., Shaffril, H. A. M., Hassan, M. S., Othman, M. S., & Samah, A. A. (2010). Prospects of waterway development as a catalyst to improve regional and community socio-economy level. *American Journal of Economics and Business Administration, 2,* 240–246. doi:10.3844/ajebasp.2010.240.246

Yoshida, M., & James, J. D. (2011). Service quality at sporting events: Is aesthetic quality a missing dimension? *Sport Management Review, 14*(1), 13–24.

Lessons learned on ecotourism in sub-Saharan Africa

Ian E. Munanura[a] and Kenneth F. Backman[b]

[a]Assistant Professor, Department of Forest Ecosystems and Society, College of Forestry, Oregon State University, Corvallis, Oregon, USA; [b]Professor, Department of Parks, Recreation and Tourism Management, Clemson University, South Carolina, USA.

Introduction

What are the real outcomes for African countries that have developed their tourism and development policies around the principals and values of ecotourism? This book attempts to address this question. A complete evaluation of the ecotourism industry in all countries is not possible due to the scope and magnitude of the task. However, the case studies across sub-Saharan Africa in this book have demonstrated both successful and unsuccessful results from ecotourism development. These lessons are valuable to scholars and ecotourism practitioners in Africa. We believe this book will stimulate scholars and practitioners to work together to formulate applied ecotourism research and policy advocacy, which will move ecotourism forward in Africa and help overcome ecotourism constraints. As seen throughout this book, the opportunity for ecotourism success in Africa is undeniable. Ecotourism in Africa has grown tremendously, and is expected to generate over 1.5 billion tourists in the next five years (Christie, Fernandes, Messerli, & Twining-Ward, 2014). As such, ecotourism is recognized as one of the fastest growing economic sectors in Africa (Backman & Munanura, 2015). The United Nations Millennium Development Goals are gaining importance in Africa, which strengthens the value of ecotourism in future political and socioeconomic discourse in Africa (Novelli, 2015; Spenceley & Meyer, 2015). It is through discussions that scholars and practitioners can together meaningfully contribute and shape the future of ecotourism in Africa. In this concluding chapter, we illustrate the ecotourism challenges that remain in Africa in the form of governance, policy, and structural constraints.

Ecotourism governance constraints

The first five chapters of the book discussed ecotourism governance in Africa. They illustrate four main ecotourism governance constraints: poor leadership skills, limited capacity of local stakeholders, uninclusive partnerships, and short-term life cycles. The case studies indicate that these constraints continue to impede ecotourism success in Africa. These constraints are briefly reviewed.

Poor leadership skills among ecotourism leaders

Skilled leadership is critical for the success of ecotourism enterprises in Africa. Visionary and committed leadership empowers local stakeholders to transcend self-serving ecotourism interests and to facilitate access to shared ecotourism interests by all stakeholders. As observed throughout this book, leadership in most social ecotourism enterprises in Africa embodies a top-down governance approach, with limited participation of stakeholders (Sebola & Fourie, 2006). Where leadership appears, it is passive and appears in the form of consultation (Brown, 2002; Koch, 1994). This creates power imbalances, which brew mistrust in leadership and conflict within the ecotourism programs (Jamal & Stronza, 2009). It is therefore not surprising to find the examples of challenged ecotourism enterprises observed in this book. Nevertheless, the value of leadership skills and commitment to the success of ecotourism enterprises should not be underestimated. Substantial resources must be invested in improving leadership capacity, quality, and performance. Efforts to improve leadership in ecotourism must embody transparency and participatory governance systems (Jamal & Stronza, 2009; Pasape, Anderson, & Lindi, 2013). Efforts should also be made to establish decision-making processes in ecotourism programs. Such decision making processes must challenge and enable leaders to facilitate inclusiveness and empowerment of all groups of local stakeholders to actively participate in ecotourism programs.

Limited capacity of local ecotourism stakeholders

Local stakeholders' capacity appeared to be one of the greatest ecotourism governance constraints. Specifically, chapter 5 revealed that ecotourism operations are predominantly led by multinational organizations, with minimal participation of local stakeholders due to limited local stakeholder capacity. At the same time, some of the multinational organizations investing in ecotourism have endeavored to improve the capacity of local stakeholders (Kline & Slocum, 2015). Progress made by multinational organizations leading ecotourism in Africa is demonstrated throughout this book. Multinational organizations have made substantial investments in local employment, training, joint venture partnerships, and the active participation of local stakeholders in ecotourism operations. However, local stakeholders' limited capacity still hinders ecotourism success. In chapter 3, for example, it was revealed that foreign-dominated tour guiding operations in Uganda have insulated local tour guides from mainstream ecotourism operations. Similar examples demonstrating how ecotourism benefits are inaccessible to local stakeholders due to poor capacity were also observed in Ghana, Tanzania, Kenya, and other countries across Africa. Some of these constraints are a result of poor government policies. For example, it was observed in chapters 3 and 11 that the limited capacity of local stakeholders has been a result of incompatible government policies. Additionally, limited access to capital, poor management skills, poor marketing and promotion skills, unaccountability, and political patronage are still some of the main constraints affecting local stakeholders' ability to optimally benefit from ecotourism. Not surprisingly, local stakeholders still feel excluded from ecotourism opportunities, which has created resentment in communities.

Experiences revealed from Uganda, Kenya, Tanzania, and Botswana suggest a pathway forward. For example, multilateral organizations' ecotourism must actively pursue ecotourism programs that enable local stakeholder to effectively participate in ecotourism through training, access to capital, and joint venture partnerships. In the future, it is important to invest in the capacity building of local ecotourism stakeholders. The importance of building local capacity in ecotourism is not new (Victurine, 2000). As demonstrated earlier, many efforts have been made to improve local capacity. The challenge, however, as noted in chapter 9, is the "one-size-fits-all" approach to training, which ignores the heterogeneity of communities, regions, and countries where ecotourism operates. The areas of ecotourism represent a diverse and complex political, sociocultural, and economic environment that requires deeper understanding and customization of prescribed local capacity-building programs. As suggested in chapters 9 and 11, capacity-building programs, such as training, joint ventures, and partnerships cannot be universal, but rather, must be specific to the realities of each country, region, and community. Applied research is therefore, needed to examine the heterogeneity of regions where ecotourism operates in Africa, and the complex local processes that affect local capacity improvement in ecotourism. Additionally, local stakeholders must be the drivers of ecotourism investment of multinational organizations to ensure local ownership and sustainability of ecotourism investment. In some situations, as in the case of Kenya, multinational-driven ecotourism operations have successfully integrated conservation and development goals of ecotourism. However, the challenge remains to sustain the continuity of ecotourism programs beyond the donor-funding period. Therefore, it is critical that local stakeholders are actively engaged and supported to develop capacity to maintain ecotourism programs beyond donor funding. Future research may explore the constraints associated with multilateral supported ecotourism operations in Africa, and implications these constraints have on ecotourism sustainability. This will enable partnerships between multilateral organizations and local stakeholders to move from technical assistance to local stakeholder empowerment.

Uninclusive ecotourism partnerships

Uninclusive partnerships are key constraints for ecotourism governance as shown in this book. Ecotourism governance is dependent on inclusive and trusted partnerships (Stone, 2015). As indicated throughout this book, many ecotourism operations have failed due to stakeholder mistrust, and exclusion of various groups of stakeholders, particularly groups representing less powerful constituencies. Chapter 2 showed how mistrust for multinational organization led to failure of ecotourism partnerships. Chapters 5–7 showed how mistrust and uninclusive partnerships have been a huge constraint for ecotourism in Tanzania. Such mistrust emerges from inability to demonstrate a tangible impact of ecotourism programs, which is a symptom of a lack of transparency and accountability, as seen in the cases of Botswana (chapter 8) and Uganda (chapter 3). Throughout Africa, lack of transparency and accountability have emerged as key challenges for ecotourism partnerships. Chapter 3 shows how ecotourism has been central to political rivalry, resource allocation-based conflicts, and mistrust in stakeholder partnerships. Mistrust in ecotourism partnerships has been attributed to lack of openness and information sharing between foreign and local ecotourism stakeholders (Brennan & Allen, 2001). Mistrust may also emerge from perceptions of uninclusive ecotourism approaches that have been enshrined in local ecotourism governance policies. This isolates local stakeholders from ecotourism, creating resentment among the ecotourism host communities (Cobbinah, Black, & Thwaites, 2015). For example, local stakeholders in Kakum Conservation Area in Ghana have been insulated from ecotourism operations. Similar sentiments are echoed in Uganda, where centralized government systems are perceived to have created barriers in the form of policies that favor foreign tour operators at the expense of local tour operators.

Moving forward, it is critical that ecotourism initiatives are built into decentralized local government systems to facilitate local ecotourism stakeholders' ability to penetrate structural boundaries created by centralized government systems. Future research may aim to identify structural barriers that challenge ecotourism success from local stakeholders'. Building trust among local stakeholders will help to cultivate inclusive and participatory ecotourism partnerships, which are important for ecotourism governance. While mistrust has been linked to partnerships led by government institutions that may not typically be transparent, it was also observed that mistrust is a problem in ecotourism partnerships led by local stakeholders (Archabald & Naughton-Treves, 2001). If not identified and managed carefully and early, mistrust has the potential to impact the collaboration and sustainability of ecotourism programs in Africa.

Mistrust of ecotourism leaders has also been attributed to the proliferation of local stakeholder interest in ecotourism, which attracts a broad spectrum of stakeholders including both powerful and weak stakeholders. The financial potential of ecotourism also draws interest from a wide scope of local groups. As seen in chapters 2 and 4, such interest has resulted in an explosion of opportunistic ecotourism partnerships driven by shorter financial benefits rather than long-term socio-economic benefits from ecotourism. One of the critical research questions that remains is, when is ecotourism growth detrimental to successful ecotourism partnerships? Further, it is crucial to identify and establish processes to help foreign ecotourism stakeholders identify credible stakeholders from a diverse pool in the shortest time possible. These concerns demonstrate the importance of facilitated partnerships for ecotourism in Africa. Ecotourism partnerships require guidance for stakeholders to optimally benefit from ecotourism (Pellis, Lamers, & Van der Duim, 2015). For example, chapter 5 discussed how nongovernmental organizations in Kenya have been critical in building trusted and inclusive ecotourism partnerships. Centralized government systems have facilitated successful ecotourism efforts. Future research may illuminate more barriers and opportunities for ecotourism across decentralized and centralized government systems. Additionally, ecotourism practitioners may pursue research on facilitated ecotourism partnerships to reveal their potential in Africa.

Elite dominance in ecotourism operations is also regarded as a challenge to inclusive partnership in ecotourism. As shown in chapters 3 and 8, ecotourism programs in Africa have failed due to power imbalances. Previously, it was observed that the elite dominance in ecotourism influenced local stakeholder dynamics and community participation in developing countries where ecotourism is dominated by powerful institutions (Blomley, Namara, McNeilage, Franks, Rainer, Donaldson, Malpas, Olupot, Baker, Sandbrook, Bitariho, & Infield, 2010; Scheyvens, 1999). In power imbalance situations, powerless local community stakeholders commonly do not have a voice in the design and implementation of ecotourism programs (Brandon & Wells, 1992; Scheyvens, 1999; Tosun, 2000). Poor consideration of such power imbalances where decisions are skewed toward the elite have resulted in ecotourism strategies that do not have substantial conservation and development impacts (Brandon & Wells, 1992; Munanura, Backman, Hallo, & Powell, 2016). A systematic assessment of the local conditions must be made to identify and prepare for management of the power imbalances at every stage of ecotourism program design and implementation. Enabling community participation at every stage of ecotourism can serve as a tool for readjusting power imbalances (Scheyvens, 1999; Tosun, 2000). Facilitated community participation empowers local residents to partner with powerful institutions and individuals to identify and communicate local wildlife conservation and human development needs.

Short-term life cycle nature ecotourism programs

Most ecotourism programs are donor funded and have short-term lifecycles ranging between three and five years. This is problematic because most organizations implementing ecotourism programs are forced to rush through the design and planning phase to ensure that the ecotourism programs begin early. Yet, the design and planning phase, is the most critical phase for ecotourism programs. In such cases, a rushed design and planning phase results in implementing organizations being pushed to design and plan ecotourism programs based on biased, quick, and simplistic site-specific assessments informed by self-interested local opinion leaders (Brandon & Wells, 1992). This is by no means limited to ecotourism programs. Most time-sensitive foreign investments in international development programs have failed due to exposure to roadside, person, and project biases (Chambers & York, 2013). Yet, ecotourism involves multiple dimensions that interact at multilevels in a nonlinear fashion. This complexity calls for a systematic assessment of ecotourism during the design phase, and flexibility for adaptation (Blomley et al., 2010). For example, threats to wildlife are typically attributed to poor residents (Nyaupane & Poudel, 2011). However, there is evidence that those who affect wildlife conservation most in some areas may be the elite whose businesses depend on forest resources (Brandon & Wells, 1992). Quick assessments have the potential for misdiagnosis of conservation and development problems that exist locally and set up ecotourism programs to fail. Such situations require extended ecotourism program design and planning periods for an effective analysis and understanding of dynamic and complex local systems (Blomley et al., 2010; Brandon & Wells, 1992; Munanura et al., 2016).

Ecotourism policy constraints

This book shows that many cases in Africa are riddled with imbalances that affect the success of ecotourism policies. Imbalance in ecotourism policies emerge from a number of issues: market-driven influences, efforts to harmonize ecotourism policies without regard to heterogeneity of ecotourism host regions, poor local market linkages, lack of understanding of basic ecotourism principles among ecotourism policy makers and divergent stakeholder interests. The success of ecotourism depends on balanced regulatory policies guiding ecotourism implementation. Such policies must represent the interests of all stakeholders, including the politically and financially challenged local stakeholders (Munanura et al., 2016; Scheyvens, 1999). Applied experiences throughout the book demonstrate progress made in establishing pro-ecotourism policies in Africa. At the same time, this book also presents a number of policy constraints that need to be addressed moving forward.

Market-driven ecotourism policies

Market-driven ecotourism policies have challenged ecotourism in Africa. Such policies are valuable to the private sector and have led to the most lucrative ecotourism operations. Yet, as seen in chapters 9 and 11, they have not helped facilitate local partnerships or access to ecotourism benefits for local stakeholders. The market-driven policies certainly remain some of the main ecotourism constraints moving forward, and have greater implications for ecotourism application in Africa. For example, we have seen in chapters 2, 5, and 9 that market-driven ecotourism policies have potential to dominate social and ecological interests of local stakeholders in ecotourism operations, exposing host communities to irreversible social and ecological impacts. There is evidence supporting the correlation between socioecological impacts of ecotourism and market-driven ecotourism policies (Mgonja, Sirima, & Mkumbo, 2015; Munanura, Backman, & Sabuhoro, 2013). The extent to which ecotourism policies address ecotourism impacts successfully remains to be seen in Africa. In the future, scholars and practitioners must explore how the trade-offs between ecotourism impacts and benefits reflect complexities in ecotourism processes in each country, region, and community, and how the trade-offs can be balanced. In addition, Additionally, future research should policy implementation constraints for desirable ecotourism policies. For example, as seen in chapters 3, 6, and 8, good policies are worthless without the capacity of local stakeholders to take advantage of them. Where there is variation in local stakeholder capacity, it is important to adapt regulatory ecotourism policies to local realities. These efforts could be supplemented with local stakeholder capacity-building programs in formulation, monitoring, and implementation. Such a combination will enable formulation and implementation of balanced ecotourism policies.

Harmonization of ecotourism policies

There was mixed reaction toward the value of harmonizing ecotourism policies across regions in Africa. Chapter 4 highlighted the disparity in ecotourism policies across East Africa as a critical challenge to ecotourism. In that chapter, the authors called for harmonization of marketing policies to remain competitive. Yet, chapter 9 called for ecotourism policies that recognize and represent the heterogeneity of host regions and the complexity of ecotourism processes, which differ across Africa. Clearly there is merit in both arguments. However, we pointed out that harmonization of ecotourism policies without recognition of heterogeneity and the complexity of ecotourism processes across regions, communities, and countries in Africa is detrimental to ecotourism success. There are many cases in this book that support this argument. For example, chapter 6 demonstrated the cost of heterogeneity assumptions in Botswana, where interests of a section of stakeholder groups were not represented in ecotourism partnerships. Such a situation creates mistrust and conflicts between stakeholders, resulting in disenfranchisement, resentment, and disincentives to provide ecotourism support among the less powerful local stakeholders. While, some broader policies may merit harmonization, such as the tourist entry visa liberalization in East Africa, most regulatory ecotourism policies needed to balance ecotourism impacts and benefits. Policy makers must recognize and take into consideration the diverse and complex ecotourism process that dictates the need for adaptive ecotourism policies. As suggested in the literature (Belsky, 2009), there are often multiple and conflicting stakeholder interests interacting at community, region, and country levels. This concern calls for careful examination and adaptation in the policy environment to ensure that policies facilitate rather than hinder ecotourism success.

Lack of basic understanding of ecotourism principles

One of the major ecotourism constraints was a lack of understanding of ecotourism principles among policy makers. Comprehensive understanding of basic ecotourism principles is critical for formulation and implementation of effective ecotourism policies (Koch, 1994). However, this has been a challenge in Africa because of limited understanding of ecotourism principles or the lack of attention to all aspects of ecotourism principles by local stakeholders (Ahebwa, van der Duim, & Sandbrook, 2012). Chapter 3 illustrated how this lack of comprehensive understanding of ecotourism principles among local stakeholders resulted in imbalanced and ineffective ecotourism policies. For example, poor local linkages to ecotourism progress in Africa were attributed to formulation of poor ecotourism policies. Even when the policies appear to be balanced, limited understanding of ecotourism principles among stakeholders, challenges policy implementation. Again, limited understanding reinforces the need for training of local stakeholders in these principles. Without a skilled labor force and knowledgeable leadership the ecotourism policies in Africa will continue to be poorly constructed. Another of the constraints is the high cost of training, particularly for small ecotourism enterprises. However, this can be overcome by cost-share efforts if groups of ecotourism enterprises organize to offer joint training programs that emphasize best practices. Such training programs will not only help to improve rural labor capital, but also have potential to improve local ecotourism market linkages.

Divergent stakeholder interests

The divergent interests of multiple stakeholders have created conflicts at times, which also affect ecotourism policy formulation and implementation. Where such conflicts exist, policies perceived to represent the interests of opposing parties often have been rejected, diminishing the potential of ecotourism. For example, it was observed at Gales Point Manatee in Belize that conflicts associated with differences in social class, gender roles, and patronage had substantial impact on ecotourism success (Belsky, 2009). Chapter 3 raises the issue of conflict between local and foreign tour operators in Uganda, where the less powerful tour operators feel despised by powerful tour operators. Chapter 9 shows the conflict between local stakeholders and government institutions at Kakum Conservation Area in Ghana, where ecotourism policies continue to isolate local residents from ecotourism operations. These conflicts emerge from the perception of imbalanced ecotourism policies by one group of stakeholders, which undermines trust and participation of local stakeholders, whose role in shaping ecotourism is critical. As seen in chapter 4, some countries in Africa have had success in minimizing stakeholder conflicts through a successful process of building trust. This success is primarily attributed to structured and facilitated partnerships by third-party institutions, where selection and active engagement of stakeholders were done carefully to balance stakeholder interests (Gray, 1985; Jamal & Getz, 1995). Future research may explore the applicability of structured and guided partnerships in ecotourism sites across Africa, and propose partnership models and policies that may effectively guide practitioners in ecotourism stakeholder governance.

Ecotourism structural constraints

Ecotourism processes encompass an enormous scope of players, including public and private institutions, international institutions, local government institutions, community-based organizations, and many more who interact at different scales. Such interactions are certainly bound to create or reveal operational constraints that have potential to affect ecotourism operations and processes. Some of these constraints include poor leadership skills, the social nature of ecotourism benefits, limited access to capital, poor local linkages, poor quality and intangible conservation, and development impacts of ecotourism efforts.

Limited entrepreneurship skills

Strong entrepreneurship skills are critical for the success of ecotourism in Africa (Victurine, 2000). Ecotourism has potential to benefit host regions in Africa, when leaders and investors are skilled entrepreneurs (Mbaiwa, 2015; Victurine, 2000). Some of the ecotourism constraints highlighted in this book, such as poor local economic linkages, perceptions of imbalanced ecotourism benefits, and failure of ecotourism initiatives, are a direct result of limited entrepreneurship skills. Chapter 8 showed that the failure of ecotourism enterprises in Botswana resulted from poor financial and marketing skills. Chapters 8, 7, and 11 pointed to lack of capital to support investment in ecotourism, among other entrepreneurship constraints in ecotourism. Chapters 4, 6, and 8 suggested that poor leadership has been one of the main constraints of ecotourism entrepreneurship in Africa. Chapter 6 illustrated that a limited commitment to ecotourism ventures is another entrepreneurship constraint in Africa. These constraints have appeared previously as critical deterrents for ecotourism entrepreneurship and must be considered when promoting ecotourism competitiveness in Africa (Kirsten & Rogerson, 2002; Victurine, 2000).

Social nature of ecotourism benefits

The collective nature of social ecotourism benefits has been criticized due to challenges associated with the "common good mentality" (Kiss, 2004; Munanura et al., 2016). However, there are cases in Africa where social enterprises have been successful (Chirozva, 2015; Mbaiwa, 2015). For example, the gorilla guardians cultural village, a social enterprise operated by former gorilla poachers at the Volcanoes National Park in Rwanda, is regarded as a successful social enterprise model. As indicated in chapter 8, those local stakeholders, who were perceived as marginalized in the private sector, controlled ecotourism destination in Africa. As Mbaiwa (2015) suggests, it is usually the marginalized stakeholders who have in the past reaped meaningful ecotourism entrepreneurship benefits. Beginning with a capital investment of $2,000 in 2006, the gorilla guardians cultural village currently generates almost $30,000 annually from community-based ecotourism activities. Another example is shown in Botswana at Chobe Enclave Conservation Trust, where a community-based ecotourism enterprise has experienced exceptional growth over 14 years (Stone, 2015). In the gorilla guardians cultural village case, those who were perceived to be powerless in ecotourism, such as poachers, have not only secured regular income from social enterprises, but have also become stewards of mountain gorilla conservation at Volcanoes National Park in Rwanda. These examples are a testimony that social ecotourism enterprises have the potential to promote integrated conservation and development goals. In the future, scholars must undertake research to examine critical factors responsible for the success and failure of social ecotourism programs in Africa. Additionally, efforts should be made to improve the performance of social ecotourism enterprises in Africa by developing leadership skills, particularly in marketing and promotion, management of shared resources, and social entrepreneurship (Mbaiwa, 2015; Victurine, 2000).

Commitment to the quality of ecotourism services

We observed that some ecotourism enterprises have failed to maximize their potential due to lack of commitment to the quality of the services they provide. Lack of commitment to quality services and the ultimate failure of ecotourism enterprises is attributed to poor leadership (Black & Crabtree, 2007). This is not surprising, because previous studies have shown leadership to be responsible for failure of most community-based organizations (Archabald & Naughton-Treves, 2001; Balint, 2006; Munanura et al., 2016). For example, some of the local community organizations in neighboring Bwindi and Mgahinga National Parks in Uganda were identified as unsuccessful because of poor leadership (Archabald & Naughton-Treves, 2001). Similar sentiments were shown in the Kimona Community in South Kenya (Southgate, 2008). On the other hand, leadership has been found to be critical in the success of organizational performance (Raghunathan, Rao, & Solis, 2013). In fact, considerable investment has been made by international development and conservation organizations, including USAID, to improve the capacity of leadership to maintain the quality of ecotourism services. Unfortunately, as many cases in this book indicate, these efforts have not been successful due to poor leadership. Future efforts must be made to facilitate ecotourism leaders to improve, monitor, and maintain quality of ecotourism services.

Commitment to the broader social entrepreneurship goals

Revenue generation is one of many social entrepreneurship goals in ecotourism. In addition to revenue, ecotourism enterprises empower weaker stakeholder groups socially, economically, and politically. As seen in chapter 8, ecotourism entrepreneurship depends on stakeholder commitment to broader goals of social ecotourism enterprises. When all the stakeholders are committed and embrace broader social entrepreneurship goals beyond financial benefits, they are better prepared to overcome long-term fatigue, financial loss, and structural constraints associated with the collective nature of ecotourism enterprises (Mbaiwa, 2015). Ecotourism stakeholder commitments will largely depend on how social ecotourism enterprises motivate every stakeholder and group involved in producing ecotourism products and services. Ecotourism stakeholders must be empowered to ensure continuous commitment to the social, economic, and political empowerment goals of their programs. For example, leaders must create conditions where active stakeholders have a voice in decision-making, have pride and confidence in their contribution, have an understanding of the overall ecotourism vision, and have been supported to maintain it.

Poor local market linkages

Local ecotourism linkage opportunities emerge from local enterprises such as hotels and lodges in rural areas where the local food can be produced and sold for income. These local enterprises provide reliable markets for local produce, and the specialized demand of the hotels can enhance creativity and development of new specialties, such as mushrooms, which are not commonly consumed in rural areas (Ashley & Roe, 1998). For this to happen, however, local producers need help to increase the quality and capacity of their production to meet demand and optimize sales. One of the challenges with building local market linkages is the lack of access to financial capital and limited access to credit among poor rural residents (Green, 2003). To address this, local government and institutions supporting ecotourism programs in ecotourism regions must facilitate the establishment of rural community development banks and credit institutions that allocate credit differently from private banks. Credit unions, revolving loan funds, and micro enterprise loan funds have proved to be effective in capitalizing rural community enterprises (Green, 2003).

Limited wildlife conservation impact

Ecotourism benefits to local stakeholders, particularly benefits from external ecotourism stakeholders such as the government and donor-funded institutions, commonly have prescribed direct benefits such as cash rewards, opportunity cost compensation and employment, and indirect incentives including schools and health centers (Brandon & Wells, 1992; Munanura et al., 2016). Even though these may have been effective in some areas, such incentives are not universally applicable, and their use without a systematic site-specific analysis is dangerous (Brown, 2002; Munanura et al., 2016). For example, direct incentives have been based on the assumption that they will influence change in local forest resource use and dependence behavior (Archabald & Naughton-Treves, 2001; Brandon & Wells, 1992). Yet, evidence has shown that where the incentives exist, they rarely provide adequate benefits to offset the opportunity cost of foregoing forest resource use (Walpole & Goodwin, 2001). Additionally among local residents, indirect incentives do not compensate the opportunity cost of coexisting with wildlife (Walpole & Thouless, 2005). For example, the conservation impact of ecotourism revenue investment in health care centers and schools in park-neighboring communities in Rwanda has not been evident (Munanura et al., 2016). While the long-term impact is undeniable, such efforts do little to address immediate economic and environmental sustainability concerns. These constraints demonstrate the need for inclusive, multilevel stakeholder identification and collaboration involving local residents in a systematic and site-specific assessment (Brown, 2002). It is only through this process that a better understanding and diagnosis of the socioeconomic, political, ecological, and institutional conditions of an area's ecotourism operations can emerge to inform ecotourism programs (Brandon & Wells, 1992; Brown, 2002).

Limited access to ecotourism benefits

Ecotourism has provides numerous economic opportunities for developing countries in Africa, such as income generation, employment, and development (Ashley & Roe, 1998). The ecotourism sustainability of ecotourism demands optimization of economic benefits and minimization of costs. Ecotourism sustainability also requires local residents have access to tourism benefits (Munanura et al, 2016; Walpole & Thouless, 2005). The reality, however, is that local benefits are constrained by limited employment opportunities and market linkages for local products. As noted earlier, to achieve economic sustainability, these constraints must be addressed and the implications for stakeholders must be understood. In most of Africa, ecotourism attracts low-skilled and low-paying employment opportunities (Ashley & Roe, 1998; Walpole & Thouless, 2005). Yet ecotourism is believed to provide much needed employment opportunities for rural communities (Mbaiwa, 2015; Mgonja et al., 2015). Lack of skilled human capital in ecotourism host regions results in skilled foreign workers at the expense of rural residents, who are left with the menial and poor-paying jobs (Ashley & Roe, 1998). For ecotourism to be economically sustainable, residents in areas adjacent to tourist destinations must be empowered with relevant skills to be competitive in the ecotourism labor market (Walpole & Thouless, 2005). As Tosun (2000) pointed out, human resources determine the character and pace of ecotourism.

Conclusion

The future of ecotourism in Africa is promising. This book discusses substantial ecotourism achievements in Africa. Experience indicates that tremendous efforts have been made to ensure local stakeholders' optimal access to ecotourism benefits. This has created incentives among local stakeholders to support widlife conservation. The trajectory of ecotourism growth, as seen throughout this book, is encouraging. However, we have also demonstrated that there are still many constraints to overcome. Some of these constraints include local enterprises' limited access to capital, stakeholders' conflicting interests imbalanced ecotourism policies, and local stakeholders' limited capacity to fully take advantage of ecotourism opportunities. In this chapter, we suggest a pathway forward for some of these constraints. However, the pace of progress toward a more vibrant ecotourism in Africa will depend on close partnerships between practitioners and scholars and their joint exploration of the critical questions raised in this chapter. Thus, we hope that this book helps initiate new discussions and partnerships between scholars and practitioners to explore questions that will help to move forward ecotourism in Africa.

References

Ahebwa, W. M., van der Duim, R., & Sandbrook, C. (2012). Tourism revenue sharing policy at Bwindi Impenetrable National Park, Uganda: a policy arrangements approach. *Journal of Sustainable Tourism, 20*(3), 377–394. http://doi.org/10.1080/09669582.2011.622768

Archabald, K., & Naughton-Treves, L. (2001). Tourism revenue-sharing around national parks in Western Uganda: early efforts to identify and reward local communities. *Environmental Conservation, 28*(2), 135–149. http://doi.org/10.1017/S0376892901000145

Ashley, C., & Roe, D. (1998). Enhancing community involvement in wildlife tourism: issues and challenges London: IIED Wildlife and Development Series.

Backman, K. F., & Munanura, I. (2015). Introduction to the special issues on ecotourism in Africa over the past 30 years. *Journal of Ecotourism, 14*(2–3), 95–98. http://doi.org/10.1080/14724049.2015.1128058

Balint, P. J. (2006). Improving community-based conservation near protected areas: the importance of development variables. *Environmental Management, 38*(1), 137–148. http://doi.org/10.1007/s00267-005-0100-y

Belsky, J. M. (2009). Misrepresenting communities: the politics of community-based rural ecotourism in Gales Point Manatee, Belizel. *Rural Sociology, 64*(4), 641–666. http://doi.org/10.1111/j.1549-0831.1999.tb00382.x

Black, R., & Crabtree, A., (Ed.). (2007). *Quality Assurance and Certification in Ecotourism.* Oxfordshire: CAB International.

Blomley, T., Namara, A., McNeilage, A., Franks, P., Rainer, H., Donaldson, A., Malpas, R., Olupot, W., Baker, J., Sandbrook, C., Bitariho, R., & Infield, M. (2010). *Development and Gorillas? Assessing Fifteen Years of Integrated Conservation and Development in South-western Uganda* (Natural Resource Issues No. 23). London International Institute for Environment and Development (IIED).

Brandon, K. E., & Wells, M. (1992). Planning for people and parks: design dilemmas. *World Development, 20*(4), 557–570.

Brennan, F., & Allen, G. (2001). Community-based ecotourism, social exclusion and the changing political economy of KwaZulu-Natal, South Africa. In David Harrison (Ed.), *Tourism and the Less Developed World: Issues and Case Studies* (pp. 203–221). New York: CABI.

Brown, K. (2002). Innovations for conservation and development. *The Geographical Journal, 168*(1), 6–17. Retrieved from http://www.jstor.org/stable/3451218

Chambers, R., & York, N. (2013). *Rural Development: Putting the Last First.* New York: Routledge.

Chirozva, C. (2015). Community agency and entrepreneurship in ecotourism planning and development in the Great Limpopo Transfrontier Conservation Area. *Journal of Ecotourism, 14*(2–3), 185–203. http://doi.org/10.1080/14724049.2015.1041967

Christie, I., Fernandes, E., Messerli, H., & Twining-Ward, L. (2014). *Tourism in Africa: Harnessing Tourism for Growth and Improved Livelihoods.* The World Bank. http://doi.org/10.1596/978-1-4648-0190-7

Cobbinah, P. B., Black, R., & Thwaites, R. (2015). Ecotourism implementation in the Kakum Conservation Area, Ghana: administrative framework and local community experiences. *Journal of Ecotourism*, *14*(2–3), 223–242. http://doi.org/10.1080/14724049.2015.1051536

Gray, B. (1985). Conditions facilitating interorganizational collaboration. *Human Relations*, *38*(10), 911.

Green, G. P. (2003). What role can community play in local economic development. In Brown, D.L., & Swanson, L. E. (Ed.), *Challenges for Rural America in the Twenty First Century* (pp. 343–352). University Park: Pennsylvania State University Press.

Jamal, T., & Stronza, A. (2009). Collaboration theory and tourism practice in protected areas: stakeholders, structuring and sustainability. *Journal of Sustainable Tourism*, *17*(2), 169–189.

Jamal, T. B., & Getz, D. (1995). Collaboration theory and community tourism planning. *Annals of Tourism Research*, *22*(1), 186–204.

Kirsten, M., & Rogerson, C. M. (2002). Tourism, business linkages and small enterprise development in South Africa. *Development Southern Africa*, *19*(1), 29–59. http://doi.org/10.1080/03768350220123882

Kiss, A. (2004). Is community-based ecotourism a good use of biodiversity conservation funds? *Trends in Ecology & Evolution*, *19*(5), 232–237.

Kline, C. S., & Slocum, S. L. (2015). Neoliberalism in ecotourism? The new development paradigm of multinational projects in Africa. *Journal of Ecotourism*, *14*(2–3), 99–112. http://doi.org/10.1080/14724049.2015.1023731

Koch, E. (1994, August). Reality or rhetoric? Ecotourism and rural construction in South Africa. *UNRISD, DP. 54.*

Mbaiwa, J. E. (2015). Ecotourism in Botswana: 30 years later. *Journal of Ecotourism*, *14*(2–3), 204–222. http://doi.org/10.1080/14724049.2015.1071378

Mgonja, J. T., Sirima, A., & Mkumbo, P. J. (2015). A review of ecotourism in Tanzania: magnitude, challenges, and prospects for sustainability. *Journal of Ecotourism*, *14*(2–3), 264–277. http://doi.org/10.1080/14724049.2015.1114623

Munanura, I. E., Backman, K. F., Hallo, J. C., & Powell, R. B. (2016). Perceptions of tourism revenue sharing impacts on Volcanoes National Park, Rwanda: a Sustainable Livelihoods framework. http://dx.doi.org/10.1080/09669582.2016.1145228

Munanura, I. E., Backman, K. F., & Sabuhoro, E. (2013). Managing tourism growth in endangered species' habitats of Africa: Volcanoes National Park in Rwanda. *Current Issues in Tourism*, *16*(7–8), 700–718. http://doi.org/10.1080/13683500.2013.785483

Novelli, M. (2015). *Tourism and Development in Sub-Saharan Africa: Current Issues and Local Realities*. London: Routledge.

Nyaupane, G. P., & Poudel, S. (2011). Linkages among biodiversity, livelihood, and tourism. *Annals of Tourism Research*, *38*(4), 1344–1366.

Pasape, L., Anderson, W., & Lindi, G. (2013). Towards sustainable ecotourism through stakeholder collaborations in Tanzania. *Journal of Tourism Research & Hospitality*, *2*(1) pp 1–14. http://doi.org/10.4172/2324-8807.1000109

Pellis, A., Lamers, M., & Van der Duim, R. (2015). Conservation tourism and landscape governance in Kenya: the interdependency of three conservation NGOs. *Journal of Ecotourism*, *14*(2–3), 130–144. http://doi.org/10.1080/14724049.2015.1083028

Raghunathan, T. S., Rao, S. S., & Solis, L. E. (2013). A comparative study of quality practices: USA, China and India. http://dx.doi.org/10.1108/02635579710367270.

Scheyvens, R. (1999). Ecotourism and the empowerment of local communities. *Tourism Management*, *20*(2), 245–249. http://doi.org/10.1016/S0261-5177(98)00069-7

Sebola, M. P., & Fourie, L. de W. (2006). Community participation in ecotourism destinations: Maleboho Nature Reserve. In *Sustainable Tourism II* (Vol. 1, pp. 193–203). Southampton, UK: WIT Press. http://doi.org/10.2495/ST060181

Southgate, C. R. J. (2008). Ecotourism in Kenya: the vulnerability of communities. http://dx.doi.org/10.1080/14724040608668448.

Spenceley, A., & Meyer, D. (2015). *Tourism and Poverty Reduction: Priciples and Impacts in Developing Countries*. London: Routledge.

Stone, M. T. (2015). Community-based ecotourism: a collaborative partnerships perspective. *Journal of Ecotourism*, *14*(2–3), 166–184. http://doi.org/10.1080/14724049.2015.1023309

Tosun, C. (2000). Limits to community participation in the tourism development process in developing countries. *Tourism Management, 21*(6), 613–633.

Victurine, R. (2000). Building tourism excellence at the community level: capacity building for community-based entrepreneurs in Uganda. *Journal of Travel Research, 38*(February 2000), 221–229. http://doi.org/10.1177/004728750003800303

Walpole, M. J., & Goodwin, H. J. (2001). Local attitudes towards conservation and tourism around Komodo National Park, Indonesia. *Environmental Conservation, 28*(2), 160–166.

Walpole, M. J., & Thouless, C. R. (2005). Increasing the value of wildlife through non-consumptive use? Deconstructing the myths of ecotourism and community-based tourism in the tropics. In Woodroffe, R., Thirgood, S., & Rabinowtz, A (Ed.), *People and Wildlife, Conflict or Co-existence?* (p. 122). Cambridge, England: Cambridge University Press.

Index

INDEX

For Product Safety Concerns and Information please contact our EU
representative GPSR@taylorandfrancis.com
Taylor & Francis Verlag GmbH, Kaufingerstraße 24, 80331 München, Germany

www.ingramcontent.com/pod-product-compliance
Ingram Content Group UK Ltd.
Pitfield, Milton Keynes, MK11 3LW, UK
UKHW051832180425
157613UK00022B/1217